PORTFOLIO

THE VEST-POCKET MBA

JAE K. SHIM, Ph.D., is professor of business at California State University, Long Beach, and CEO of Delta Consulting Company, a management consulting and training firm. He received his M.B.A. (Business Economics) and Ph.D. (Operations Research) degrees from the University of California at Berkeley (Haas School of Business). Dr. Shim has been a consultant to commercial and nonprofit organizations for more than thirty years and has published numerous articles in such journals as *Financial Management, Econometrica, Decision Sciences, Management Science, Long Range Planning, OMEGA,* and *Journal of the Operational Research Society.* He has more than fifty college and professional books to his credit, including *Operations Management, Managerial Economics, Financial Management, Managerial Accounting, 2003 U.S. Master Finance Guide, Barron's Accounting Handbook, Investment Sourcebook, Dictionary of International Business Terms, 2003 Corporate Controller's Handbook of Financial Management, The Vest-Pocket CPA,* and *The Vest-Pocket CFO.* His books have been published by Aspen, Prentice-Hall, McGraw-Hill, Barron's, CCH, Southwestern, John Wiley, Amacom, Fitzroy Dearborn, CRC Press, and the American Institute of CPAs (AICPA). Dr. Shim has been frequently quoted by such media as the *Los Angeles Times, Orange County Register, Business Start-ups, Personal Finance,* and *Money Radio.* Dr. Shim was the recipient of the 1982 Credit Research Foundation Award for his article on financial modeling.

JOEL G. SIEGEL Ph.D., CPA, is a professor of accounting and finance at Queens College of the City University of New York and a financial consultant to management. He is the author of sixty-five published books and more than three hundred articles. Dr. Siegel's articles have appeared in professional journals, including *The Financial Executive, The Financial Analysts Journal, The CPA Journal, The National Public Accountant, Credit and Financial Management,* and the

International Journal of Management. He has served as consultant and/or advisor to numerous organizations, including the AICPA, Citicorp, and ITT. He was affiliated with Coopers and Lybrand, CPAs, and Arthur Andersen, CPAs. In 1972 Dr. Siegel was the recipient of the Outstanding Educator of America award. He is listed in *Who's Where Among Writers* and in *Who's Who in the World.*

ABRAHAM J. SIMON, Ph.D., CPA, is professor of accounting and information systems at Queens College of the City University of New York. He has served as consultant to several organizations and to the City of New York. He has authored professional books for the AICPA and the Council on Municipal Performance. Dr. Simon's articles have appeared in many journals, including the *International Journal of Accounting Education and Research,* the *National Public Accountant,* and *Credit and Financial Management.* Professor Simon has practiced extensively as a CPA.

The
Vest-Pocket
MBA

THIRD EDITION

Jae K. Shim, Ph.D.
Joel G. Siegel, Ph.D., CPA
Abraham J. Simon, Ph.D., CPA

Portfolio

DEC 1 7 2007

PORTFOLIO
Published by the Penguin Group
Penguin Group (USA) Inc., 375 Hudson Street, New York, New York 10014, U.S.A.
Penguin Group (Canada), 10 Alcorn Avenue, Toronto, Ontario, Canada M4V 3B2 (a division of Pearson Penguin Canada Inc.)
Penguin Books Ltd, 80 Strand, London WC2R 0RL, England
Penguin Ireland, 25 St Stephen's Green, Dublin 2, Ireland (a division of Penguin Books Ltd)
Penguin Group (Australia), 250 Camberwell Road, Camberwell, Victoria 3124, Australia (a division of Pearson Australia Group Pty Ltd)
Penguin Books India Pvt Ltd, 11 Community Centre, Panchsheel Park, New Delhi - 110 017, India
Penguin Group (NZ), cnr Airborne and Rosedale Roads, Albany, Auckland 1310, New Zealand (a division of Pearson New Zealand Ltd)
Penguin Books (South Africa) (Pty) Ltd, 24 Sturdee Avenue, Rosebank, Johannesburg 2196, South Africa

Penguin Books Ltd. Registered Offices:
80 Strand, London WC2R 0RL, England

First published in the United States of America by Prentice-Hall, Inc. 1986
Second edition published 1997
This third edition published by Portfolio, a member of Penguin Group (USA) Inc. 2004

10 9 8 7 6 5

PUBLISHER'S NOTE
This publication is designed to provide accurate and authoritative information in regard to the subject matter covered. It is sold with the understanding that the publisher is not engaged in rendering legal, accounting, or other professional services. If you require legal advice or other expert assistance, you should seek the services of a competent professional.

ISBN 1-59184-051-1
cip data available

Printed in the United States of America
Set in 9/10 Times Ten Roman
Designed by GGS Book Services, Atlantic Highlands

Preface

Here is a handy pocket problem-solver for today's busy executive. It's a working guide to help you quickly pinpoint in the complex world of business:

What to look for

What to do

What to watch out for

How to do it

Throughout this book you'll find ratios, formulas, guidelines, and rules of thumb to help you analyze and evaluate any business-related problem. You'll find this book practical, quick, and useful; uses for this book are as varied as the topics presented herein.

Part I (Chapters 1, 2, 3, and 4) takes you through the world of business strategy, management, marketing, and legal environments of business. You will learn strategic analysis, various management techniques, production/operations management, the marketing process of planning and distribution, and how to price and promote products. These management and marketing techniques and processes have been presented in an extremely understandable and practical format to make them as useful as possible. The statutory and case law affecting business operations and decisions are also presented, as legal requirements must be known in order to protect the business entity.

Part II (Chapters 5, 6, and 7) covers accounting principles and guidelines for evaluating a company's financial health. You will gain understanding of various financial statements and their implications. You will be exposed to Corporate Responsibility Law, better known as the Sarbanes-Oxley (SOX) Act. You'll learn techniques for analyzing another company's financial position should you wish to invest, extend credit, or compare. You will also learn how to improve a company's corporate profitability and shareholder value. We will present internal managerial accounting applications to help you evaluate your own company's performance, profitability, marketing effectiveness, and budgeting process. You'll learn how to highlight problem areas with variance analysis. You will also learn some valuable new tools, such as activity-based costing (ABC), life-cycle costing, target costing, and corporate balanced scorecard.

Part III (Chapters 8, 9, and 10) takes a look at financial analysis tools, financial metrics, and financing methods for decision making. Through break-even and sensitivity analysis, you'll be able to move your company toward greater profits. For investment purposes, this part presents guidelines for evaluating proposals, whether they be short- or long-term, for profit potential and risk-return comparisons. You'll learn management and financing techniques to ensure the best possible strategies for maximizing and acquiring cash. Also covered are basic financial tenets of portfolio theory, the capital asset pricing model (CAPM), and the arbitrage pricing model (APM).

Part IV (Chapters 11 and 12) delves into the seemingly complex world of quantitative analysis. You'll use statistics for forecasting and validity testing. Decision theories include linear programming, learning curve theory, and queuing models; these are presented concisely and comprehensively to help you use sophisticated techniques with relative ease. And you'll learn how computer applications facilitate these complex procedures. Computer applications are heavily stressed throughout these chapters.

Part V (Chapters 13 and 14) covers the economic issues of interest to business managers because they have a significant impact upon corporate success or failure. Attention should be given to the changing economic environment, as well as economic indices and statistics, in making financial and investment decisions. Many companies are multinational, so business managers must understand the opportunities and difficulties associated with international business and multinational finance. Some relevant issues of concern to businesspeople are foreign exchange rates, currency risk management, political risk, and international sources of financing.

This book has been written in a question-and-answer format in order to address the pertinent issues that come up during the course of business. The questions covered here are typical, and are frequently asked by persons like you. The answers provided are clear, concise, and to the point. In short, this is a veritable cookbook of guidelines, illustrations, and "how-tos" for you, the modern decision maker. Keep it handy for easy reference throughout your busy day.

Contents

The Vest-Pocket MBA

PART ONE

Business Strategy, Management, Marketing, and Legal Strategies

CHAPTER 1

Strategic Management and Operations Management (OM)

This chapter provides a discussion of strategic management and production and operations management (P/OM), including

- Mission statement
- Strategic management
- Strength, Weaknesses, Opportunities, and Threats (SWOT) analysis
- Management decision making
- Simulation
- Capacity management
- Location analysis
- Time-study procedures
- Aggregate planning schedules
- Inventory management
- Scheduling, including project scheduling

Strategy can be defined as a course of action or a plan, including the specification of resources required, to achieve a specific objective. All business organizations have objectives, but because of the dynamic nature of the organizations' environments, overall plans or strategies are needed to specify in broad terms just how the objectives of the organizations can be achieved, given the uncertainty of the environments.

Strategic management is therefore concerned with deciding on a strategy and planning how that strategy is to be effected. As such, strategic management has general relevance in that it is relevant for managers in all types of organizations—profit-seeking and nonprofit organizations, state and private sector.

Production and operations management (P/OM) is a vital management activity in both manufacturing and service organizations. It is primarily concerned with the process of transforming organizational resource inputs into final organizational outputs. It is a comprehensive process that treats the organization as a system of interconnected functions. The major functions of P/OM incorporate design, planning, decision making, operations, and system controls.

1.1 THE ORGANIZATIONAL MISSION STATEMENT

What is the purpose of a mission statement?

A mission statement describes the basic operational intent of an organization. It takes a long-term perspective and states the reason for a firm's existence. Its function is to provide guidance for the firm's shareholders, customers, and employees about the organization's overall direction and rationale.

How is a mission statement developed?

A mission statement should be consistent with the organization's history, including past achievements, organizational culture, attributes, and basic policies. A new organization will take into consideration the history of the industry it is joining as well as the purpose it wishes to serve. Successful mission statements emphasize areas in which an organization has its greatest strengths and resources.

What are the key elements of a mission statement?

A mission statement must be

- Meaningful for the organization's client or customer base. Organizations must be constantly aware of who their clientele is, and of its requisite needs.
- Realistic and attainable. Unrealistic mission statements will cause an organization to fail.
- Stimulating and inspiring. A motivational mission statement will enhance employee creativity and commitment.
- Definitive and explicit. Unclear mission statements result in dispersed and unsuccessful organizational strategies.

Example 1.1

An independent power producer states that its mission consists of four central values:

Integrity: To act with integrity and honor commitments.

Fairness: To treat fairly employees, customers, suppliers, and the governments and communities in which the organization operates.

Fun: To create and maintain an atmosphere in which employees can advance in their skills while enjoying their time at work.

Social Responsibility: To undertake projects that provide social benefits, such as lower costs to customers, a high degree of safety and reliability, increased employment, and a cleaner environment.

Example 1.2

A rapidly growing petroleum company states that its mission is to create value by adding substantial oil and gas reserves while minimizing geological risk and leveraging staff expertise.

Example 1.3

A company that introduced the first independent electronic product information database that uses the industry standard Universal Product Code (UPC) numbering system states that its mission is to provide quality electronic merchandise management services and technologies to the retail industry.

1.2 STRATEGY DEVELOPMENT PROCESS

What is the purpose of an organizational strategy?

The purpose of an organizational strategy is to achieve the goals of the mission statement. This is done by developing a logical plan for utilizing the organization's strengths and resources. An organizational strategy provides direction for the organization's activities and its human resources within the context of its mission statement's objectives.

What strategy must an organization develop to achieve its mission?

An organizational strategy must be developed for each functional area within an organization's mission statement. The resulting strategies contain

1. A clear purpose
2. Measurable expected outcomes
3. Fall-back plans in the event the primary strategy cannot be implemented
4. Costs and benefits

Developing an organizational strategy using the Strength, Weaknesses, Opportunities, and Threats (SWOT) analysis.

To use SWOT analysis is to combine the assessment of the environment with the analysis of the organization's internal resources and capabilities. The key objective is to arrive at a strategic fit—the matching of strength to opportunities, the elimination or avoidance of threats, and the strengthening or avoidance of weaknesses.

Elements analyzed within the organization's environment consist of the following variables:

1. culture
2. demographics
3. economic technology
4. organizational publics
   a. capital originators including shareholders, creditors, bankers, and underwriters
   b. raw material and component providers
   c. customers
   d. human resources
   e. competitive rivals
   f. governmental and legal entities, including regulators
   g. special-interest lobbying groups

The SWOT analysis allows managers to develop a strategic plan by examining organizational strengths and weaknesses in terms of the opportunities and threats presented by the organization's environmental elements. Subsequent strategies and tactical decisions can produce a competitive advantage.

What does strategic analysis seek?

Strategic analysis seeks to understand the strategic position of the organization. The analysis should encompass the environment, resources, objectives, expectations, and behaviors of the organization. Strategic choice concerns the formulation of possible courses of action, the evaluation of the courses of action, and the choice between them. Strategic implementation is the planning of how the strategy can be put into effect. Implementation affects all aspects of the organizational system.

More specifically, strategic analysis is concerned with the understanding of the strategic position of the organization, and will thus seek to analyze

The mission—What business are we in? Why does the business exist at all? What is the value system of the business?

The goals—The goals reflect the specific relevance of the mission to the various stakeholders.

The objectives—Embodying the mission, objectives are quantifiable and are used to measure actual performance.

The external environment—This analysis involves the scanning of the environment for factors relevant to the organization's current and future activities.

The internal appraisal or position audit—This is an assessment of the current state of an organization in terms of resources, assets, facilities, and performance values.

The corporate appraisal—This is the evaluation of the strength, weaknesses, opportunities, and threats (SWOT) in relation to the environmental factors.

The gap analysis—This involves identifying the gap between where we are now, where we will be when extrapolated, and where we desire to be.

What are the three levels of planning? How are they related?

There are, in general, three levels of strategy: corporate strategy, business strategy, and functional strategy. Corporate strategies define what business or businesses the firm is in or should be in, and how integrated these businesses should be with one another. Business strategies define how each business attempts to achieve its mission within its chosen area of activity. Functional strategies govern how the different functions of the business (marketing, production, sales, finance, HRM, IT, etc.) support the corporate and business strategies.

These levels of strategies are matched by the three levels of planning: strategic planning, tactical planning, and operational planning. Strategic planning defines the objectives of the organization, changes in these objectives, the resources needed to attain these objectives, and the policies that are to govern the acquisition, use, and disposition of said resources. Tactical planning ensures that the resources are obtained and used effectively and efficiently in the accomplishment of the organization's objectives. Operational planning ensures that specific tasks are carried out effectively and efficiently.

1.3 MANAGERIAL DECISION MAKING

All managers suffer from a shortage of knowledge, resources, and time. Working within these parameters, the management process culminates in decisions to implement various actions. Decision making is the focal point of all organizational dynamics, and management effectiveness is judged on the basis of the quality of these decisions.

What is managerial decision making?

Managerial decisions are deliberate choices made from a range of alternatives. Before making a decision, a manager must evaluate each choice according to its projected outcomes in terms of the organization's resources as well as the amount of information and time available. Thus, every managerial decision is a best-effort compromise made in an environment of uncertainty.

What are the types of management decisions?

From a management perspective, there are three types of decisions:

1. Long-term strategic decisions concerning the external environment of the organization
2. Administrative decisions intended to order the functions of the organization in the most cost-effective way
3. Operational decisions designed to maximize a firm's profitability through productive procedures

What are the types of strategic decisions?

There are many types of strategic decisions in P/OM:

1. *Product or service strategy.* Management decisions regarding product-line market strategies (including design, quality, and cost) determine production cost parameters.
2. *Process strategy.* Management decisions regarding process methods are critical in determining technological and organizational production requirements. The process strategy decision is also crucial in determining capital and financial requirements.
3. *Research and Development (R&D) strategy.* R&D is critical for organizational survival in today's rapidly changing marketplace. The R&D strategy

includes total resources being devoted to an effort and the type of research to be performed, including pure vs. applied research, manufacturing vs. market research, and product vs. process development.

4. *Location strategy.* Often the success or failure of a business, production, or service is determined by a location decision.

5. *Inventory management strategy.* It is essential to develop a strategy for coordinating production needs with raw material and component inventories. However, the inventory strategy is determined by whether the demand is dependent on or independent of the demand for other components. If the demand for one product, such as air conditioners, is independent of that for another product, such as kitchen chairs, an independent inventory management strategy is required. However, if the overall component demand is dependent on the demand for the product, a Material Requirements Planning (MRP) strategy is needed. MRP is a component-manufacturing planning method in which items required for a manufacturing process are indexed to overall product demand. With MRP it is not essential that all inventory items be available at all times, but that they be available only when they are required in the production process. Thus, under MRP, inventory needs are coordinated with production needs. (See Chapter 12, on inventory management, for a more complete discussion.)

6. *Human resource planning and management strategy.* As a rule of thumb, more than 75 percent of a firm's operating expense is for human resources. Therefore, adequate hiring, training, and utilization of human resources is a critical operational strategy for achieving success.

Example 1.4

The management of an organization makes a strategic decision to develop a five-year marketing plan to achieve a competitive advantage through the introduction of a new service.

Example 1.5

An automobile manufacturer makes a process strategy decision to offer a standard group of options on its automobiles in order to reduce the variation in its production needs and lower unit costs.

Example 1.6

A computer-chip manufacturer makes a strategy decision to increase R&D expenditures on an advanced CPU chip design, enabling compatibility with multiple computer operating systems.

Example 1.7

A firm makes a location strategy decision to conduct a nationwide survey of state industrial development agencies to evaluate in which locations the company would receive the greatest financial and environmental benefits.

Example 1.8

A lawn-mower and snow-blower manufacturer makes an inventory management decision to use an MRP system to coordinate the need for lawn-mower and snow-blower components with seasonal manufacturing schedules.

Example 1.9

A manufacturer makes a human resource strategy decision to give more responsibility to its employees by creating work teams to assemble entire products rather than components in the belief that it will obtain greater productivity as a result of job enrichment.

What are the types of administrative decisions?

1. *Programmed decisions.* Decisions typically made regarding highly routine situations, in which little discretion is required.
2. *Nonprogrammed decisions.* Decisions made in unstructured situations, in which problem conceptualization and original thinking are required.

Example 1.10

Management makes a programmed administrative decision to establish a vehicle maintenance schedule.

Example 1.11

Management makes a nonprogrammed administrative decision to implement an organizational downsizing plan to reduce duplication of services, decrease costs, and increase profitability.

What are the types of operational decisions?

1. *Quality.* Decision making regarding product and service quality is a vital operations responsibility necessitating comprehensive organizational support. Quality decisions are made in the design stage of the product or service plan and require the creation and maintenance of standards.

2. *Process.* Operational decisions are made regarding the design of the process used in the manufacturing or servicing of a final product. Process decisions are normally long-range and cannot be easily reversed.

3. *Capacity.* Operational capacity decisions are concerned with the long-term capability of an organization to produce the required amount of output over time. Capacity planning determines not only the size of an organization's physical productive capability, but also its human resource needs.

4. *Inventory.* Inventory decisions are crucial in fulfilling management's inventory management strategy. The challenge for operations management is to create a balance in inventory between product demand, cost, and supply needs.

5. *Human Resources.* Human resources are an extremely important operational management responsibility. Organizations pay a major portion of their revenues to employees. Therefore, effective selection, hiring, training, termination, and general management of human resources are critical for the future of the organization.

Example 1.12

The franchise management of a fast-food retail chain makes a determination concerning quality standards in terms of the content and temperature of the food when it is served to the customer. It implements a program to ensure that individual franchises meet the quality standards.

Example 1.13

The management of a car-washing company makes a process decision to utilize a brushless car-washing facility that requires fewer workers, results in less damage to car finish, and is more productive.

Example 1.14

A seasonal manufacturer of lawn equipment makes a capacity operational decision to hire and train a second shift of employees during peak demand periods rather than increase overall plant capacity. This makes more productive use of existing capacity without increasing long-term overhead costs, including plant maintenance and capital financing costs.

Example 1.15

The franchise manager of a chain of job printers makes an operational decision to allow the individual store managers to buy their own printing supply inventory as long as they use the franchise's equipment.

Example 1.16

A franchise manager makes a human resource operational decision to allow individual franchisees to hire, train, and supervise their own employees. Thus, the individual franchisee has the entire human resource operational responsibility.

What are the steps in the decision-making process?

Making good decisions is essential to the management process. As discussed, decisions are made based on rational choices from among a group of alternatives. Good decisions are the result of a sequential series of analytical steps.

1. *Identify and delineate the problem.* No management action can occur unless there is a need to resolve an issue. Additionally, when identifying a problem, management must assess the seriousness of the issue. Highly critical issues require more immediate attention and place a greater demand on existing resources. Difficulties in identifying problems include:

   Perceptual errors. Often problems are not identified because of personal biases, which do not allow an individual to perceive that there is a problem that needs attention. Preconceived notions of how something should be (as well as personal preferences) will interfere with the ability to identify a problem.

   Insufficient information. Insufficient research about a specific problem can result in misleading and unwarranted conclusions regarding the true nature of the problem and its possible solution.

Mistaking a symptom as the cause of the problem. An apparent cause of a problem may just mask a systemic cause. Again, further research is essential to find the cause and nature of a problem.

2. *Establish decision priorities and goals.* Managers constantly deal with problems. However, all organizations have limited resources. They must assign priorities to problems in terms of their importance relative to the organization's goals. This process results in a matching of organizational resources with priorities, and creates a management methodology for administering solutions to problems.

3. *Ascertain the cause of the problem.* In order to develop a solution to a problem, management must understand the problem's cause. This requires a systemic understanding of the dynamics of the situation that has caused the problem.

4. *Develop realistic alternatives.* It is important for the manager to develop a range of alternative, realistic solutions. This means doing extensive research into the nature of the problem and discovering what alternatives would provide a good solution.

5. *Weigh the best alternative.* This requires extensive evaluation and comparison using a cost-benefit analysis. Alternative solutions are developed within the constraints of limited time and resources, and with a degree of uncertainty.

6. *Choose a solution.* After conducting extensive research, a decision will have to be made regarding an optimal solution. Managers operate within an environment of incomplete information, time deadlines, and limited resources. All solutions represent choices with limited outcome predictability. Therefore, managers must make decisions within a range of known alternatives having unknown outcomes.

7. *Implement the decision.* This requires developing human resources to carry out the decision. This mandates a high communication level between the manager and the human resource team.

8. *Follow up.* All decisions require constant monitoring. Changes will have to be made over time to ensure optimum results. This requires an effective organizational control and evaluation system for future organizational decisions

Example 1.17

A word-processing software manufacturer that has been very successful in the text-based operating system market faces a crucial decision when the industry standard operating system is changed to a graphical user interface (GUI) system. The company's text-based word processor is extremely successful and has a large following. The commands used in the text-based word processor are difficult to learn, but once learned, it is a very versatile word processor.

If the word processor is converted to a graphical user interface, a portion of the installed user base may be lost, and its competitive advantage, based on powerful nonintuitive commands, may also be compromised. However, failure to convert the word processor to a graphical user interface will mean losing market share since the major competitors have already released GUI word processors.

After deciding to develop a GUI word processor, the company has to decide whether to do a fundamental rewrite of the program, which could take at least two years, or to simply update it and make it GUI-compatible. The company decides to release a GUI update to its word processing program, with a fundamental GUI rewrite scheduled for a future date.

What is decision making under certainty and conflict?

Decision making involves managing three major elements:

Decision strategy. A decision maker develops a plan affecting long-term organizational outcomes, utilizing existing organizational resources.

States of nature. These are elements of the environment over which the manager has little or no control. States of nature include weather, political environment, the economy, technological developments, etc. These can dramatically affect the outcomes of any decision strategy.

Outcome. This is the result of the interaction of the implementation of a decision strategy with the states of nature. Because of the many variables within the states of nature, outcomes can be extremely difficult to forecast.

Thus, outcomes of a decision strategy, O (the dependent variable), is a function of the interaction of the two independent variables D (decision strategies) and S (the states of nature). Figure 1.1 shows a decision matrix. The rows are strategic choices a manager can make, while the columns represent decision outcomes. An outcome O_{ij} is a function of a decision strategy D_i and a state of nature S_j.

Figure 1.1 Decision Matrix

	States of Nature					
Strategies	S_1	S_2	S_X	S_X	S_X	S_j
D_1	O_{11}	O_{12}	*	*	*	O_{1j}
D_2	O_{21}	O_{22}	*	*	*	O_{2j}
D_x	*	*				*
D_x	*	*				*
D_j	O_{i1}	O_{i2}	*	*	*	O_{ij}

Mathematically, this relationship can be expressed as follows:

$$O_{ij} = f(D_i, S_j)$$

What are decision trees and decision tables?

Developing a graphical display is an effective way of mapping the alternatives and probable events that can occur in a complex decision-making environment. Decision trees use symbols consisting of squares and circles. Branches of the decision tree that extend from a square depict an area in which several choices can be made, while a circle connotes a unique state of nature having certain outcomes.

A decision tree is analyzed in reverse order, from right to left, going back chronologically. Decision trees are normally accompanied by a payoff or decision table, where all the alternatives are listed down the left side of the table, with states of nature listed across the top of the table, and payoffs stated in the main part of the table.

Example 1.18

The Jackson Lawn Products Corporation is studying the possibility of manufacturing a new line of lawn mowers. Since the market for the new mowers is uncertain, the corporation must decide whether to construct a large or small plant, or do nothing. Figure 1.2 presents a decision tree depicting the Jackson Lawn Products decision choices.

Figure 1.2 Jackson Lawn Products Corporation Decision Tree

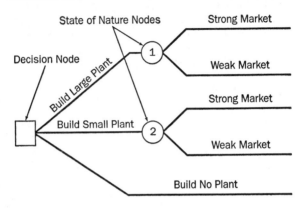

A payoff or decision table can be developed to assist Jackson Lawn Products in determining what type of lawn-mower plant they should build. There is an outcome for each decision and state of nature that can be described in units of monetary value. The units of monetary value are also described as conditional values.

Exhibit 1.1 describes all of Jackson's decision alternatives in the left column of the exhibit, the states of nature across the top, and the payoffs (conditional values) in the main part of the exhibit. In the case of building a large plant, a strong market will produce a $250,000 net profit, whereas a weak market will result in a $125,000 net loss. If a small plant is built, a strong market will produce a $125,000 net profit, with a $60,000 net loss in a weak market.

Exhibit 1.1 Decision Table with Conditional Values for Jackson Lawn Products Corporation

	States of Nature	
Decision Alternatives	*Strong Market*	*Weak Market*
Build Large Plant	$250,000	−$125,000
Build Small Plant	$125,000	−$60,000
Build No Plant	$0	$0

What is decision making in a total quality environment?

Total Quality Management (TQM) evolved from W. Edwards Deming's fourteen points, which were termed Total Quality Control. Decision making in a total quality environment essentially involves the elements of a continuous process, focusing on three essential components: continuous improvement, assessment management, and teamwork.

Implementing decision making in a total quality environment requires

Making quality improvement a central organizational focus

Extensive and continuous employee training

Total involvement of the employees and management concerning the organization's mission, goals, and operational objectives

Continual improvement of organizational processes rather than focusing on employees as the source of quality failures

Team decision making

The recognition that the customer defines quality, and that a total quality decision objective is to meet or exceed customer satisfaction standards.

Decision making in a TQM environment is a shared experience for all employees throughout an organization. Information is an organizational resource essential for making quality decisions. Increased quality leads to increased productivity, lower unit costs, and higher customer satisfaction.

Example 1.19

A transmission manufacturing company was machining highly exacting parts to be used in automatic transmissions. The parts consisted of gears, bearings, and assorted spacers and shafts. The parts were engineered to be within the industry standard of + or − .003″ of specifications. However, other manufacturers were able to produce the same transmissions at two-thirds of the price and achieve higher productivity and quality.

Management decided to make a 300 percent improvement in the tolerances of the parts by reducing them to + or − .001″ tolerance. The net results were fewer returns, lower unit costs, and higher overall customer satisfaction. Consequently, productivity and profits grew substantially.

1.4 SIMULATION MODELS

Management uses simulation techniques to replicate the characteristics and dynamics of a real system. Simulations enable management to test models of performance when it is too expensive, risky, or time consuming to use the real materials, workers, and equipment. Using simulation, a manager can test the effects of a decision in a wide variety of situations, including time compression scenarios, without disrupting an operational system. It allows the manager to evaluate alternative system designs when implementing a given operational strategy.

Additionally, simulation permits the manager to evaluate the effects of interactions between individual system components and various when/if tactics.

The weaknesses of simulations are that they are syllogistic in that they can evaluate only the information built into the model. Therefore, variables not included or not capable of being included in the model cannot be evaluated. Another limitation of simulation is that it is typically designed for unique situations, thus restricting transferability to other scenarios.

How is simulation implemented by management?

When implementing a simulation model, management is required to

1. Delineate the problem.
2. Categorize the factors associated with the problem.
3. Develop an analytical model.
4. Construct strategic alternatives for testing.
5. Implement the simulation.
6. Analyze the outcomes of the simulation.
7. Apply the analysis to an operational system.

What is the Monte Carlo simulation?

When a scenario contains elements of chance, the Monte Carlo simulation can be used to estimate outcomes. The Monte Carlo simulation analyzes the probability distribution of variables in a problem and uses random sampling of the data. Using random sampling, these probabilities are calculated to estimate a problem's solution. The Monte Carlo simulation is developed through the following procedures.

1. Probability distributions for major elements of the problem are established. (A critical feature of the Monte Carlo simulation is the generation of probability distributions. The probability distribution must correspond to the actual data as closely as possible in order for the simulation to be valid and reliable. A commonly accepted method for doing this is historical frequency.)
2. Cumulative probability distributions are developed for each variable. After establishing a probability distribution for each variable in the model, the probabilities are sequentially totaled.

3. Random samples are established using the cumulative probability distributions to obtain specific element values for each observation. A random-number table is often used to generate numbers for the sampling distribution.

4. Several simulation trials are performed. The actual number of trials needed is determined by statistical tests of significance.

Monte Carlo simulations have a wide number of applications, including estimating inventory demand on a time-interval basis, times between machine failures, project scheduling times, and servicing schedules. Exhibit 1.2 presents a Random Number Table.

Example 1.20

A computer memory-chip manufacturer's records show the following failure rates of a particular memory chip when tested individually:

Memory Chip Failures

Failures	Frequency of Failure in Hours
2	10
5	20
6	30
8	40
2	50
1	60
Total Hours	210

Memory Chip Failures, Frequency of Failure, Failure Probability, Cumulative Probability, and Monte Carlo Numbers

Failures	Frequency of Failure in Hours	Probability (Frequency/ Total Hours)	Cumulative Probability	Monte Carlo Numbers
2	10	0.05	0.05	01–05
5	20	0.10	0.15	06–15
6	30	0.14	0.29	16–29
8	40	0.19	0.48	30–48
3	50	0.24	0.72	49–72
1	60	0.29	1.01*	73–00
Total Hours	210	1		

* Rounding error

Random numbers are then assigned, using a computer-generated table of random numbers:

Exhibit 1.2 Random-Number Table

75	55	41	96	97	38	33	79	91	22	20	24
39	75	58	48	68	6	62	30	21	96	4	56
91	88	78	58	94	5	51	61	59	90	40	14
79	93	62	48	73	88	17	56	48	22	53	3
50	22	76	38	2	46	68	94	89	17	83	76
5	21	35	52	95	79	19	51	26	46	2	10
76	44	51	15	98	71	33	75	26	47	58	99
77	71	51	20	75	9	91	92	22	99	33	11
4	89	54	62	67	9	65	79	47	39	25	77
88	18	17	46	7	16	98	90	54	56	95	66
56	31	44	50	29	74	66	35	55	81	43	76
55	61	97	16	32	31	66	29	65	61	6	26
65	82	50	68	26	53	76	6	99	98	14	46
30	1	20	47	92	61	76	17	72	15	57	94
95	45	83	50	100	49	58	32	19	0	13	79
70	94	39	19	64	33	28	61	81	6	88	99
87	38	16	34	9	89	19	69	77	24	33	84
47	26	29	96	9	96	2	70	9	34	42	91
85	90	31	79	89	3	86	75	61	59	40	73
48	94	57	21	70	72	23	57	97	50	4	39

The next step is to simulate the memory-chip failures. In this example, twenty simulations are run using random numbers from the first column of the random-number table. The number of memory chip failures is derived from where the random number coincides with the Monte Carlo interval, as shown in Exhibit 1.3.

Exhibit 1.3 Failure Rates

Simulation	Random Number	Simulated Failures
1	75	1
2	39	8
3	91	1
4	79	1
5	50	3
6	5	2
7	76	1

Exhibit 1.3 Failure Rates (*continued*)

Simulation	Random Number	Simulated Failures
8	77	1
9	4	2
10	88	1
11	56	3
12	55	3
13	65	3
14	30	8
15	95	1
16	70	3
17	87	1
18	47	8
19	85	1
20	48	8
Total Number of Failures		60
Average Failure Rate 60/20 =		3

A frequency distribution for the hours and failures of the simulation can now be tabulated, as shown in Exhibit 1.4.

Exhibit 1.4 Simulation Frequency Distribution

Hours	Failures	Probability of Failure
10	4	0.07
20	0	0
30	0	0
40	32	0.53
50	15	0.25
60	9	0.15
		1

In this simulation, the average failure rate for the memory chips is 3; however, the greatest number of failures occurs between 40 and 50 hours of operation. Assuming enough simulated iterations occurred, the simulated outcomes will represent real operations.

In this example, running more simulations could have changed the average failure rate for the memory chips. The expected failure rate for the memory chips can be calculated from the failure rates and their probabilities:

$$\text{Expected failure rate} = \sum_{i=1}^{5} (\text{probability of } i \text{ units})$$
$$\times (\text{failure rate of } i \text{ units})$$
$$= (.05)(2) + (.10)(5) +$$
$$(.14)(6) + (.19)(8) +$$
$$(.24)(3) + (.29)(1)$$
$$= .1 + .5 + .84 + 1.52 + .72 +$$
$$.29$$
$$= 3.97 \text{ failure rate}$$

The expected failure rate for the memory chips is higher than the average for the sample simulation. Assuming more simulations were run, the average failure rate would more closely approximate the expected failure rate.

1.5 CAPACITY MANAGEMENT

Capacity is the total productive capability of a system during a unit of time. For a manufacturing facility, capacity is simply the maximum output that can be attained with the existing capital equipment during a certain period of time. Thus, an automobile manufacturer may define its capacity as the number of cars that can be assembled in an hour, day, week, or month. Capacity is critically important for a productive organization because

- It provides the output required to meet product demand.
- It directly impacts the cost and efficiency of productive capability.
- It is a major organizational investment.

What is design capacity?

Design capacity is the total achievable capacity under perfect conditions. Normally, perfect conditions are not achievable, and few organizations operate for any period of time at design capacity. Furthermore, operating at design capacity can cause rapid wear and breakdowns. Operating at design capacity essentially means operating at the organization's productive limits.

What is effective capacity or utilization?

Effective capacity or utilization is a ratio between the expected capacity of a firm and its design capacity. It can be computed using following formula:

$$\text{Effective capacity} \atop \text{or utilization} = \frac{\text{Expected capacity}}{\text{Design capacity}}$$

Effective capacity is affected by an organization's product mix, production scheduling, equipment age, and maintenance standards.

Example 1.21

A television manufacturing company has a design capacity of fifty televisions per hour, but due to intensive quality control standards, it normally produces only forty televisions per hour. The effective capacity or utilization of the television manufacturing company is calculated in the following manner:

$$\frac{\text{Effective capacity}}{\text{or utilization}} = \frac{\text{Expected capacity}}{\text{Design capacity}}$$

$$\frac{\text{Effective capacity}}{\text{or utilization}} = \frac{40}{30} = 80\%$$

What is capacity efficiency?

Capacity efficiency is the ratio of production output to effective capacity. It is a measure of effective management in utilizing effective capacity. It is calculated using the following formula:

$$\text{Efficiency} = \frac{\text{Actual output}}{\text{Effective capacity}}$$

Example 1.22

The effective capacity of a candy manufacturing company is 1,000 units of candy per hour; however, it actually produces only 850 units per hour. The efficiency of the candy manufacturing company can be computed in the following manner:

$$\text{Efficiency} = \frac{\text{Actual output}}{\text{Effective capacity}}$$

$$\text{Efficiency} = \frac{850}{1,000} = 85\%$$

What is rated capacity?

Rated capacity is a determination of the maximum usable capacity of manufacturing capability. Rated capacity can never exceed design capacity. It is a product of design capacity times effective capacity times efficiency. The formula used to calculate rated capacity follows:

$$\text{Rated capacity} = \text{Design capacity} \times \text{Effective capacity} \times \text{Efficiency}$$

Example 1.23

A computer-printer manufacturer has a manufacturing facility operating at an effective capacity of 80 percent with 85 percent efficiency. It has two assembly lines operating five days a week, with two shifts a day. Each assembly line has a design capacity of forty printers per hour. The rated capacity of the computer-printer manufacturer is calculated by multiplying the design capacity by the effective capacity by the efficiency of the plant. To determine the design capacity, the two production lines have to be multiplied by the number of printers times the combined number of hours of production:

Design capacity = 40 printers/hour × 2 assembly lines × 80 hours = 6,400

Rated capacity = Design capacity × Effective capacity × Efficiency

Rated capacity = 6,400 × 0.8 × 0.85 = 4,352 printers per week

What factors affect capacity?

Many factors affect an organization's productive capacity. Some are within management's control, others are not. Factors that are within management's control include the acquisition and supervision of land, physical resources, and the utilization of labor.

Management challenges affecting organizational capacity include personnel issues, technological maximization, and issues that are not directly controllable, such as the impact of weather events, political issues, or war.

1.6 LOCATION ANALYSIS

Few decisions have more long-lasting and critical-cost implications than plant location. Costs affected by location decisions include

- *Transportation.* The geographic location will determine how far products must be transported to markets.

- *Energy.* Utility geographic service areas determine the respective energy costs for any particular location. These costs vary widely.

- *Taxation.* Local and state tax rates vary widely. Location decisions have major taxation cost implications.

- *Wages.* Wage levels vary widely, depending on geographic regions. However, a location decision made solely on the basis of wage levels without considering labor productivity is counterproductive.

- *Raw materials.* Certain industries are extremely dependent on the ready availability of specified raw materials, such as wood or iron ore. Location analysis, therefore, must include the availability of such raw materials.

What is locational break-even and profit analysis?

Locational break-even analysis is an economic comparison of locational options based on a cost-volume examination. Location decisions can be compared in graph form using alternative production/sales volumes. In order to perform locational break-even analysis, it is essential to

1. Establish the fixed and variable costs for each location.

2. Graph the costs for each location, where costs are on the Y axis and production/sales volume is on the X axis of the graph.

3. Determine which location has the lowest production/sales volume.

Example 1.24

A washing-machine manufacturer is analyzing three possible locations—Buffalo, New York; Toledo, Ohio; and Orlando, Florida—to build an additional manufacturing facility. Research analyses indicate the annual fixed costs for the sites are, respectively, $45,000; $60,000; and $95,000. The variable unit costs, respectively, are $235, $205, and $185. The anticipated selling price for the washing machines is $350. The company is seeking the most economical location for an expected volume of five thousand units annually.

The total cost for each city at the expected volume of five thousand units is calculated using the following formula:

Total cost = Fixed cost + Variable cost × Total volume

Buffalo:

Total cost = $45,000 + $235 × 5,000 = $1,220,000

Toledo:

Total cost = $60,000 + $205 × 5,000 = $1,085,000

Orlando:

Total cost = $95,000 + $185 × 5,000 = $1,020,000

Expected annual profits for each location can be calculated using the following formula:

Total revenue = (Selling price × 5,000) − Total cost (Fixed cost + Variable cost × total volume)

Buffalo:

$1,750,000 − $1,220,000 = $530,000

Toledo:

$1,750,000 − $1,085,000 = $665,000

Orlando:

$1,750,000 − $1,020,000 = $730,000

Assuming a maximum production of five thousand units, Orlando provides the lowest cost location, at $1,020,000, and the highest annual profit, $730,000.

Figure 1.3 shows the locational break-even analysis. At five hundred units, Buffalo and Toledo are both cheaper than Orlando. At fifteen hundred units, Toledo is the cheapest location, but at two thousand units of production, Orlando becomes the cheapest. Therefore, the crossover points in the break-even analysis are five hundred and fifteen hundred units of production.

Figure 1.3 Locational Break-Even Analysis

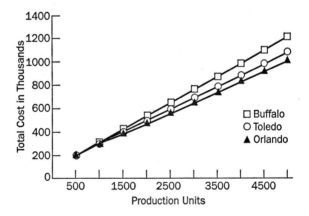

Figure 1.4 shows the locational profit analysis. At 500 units both Buffalo and Toledo earn a profit of $12,500. At 1,000 units Toledo earns a profit of $85,000, while Buffalo and Orlando earn $70,000. At 1,500 units Buffalo shows a profit of $127,500, while Orlando shows a profit of $152,500 and Toledo shows a profit of

$157,500. From 2,000 to 5,000 units Orlando is clearly more profitable than either Buffalo or Toledo. The crossover points are 500; 1,000; 1,500; and 2,000 units for locational profitability.

Figure 1.4 Locational Profit Analysis

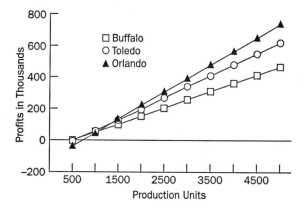

Therefore, from both a cost analysis and profit analysis standpoint, Orlando at two thousand units and more is the best locational choice.

What is the center-of-gravity location method?

The center-of-gravity location method relies on mathematical analysis to determine where a warehouse should be located in order to service a number of retail stores in disparate locations. The method considers three factors:

- Market location
- The volume of goods handled in these markets
- Shipping expenses to each location

In order to develop the center-of-gravity location method, each retail outlet has to be given coordinates within a map grid system where the geographical distances are correctly established.

The center of gravity is determined by using the following formula:

$$C_x = \frac{\sum i\, d_{ix}\, V_i}{\sum i\, W_i}$$

$$C_y = \frac{\sum i\, d_{iy}\, V_i}{\sum i\, V_i}$$

where

C_x = x coordinate of the center of gravity

C_y = y coordinate of the center of gravity

d_{ix} = x coordinate of the center of gravity

d_{iy} = y coordinate of the center of gravity

V_i = volume of goods moved to or from location i

In order to accurately reflect the true cost of distance on shipping, the center-of-gravity method evaluates the distance as well as the total volume actually being shipped to any respective location. The ideal location for a warehouse servicing several retail outlets is that which has the lowest weighted cost of distance and volume of units actually shipped.

Example 1.25

Good Worth Hardware is a chain of six retail hardware stores being supplied by an outdated warehouse close to its first store. Stores are located in cities A, B, C, D, E, and F in Ohio, Pennsylvania, and New York.

The monthly volume of goods shipped to the respective stores is shown in Exhibit 1.5.

Exhibit 1.5 Monthly Volume of Goods Shipped to Stores

Hardware Store Location	Volume of Monthly Shipments
City A	600
City B	800
City C	900
City D	1,200
City E	850
City F	1,100

The company needs to find a more centralized location in which to locate a modern warehouse to supply all the hardware stores. The data from the coordinate locations is then used in the formulas for coordinates x and y.

$$C_x = \frac{(40)(600) + (100)(800) + (150)(900) + (165)(1,200) + (50)(850) + (110)(1,100)}{600 + 800 + 900 + 1,200 + 850 + 1,100}$$

$$C_y = \frac{(30)(600) + (90)(800) + (140)(900) + (180)(1,200) + (60)(850) + (120)(1,100)}{600 + 800 + 900 + 1,200 + 850 + 1,100}$$

The center-of-gravity coordinate is shown in the co-ordinate locations in Figure 1.5.

Figure 1.5 Coordinate Locations for Hardware Stores

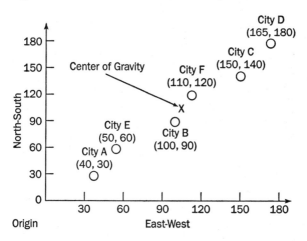

1.7 TIME STUDIES

The classical approach to time studies, developed by Frederick W. Taylor in 1911, is the accepted procedure for production analysis. A time study, also termed a stopwatch time study, is an analysis of a worker's performance against a time standard. Time studies are normally performed on short, repetitive, production types of tasks.

How is a time study performed?

There are several basic steps which must be followed in any time study:

1. Define the job to be analyzed.
2. Break the job into discrete tasks.
3. Measure the actual time required for each task.
4. Develop a statistically significant sample size of the task work-cycles to be measured. Work measurement depends on sampling the work process. However, in order to counter inherent variability in the work samples, a sufficient representation of the sample universe must be selected. Therefore, it is essential to determine an adequate work-cycle sample size. In order to do this, a preliminary analysis, usually consisting of anywhere from five to twenty repetitive work cycles to determine variability, must be performed.

The work-cycle sample size is dependent on three factors:

a. Observed variance in the work-cycles.

b. How closely the sample will conform to the average work-cycle (accuracy).

c. The desired statistical level of confidence.

The work-cycle element having the greatest variability will determine the sample size needed to obtain an acceptable statistical level of confidence. The typical statistical level of confidence expected is 95 percent, with a reliability of t = 5%. The following formula will determine required sample sizes:

$$N = \frac{nZ^2[n\sum X^2 - (\sum X)^2]}{(n-1)^{a^2}(\sum X)^2}$$

where

n = initial sample size

X = cycle time

a = accuracy

Z = confidence level (Z = 1 for 68.3% confidence level, Z = 2 for 95.5% confidence level, and Z = 3 for 99.7% confidence level)

5. Calculate the average time required for each job element using the following formula:

$$\text{Average job element time} = \frac{\text{Sum of the time needed to perform each task}}{\text{Number of job cycles}}$$

Rate the performance of each worker (performance rating). Calculate the normal time required for each job element using the following formula:

$$\text{Normal time} = \sum \left[\frac{(\text{average element time})}{\dfrac{\text{performance rating}}{100}} \right]$$

Here the observed time, normal time, for a particular employee is rated against the average job element time.

Determine allowances that may be permitted for a particular job task. This may take into consideration personal factors as well as unavoidable constraints encountered in the work situation. Allowances include all unavoidable delays, but rule out avoidable delays. An allowance factor represents time lost due to personal factors, shift adjustments, improper equipment, fatigue, and related issues. The performance rating is adjusted for any allowances.

Calculate the standard time. When calculating the standard time, three different types of time are actually utilized. Actual time is the time a particular employee actually takes to perform a particular job operation. Normal time is the time needed to complete an operation by an employee working at 100 percent efficiency with no delays. Standard time is the time needed to complete an operation by an employee working at 100 percent efficiency with unavoidable delays:

$$\text{Standard time} = \text{normal time} + \text{allowance fraction}$$

$$\text{Standard time} = \frac{\text{normal time}}{1 - \text{allowance fraction}}$$

Example 1.26

A work operation consisting of three procedures is observed using a stopwatch time procedure. The allowance for the work operation is 15 percent. It is necessary to determine the standard time for the operation, and what the standard should be in hours per fifteen hundred units. The observed data appear in Table 1.1.

Table 1.1 Stopwatch Time Study

Job Element	Performance rating (%)	Observations (seconds/element)										Mean Time (sec)	Normal Time (sec)
		1	2	3	4	5	6	7	8	9	10		
1	85	10	4	9	8	5	6	8	6	8	8	7	6
2	90	11	9	12	12	14	11	10	9	11	13	11	10
3	105	8	9	9	7	8	6	10	7	8	9	8	9
												Total:	25

The standard time is 28.94 seconds/unit, and the standard for 1,500 units is 12.06 hours.

Example 1.27

A manager wants to determine the required sample size for three different work-cycle elements after having performed twelve sample observations. The manager is seeking a 95.5 percent statistical confidence level, with an accuracy of plus or minus 5 percent. Refer to Exhibit 1.6.

Exhibit 1.6 Required Sample Size at .005 Level of Confidence

Sample Observation	Element 1		Element 2		Element 3	
	X	X^2	X	X^2	X	X^2
1	8	64	12	144	7	49
2	7	49	13	169	6	36
3	10	100	14	196	9	81
4	9	81	16	256	8	64
5	6	36	18	324	9	81
6	8	64	15	225	7	49
7	9	81	16	256	9	81
8	10	100	17	289	8	64
9	9	81	14	196	7	49
10	9	81	15	225	8	64
11	7	49	16	256	7	49
12	8	64	14	196	9	81
Total	100	850	180	2,732	94	748

Z = 95.5% confidence level = 2

Element 1:

$$N = \frac{nZ^2[nX^2 - (X)^2]}{(n-1)a^2(X)^2}$$

$$= \frac{12(4)[12(850) - 10,000]}{11(.0025)\,10,000} = 34.91$$

Element 2:

$$N = \frac{12(4)[12(2.732) - 32.400]}{11(.0025)\,32,400} = 20.69$$

Element 3:

$$N = \frac{12(4)[12(748) - 8,836]}{11(.0025)\,8,836} = 27.66$$

Element 1 has the largest required sample size of 35. Therefore, the manager needs to make another 23 sample observations to complete the total sample size of 35.

1.8 WORK SAMPLING

Work sampling is a work measurement methodology that estimates the time an employee utilizes in performing assigned job tasks. The methodology uses random observations of actual worker activity and is dependent on the laws of probability. Since it does not require a formalized time study procedure conducted by qualified stopwatch analysts, it is less costly. The methodology requires that the manager simply determine whether an employee is actually working or is idle during any particular observation.

After all the observations have been completed, the percentage of working observations is computed from the total observations. The greater the number of observations, the more accurate the technique.

How is work sampling used?

Work sampling is used for the following:

1. *Ratio delay studies.* Worker allowances are determined by calculating the percentage of time an employee spends on unavoidable delays.

2. *Percent utilization of equipment.* This technique is used to determine the actual utilization of machinery and other equipment.

3. *Determining labor standards.* This technique is useful in determining work standards for various tasks by rating the employee's performance.

4. *Evaluating employee performance.* A performance standard can be calculated utilizing the work sampling procedure and resulting standards.

How is work sampling performed?

1. *Sample observations.* Several sample observations are performed, to act as the basis for developing a correct sample size based on the problem's parameters.

2. *Compute the actual sample size.* The sample size is dependent on the desired level of statistical confidence and accuracy.

   Normally, the acceptable level of confidence is 95 percent, with an accuracy level of plus or minus 5 percent. The following formula determines the actual sample size necessary for a work sampling procedure:

$$N = \frac{Z^2 (1 - p)}{a^2 p}$$

where

P = estimate of time utilized in an activity

$1 - p$ = estimate of time not utilized in an activity

a = accuracy level fraction

Z = confidence level ($Z = 1$ for 68.3% confidence level, $Z = 2$ for 95.5% confidence level, and $Z = 3$ for 99.7% confidence level)

A higher confidence level and a reduced accuracy level fraction will increase the required sample size. The 95 percent confidence level and ± 5 percent accuracy level establish that in 95 cases out of 100 the sampling activity will be accurate within ± 5 percent of the proportion of time utilized in an activity (p).

3. *Prepare a random schedule of employee observations.*

4. *Observe and rate the employee's work performance.*

5. *Total the number of units produced, and calculate the normal time per unit.*

6. *Compute the standard time per unit.*

Example 1.28

The supervisor of a large production organization wants to determine what the idle time is with a confidence level of 95.5 percent and an accuracy level of 5 percent. After performing a random sample of seventy-five observations, it is determined that there is 20 percent idleness. Analyze the percentage of operational idleness. The required sample size is determined using the following formula:

$$Z = 95.5\% \text{ confidence level} = 2$$

$$N = \frac{Z^2 (1 - p)}{a^2 p} = \frac{4 (1 - .20)}{0.0025(0.2)} = 6,400$$

Additional observations needed for sample = $6,400 - 75 = 6,325$

For establishing labor standards, work samples are used in a manner similar to time studies. However, work samples are more appropriate for operations having long production cycles, group service or production operations, and work using indirect labor. A determination is made as to whether an employee is busy or idle during the observation, a ratio is given to the employee, and the units produced are totaled in order to produce an average. Using this data, the normal time and standard time can be determined:

$$\text{Normal time} = \frac{(\text{Total study time}) \times (\text{working time percent}) \times (\text{performance rating})}{\text{numbers of units produced}}$$

The standard time is the normal time plus allowance time:

$$\text{standard time} = \text{normal time} + \text{allowance time}$$

$$= \frac{\text{normal time}}{1 - \text{allowance time}}$$

Example 1.29

A work-sample study of a production operator was conducted over sixty hours (thirty-six hundred minutes) and disclosed the following data:

Number of pieces produced	580
Total number of observations	800
Total number of observations working	650
Average performance rating	95%

The total allowance given by the company for this operation is 15 percent. What is the standard time for each operation?

$$\text{Normal time} = \frac{\text{(Total study time)} \times \text{(working time percent)} \times \text{(performance rating)}}{\text{numbers of units produced}}$$

$$= \frac{(3,600 \text{ min.})(0.8125)(.95)}{580}$$

$$= 4.8 \text{ minutes/unit of production}$$

$$\text{Standard time} = \frac{\text{normal time}}{1 - \text{allowance time}}$$

$$= \frac{4.8}{1 - .15} = 5.65 \text{ minutes/unit of production}$$

1.9 AGGREGATE PLANNING STRATEGIES

Planning is a primary management responsibility. Aggregate planning is concerned with organizing the quantity and timing of production over a medium period of time, up to eight to ten months, with undetermined demand. Specifically, aggregate planning means combining all of an organization's resources into one aggregate production schedule for a predetermined intermediate time period. The objective of aggregate planning is to maximize resources while minimizing cost over the planning period.

The aggregate production plan is midway between short-range planning and long-range planning. Aggregate planning includes the following factors:

1. Workforce size and composition
2. Demand forecasts and orders
3. Raw material planning
4. Plant capacity management
5. Use of outside subcontractors
6. Inventory management

Aggregate planning is the link between short-term scheduling and long-term capacity planning.

What are aggregate planning strategies?

There are three types of aggregate planning strategies:

Pure strategy. In this strategy, only one production or supply factor is changed.

Mixed strategy. This strategy simultaneously alters two or more production or supply factors, or some combination thereof.

Level scheduling. This strategy has been adopted by the Japanese; it embodies maintaining constant monthly production schedules.

What aggregate planning strategies influence demand?

Aggregate planning can influence demand in the following ways:

1. *Pricing strategies.* Pricing can be used to increase or reduce demand. All things being equal, increasing prices reduces demand, while lowering prices increases demand.

2. *Advertising and promotion strategies.* Advertising and promotion are pure demand management strategies in that they can increase demand by making a product or service better known, as well as positioning it for a particular market segment.

3. *Delayed deliveries or reservations.* Managing future delivery schedules is a strategy for managing orders when demand exceeds capacity. The net effect of delayed deliveries, or back ordering, and reservations is to shift demand to a later period of time—often to a more slack period—which provides a smoothing effect for overall demand. However, the negative is that a percentage of orders will be lost as consumers are unwilling or unable to wait the additional amount of time.

4. *Product mix diversification.* Product mix diversification is a method used to offset demand seasonality. For example, a lawn-mower manufacturing company may diversify into snow-removal equipment to offset the seasonality of the lawn-mower industry.

What aggregate planning strategies influence supply?

Aggregate planning is also used to manage supply considerations by using the following strategies:

Subcontracting. Subcontracting is a method of increasing capacity without incurring large capital investment charges. It can turn the competitive advantage of other corporations to the contracting organization's advantage. However, subcontracting can be costly and also reveals part of the business to potential competitors.

Overtime and idle time. A direct short-term strategy for managing production capacity is to either increase or decrease the size of the workforce. This strategy has the advantage of utilizing the currently existing workforce. However, overtime is expensive and can produce job burnout if relied upon too extensively. On the other hand, enforcing idle time on the workforce can result in resistance as well as a drop in morale.

Hiring and laying off employees. Hiring and laying off employees is a medium- to long-term strategy for increasing or decreasing capacity. Hiring employees usually involves the cost of training, while laying off employees can incur severance charges. Laying off employees can also cause labor difficulties with unions and reduce morale.

Stockpiling inventory. Accumulating inventory is a strategy for smoothing variances which may occur between demand and supply.

Part-time employees. Certain industries have seasonal requirements for lower-skilled employees. Aggregate planning can be used to manage these seasonal requirements.

What is the charting method of aggregate planning?

Charting is a highly utilized trial-and-error aggregate planning method. It is relatively simple to use and is easily understood. Essentially, the charting approach uses a few variables in forecasting demand and applying current production capacity. While the charting method does not assure an accurate prediction, it is simple to implement, requiring only minimal calculations.

The charting method requires five steps to implement:

1. Calculate each period's demand.
2. Calculate each period's production capacity for regular time, overtime, and subcontracting.
3. Determine all labor costs, including costs for hiring and layoffs, as well as the cost of holding inventory.

4. Evaluate organizational employee and stock policies.
5. Create optional policies and evaluate their costs.

Example 1.30

A Florida men's suit manufacturer has created expected demand forecasts for the period June–January, as shown in Table 1.2.

Table 1.2 Expected Demand for Men's Suits, Production Days, and Daily Demand

Month	Expected Demand	Production Days	Daily Demand
July	5,500	20	275
August	5,200	22	236
September	5,300	21	252
October	4,800	21	229
November	4,300	19	226
December	4,100	20	205
Average			237

The daily demand is calculated by dividing the total expected demand by the number of monthly working days:

$$\frac{\text{Average}}{\text{demand}} = \frac{\text{Total expected demand}}{\text{Number of production days}}$$

Figure 1.6 Monthly and Average Men's Suit Demand

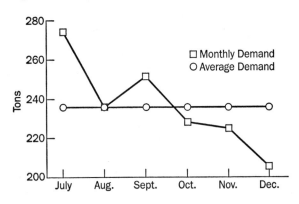

The graph in Figure 1.6 illustrates that there is a substantial variance between the the monthly and average men's suit demand.

What are the costs of aggregate planning?

Aggregate planning is a systems methodology that has major organizational impacts. Every strategy has associated costs and benefits. Increasing hiring means increasing training costs and incurring the associated employment benefit costs. Increasing inventory increases carrying costs, which consist of capital and storage costs, deterioration, and obsolescence. Using part-time employees involves the costs and risks of using improperly trained and inexperienced personnel, as well as possibly creating union conflicts. Using subcontractors has the cost of exposing an organization to potential competitors.

Example 1.31

Using the data in Example 1.30, it is possible to develop cost estimates for the men's suit manufacturer. Basically, the manufacturer has three choices:

- The manufacturer can meet expected monthly production fluctuations by varying the workforce size—hiring and laying off employees as needed. In this scenario, an assumption is made that the men's suit manufacturer has a constant staff of fifty-five employees.

- Another alternative is to maintain a constant workforce of fifty-one employees and subcontract for additional expected demand.

- A third alternative is to maintain a workforce of sixty-nine employees and store suits during the low-demand months.

Organizational Costs	
Inventory Holding Cost Per Unit Per Month	$3
Subcontracting Cost Per Unit	$25
Labor Hours Per Men's Suit	$2
Layoff Cost Per Employee	$500
Hiring and Training Cost Per Employee	$650

THREE PLAN SUMMARY COSTS

Items	Plan 1 Hiring & Laying Off	Plan 2 Sub- contract	Plan 3 Store Inventory
Hiring Costs	19,278		
Layoff Costs	2,000		
Inventory Holding Costs			14,244
Subcontractor Costs		102,700	
Total	21,278	102,700	14,244

In this example, the best production plan is Plan 3, which maintains a workforce of sixty-nine employees and stores men's suit inventory during low-demand months.

1.10 TRANSPORTATION METHOD

The objective of the transportation method is to limit shipment costs from several points of origin to several points of destination. Organizations that have an origin and destination network must maximize effectiveness in order to limit costs while expediting the shipments.

How is the transportation method implemented?

The transportation method is implemented initially by determining point of origin, predictive capacities, destination requirements, and shipment costs to the various destinations from the point of origin. The analysis utilizes a matrix containing these factors.

Example 1.32

A company manufactures furnaces in three different cities—A, B, and C—located in various regions of the country. They are shipped to three different warehouses—D, B, and F—also located in various regions of the country. Each manufacturing site has different capacities, and each warehouse has different requirements. A transportation matrix is developed to illustrate the data in Figure 1.7 on page 44.

Plan 1

Month	Required Number of Suits	Required Production Hours (Suits Required × 2)	Hours Available per Employee per Month (No. of Days × 8)	Workers Required (Required Production Hours/ Hours Available)	Workers Hired	Workers Laid Off	Hiring Cost (Workers Hired × $650)	Layoff Cost (Workers Laid Off × $500)
July	5,500	11,000	160	69	14	0	8,938	
August	5,200	10,400	176	59	4	0	2,659	
September	5,300	10,600	168	63	8	0	5,262	
October	4,800	9,600	168	57	2	0	1,393	
November	4,300	8,600	152	57	2	0	1,026	
December	4,100	8,200	160	51		4		2,000
Total							19,278	2,000

Plan 2

Month	Required Number of Suits	Available Production Hours (No. of Days × 8 × 51)	Number of Suits Produced (Available Hours/2)	Suits Subcontracted	Subcontractor Cost (Tons Subcontracted × $25)
July	5,500	8,160	4,080	1,420	35,500
August	5,200	8,976	4,488	712	17,800
September	5,300	8,568	4,284	1,016	25,400
October	4,800	8,568	4,284	516	12,900
November	4,300	7,752	3,876	424	10,600
December	4,100	8,160	4,080	20	500
Total					102,700

Plan 3

Month	Required Number of Suits	Available Production Hours (No. of Days × 8 × 69)	Number of Suits Produced (Available Hours/2)	Ending Inventory of Suits	Inventory Holding Cost (Ending Inventory × $3)
July	5,500	11,040	5,520	20	60
August	5,200	12,144	6,072	872	2,616
September	5,300	11,592	5,796	496	1,488
October	4,800	11,592	5,796	996	2,988
November	4,300	10,488	5,244	944	2,832
December	4,100	11,040	5,520	1,420	4,260
Total					14,244

Figure 1.7 A Transportation Matrix

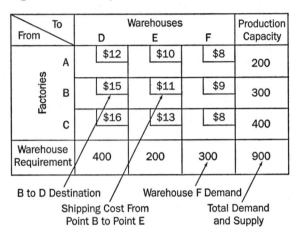

To / From		Warehouses			Production Capacity
		D	E	F	
Factories	A	$12	$10	$8	200
	B	$15	$11	$9	300
	C	$16	$13	$8	400
Warehouse Requirement		400	200	300	900

B to D Destination

Shipping Cost From Point B to Point E

Warehouse F Demand

Total Demand and Supply

What is the Northwest corner rule?

In the Northwest corner rule, the maximum amount of a shipment is shipped from the upper left-hand corner (Northwest corner) of the matrix and distributed through the other cells, going to the right and down throughout the matrix until all demands are met.

Example 1.33

An initial feasible transportation solution from the previous example is shown in Figure 1.8. The following shipments are assumed to have occurred:

1. 200 furnaces are shipped from A to D (this consumes A's production capacity).

2. 200 furnaces are shipped from B to D (this fulfills D's warehouse requirement).

3. 100 furnaces are shipped from B to E (this consumes B's production capacity).

4. 100 furnaces are shipped from C to E (this fulfills E's requirement).

5. 300 furnaces are shipped from C to F (this fulfills F's warehouse requirement and C's production capacity).

Using this information, furnace shipping costs are calculated for each respective destination, as shown in Table 1.3.

Figure 1.8 Warehouses, Demand, and Shipping Costs

To / From	Warehouses			Production Capacity
	D	**E**	**F**	
A	$12 / 200	$10	$8	200
B	$15 / 200	$11 / 100	$9	300
C	$16	$13 / 100	$8 / 300	400
Warehouse Requirement	400	200	300	900

(Factories: A, B, C)

Table 1.3 Respective Furnace Shipping Costs for Each Destination

Route	Furnaces Shipped	Unit Cost	Total Cost
From A to D	200	$12	$1,200
From B to D	200	$15	$3,000
From B to E	100	$11	$1,100
From C to E	100	$13	$1,300
From C to F	300	$8	$2,400
Total Cost			$9,000

This is an initial solution, in which all demands and capacities are utilized. However, this may not be the least expensive transportation solution for this set of variables because no consideration was given to limiting costs.

What is the stepping-stone method, and how does it reach an optimum transportation solution?

The stepping-stone method is a technique for optimizing an initial transportation solution. The methodology calculates cost by testing each unused square in a transportation table. The following methodology is followed to calculate an optimal transportation solution:

1. Choose any unused square in a transportation table, such as Figure 1.8.
2. Develop a closed horizontal and vertical path back to the original square through the squares that are being used. Unused squares are skipped in the process.

3. The first unused square is marked with a plus (+) sign and subsequent corner squares in the developed closed path are alternately marked with minus (−) and plus (+) signs.

4. An evaluation index is created by adding the unit cost figures in each square containing a plus sign, and then subtracting the unit costs in each square containing a minus sign.

5. The methodology repeats all of these steps until an evaluation index is calculated for all the unused squares. An optimal solution is achieved when all the results are equal to or greater than zero. If a square evaluation is negative, cost reductions can be accomplished by transferring as many units as possible to that square.

Example 1.34

Using the transportation matrix for the furnace company, the stepping-stone method can be used to evaluate an optimal shipping route. Every empty cell must be tested using a closing pathway of engaged cells. In the stepping-stone method, the number of engaged squares has to equal the number of rows in the table plus the number of columns minus one (R + C − 1 = number of engaged cells). In the furnace example we have

$$R + C - 1 = \text{number of engaged cells}$$
$$3 + 3 - 1 = 5$$

If there are fewer engaged cells than the stepping-stone rule calls for, there is a degeneracy, meaning it is not possible to trace a closed path for one or more unoccupied squares. Trace shipping route A to E: starting in empty cell AE, a route is traced using only engaged squares. Thus, a route is traced from AE to AD to AB to BE, and alternate plus and minus signs are placed in each square. This is shown in Figure 1.9.

A shipping cost index for route AE is calculated using the shipment costs in the upper right-hand corner of each square:

$$\$10 - \$12 + \$15 - \$11 = +\$2$$

Thus, for route AE, an additional cost of $2 would be incurred for each furnace shipped.

Figure 1.10 shows shipping route AF.

Figure 1.9 Shipping Route AE

From \ To	Warehouses			Production Capacity
	D	E	F	
A	$12 − 200	$10 +	$8	200
B	$15 + 200	$11 →100 −	$9	300
C	$16	$13 100	$8 300	400
Warehouse Requirement	400	200	300	900

The shipping cost index for shipping route AF is

$$\$8 - \$12 + \$15 - \$11 + \$13 - \$8 = +\$5$$

Using route AF will increase furnace shipping costs by $5 per unit.

Shipping route BF (not shown) would start in square BF, going to square BE, to square CE, and back to square BF. The shipping cost index for shipping route BE is

$$\$9 - \$11 + \$13 - \$8 = +\$3$$

Using route BE will increase furnace shipping costs by $3 per unit.

Figure 1.11 presents route CD. The shipping cost index for route CD is

$$\$16 - \$13 + \$11 - \$15 = -\$1$$

Of the three routes, shipping route CD is the optimum because it would reduce the furnace shipping costs by $1 per unit.

Figure 1.10 Shipping Route AF

From \ To	Warehouses			Production Capacity
	D	E	F	
A	$12 − 200	$10 +	$8	200
B	$15 + 200	− $11 →100	$9	300
C	$16	+ $13 100	$8 →300	400
Warehouse Requirement	400	200	300	900

Figure 1.11 Shipping Route CD

To From	Warehouses			Production Capacity
	D	**E**	**F**	
A	$12 200	$10	$8	200
B	$15 − 200◄----¬100	+ $11	$9	300
C	¦$16 + └----→¹100	−¦ $13	$8 300	400
Warehouse Requirement	400	200	300	900

The total amount that may be shipped on the optimum route is the smallest number in the squares having minus signs. Thus, in shipping route CD, one hundred furnaces (found in square CE) is the greatest amount that can be shipped. Using shipping route CD reduces furnace shipping costs by $100 (100 units × $1 = $100).

1.11 SCHEDULING

Scheduling is the management of organizational resources to achieve an orderly and uninterrupted workflow process. The basic objective of scheduling is to maintain high organizational productivity, low inventory levels, and high levels of customer satisfaction. Scheduling involves the use of time and the setting of priorities into operational rules. Scheduling is generally categorized into forward and backward scheduling.

What is forward scheduling?

Forward scheduling begins as soon as demand is known. This type of scheduling is generally used by custom fabricators and manufacturers who rely on individual customer orders. Normally, forward scheduling assumes a very short delivery date. It is essential that fabrication and manufacturing times be accurately estimated in order to develop reliable deadlines. This mandates the development of reliable estimates of fabrication and manufacturing capacities.

What is backward scheduling?

In backward scheduling, start and due dates, as well as the required capacity for individual jobs, are developed by calculating processing times and required capacities sequentially from the last job back to the first.

What is shop loading?

Shop loading is the apportioning of jobs to production centers. Although this method determines which manufacturing centers receive specific jobs, it does not specify processing priorities. When job orders can be performed equally well by several manufacturing centers, prioritizing the manufacturing centers becomes necessary.

What are the two shop-loading methods?

The two shop-loading methods are infinite loading and finite loading. Infinite loading does not consider capacity limitations when apportioning jobs to work centers, whereas finite loading apportions work to manufacturing centers consistent with their production capacities.

Infinite loading monitors and measures production underloads and overloads and projects the timing sequence of their occurrence. The net result of infinite loading's monitoring and measuring of the production process results in a determination of capacity requirements. An overload occurs when a manufacturing center cannot finish scheduled jobs because of capacity constraints; an underload occurs when a manufacturing center experiences periods of idleness because of insufficient job scheduling.

Because finite loading does not permit capacity overloads, it mandates job rescheduling based on existing manufacturing capacities.

What are the advantages of finite and infinite loading?

All jobs must be prioritized before finite loading can be implemented. Since finite loading cannot exceed capacity, it should generate more realistic completion times. Those jobs not having the highest priority are rescheduled for a later time.

Infinite loading's advantage is that it does not consider capacity. Therefore, it gives a more realistic assessment of what production capacity is really required to complete designated jobs. Using the capacity requirements that infinite loading provides allows management to more accurately schedule work among the available manufacturing centers.

How are Gantt charts useful in loading and scheduling?

The Gantt load chart depicts the apportioning of jobs to a production center. Many variations exist, but usually the load chart is a table depicting the production center, assigned jobs, hours required for the assigned jobs, and remaining capacity in hours arranged along horizontal and vertical lines.

A Gantt schedule chart is a graph used to analyze the progress of currently scheduled jobs. It is a visual method for surveying the actual progress of jobs in production.

What are the advantages and disadvantages of the Gantt loading and scheduling charts?

Gantt charts are a very popular management tool for assessing job loading for production centers, as well as for analyzing actual job progress in the production centers. They are easy to develop and understand.

However, critics feel that Gantt charts are unsophisticated in the sense that no allowance is provided for uncontrollable production delays resulting from human error, unavoidable technical failures, or material shortages. The charts also require continual adjustment as conditions change. Furthermore, when there is more than one production center that is equally capable of processing job orders, the Gantt methodology does not provide the required sophistication to help management make decisions as to which production center should process particular jobs. Essentially, Gantt charts tend to be more useful in simply maintaining records regarding current operations.

Figure 1.12 Gantt Load Chart

| | Production Center | | | | | |
| | No. 1 | | No. 2 | | No. 3 | |
Job Number	Re- quired	Avail- able	Re- quired	Avail- able	Re- quired	Avail- able
1	7	70	2	50	3	60
2	3	63	4	48	6	57
3	6	60	5	44	4	51
4	4	54	3	39	7	47
5	9	50	7	36	8	40
6	2	41	6	29	4	32
7	4	39	4	23	8	28
8	7	35	8	19	5	20
9	3	28	4	11	7	15
10	4	25	5	7	2	8
Remaining Hours		21		2		6

Example 1.35

It is necessary to chart the loading of ten jobs and to calculate the remaining production hours available in three different production centers. A Gantt load chart, shown in Figure 1.12, is prepared to demonstrate the loading of the jobs.

Example 1.36

Management needs to visualize the scheduling and production status of four different job orders, 1, 2, 3, and 4. A Gantt scheduling chart, shown in Figure 1.13, displays the scheduling and production status of the four products.

Figure 1.13 Gantt Scheduling Chart

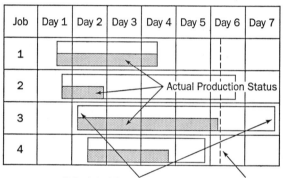

Scheduled Production Time   Observation Date

1.12 SEQUENCING

Gantt charts are useful for tracking job loading, but they do not have the sophistication to help management determine what job order priorities should be. Sequencing is a process that prioritizes job orders in the manufacturing process.

What are priority rules?

The basic function of priority rules is to provide direction for developing the sequence in which jobs should be performed. Priority rules assist management in ranking job loading decisions for manufacturing centers.

There are several priority rules that can be applied to job loading. The most widely used priority rules are

DD—Due Date of a Job. The job with the earliest due date has the highest priority.

FCFS—First Come, First Served. The first job to reach the production center is processed first.

LPT—Longest Processing Time. Jobs with the longest processing time have the highest priority.

PCO—Preferred Customer Order. A job from a preferred customer receives the highest priority.

SPT—Shortest Processing Time. The job with the shortest processing time has the highest priority.

Example 1.37

Using the data contained in the following table, Job Processing Data, it is necessary to schedule orders according to the priority rules of Due Date (DD); First Come, First Served (FCFS); Longest Processing Time (LPT); Preferred Customer Order (PCO); and Shortest Processing Time (SPT).

	Job Processing Data		
Job	*Preferred Customer Status (1 = Highest)*	*Processing Time (days)*	*Due Date (days)*
A	3	7	9
B	4	4	6
C	2	2	4
D	5	8	10
E	1	3	5

PRIORITY RULES AND JOB SEQUENCING OUTCOMES

	Priority Rules			
Due Date	*First Come, First Served*	*Longest Processing Time*	*Preferred Customer Order*	*Shortest Processing Time*
C	A	D	E	C
E	B	A	B	E
B	C	B	A	B
A	D	E	C	A
D	E	C	D	D

What is the critical ratio method?

The critical ratio method assigns a priority based on a continually updated ratio between the time remaining until the due date and the required job processing time. When used in conjunction with other jobs waiting to be processed, the critical ratio method is a relative measure of critical job order priority. The critical ratio gives the highest priority to jobs that must be done to maintain a predetermined shipping schedule. Jobs that are falling behind a shipping schedule receive a ratio of less than 1; a job receiving a critical ratio greater than 1 is ahead of schedule, and is, therefore less critical. A job receiving a critical ratio score of 1.0 is precisely on schedule.

The critical ratio is calculated by dividing the remaining time until the date due by the remaining process time using the following formula:

$$\text{critical ratio} = \frac{\text{remaining time}}{\text{remaining process time}}$$

$$= \frac{\text{due date} - \text{today's date}}{\text{days of remaining process time}}$$

Example 1.38

On day 16, four jobs—A, B, C, and D—are on order for Ferguson's Kitchen Installation Service:

	Jobs on Order	
Job	*Due Date*	*Days of Remaining Process Time*
A	27	8
B	34	16
C	29	15
D	30	12

Using this data, the critical ratios and priority order are computed.

	Critical Ratios and Priority Order	
Job	*Critical Ratio*	*Priority*
A	(27 − 16)/8 = 1.38	4
B	(34 − 16)/16 = 1.13	3
C	(29 − 16)/15 = .87	1
D	(30 − 16)114 = 1	2

Job C has a critical ratio of less than 1, indicating that it has fallen behind schedule. Therefore, it gets the highest priority. Job D is exactly on schedule, but jobs B and A have respectively higher critical ratios, indicating they have some slack time. This gives them respectively lower priorities.

What is Johnson's rule for scheduling N jobs in two production centers?

Johnson's rule provides an optimum prioritization based on minimum processing time when N jobs have to be sequentially processed in two production centers. The net result of utilizing Johnson's rule is a minimization of total idle time at a production center.

The procedure for using Johnson's rule follows:

1. Show all the processing times for all orders at each respective processing site.
2. Find the job with the shortest processing time. If the job is at the first processing site, schedule it first; however, if it is at the second processing site, schedule it last.
3. Once the job is scheduled, it receives no further consideration.
4. The remaining jobs are scheduled using rules 2 and 3.

Example 1.39

Five job orders must be sequentially processed through two processing centers. The orders need to be sequenced to achieve minimum idle time.

Processing Time for Jobs in Hours		
Job	Processing Center 1	Processing Center 2
A	11	3
B	6	8
C	9	4
D	2	9
E	10	6

Now it is necessary to sequence the jobs, starting with the smallest processing time. The smallest job is Job D, in Processing Center 1. Since Job D is in Pro-

cessing Center 1, it is sequenced first, and then eliminated from further consideration.

D				

The second smallest processing time is Job A in Processing Center 2. Job A is placed last, because it is at
Processing Center 2, and eliminated from further consideration.

D				A

The next smallest processing time is Job C, in Processing Center 2. Job C is placed next to last.

D			C	A

For the next smallest processing time, there is a tie
between Job B, in Processing Center 1, and Job E, in
Processing Center 2. Job B is placed in the next highest
sequence after Job D, and Job E is placed directly after
Job B.

D	B	E	C	A

The resulting sequential processing times are

Processing Center 1	2	6	10	9	11
Processing Center 2	9	8	6	4	3

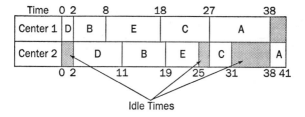

Idle Times

In Processing Center 2, the five jobs are completed
in forty-one hours, and there are eleven hours of idle
time.

1.13 PROJECT MANAGEMENT TECHNIQUES: PERT AND CPM

What is PERT?

The Program Evaluation Review Technique (PERT) was originally developed for the U.S. Navy's Polaris submarine project. The primary purpose of PERT is to plan, schedule, and coordinate the sequential activities required in one time-complex project. The PERT model develops a graphical depiction of the sequential activities required to complete a project. It then determines the total anticipated time needed for the project's completion. PERT is considered a network method of project scheduling because activities are depicted as arrows, while intermediate goals, or events, are depicted as circles. There are four steps necessary in developing a PERT network project schedule:

1. A comprehensive project analysis is performed.
2. All the required project activities are categorized according to their order of precedence.
3. A PERT chart is drawn; all the activities preceding an event are shown using lettered arrows, and events are numbered using circles.
4. Time and/or cost estimates are assigned to each activity.

Example 1.40

It is necessary for a manager to develop a PERT network using the following information, listing activities and their respective predecessors.

Activity	Preceding Activity
A	—
B	—
C	B
D	B
E	B
F	C
G	D
H	E

A PERT chart is drawn as in Figure 1.14, where all the activities are lettered using arrows, and the events are numbered using circles.

Figure 1.14 PERT Network Project Schedule

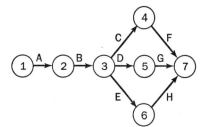

Activities can also be designated by their beginning and ending events. For example

Beginning Event	Ending Event	Activity
1	2	1–2
2	3	2–3
2	4	2–4
3	4	3–4
4	5	4–5
4	6	4–6
5	7	5–7

What is the critical path method (CPM)?

The critical path method was originally developed to schedule the startups and shutdowns of major production plants. This method is based on developing three activity-time estimates for calculating project completion time with variances. The three time estimates are optimistic time (a), pessimistic time (b), and most likely time (m).

What are the optimistic, pessimistic, and most likely times?

Optimistic time (a) is an estimate of the least, or minimum, time an activity will take to complete. Pessimistic time (b) is an estimate of the most, or maximum, time an activity will take to complete. Most likely time (m) is an estimate of the average, or normal, amount of time an activity would take, assuming it were to be repeated several times.

In arriving at an expected time (t) for a given project activity, a beta probability distribution is employed in PERT. The three time estimates are combined and averaged to calculate a single time estimate. Normally, in PERT applications the most likely time (m) is given a weight of four, while the optimistic time (a) and pessimistic time (b) are each given a weight of one. The variance (v) for each activity is also calculated:

$$t = \frac{A + 4m + b}{6}$$

and

$$v = \left[\frac{b - a}{6}\right]^2$$

The expected times (t) and variance (v) are calculated for each activity after the network for the PERT analysis is completed.

Example 1.41

There are five activities in a project. It is necessary to compute the expected times and variances for the project:

Activity	Optimistic Time (a)	Most Likely Time (m)	Pessimistic Time (b)	t $\frac{a + 4m + b}{6}$	V $\frac{b - a}{6}$
1–2	5	7	9	7	0.67
1–3	1	3	5	3	0.67
2–4	2	3	4	3	0.33
3–4	4	6	8	6	0.67
3–5	3	7	9	6.67	1

What is critical path analysis?

Critical path analysis consists of analyzing a sequence of activities from the beginning event to the ending event. The critical path is the time it takes to finish all the project's activities without any slack time. This is critical to the completion of a project because it controls the project's completion time. To calculate the critical path, data must be obtained on the earliest start and finish times, the latest start and finish times, and the available slack time:

1. *ES.* Earliest activity start time. The time at which all preceding activities are finished; the earliest an activity can commence.

2. *LS.* Latest activity start time. The time at which all successor activities have to be finished without delaying the entire project. The latest activity start time is calculated by subtracting the expected time of the activity (t) from the latest finish time (LF), and then subsequently subtracting (t) for the longest path(s).

3. *EF.* Earliest activity finish time. The earliest activity finish time equals the earliest activity start time (ES) of the activity, plus expected time (*t*) for the activity.

4. *LF.* Latest finish time. The time at which the project must be finished. The latest activity finish time equals the latest start time (LS), plus the expected time (*t*) of the activity.

5. *S.* Slack time. An activity's total slack is the difference between the latest and earliest activity start times (LS − ES) or the latest and earliest activity finish times (LF − EF).

After calculating the preceding data for each activity, the overall project can be analyzed. This includes the critical path, which is the time it takes to finish all the project's activities, without any slack time.

Example 1.42

Using the PERT chart in Figure 1.15, calculate the ES and EF for each activity.

Figure 1.15 PERT Chart

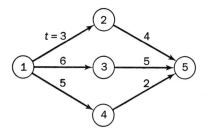

Now the earliest start (ES) and earliest activity finish times (EF) are determined. In order for an activity to begin, all preceding activities must be finished. EF is calculated by adding the expected time (*t*) to the ES for each activity.

Activity	*t*	*ES*	*EF* (*t* + *ES*)
1–2	3	0	3
1–3	6	0	6
1–4	5	0	5
2–5	4	3	7
3–5	5	6	11
4–5	2	5	7

The latest activity finish time (LF) of the project is 11, since the earliest activity finish time (EF) for activity 3–5 is 11.

In order to calculate a project's critical path, it is necessary to determine the latest start time (LS) by subtracting the expected time (t) of the activity from the latest finish time (LF). It is also necessary to determine the slack time for each activity by subtracting the earliest activity start time (ES) from the latest activity start time (LS).

Example 1.43

Using the above data, what are the project's slack time and critical path?

Activity	t	ES	EF (t + ES)	LS	LF (LS + t)	S (LS − ES)
1–2	3	0	3	4	7	4
1–3	6	0	6	0	6	0
1–4	5	0	5	4	9	4
2–5	4	3	7	7	11	4
3–5	5	6	11	6	11	0
4–5	2	5	7	9	11	4

The critical path is the activity with 0 slack time, or activity 3–5. The total completion time of the project is 11, since activity 3–5 is the longest path to completion. Figure 1.16 presents the critical path.

Figure 1.16 PERT Chart Showing Critical Path

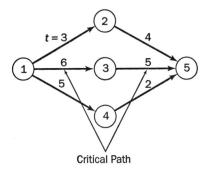

Critical Path

CHAPTER 2

Management

Management is a process that utilizes various functions and activities to help an organization accomplish its goals. Managers are charged with the responsibility of achieving the organization's goals by getting things done. Above all else, the management process is dependent on coordinating and motivating people in the organization to achieve high-quality outcomes. The study of management involves theories, principles, and concepts used in this process.

2.1 JUST-IN-TIME (JIT) INVENTORY

Inventory is maintained in order to prevent production problems caused by the lack of supply of needed materials. Just-in-time (JIT) is an inventory system that maintains the smallest amount of inventory necessary to continue the organizational production process and to minimize costs.

What is the cost of inventory?

Inventory entails many hidden and obvious costs. Among these are the costs of carrying, ordering, and storing supplies, as well as the risks of obsolescence, spoilage, shrinkage, inadequate insurance, and undetected defects. Inventory costs can involve an enormous amount of money.

How does the Just-in-Time (JIT) Inventory Management System work?

The Just-in-Time Inventory Management System seeks to provide the exact amount of production materials when needed, without shortages or excess inventory. In order to maintain this exacting performance specification, the methodology is designed to minimize system variances both inside and outside of the production process.

What are system variances, and what causes them?

Basically, production system variances occur because of ineffective management practices and insufficient utilization and/or processing of production materials—i.e., waste. One bottleneck can be an ineffective procurement system, which includes purchasing, source, supply, and materials management.

Waste occurs because

- Production results have unacceptable quality, quantity, or timeliness due to poor employee training, low quality production resources, or poor-quality materials.
- Design specifications are faulty.
- Customer specifications are incomplete or unrealistic.

How does JIT minimize production variances?

JIT minimizes production variances in the following ways:

- Small lot sizes are used. Small lot sizes require smaller material inventory needs, and delivery times can be more reliably estimated and managed.
- The stages of the manufacturing process are carefully synchronized. This prevents unanticipated material demands.
- Inventory is used only when required instead of accumulating while waiting for need. This is called an inventory "pull" strategy, as opposed to a "push" strategy.
- Smaller lot size produces a steadier inventory demand because maximum and minimum inventory levels are reduced. This can be demonstrated by calculating a mean inventory level:

Mean inventory level = Maximum inventory
+ Minimum inventory level ÷ 2

Example 2.1

A manager wants to understand the mean inventory levels in two different production departments. The first has large lot production of five thousand units, while the second only produces in small lot sizes of two hundred units. The manager must calculate the mean inventory levels:

Lot Size	Minimum Inventory	Maximum Inventory	Mean Inventory Level = Max. Inventory + Min. Inventory/2
5,000	500	9,000	4,750
200	150	250	200
Difference			4,550

The large lot size has a mean inventory level of 4,750, while the small lot size has a mean inventory level of 200. The difference between the large and small lot sizes in mean inventory levels is 4,550.

2.2 MATERIAL REQUIREMENTS PLANNING (MRP)

A material requirements planning (MRP) system provides a methodology for analyzing and forecasting material needs for the purpose of developing a schedule of the material necessary to complete production goals. An MRP system requires a production schedule, a bill of material, inventory and purchase records, and lead times for each production item. The MRP graphically demonstrates when inventory materials need to be ordered, or when production on an item must begin so a particular item will meet the production schedule.

Normally, MRP is computerized. MRP is a widely used inventory management system in companies involved in mass assembly.

Example 2.2

A company produces a consumer item that consists of several components also manufactured by the company. Using these items, an MRP is constructed:

Component Deadline and Start Date	Weeks 1	2	3	4	5	6	7	8	Lead Time
A. Deadline Date								75	1 week
Start Date						75			
B. Deadline Date							150		3 weeks
Start Date			150						
C. Deadline Date							200		2 weeks
Start Date				200					
D. Deadline Date					350				1 week
Start Date			350						
E. Deadline Date				400					1 week
Start Date			400						
F. Deadline Date			550						1 week
Start Date		550							
G. Deadline Date		400							2 weeks
Start Date	400								
H. Deadline Date		500							2 weeks
Start Date	500								

Gross Material Requirements Plan for 75 Units of A

In this gross material requirements example, in order to produce 75 units of A in Week 8, their manufacture must begin in Week 7. However, that requires that 150 components of B and 200 of C be available at that time. In turn, that means manufacture of components B and C must start at Weeks 4 and 5, respectively. The MRP shows the start and deadline dates of the other required components in the manufacturing chain. Transforming these dates into an actual calendar allows managers to quickly view their progress in the manufacturing process.

How is an MRP adjusted when there is inventory on hand?

When there is inventory on hand, the MRP manufacturing schedule is adjusted to the actual net requirements to meet the production deadlines.

2.3 PLANNING

What is planning?

Planning is a fundamental management process that influences an organization's mission, goals, and objectives so management can determine a future course of action. Planning is dynamic and continually responds to changes in the business environment. Rather than requiring management to react to changes, planning allows the proactive control of future environmental variables. The planning process normally results in a management plan that can be widely distributed throughout the organization.

Why is planning essential?

Planning compels an organization to consider its future actions. The reality is that the organizational environment is becoming far more competitive and complex because of increasing international competition and technological progress. While research and development expenditures are increasing, product life cycles are becoming steadily shorter. Planning is absolutely essential in order to develop an understanding of where an organization should be devoting its resources and energy. Without planning, proactive strategies and programs cannot be developed to secure the organization's future success. Planning allows an organization to develop a rational method for controlling and developing the future.

Who is responsible for planning?

The real question in planning authority is whether the planning is centralized or decentralized. Traditionally, the planning function was centralized as a staff management responsibility. The role of the centralized planner was to help shape the organization's mission, goals, and objectives, and to develop management strategies for future actions. This was predicated on the advantage management traditionally had in accessing strategic information. It was only natural for planning to be positioned in a centralized management environment.

As the organizational environment has become more dynamic, with management information systems becoming more sophisticated and ubiquitous, information management capabilities have proliferated throughout all levels of an organization. Thus, the planning function has become integrated into the operational levels of organizations. This provides for a dynamic environment in which the organization's mission, goals, and objectives are continuously being tested and shaped by those with the responsibility for operationalizing them.

What are the advantages of planning?

Planning makes it possible for an organization to

- Achieve a coordinated system in which all levels of the organization have input into operationalizing its mission, goals, and objectives.
- Control and manage the future in a manner consistent with the organization's capabilities and resources.
- Develop a sophisticated management information system so the organization can increase its information-processing capability.
- Define organizational and performance objectives to achieve higher quality and productivity.
- Coordinate an overall management development effort throughout the organization.

What are the types of planning?

There are several ways of categorizing plans. Two methods are specificity and timeliness:

1. *Functionally specific plans.* These plans apply to individual organizational functions, including human resources, operations, financial, and marketing management.

2. *Time range of the plan.* The time range of a plan can correspond with the time parameters of objectives from short- and medium-range to long-range.

Organizational plans are normally classified into several general categories which encompass a wide range of activities and functions:

- *Strategic Planning.* Strategic planning encompasses the broadest and most comprehensive type of planning. It includes the main purpose of the organization, its mission, and the organization's short-, intermediate-, and long-range objectives, including the specific details of how the objectives and goals will be achieved. Strategic planning contains within it operational and tactical planning as well as standing and single-use plans.

- *Tactical Planning.* This type of planning is concerned with specific methods of implementing an overall strategic plan. If, for example, an organization would like to enter a new market, tactical planning would focus on the types of products or services that might be necessary to do that.

- *Operational Planning.* Operational planning is very specific and is concerned with actual methods of operationalizing tactical plans, which are designed to implement the overall strategic plan. For example, an operational plan might be concerned with managing a manufacturing process to produce a specific product developed by a tactical plan.

- *Single-Use Plans.* Single-use plans have very specific time limits and purposes. Single-use plans are used to implement a program, product, project, or service. A single-use plan might, for example, be used for designing and implementing a specific manufacturing process for the production of a particular product within a clearly defined time frame.

- *Standing Plans.* Standing plans are ongoing management plans for particular organizational policies.

What are the steps in the planning process?

There are six basic steps in the planning process:

1. *Survey the current organizational environment.* Before a strategic plan can be established, management must conduct a thorough review of the organization's overall environment. This review must examine the firm's strengths and weaknesses, the competitive and regulatory environ-

ment, and the current economic and market developments. This review will help the organization form a strategic plan; however, this plan must be coordinated with the organization's operational plan, which is based on current cash flow, market performance, and overall capabilities.

2. *Develop goals and objectives.* The survey of the organization's current environment assists the organization in determining short-term objectives and future goals. Organizational objectives have different time spans, depending on the nature of the objectives and the type of organization. Long-range plans can be as long as twenty-five years. Short-term plans can last up to one year, while intermediate-term plans can last from one to five years. All objectives must be met prior to achieving the organization's long-term goals. Complex organizations often have multiple objectives, which create additional planning and budgeting challenges.

   There are several types of organizational objectives:

   • *Quality and productivity objectives.* Quality and productivity go hand in hand. Productivity is a ratio of the input of organizational resources to its output. An example of such a ratio is labor to units produced. However, without some standard of quality, there can be no productivity; conversely, high quality increases productivity by decreasing imperfections and waste.

   • *Marketing objectives.* Marketing objectives are based on the degree of success the organization is experiencing in achieving market, product, and service growth. Management also seeks to evaluate an organization's overall market mix in order to determine where resources should be allocated.

   • *Profitability objectives.* Profitability objectives include the total increase in profits relative to sales and net assets. Numerous financial ratios are used to measure profitability. Profitability objectives are important to management for monitoring an organization's financial progress.

3. *Create an organizational action plan.* The net result of the planning process is the establishment of an organizational action plan designed to achieve short-term objectives and longer-term goals. An organizational action plan is derived from the careful definition and understanding of the organization's

short-term objectives, which are consistent and instrumental in achieving intermediate- to longer-term objectives. After establishing a consensus with those responsible for carrying it out, the plan is transformed into a clearly written document. While the plan must encompass all of the short-, intermediate-, and long-term objectives in order to achieve the organization's longer-term goals, it must also be flexible enough to permit adaptation to future changes in the organizational and external environment.

4. *Earmark resources.* In order to implement an action plan, a careful assessment of the quantity and nature of the necessary resources is required. A budget is developed for the purpose of allocating the required resources. The budget is based upon a priority analysis of each objective. The budget must be consistent with the organizational action plan's short-, intermediate-, and longer-term objectives. Budget allocations require constant monitoring to measure their success in achieving objectives.

5. *Execute the plan.* An organizational action plan will have no effect unless it is carried out. Organizational action plans are executed through the cooperation and teamwork of those within the organization. Management efforts must be coordinated while employees are oriented and trained in the plan's implementation.

6. *Manage the plan.* The management process involves constant feedback regarding the success of the plan in achieving its stated objectives. The use of a management information system would be extremely instrumental in managing the plan's implementation.

Example 2.3

A beer brewery is planning to establish an organizational action plan. The company has several short-term objectives designed to achieve its long-term goal of increasing its overall market share:

- *Offset server liability.* One of the objectives of the company is to offset the server's legal liability when selling alcoholic beverages. The company creates a series of posters to be posted in establishments serving alcoholic beverages. Some posters illustrate the effects of drunk driving, and others cite the necessity of choosing a designated driver. The company also develops beer with a lower alcohol content.

- *Support the actions of Mothers Against Drunk Driving (MADD) and other groups such as Students Against Drunk Driving (SADD).* The company decides to initiate a social responsibility campaign that emphasizes two points: not consuming more than an individual's limit, and the need for responsible automobile driving.

- *Change the image of its products.* In addition to introducing a low-alcohol beer, the company also introduces a low-calorie "lite beer," as well as a non-alcoholic product.

- *Develop a sales training program.* In order to achieve higher sales, the company develops a sales training program that emphasizes the importance of educating customers about the company's variety of beer products, including low-alcohol and low-calorie beverages. It also seeks to demonstrate the company's commitment to social responsibility.

After creating a consensus regarding its organizational action plan, the brewery initiates a training program in which its sales managers and representatives are trained in the significance of the newly developed plan. The company also develops a sophisticated management information system containing a large database, which sales representatives can continuously update from remote locations using telecommunications.

Over time, the company makes steady progress in increasing its market share while improving relations with MADD and SADD. The company has also achieved success in reducing the number of server liability cases as well as driving-while-intoxicated convictions in its market area.

Finally, the company's market share, net profit, and stockholder equity show steady growth.

2.4 TOTAL QUALITY MANAGEMENT (TQM)

Total quality management (TQM) is an extremely well-publicized organizational methodology. It is intended to involve all parts of the organization, beginning with total commitment from top management. It is a system-wide concept in that all parts of the organization must function congruently in order for it to be functional. A major component of TQM is employee involvement, which management strongly encourages in every step of the decision-making process. This is accomplished through in-depth training and the delegation of extensive quality responsibility to operational employees.

What are the main components of TQM?

The following are some of the basic components of TQM:

- Organizations succeed through constant product and service development and innovation.
- Organizations must embrace a new management philosophy, rejecting traditional management views.
- Quality is achieved by design rather than by inspection.
- Purchasing must be based on total cost. Short-term material savings could be disastrous if the quality of materials is unacceptable.
- Production and service methods must be continuously improved. Single or occasional standard review and revision are unacceptable.
- Employees must receive training.
- Management must demonstrate leadership by teaching others what must be done on a continuous basis.
- A positive and personally rewarding organizational environment must be established in order for employees to be productive.
- Organizational communications must be open and free at all levels.
- Slogans and short-term employee objectives are not successful.
- Quotas are not successful motivators.
- Employees should be recognized and rewarded for the work they do.
- Continuous education and training programs should be made available to employees.
- A management program must be created to implement TQM or it will never happen; implementing TQM requires the active support of top management.

What is the role of quality in TQM?

Quality is a central focus in TQM. The concept of quality goes far beyond the acceptance of a standard minimum number of defects; it essentially means preventing defects from occurring in the first place. This concept has come to be known as "zero defects." However, TQM does not limit itself to zero defects in products—it also means providing superb service to develop loyal customers who are so impressed with the quality of the service and products that they recommend the organization to others. TQM's operational definition of quality is nothing less than total customer satisfaction. This is achieved by meeting or exceeding the customer's expectations.

Quality itself is not a fixed objective. Rather, it is a continuously evolving target. Organizations cannot be satisfied merely with achieving zero defects in a product or a high level of customer satisfaction. Continuous improvement is essential; previous quality levels should be used as the basis for future improvements.

What is necessary to achieve continuous improvement?

Continuous improvement is dependent on continuously improving work methods, where employees and customers have unlimited opportunities to express their points of view. This involves developing a dynamic, continually changing, flexible, broad, organizationally based quality planning process. This process will lead not only to new levels of quality performance, but also to new opportunities.

How does TQM compare with the traditional view of management?

TQM goes far beyond the traditional view of management, where a defect standard was defined as acceptable. Table 2.1 compares the traditional management view with TQM.

Table 2.1 Traditional Management View Compared with TQM

Traditional Management View	TQM
High quality is unaffordable.	Low quality is unaffordable.
Low quality produces lower costs.	High quality produces lower costs.
A percentage standard of defects is acceptable.	Only zero defects are acceptable.
Defects are a function of employees.	Defects are a function of the system designed by management.

Table 2.1 (continued)

Traditional Management View	TQM
Annual quality standards are established.	Continuously improve quality standards to maintain competitive advantages.
Manage by using quotas and standards.	Eliminate quotas and standards.
Employees are a cost center.	Employees are a profit center.
Manage by fear.	Drive out fear.
Low costs create profits.	Loyal customers create profits.
Buy on the basis of price.	Buy on the basis of total costs.
Manage on the basis of profits.	Profits are historical and do not predict the future.

2.5 OTHER QUALITY-CONTROL TECHNIQUES

What are the Baldrige National Quality Award criteria?

In 1987, the Malcolm Baldrige National Quality Award (MBNQA) was created to recognize companies outstanding in quality management and control. The criteria specified in the MBNQA are leadership, information and analysis, strategic quality planning, human resource utilization, quality assurance, quality results, and customer satisfaction. Each company uses its own unique approach to win the award, individually defining the management strategies and techniques required for each category.

The winning companies share certain characteristics:

- They dedicate themselves to changing former management practices in order to implement newer strategies, often requiring radically different operational procedures.

- They display a singular resolve in committing the organization to the new strategy for the long term. They do not expect quick "fixes" to solve their problems.

- Various innovative practices often emerge, including outside partnering, human resource empowerment, and developing operational strategies to achieve new objectives and long-term goals.

What is the ISO 9000 standard?

ISO 9000 is the general name for the quality standard accepted throughout the European Economic Community (EEC). ISO 9000 was initially adopted in 1987. ISO is a series of documents on quality assurance published by the Geneva-based International Standards Organization. The five documents outline standards for developing total quality management and a quality improvement process. ISO 9000 consists of guidelines for the selection and use of the quality systems contained in ISO 9001–9003. ISO 9001 outlines a model for quality assurance in design, development, production, installation, and servicing. ISO 9002 outlines a model for quality assurance in production and installation. ISO 9003 outlines a model for quality assurance for finance inspection and testing. ISO 9004 is not a standard but contains guidelines for quality management and quality system elements.

Today, more than fifty trading countries, including the United States, use the ISO 9000 standard. It is anticipated that certification in the ISO 9000 standard will be mandatory for firms involved in international trade. Companies doing business with many U.S. agencies are required to meet ISO 9000 standards.

What is Statistical Process Control (SPC)?

Statistical process control (SPC) is a widely used statistical variation measurement system that plots data graphs over time to illustrate upper and lower control limits for a particular process. The basic concept seeks to monitor excessive variations in a process.

What is special cause variation?

Special cause variations are process variations caused by external influences. In order to use SPC effectively, management must undertake the demanding process of detecting and eliminating all special cause variations from a process. For example, a special cause variation may be electrical surges experienced from a power source, causing manufacturing equipment failures. In order to eliminate this special cause, management installs a surge protector on the line.

What is common cause variation?

Common cause variations are random variations in a process. While management procedures can be developed to control for common cause variation, its complete elimination is unrealistic. However, common cause that exceeds upper or lower control limits around a predetermined mean value must be carefully investigated by management.

What is a stable system?

A stable system is a process operating within the tolerances of common cause variation. This can also be described as operating in statistical control. This does not mean there is no variation in the process; rather, it is operating within the upper and lower control limits of common cause variation around a predetermined mean value.

How is SPC computed?

Standard deviation measures of a data sample mean are used to establish upper and lower process control limits. A process operating in statistical control should be within three standard deviation units from the mean. (See Figure 2.1.)

Figure 2.1 Production Process Variability

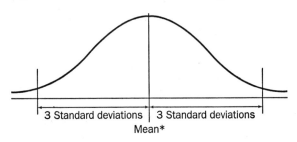

3 Standard deviations | 3 Standard deviations
Mean*

*99.7% confidence level

What are control charts?

Control charts are used to assist management in determining when excessive variation is occurring in a process. This is determined by setting upper control limits (UCL) and lower control limits (LCL) for a given data sample.

A method for determining upper and lower control limits for the percent defective in a large sample, a p-chart, is as follows:

$$UCL = \bar{p} + z\sigma_p$$
$$LCL = \bar{p} - z\sigma_p$$

Where

$\bar{p}$ = average defects in a sample

z = number of standard deviations
(3 = 99.7% confidence level)

σ_p = standard deviation of the sample
population

n = sample size

σ_p is calculated by the following formula:

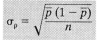

$$\sigma_p = \sqrt{\frac{\bar{p}(1-\bar{p})}{n}}$$

Example 2.4

An automobile-tire manufacturing company is seeking to develop a statistical process control chart of defective tires manufactured over a period of time. The manufacturer takes a weekly sample of one hundred tires over a twenty-week period.

Weekly Sample	Number Defective	Fraction Defective	Weekly Sample	Number Defective	Fraction Defective
1	11	0.11	11	7	0.07
2	3	0.03	12	3	0.03
3	4	0.04	13	4	0.04
4	6	0.06	14	9	0.09
5	9	0.09	15	5	0.05
6	5	0.05	16	8	0.08
7	4	0.04	17	10	0.10
8	14	0.14	18	13	0.13
9	10	0.10	19	7	0.07
10	15	0.15	20	5	0.05
Total Defects				152	
Mean					0.076

$$\bar{p} = \frac{\text{Total number of tires examined}}{\text{Total number of defects}}$$

$$= \frac{152}{(100 \times 20)} = .076$$

$$\sigma_p = \sqrt{\frac{(.076)(1-.076)}{(100)}} = 0.0265$$

$$UCL_p = \bar{p} + z\sigma_p = .076 + 3(.0265) = .1555$$

$$LCL_p = \bar{p} + z\sigma_p = .076 - 3(.0265) = .00*$$

*Cannot have a negative LCL

When the process chart for the tire manufacturer is developed, it becomes apparent that no sample of defects exceeds the control limits, and it is therefore in statistical control. Only in Week 10 does it approach the upper control limit, with fifteen defects. (See Figure 2.2.)

Figure 2.2 Tire Manufacturer Process (p) Chart

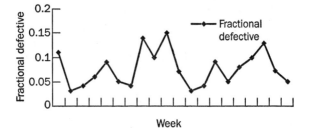

2.6 MANAGING QUALITY CONTROL

Quality control management is a crucial organizational responsibility. Now, as never before, organizations are vigorously competing on the basis of quality. ISO 9000 standards and global competition are pushing quality performance standards to ever-higher levels. A major responsibility of quality control management is to develop procedures to locate quality bottlenecks and to ensure that products are made right the first time.

How should a quality control program be designed?

Management should develop and implement a quality control program using the following four steps:

1. *Delineate product and service quality requirements.* The quality interrelationship between products and services and market requirements has to be carefully established. Performing market surveys in appropriate market segments may be helpful in understanding the level of quality available and required by the marketplace. Management, however, has greater understanding of products and services than customers do, and this knowledge can be used to develop their full quality potential and competitive advantage.

2. *Develop quality standards.* Products and services should be designed to the highest quality standards available. Manufacturers who use computer-aided design (CAD) and computer-automated manufac-

turing (CAM) are able to achieve the highest technical standards possible in achieving lasting quality. It is quantitatively cheaper to design quality prior to manufacturing or delivering a service than to correct flaws at the customer level, where the costs escalate beyond control. Additionally, global competition demands the highest quality standards available.

3. *Develop a quality analysis program.* Management must develop a consistent and systematic program for ensuring high quality. Not only does this mean selecting samples for a continual review process, it also means constantly improving products and services to achieve ever-improving quality standards.

4. *A total organizational commitment to quality must be established.* Management has the obligation of not only designing quality requirements and standards, but also the responsibility to ensure a total organizational commitment to achieving them. This means developing an employee training program in which all will gain the ability to perform to their highest potential.

What is benchmarking, and how is it useful?

Benchmarking is a process of comparing an organization's products or services against those considered to be the best in a particular industry or market segment. There are several types of benchmarking. These include

- Comparison of internal departments within one organization, including its subsidiary elements.
- Careful examination of the functional units of several different organizations.
- An analysis of the competitive practices of several different industries within a particular market segment.

The benchmarking procedures that should be followed include the following:

- Identify a particular product, service, procedure, or function that could be improved.
- Create a benchmarking team.
- Target a particular organization or group of organizations with characteristics that would be most suitable for analysis.
- Evaluate the most productive practices, procedures, and functions within a given market, and then adapt and implement those that would be most useful to the target organization.

What are quality circles (QC), and how are they used?

The purpose of quality circles (QC) is to allow a forum within an organization where those who are charged with the operational responsibilities interact with colleagues to improve the quality and productivity of the workplace and organization. Most QC groups have ten or fewer members, and all are volunteers.

Normally, although their schedules are flexible, most quality circles meet weekly or monthly, depending on the group's needs. The most successful QC groups consist of highly dedicated and disciplined members who strongly desire to improve the work methods and procedures followed in the organization. They seek to work together as a group to share their experience and abilities to solve common problems.

QC groups work best when they are integrated into an ongoing organizational quality control program with strong management support. QC programs are ongoing and seek to improve the overall organization through constant quality improvements.

The benefits of QC groups include dramatic increases in organizational productivity and quality, increased job satisfaction, and lowered rates of absenteeism, job-related accidents, and turnover.

2.7 QUALITY CONTROL TOOLS

What is a flow chart, and how is it used?

Flow charts are graphical depictions of a logical sequence of activities for a particular process. Management uses flow charts to understand the dynamics of an ongoing process. The objective analysis of the interrelationships of the parts of a process provided by a flow chart allows management to conceptualize alternative process configurations.

Example 2.5

A furniture manufacturer wishes to draw a flow chart of the processes involved in the fabrication of its product, from receipt of unfinished wood to final sales. (See Figure 2.3.)

What are fishbone charts, and how are they used?

Fishbone charts are graphical charts used to help identify sources of quality deficiencies. In appearance they resemble fishbones. The deficiency, defined as the

Figure 2.3 Flow Chart for a Furniture Manufacturer

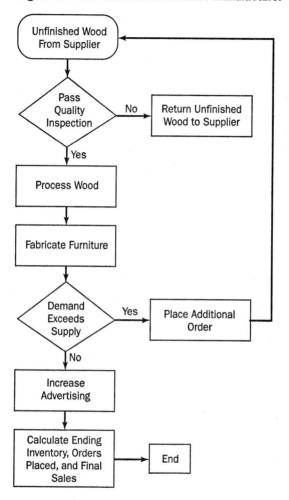

effect, is at the "head" of the fishbone, while the procedures contributing to the effect are termed causes, and they are the "bones." The bones are viewed as the potential causes of the problem that is being examined.

Example 2.6

An automobile manufacturer wants to prepare a fishbone chart to discover what is causing defects in the cars being produced. (See Figure 2.4.)

Figure 2.4 Fishbone Chart for an Automobile Manufacturer

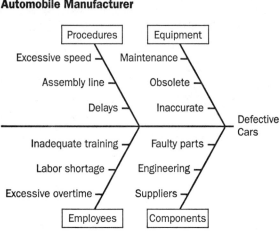

What is a Pareto chart?

A Pareto chart is a bar-graph display of the number of component errors that occur in a specified period of time. Pareto charts allow management to focus on individual component errors in order to isolate problem areas.

Example 2.7

A computer manufacturer wants to prepare a Pareto chart to do an analysis of weekly component defects. (See Figure 2.5.)

Figure 2.5 Weekly Component Defects

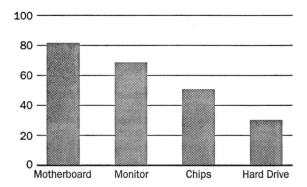

What is a histogram?

Histograms are bar-graph displays of measurements of a particular component within a specified period of time. This allows management to observe the aspects of a particular component or process over time.

Example 2.8

A firm wants to prepare a histogram in order to have a weekly breakdown of data errors at its various sites. (See Figure 2.6.)

Figure 2.6 Weekly Data Errors

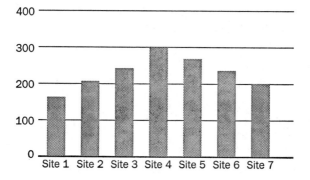

2.8 GROUP DECISION MAKING

Group decision making involves the activities of two or more people working together to resolve a particular issue. The relative merits of group decision making versus individual decision making is a controversial issue. There is general agreement that group decision making is superior when nonprogrammed decisions are required; that is, when an unusual or unique set of events needs to be conceptualized involving several related elements of information.

What are the advantages and disadvantages of group decision making?

Advantages

1. Groups have greater knowledge and insight for evaluating group goals and objectives.
2. A group of organizational members brings broader knowledge for developing situational alternatives.

3. Groups bring greater knowledge and a wider breadth of experience for evaluating alternatives.

4. Groups bring more resources to bear when doing research for particular subjects of interest.

5. Those who participate in the forming of a group decision are highly motivated to implement resulting decisions. Consensus is a strong motivator.

6. Group decisions can be much more creative than individual decisions because many points of view are considered.

Disadvantages

1. Group decisions may result in the risky shift phenomenon, as groups will take greater risks than individuals will. However, individual managers have the responsibility for implementing group decisions.

2. Group scheduling difficulties can result in long delays between meeting times.

3. Group decisions are very costly because they take much longer to develop than individual decisions.

4. "Group think" can develop, where conformity to the consensus is more important than individual expression of ideas.

5. Groups can be used as scapegoats for managers seeking to avoid responsibility for implementing group decisions.

6. Dominant personalities or supervising managers can result in group members being reluctant to express their points of view and conforming to one individual's point of view.

What is brainstorming and how is it used?

Brainstorming is a group decision-making technique in which the group operates under the rules that no one's idea should be criticized, no matter how outrageous it may appear. The basic purpose of this technique is to generate ideas and original thinking. Ideas generated through brainstorming can be discussed at a later period and may act as the genesis for new organizational policies.

What is the Delphi technique?

The Delphi technique is a process of soliciting ideas from a group of anonymous volunteers using a series of mailed questionnaires together with a summary of previous results. Using the summaries from earlier responses, the respondents are subsequently asked to further evaluate and focus their positions on the same range of issues. The basic goal is to reach a consensus among the respondents after at least two sets of questionnaires have been circulated. Normally, though many rounds of questionnaires can be circulated, after two responses a consensus begins to emerge.

What is the nominal group technique (NGT)?

In the nominal group technique a group of people initially discusses ideas in writing rather than having an open discussion. At a later point, the group members individually express their ideas to a moderator, who records them in full view, often using a flip chart.

After all the ideas have been recorded, a vote is taken and the ideas are prioritized. The rankings of the group members are then tallied to reach a final consensus on the relative priorities of the ideas discussed.

2.9 ORGANIZATIONAL STRUCTURE

Organizational structure consists of the methods used for disseminating power and authority throughout an organization. The rationale of an organization is that people work together more effectively than they do alone. This is the basis for synergy. However, an organization must be structured effectively to achieve synergy.

A traditional discussion in organizational theory is whether to centralize or decentralize an organizational structure.

What functions do centralization and decentralization perform?

The processes of centralization and decentralization determine who will have authority and power in an organization. In a centralized organization, authority and power are retained by just a few managers, whereas in a decentralized organization authority and power are disseminated to many managers through several levels.

Centralization allows high-level management to retain direct control over the organizational operations. Decentralization creates an environment in which decisions are made by those with responsibility at the organization's operational level.

Centralization's advantage of direct control is offset by its distance from and possible misunderstanding of the organization's operations. This is particularly acute when the organization has geographically dispersed operations.

Decentralization's advantage of giving operational managers direct decision-making authority is offset by a lack of coordination at the organization's staff-management levels. Some of these disadvantages can be offset through the implementation of a management information system that permits direct access to management-staff levels.

In reality, organizations often are both centralized and decentralized in that certain functions, such as finance, are directed through a centralized management control system, while other operational functions are decentralized. This permits an organization to have direct staff-management control over certain designated functions, such as finance, while permitting flexible decentralized control where it is most functional.

What is the chain of command?

The chain of command is the line of authority that connects superior and subordinate positions in a hierarchical organization. Following the chain of command, subordinate positions must seek approval from the next immediately superior position prior to going to the next superior position for authorization. Similarly, superior positions must follow the chain of command going downward when passing instructions to lower levels of the organization (see Figure 2.7). In flat organizations, the chain of command often has little relevance.

Figure 2.7 Chain of Command

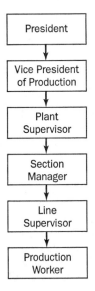

What is the line and staff division of authority?

Line and staff is a concept first developed by the military. Respectively, line and staff describe the direct functional roles and advisory relationships existing in an organization. In modern terms, line functions are those that have direct operational responsibilities, such as production or customer service. Staff responsibilities are essential management services provided to line functions. Staff responsibilities include human resource management, strategic planning, quality control, and marketing (see Figure 2.8).

Figure 2.8 Line and Staff Management

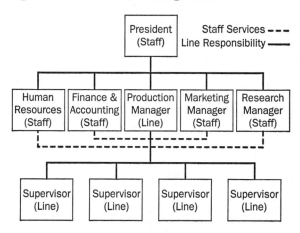

2.10 DEPARTMENTATION

Departmentation is a method of grouping organizational activities in order to achieve organizational objectives. A primary purpose of departmentation is to provide an organization with similar specialized services or activities. For example, a marketing department normally consists of people primarily concerned with developing markets for particular products and services an organization may offer. It is not concerned with production, although it may interface from time to time with the production department in order to better understand products and the department's functional capabilities.

Departments are created to fulfill the following objectives:

- *Functional.* A functional department performs a specific role. Functional departments would include accounting and finance, human resources, marketing, production, research, and development.

- *Product.* A product department is created to build or complete a specific product. Job duties are highly functional in nature, and have the completion of a particular product as the end goal. General Motors, for example, is organized according to automobile product divisions.

- *Customer.* These are departments created to serve specific customer needs. For example, a department store may have the following customer departmentation: babies, boys and girls, teens, ladies' and men's wear, maternity, etc. Customer departmentation allows an organization to group its activities to best serve specific customer requirements.

- *Geographic.* National or international organizations have specific geographic needs. It is unrealistic to have one central management center for an organization that has large nationwide and/or international operations. The communication and logistical needs are simply too great. Geographic departmentation can be used to manage specific regional needs. For example, an organization may have southern, western, eastern, and northern divisions, or Asian, European, and Latin American divisions.

2.11 PERFORMANCE EVALUATION

Performance evaluation is the appraisal of employee performance using a systematic method of analysis. The essential process of performance evaluation is predicated on observation and judgmental analysis. The judgmental nature of performance evaluation precludes the possibility of completely eliminating subjective evaluations. Therefore, rigorously following an objective methodology is essential to creditable evaluations.

What is the graphic rating scales performance evaluation method?

Graphic rating scales show a number of employee performance rating factors on which a supervisor bases an evaluation. Rating factors include quantity and quality of work, attendance, timeliness, behavior, attitudes, willingness to learn new techniques, and other factors that management feels are important. These factors are then rated using an evaluation scale. In a five-point rating system, the highest rating is usually given a value of five while the lowest rating is given a value of one. All the points are added up to form a total for each employee.

Example 2.9

A manager wants to create a graphic rating scale for the purpose of rating the employees in a production environment. To do this, the manager creates a form with a series of performance categories and rating criteria to be used by the production supervisors for rating their employees.

Graphic Rating Scales					
Employee Name:			Date:		
Dept.:					
Rating Scale	Exceptional	Good	Average	Acceptable	Poor
Units of work normally produced					
Work quality					
Timeliness					
Attendance					
Work attitude					
Cooperativeness					
Dependability					

What are behaviorally anchored rating scales (BARS)?

Behaviorally anchored rating scales are developed by rating specific job-related behaviors. Several scales can be developed covering various job-related behaviors, and BARS points can be given for various aspects of the job behavior. Figure 2.9 shows one area to be evaluated for a teacher.

Figure 2.9 Behaviorally Anchored Rating Scales

Teaching Ability		
(the ability to successfully interface with students and teach subject materials)		
Above Average Performance Outstanding teacher who is rated well by students.	___ 4 ___ 3.75 ___ 3.5 _X_ 3.25 ___ 3	Teacher is considered an expert in the field, communicates well, and has strong student acceptance. Teacher receives numerous student recommendations.
Average Performance Enthusiastic teacher who is very familiar with the material.	___ 2.75 ___ 2.5 ___ 2.25 ___ 2 ___ 1.75	This teacher can be relied upon to do a professional job, and to be well prepared.
Poor Performance Teacher shows little professional interest	___ 1.5 1.25 ___ 1	Teacher is not well prepared and has poor interaction with students. Frequent student complaints.

2.12 COMPENSATION

Compensation is often the largest organizational budgetary expense. It consists of the direct financial earnings an employee receives for work performed, as well as associated employee benefits. Generally, direct financial earnings include one or more of the following: salary, commission, bonuses, and/or merit pay. Benefits, which can represent an additional 40 percent of the total compensation package, may include health, life, and other forms of insurance; subsidized pension plans; compensated time including vacations, personal and/or sick leave; stock options; and subsidized services including cafeterias and recreational facilities.

Is there a relationship between compensation and performance?

The relationship between compensation and performance is controversial. Some research indicates a direct and positive relationship between the compensation levels and the quantity and quality of production. Others argue that tying compensation to performance destroys intrinsic motivation. It does seem fair to say that some behaviors can be more effectively motivated by compensation than others.

What common compensation methods exist, and how successful are they?

Generally, management seeks to fairly compensate its employees. However, management also expects comparable output for its compensatory policies. In the final analysis, employee productivity is necessary to generate the profits essential to forming the basis of a compensation plan.

A basic type of salary compensation is a straight-time compensation plan. However, others may choose to provide employee incentives:

- *Flat rates*. Wage rates are based on an established pay scale for a specified job in a straight-time compensation plan. Flat-rate plans do not recognize seniority, performance, or other individual differences. For example, an assembler on a particular job gets paid a flat rate of $7 per hour, irrespective of experience. Flat rates are often found in unionized environments where the union does not wish to distinguish between individual capabilities. Flat rates prevent management from creating employee performance incentives.

- *Incentive plans.* The piece-rate system and commission plans are types of individual incentive plans. In a piece-rate system the employee works from an established pay level, with additional stated levels of compensation being paid for production exceeding a base quota. The base production level is established after production research is completed.

  The commission plan is usually associated with sales personnel. It is an established rate that is paid on the basis of sales. The greater the sales, the greater the commission. It is probably one of the oldest forms of incentive plans.

  A gainsharing plan is an incentive plan that shares compensation, normally in the form of cash bonuses, with a group's members based on their performance. It is probably one of the most successful forms of employee incentive plans.

2.13 MOTIVATING PERFORMANCE THROUGH JOB DESIGN

Job design is essential to the organizational process. Job design not only structures the way work is done in the organization, it is also a critical factor in determining how an employee is motivated to perform useful work. There are several forms of job design.

What is job specialization?

Job specialization is the process of dividing work into smaller processes for the purpose of simplification. Job specialization, originally alluded to by Adam Smith, was fully developed by Frederick W. Taylor in *Principles of Scientific Management* (New York: Harper Bros., 1911) for the purpose of increasing production efficiency. Job specialization makes work so simple that workers become interchangeable. The disadvantage is that the lack of challenge in simplified work processes often leads to boredom and subsequent accidents.

What is job rotation?

Job rotation is a form of job design in which employees are systematically moved, or rotated, from one job to another. An objective of job rotation is to diminish the boredom and accidents often associated with job specialization. One advantage of job rotation is that employees have an opportunity to experience a cross section of jobs in the workplace and thus become familiar with them all.

Nonetheless, when each individual job is specialized, the objective of avoiding the boredom and accidents associated with job specialization is unrealistic.

What is job enlargement?

Job enlargement simply consists of expanding the number of job responsibilities an individual has without increasing his or her authority to decide how the work is to be accomplished or what priorities work should receive. The rationale for job enlargement is that it increases worker motivation; however, the only change is that the employee has more to do than before the job was enlarged. If the work consists of specialized tasks, the rationale for work enlargement has little inherent justification.

What is job enrichment?

The concept of job enrichment was developed by Frederick Herzberg in the late 1960s. The essential component of job enrichment is increasing the extent of control an employee has over the work for which he or she is responsible. The assumption in job enrichment is that the work itself is the motivator. The employee controls the type of work, the work methods, and the degree of freedom or autonomy he or she has in making decisions regarding work issues.

What is flextime?

Flextime is a method of developing work schedules that reflect worker preferences and needs. Using a range established by management, employees can determine at what hours they will begin and end the workday. Flextime is particularly useful for employees who must balance family and work responsibilities. It has proven to be popular, useful, and productive for employees and organizations.

What is the quality of work life?

The quality of work life is the personal significance the work environment has for individual employees. A high-quality work life is personally fulfilling and has a high degree of significance. A low-quality work life will produce worker alienation. A positive quality of work life is associated with lower absenteeism and tardiness as well as higher productivity.

2.14 EFFECTIVE LEADERSHIP

Leadership is an extremely important concept in organizational dynamics. Basically, leadership consists of the
manipulation of power. Power is the leader's ability to
get others to do what the leader wants. The way power is
managed distinguishes one leader from another.

What are the sources of leader power?

There are several sources of leader power:

- *Legitimate power.* Legitimate power is conferred
  by the organization itself, not by the person who
  occupies a particular position. For example, the
  role of bank president confers an ability on the
  person occupying the role to manage the overall
  affairs of the bank as well as to have a certain
  level of conferred status.

- *Reward power.* Managers have the ability to grant
  financial, status, and promotional rewards to the
  organization's human resources. This is an important source of management power.

- *Coercive power.* Coercive power is the ability of
  the manager to force others to carry out functions
  they would not otherwise perform because of the
  manager's ability to impose sanctions.

- *Expert power.* Expert power is derived from the
  particular knowledge and expertise an individual
  has. For example, a computer expert is one who
  has demonstrated accumulated insight into the
  functioning of computers and is able to make
  computers perform as desired.

- *Information power.* Information power is derived
  from access to sources of information that others
  do not have. Thus, those with information power
  have the ability to gain particular organizational
  and competitive advantages.

- *Referent power.* Referent power is power derived
  from the esteem in which one is regarded by others. Those with referent power are therefore able
  to more effectively lead an organization.

What skills do leaders need?

Effective leadership depends on the exercise of several skills:

- *Flexibility.* Flexibility is an essential skill for managers. Not only is the environment of business

extremely dynamic, the workplace itself consists of great cultural diversity, which requires constant modification of organizational culture.

- *Communication.* The understanding, processing, and transferring of information is a central management function. The ability to interface with others in the organizational and business environments requires excellent communication skills.

- *Human resource management.* Organizations consist of people. A critical management role is managing the organization's human resources. This consists of developing and managing training programs, setting organizational development strategies, counseling, and other skills.

- *Conceptualization.* This is the ability to understand the implications of information and strategic developments; conceptualization is required for managers to succeed in a progressively evolving technological and internationally competitive environment.

CHAPTER 3

Marketing

Marketing is an essential business function. It is the process of planning and distributing the exchange of products and services using the concepts of pricing and promotion. In this sense, marketing is not only an essential function, it is also a creative process.

3.1 THE DEFINITION OF MARKETING

The basic concept of marketing is based on the idea of an exchange of equal market values for the purpose of satisfying human needs or wants. This definition raises several additional questions.

What is an exchange?

A marketing exchange occurs when an individual gives something of value for a sought-after product or service. The vehicle most often used for an exchange transaction is money. Barter is another form of exchange which does not require the use of money. Instead, in a barter system, there is an exchange of property or services. An example of a barter system is marketing consulting services given in exchange for the purchase of a computer system.

What is market value?

Market value is established by actual or potential buyers and sellers. A marketplace can be centralized, such as a stock market, or decentralized, as is the case with a national marketplace. In the decentralized marketplace, advertising and mass communication inform the buyers and sellers as to market values.

What is a need?

A need is an unfulfilled desire that an individual has and that acts as a strong motivator. The individual seeks to fulfill a need. Needs include physical, social, and psychological desires. Marketing can create individual needs.

What is a want?

A want is an unfulfilled need. Wants are culturally based in the sense that when an individual has a need for shoes, for example, he or she will think of a particular brand name to satisfy the need. Individuals who have a need for a chocolate bar may state they want a "Hershey Bar," when really any brand of chocolate bar will suffice. Wants and needs are often confused. For instance, some computer manufacturers emphasize the speed and power of a computer, when many consumers only need a simple word processor to type a letter. Thus, computer manufacturers can take advantage of the confusion by bundling word processing software with the computer and emphasizing its simplicity and usefulness for word processing, rather than its technological features, and gain market share.

What is the role of products and services in marketing?

Marketable products and services are used to satisfy the wants and needs of consumers in the marketplace. An individual with a need to appear successful may want to purchase expensive clothing or a luxury car to satisfy the need.

3.2 DEFINING THE MARKET

A market is a group of individuals and/or organizations who want a particular product or service, and who have the financial ability to acquire it. This group of people and/or organizations is termed the target market. However, in order to be considered part of the market, the target group must be actively willing to purchase the product or service in question and have the authority to do so. Otherwise, they are out of the market.

What is mass marketing?

Organizations using mass marketing essentially assume "one size fits all"—that is, one particular product mix will satisfy everyone in a particular market, and it is not necessary to identify and service different aspects of the overall market. The example that is usually cited to illustrate mass marketing is Henry Ford's marketing of the Model T; he said people could have any color they wanted "as long as it is black." The rationale for mass marketing is that the greatest learning curve and economies of scale result in the lowest unit costs and prices. Increasingly, however, companies are moving away from mass marketing and toward target marketing.

What is target marketing?

Target marketing consists of breaking a total market into market segments representing smaller, homogeneous markets. Once this analysis is performed, it is possible to identify those market segments that can be targeted for a particular product or service based on the conformity of their homogeneous characteristics to the product or service specifications. Using market segmentation, target marketing allows marketing managers to develop more effective marketing strategies.

What is the marketing mix?

The marketing mix consists of four variables—the four Ps—that a marketing manager can control: product (P_1), place (P_2), promotion (P_3), and price (P_4).

- *Product.* The most basic element of the marketing mix is a company's product or service. The product component includes quality, features, brand name, types of packaging and design, and product-related services including maintenance and warranties.

- *Place.* Place concerns the processes management uses to make products and services available to the target market. This includes developing marketing intermediaries in order to provide the product or service to market locations. The methods used to distribute products and services are also an essential place component.

- *Promotion.* Promotion involves the methods used to transmit product information to the target market. This involves creating and using advertising, choosing the appropriate media, developing a sales force, utilizing direct marketing where appropriate, and using other promotional methods.

- *Price.* Pricing is an important element of marketing a product or service. Management must choose pricing objectives that are consistent with the target market's expectations as well as the estimated product demand and the costs of producing the product or service. Competitive factors also play an important role in achieving product or service pricing.

Table 3.1 The Marketing Mix

Product

Quality

Type of feature

Brand name

Kind of packaging

Design type

Product-related services (service, warranties, maintenance policies)

Place

Number and type of marketing intermediaries

Market location

Warehouse location

Distribution methods

Promotion

Promotion budget

Advertising message

Types of advertising media

Sales force

Types of direct marketing

Methods of sales promotion

Price

Pricing objective

Product demand

Costs

Product mix pricing

Competitive factors

The marketing mix management chooses at any particular moment is a combination of these four Ps. The total marketing-mix combinations available at any particular time are the product, place, promotion and pricing alternatives available to management. Thus,

marketing mix combinations = $(P_1 \times P_2 \times P_3 \times P_4)$.

Example 3.1

A toy manufacturer wants to determine its possible marketing-mix combinations at a particular time. It has the following possible product, place,

promotion, and price combinations, respectively:
5, 10, 8, 7.

marketing mix combinations $= (P_1 \times P_2 \times P_3 \times P_4)$

$$\text{marketing mix combinations} = (5 \times 10 \times 8 \times 7)$$
$$= 2,800$$

What is product positioning?

Product position is the perception consumers have
regarding a market offering relative to its competitors.
Product positioning is the act of analyzing and managing consumer product position perceptions. Management develops product position maps to analyze how
consumers position products relative to the competition. Product position maps can be developed prior to
introducing a product or service or subsequent to introduction in order to obtain further market information.

Example 3.2

XYZ Food Corporation is considering targeting the
retail consumer food market by introducing packaged orange juice. The question the corporation must
answer is whether to introduce a high-quality whole
orange juice product packed fresh at the citrus grove,
a lower-quality concentrate also packed at the citrus
grove, or a reprocessed concentrate packed locally.
Company A has the high-quality whole orange juice
medium-price market; company B has the medium-
quality and -price concentrate market; company C
has the low-quality reprocessed concentrate low-
price market. Corporation XYZ decides to offer a
high-quality premium-priced whole orange juice
product although there is room in the market to
offer a low-quality reprocessed concentrate at a high
price.

Figure 3.1 Product Positioning Map for Orange Juice

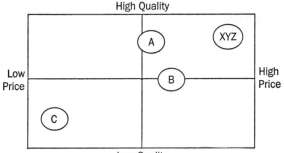

How is market demand determined?

Determining market demand is a critical management concern. Numerous variables ultimately determine market demand. These include demographics (such as age, sex composition, and per capita income of buyers), the state of the economy, past industry sales, and other factors. Thus, market demand is dependent on the current environment. Three methods management can use to project current market demand are total market potential, total industry sales, and market shares.

What is total market potential and how is it calculated?

Total market potential is a calculation of the potential market sales for an entire industry, assuming a predetermined marketing effort under a given set of market conditions.

The formula for calculating total market potential is

$$M = nap$$

where

n = number of buyers in the particular product/market, assuming given market conditions

a = average quantity purchased by buyers

p = average unit price

Example 3.3

Calculate the total market potential for ballpoint pens in the United States in any given year. Out of a population of approximately 250 million, it is necessary to calculate the estimated number of buyers of ballpoint pens. After researching the market, it is determined that the average age of ballpoint pen buyers range from ages ten to seventy-five. This eliminates approximately 55 million people from the pool. In addition, if another 30 million people are eliminated because they are institutionalized or are illiterate, the total pool of potential buyers (n) is 165 million (250 − 55 − 30 = 165). Additionally, market research tells us that annual per capita ballpoint pen purchases (a) are 8, and that the average price (p) is $1.50 per pen.

The total market potential for ballpoint pens is

$M = nap$

$M = (165,000,000 \times 8 \times \$1.50) = \$1,980,000,000$

What is area market potential?

It is necessary for companies to choose the best marketing territories for their products and services. Being able to estimate the market potential of areas, including cities and states, is essential prior to committing a company's financial resources.

How are industry sales and market shares determined?

Trade associations normally provide gross industry sales data. By tracking its own sales against those of the entire industry, a firm can accurately determine its market share and whether it is increasing or decreasing. Additionally, marketing research firms monitor product-category sales in various retail outlets. This data allows a company to compare its own sales both with the overall industry and with particular competitors.

3.3 MANAGING THE MARKETING PROCESS

Marketing management involves marketing analysis and planning, implementing, and controlling a marketing strategy. Marketing management involves product and service development as well as supervising basic marketing functions such as promotion, pricing, and distribution.

What is marketing planning?

Marketing planning consists of making decisions about the overall direction of a marketing effort and is a function of effective marketing research. Areas that have to be planned include the company's marketing mix, the marketing budget and priority allocations, distribution methods, brand names, and packaging.

A marketing plan should have a brief executive summary giving the plan's highlights and major conclusions. It should also discuss the current market, product, competitive, and distribution environment. All relevant variables and data are discussed with an analysis of how they impact the marketing plan. Analyses of current opportunities, product market strengths and weaknesses, and major issues needing attention are provided. Financial and market objectives are also detailed. The marketing plan is used for developing an overall marketing strategy.

What is marketing strategy?

A marketing strategy is a comprehensive marketing methodology that is developed as a result of extensive marketing planning. A marketing strategy details the following factors: target markets, product line, product positioning, price, distribution channels, sales force, service procedures, advertising and promotion methodologies, product research and development expenditure targets, and marketing research.

How are marketing departments organized?

Many types of marketing organizations currently exist. Companies often create various combinations of marketing organizations. The basic types of marketing organizations include the following: functional, geographical, product and brand management, and by market.

What is a functional marketing organization?

A functional marketing organization consists of marketing personnel, typically managed by a marketing vice president. This is the most widely used marketing organization. Since a functional marketing organization is not specialized, it is the simplest to manage. While this is a strength when a firm has relatively few products and services, it can also be a liability as a firm's market offerings become more diversified and specialized. Since a functional marketing organization has broad responsibilities, marketing personnel can compete with each other for specialized product or service resources. Figure 3.2 shows a typical functional marketing organization chart.

Figure 3.2 Functional Marketing Organization Chart

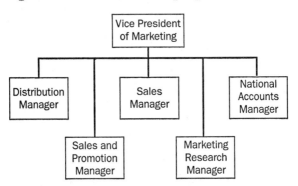

What is a geographical marketing organization?

National companies often find it is more effective to have regional sales personnel and managers reporting to one national sales manager. The regional sales managers directly supervise a certain number of sales personnel. This facilitates regional market responses while freeing the national sales manager from excessive responsibility. Figure 3.3 shows a geographical marketing organization.

Figure 3.3 Geographical Marketing Organization

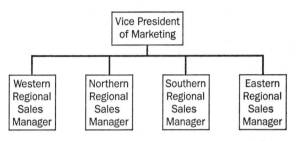

What is a product- and brand-directed marketing organization?

Product- and brand-oriented marketing structures normally occur when organizations have experienced a large increase in products being offered to the market. Corporate management finds managing individual products and brands to be too time intensive and therefore chooses individual managers who specialize in a particular product or brand. Product and brand organizations are essentially separate entities that interface with all elements of the larger organization. Thus, product and brand managers interface with the overall organization's production, promotion, advertising, legal, budgetary, research, purchasing, and related functions.

Product- and brand managers become deeply knowledgeable about their product areas and can react quickly to market changes. However, product and brand management organizations often multiply to include even minor products. This imposes a large financial cost on the overall organization. Additionally, product and brand managers often compete with each other for organizational resources, creating a highly charged corporate environment.

What is a market organization?

Companies often deal with many different target markets. However, each target market has its own distinctive needs (for example, some companies sell products or services to various industrial sectors as well as to federal, state, and local governments). Often, products are developed just for certain target markets (for example, a book publisher will produce books for the primary, secondary, college, and trade markets). When the market potential is great enough, companies often organize departments to coincide with those specific markets.

The market organization focuses attention on the marketing function. It allows for greater concentration of effort on the markets that are essential to the organization's success. Figure 3.4 shows a market organization for a publisher.

Figure 3.4 Market Organization for a Publisher

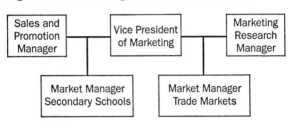

How are marketing plans implemented?

An organizational marketing plan has no values unless it is put into action. A close management interface with all aspects of the organization including production, promotion, marketing, research, and design is essential to successfully implement the plan. Successful implementation requires creating a specific management plan to carry out elements of the marketing plan.

3.4 MARKET RESEARCH

Marketing research seeks to answer the question of what market needs exist and where they are located, what purchasing patterns exist and where they are located, and other factors such as pattern of growth. Modern marketing research depends on the development of an extensive management information system, normally with a large product and consumer database at its core. The research process is ongoing and data about products, manufacturers, customers, and competitors is continually being collected and analyzed.

The market-research process follows a series of steps, which include understanding the problem to be researched, creating a research design for the problem, designing data sources (including designing the data collection methods), implementing the study, analyzing and processing the collected data, and developing the research report. Figure 3.5 illustrates the market-research process.

Figure 3.5 Market-Research Process

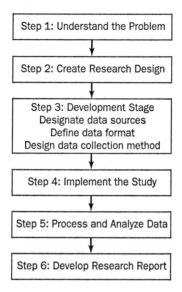

Step 1: Understand the Problem

Step 2: Create Research Design

Step 3: Development Stage
Designate data sources
Define data format
Design data collection method

Step 4: Implement the Study

Step 5: Process and Analyze Data

Step 6: Develop Research Report

Understanding the problem to be researched

A marketing manager, usually working with a marketing research group, must examine a problem carefully to understand its nature and complexity. A careful definition of the problem's parameters is crucial in developing a research project's goals.

There are various types of research problems. Some research is merely exploratory in nature, which allows management to develop a clearer conceptualization of a problem. A more in-depth market study may be concerned with describing a particular problem in detail. A third type of research is interested in understanding the dynamics of a particular situation in terms of what causes it, or related issues, to occur. The objective of the research is the critical factor in determining the nature of the research design.

How is the research design created?

After developing an understanding of the problem to be researched, the next question to be answered is what potential market value the research has when launching a new product.

Example 3.4

Management seeks to determine the market value when launching similar products in a market segment to form the basis for a research budget. It can be determined that other product launches had an average annual profit of $35 million when market research was conducted, and only $15 million without market research.

market research value = average profits with
market research
− average profits without
market research

market research value = $35 million
$$\frac{- \$15 \text{ million}}{\$20 \text{ million}}$$

In this example, it would be possible to justify a $20 million research budget.

Once a budget can be determined for the research project, it is then necessary to determine what types of data will be used. Two types of research data, primary and secondary, may be used in market research. Primary data, such as census data collected by the government, is original data that is either collected directly or is provided by a source who collects it directly. Secondary data is data reported on by a secondary source, such as another market report or a periodical, that provides results of primary data used in preparing the report. For the most part, market research uses primary data, although secondary data can be a useful theoretical source, and can validate results obtained from primary data collection studies.

In the development stage, how is marketing-research data collected?

Marketing data is obtained using four basic research approaches: observational, focus group, survey, and experimental.

- *Observational.* This is the most unstructured method of collecting data. The data collection method will depend on the context of the situation. For example, if one were to collect data regarding the cruise-ship industry, one observational approach would be to book a cruise on one or several selected cruise ships and observe the activities on board and the food being served, as well as to listen to passengers' before and after comments during embarkation and disembarkation.

- *Focus group.* In the focus-group methodology, a small group of selected individuals are invited to discuss a certain topic. Using the cruise-ship example, questions would be focused on the group's overall impressions regarding the cruise-ship industry, with special attention given to particular cruise lines. Data obtained from a focus-group session can be very useful when designing a more in-depth research study.

- *Survey research.* Surveys are the most commonly used form of marketing research. A survey is a systematic research tool used to obtain descriptive data. The three basic types of surveys are mail surveys to specified geographical areas, systematic telephone surveys within a calling area, and one-on-one personal interviews with an individual or a group.

- *Experimental research.* This type of research has the most methodological accuracy. In experimental research, measures of the effects of variation in independent variables on the subject dependent variable are taken. This is done using as controlled an environment as possible, in either a laboratory or field setting. An example of experimental research is testing the impact of various types of advertising on resulting sales. Different types of advertising can be used in different regional markets for the same product to determine if there is any measurable difference in resulting sales. However, controls for inherent regional differences must be predetermined.

How is a sampling plan developed?

A sampling plan is developed for the purpose of ensuring that the collected data is valid and reliable for the selected population. A sampling plan addresses three issues: the sampling unit, the sampling method, and the sample size.

- *Sampling unit.* This is a definition of a particular target population. If a company wants to sample opinions of people using a particular product, it is necessary to define who that target population actually is.

- *Sampling method.* Researchers can use either a probability or nonprobability sample of the target population. A probability sample is a statistical calculation of the sampling error of a target population. At the 1 percent level of confidence, there is a 99 percent probability of gaining a valid and reliable sample of the target population, while 1 percent would be inaccurate. In a nonprobability sample, the researcher makes a judgment about what portion of a target population should be included in a sample.

- *Sample size.* Since it usually is impractical to sample opinions of an entire target population, it becomes necessary to develop a representative sample of the target population. Of course, the larger the sample, the more reliable and valid are the results. Sample sizes, either at the 5 percent or 1 percent level of confidence, are chosen according to the scope of the study, the resources available, and the criticality of the need for reliability.

How is the market-research study implemented?

In the implementation stage, the researcher actually collects the required data. This is the most expensive and error-prone stage of the marketing-research process. Data collection methods include mechanical means, computers (including bar coding and interactive data input), questionnaires, and interviewing. The major concern here is that data collection methods ensure valid and reliable data.

How is the data processed and analyzed?

The data processing and analysis stage involves the processes of reviewing, categorizing, and analyzing. First the data must be reviewed for collection errors and omissions to ensure that all areas have been completed accurately. Then the data has to be placed in categories so that similar data can be compared. The analysis step is crucial for the study's final outcomes. Various statistical analysis methods such as repression analysis are utilized for interpreting results.

How is the research report developed?

Final reports should be succinctly written. Results should be interpreted and presented in an understandable format. Management requires report formats that are easily interpreted and conceptually coherent. The appropriate use of graphics can be helpful in explaining outcomes. Oral presentations by researchers are often used to further explain the study.

3.5 MARKET SEGMENTATION

Markets consist of buyers. Buyers have many different characteristics which are important in determining their willingness to purchase products and services. These differences are predicated on geography, demographics, buying power, occupation, education, and buying behavior. Markets can be divided into four clearly defined segments based on these characteristics: geographic, demographic, psychographic, and consumer behavior.

What is geographic segmentation?

Markets can be divided geographically by zip codes, cities, states, regions, or countries. A company that has a nationwide distribution system may detect differences in national demand depending on the region of the country. A particular product may sell better in certain regions than in others. The product can then be sold, advertised, and tailored to certain designated geographic regions.

What is demographic segmentation?

Demographic segmentation uses various population measures, including age, sex, income, nationality, education, and occupation as the basis for dividing people into specific markets. Demographic segmentation is easy to measure and is widely used.

- *Age.* This demographic variable is often used to divide markets (for example, a clothing department store divides departments chronologically: infants, girls and boys, young teens, young women and young men, ladies and men). For a clothing department store, demographic segmentation based on age works well. However, in other areas, age may not be so effective, as everyone wants to be perceived as being young.

- *Sex.* Gender is a widely used method of demographic segmentation, particularly in the clothing, hairdressing, health, hygiene, and print markets. While gender is an easily measured demographic variable, market trends and applications may change quickly. The role of women is evolving rapidly in modern society. Automobile marketing, for example, is now targeting the large numbers of female automobile owners using options and designs desired by women.

- *Occupation.* Market segmentation by occupation is also effective because of associated lifestyles (for example, businesspeople are targeted by the travel and clothing industries because they do more traveling and purchase more business clothing).

- *Education.* Level of education is an important demographic segmentation variable, primarily because higher levels of education are associated with higher levels of income and higher proportions of disposable income.

- *Nationality.* Nationality, racial, and cultural groupings are important American demographic segmentation variables because the United States has such a diverse population. However, these variables can be difficult, as it may be a mistake—as well as a misrepresentation—to believe that these demographic groupings all have the same desires and purchasing patterns.

What is psychographic segmentation?

Psychographic segmentation divides markets on the basis of social class, personality traits, and/or lifestyles.

- *Social class.* Dividing the population on the basis of social class primarily uses income as a determinant of the buying behavior and lifestyles people exhibit in the various groupings. Social class ranges from lower to middle to upper class. The classes can be further stratified into upper-lower, upper-middle, and upper-upper. Social class is a strong determinant of individual purchasing preferences in consumer goods as well as in services such as education, travel, and tourism.

- *Personality traits.* This is a method of segmenting markets based on a perception of how differences in consumer personalities affect buying behavior. Products and services will be marketed in a manner that will appeal to these personality traits (for example, those who are considered more conservative are perceived as desiring products having darker colors and more reserved styles of dress). There is no clear evidence that personality-trait market segmentation is successful in accurately identifying target markets and individual personalities.

- *Lifestyle.* A person's lifestyle can best be defined as how that person adapts to and interacts with the environment. Some people may be more artistic or entrepreneurial than others. Segmenting the market according to lifestyle attempts to identify common interests that a group of people has and to target this group for particular products and services (for example, those identified as having an adventurous lifestyle would be perceived as having a greater desire to go on a sailing vacation than to stay at a resort).

- *Consumer behavior.* An additional method of segmenting markets is based on consumer behavior relating to specified products and services. One category included under consumer behavior would be the amount of use of a particular product. Here consumers can be classified as heavy, moderate, or light users. Consumer profiles by usage category help determine the characteristics each group displays and how to appeal to the groups. It is also important to determine who does *not* use the product in order to determine whether a target marketing program would be justifiable.

  Another market-segment area of consumer behavior is brand loyalty. It is important to determine what the nature of consumer brand loyalty is for a specific product or service. By understanding which consumers are extremely loyal and which migrate, it may be possible to develop and implement strategies to increase or maintain consumer loyalty.

  Still another method of segmenting consumer behavior is based on the benefits consumers seek by purchasing particular products and services. Some consumers may seek the speed of service associated with retail fast food. Others may seek the hygienic qualities associated with certain consumable products such as toothpaste, household cleaners, or paper tissues. After determining the benefits consumers actually seek from specified products, the characteristics of the consumers must also be examined. Marketing strategies might be developed, promoting new or expanded benefits to the consuming groups.

3.6 BRAND MARKETING DECISIONS

The objective of brand marketing is to increase consumer product or service awareness in order to generate increased and predictable demand, leading to consumer willingness to buy and display loyalty. Brand-marketing decisions involve a wide range of issues.

What is a brand?

A brand is a name, logo, sign, or shape that singularly, or in combination, allows the consumer to differentiate the product or service from others in the marketplace.

What is a brand name?

A brand name is a word, numbers, or some combination thereof, which can be verbally expressed (for example, 3Com is a brand name).

What is a brand mark?

A brand mark is a symbol, graphic image, or shape, often used as a logo, which describes either a brand manufacturer or product.

What is brand loyalty?

Brand loyalty is repetitive consumer buying behavior resulting from consumer satisfaction with a particular brand.

What is brand recognition?

Brand recognition allows consumers to differentiate a branded product from other brands, or from those that are not branded.

What is brand acceptance?

At the minimum, marketers hope to generate brand acceptance, where the consumer finds the brand meets their expectations. Therefore, they will purchase the product and not resist it.

What is brand preference?

Successful brand marketing causes brand preference, where consumers prefer a particular brand over another.

What is brand insistence?

Extremely successful brand marketing may cause brand insistence, where consumers insist on having one brand over another. True brand insistence is extremely difficult to generate.

What is brand rejection?

Brand rejection occurs when the consumer is familiar with a particular product but refuses to purchase it because of dissatisfaction with previous purchases.

Brand rejection is extremely costly and difficult to reverse because the buyer's bias prevents him or her from considering any more purchases.

What is brand equity?

Brand equity is added value brought to a product by a brand name. This can be enhanced through the use of labels and logos. (Certain clothing and sports-accessory manufacturers prominently display their name and/or logo on the product.) Brand equity often will allow the manufacturer to charge a premium price for its products.

How is branding useful?

Branding is an overwhelming market force. It gives the seller numerous advantages:

- Brands divide products into identifiable classes, providing the ability to accurately measure sales and provide follow-up.
- Brands provide a methodology for market segmentation.
- Brands can be legally protected and trademarked, preventing competitors from usurping products and their respective market share.
- Brands encourage consumer familiarity and loyalty.
- Brands help to create a company image.

How are branding decisions made?

Normally, a firm makes branding decisions only after extensive debate, research, and discussion. Occasionally, companies even offer a public contest to choose a brand name (for instance, Ford Motor Company sponsored a national contest when it sought a brand name for the car that later became known as the Edsel). Companies often use marketing research firms, as well as more specialized brand-name consultants, to choose a brand name.

What is brand strategy?

Brand strategy is the marketing objective sought by giving or associating products or services with a particular brand. There are at least four brand strategies that a firm can pursue: corporate-blanket brand, family-blanket brand, product-range brand, and new-product brand.

- *Corporate-blanket brand.* A corporate-blanket brand occurs when a company uses its name as the primary identifier of its products. The products, such as breakfast cereals, are usually in just one market, and the corporation seeks corporate-brand identification.

- *Family-blanket brand.* Family-blanket brand is used to cover a series of products in a variety of markets. One brand name covers them all.

- *Product-range brand.* Product-range brands are used to describe a series of products that have clear links in one market. An example would be a variety of shampoos with the same brand name but formulated for different hair conditions.

- *New-product brand.* A new-product brand is used when a firm introduces a new product in a totally different market that has no relationship to previous products the firm has on the market. If the firm expects the product will have a long product life cycle, and that it will generate sufficient profits to warrant a separate launch, a new product brand may be justified.

3.7 SERVICE FIRM MARKETING STRATEGIES

As of 2004, more than 70 percent of all U.S. employment was in the service-producing sector. Additionally, services account for more than 70 percent of the gross domestic product and will produce 90 percent of all new jobs in the next ten years.

What are the characteristics of the services industry?

- *Intangibility.* Marketing services are intangible—they cannot be seen, tasted, felt, or sensed. Services are unknown until they are performed (for example, a woman seeking a new hairdo from the hairstylist does not know what it will be like until it is actually done). Because of the unknown nature of services, marketers must create an image of quality, reliability, and value for the consumer.

- *Immediate production and consumption.* Services are consumed as fast as they are produced. A lawn service leaves a trimmed lawn as soon as it is finished. Therefore, developing a strong relationship with the consumer is critical for the marketer's success.

- *Perishability.* Services cannot be saved or stored. It is difficult for service firms to provide the ideal level of service at all times. During periods of peak demand, resources may be overtaxed, while during periods of low demand, resources are underutilized. For instance, organizations providing mass transit often find that trains or buses are overloaded taking passengers to the urban area during the morning rush, but empty on the return ride.

- *Inconsistency.* There is no standard in services. The level of quality varies, depending on who provides the service as well as when and where it is provided. Résumé writers provide a wide variety of résumés depending on who is writing it, what their industry depth of knowledge is, how well they write, and what level of interest they have in the consumer.

How is marketing performed for the service sector?

Marketing for the service sector is more complex than for tangible products primarily because of the difficulty in defining quality service and managing productivity.

- *Service market differentiation.* The greatest challenge for service marketers is differentiating between service providers. If consumers perceive that service providers have indistinguishable offerings, price competition becomes the only differentiating feature. A method of differentiating services from the competition is to add innovative features. Thus, the marketer adds to the primary service package by offering a secondary service package. (For instance, an automotive lubrication service provider might add a secondary service package of automotive manufacturer certification, speed of service, and a consumer-comfort facility to distinguish its service from the traditional service station or automotive dealership.)

- *Service productivity.* The service industry is experiencing a need to increase its productivity to remain competitive. However, the service industry is highly labor intensive. Increasing productivity, therefore, is extremely challenging. The following methods can be utilized in the service industry to increase productivity.

    Better utilization of labor. Management can research and develop more effective service procedures. Employee skills can be upgraded through training to make their service activities more effective.

    Trade off quality for quantity. In order to improve productivity, organizational procedures are developed whereby less time is spent per service unit. This may require changing the nature of the service, as well as how services are delivered (for example, using an automatic phone router that screens and routes phone calls).

Automate the provision of services. The implementation of technology often can reduce the need for labor while increasing consumer satisfaction (such as installing a fax-back system that immediately provides consumers with requested information).

Update current employees. Utilizing training and certification programs, it may be possible to upgrade lower-paid employees to perform specified services performed by professionals (for example, nurses are now performing many medical services previously performed by doctors).

Allow consumers to perform self-service. Increasingly, consumers are substituting their own labor for procedures formerly performed by employees (as in self-service gas stations).

How can service delivery differentiation be achieved?

Service delivery can be differentiated with the "three Ps" of service marketing: people, physical environment, and process. Having better-trained and more competent people can be extremely important in the service delivery process. Improving the physical aspects of the service delivery environment is also extremely important (for example, having a clean and cheerful waiting room can be crucial in improving the overall image of an organization). Finally, improvements and innovations in the process can make a critical difference in service differentiation (for instance, the installation of bar-code scanners in supermarkets expedites the check-out process with improved accuracy, while enabling management to maintain a real-time management information system).

3.8 PRODUCT LINE DECISIONS

A product line is a group of products related on the basis of similar customers, marketing methods, or product characteristics. The range of product lines establishes a product mix. The two types of product lines are those with complementary and substitute products.

What are complementary products?

In a product line, complementary products are those designed to add to the original product. For example, a company that produces computers would also manufacture other items, such as printers and software.

What are substitute products?

Substitute products are those that appeal to the same basic market segment but have different specific characteristics. For example, a soup company may have a full line of soups, including chicken, tomato, turkey, pea, and so on. Each soup can easily be substituted for the other.

How long should a product line be?

Product-line length is determined by the number of products supported in a particular product line. Companies seeking high market share and growth have longer product lines.

Profitability is also affected by product-line length. A product line has too many products if adding to the line reduces profits; it has too few products if profits can be increased by adding products.

Increasing product length tends to increase associated costs, including engineering, inventory, ordering, and transportation costs. Companies with successful products often tend to increase product-line length in order to increase profits. However, overextended product lines can cause diminishing returns.

Lines can be extended by stretching and filling.

What is product-line stretching?

Product-line stretching develops when a firm adds additional products to a product line. Product lines can be stretched downward, upward, or both.

What is downward product-line stretching?

A company that produces "high-end" products, in the more expensive range of the market segment, stretches downward by offering lower-priced products in the market segment. Offering lower-priced products will appeal to a wider range of consumers, who may upgrade upon seeing the feature differences between the low- and high-end products. Using the "downward stretch" can be a competitive marketing strategy to challenge competitors at either the high or low end of the market segment.

What is upward product-line stretching?

A company that produces "low-end" products, in the least expensive range of the market segment, stretches upward by offering higher-priced products in the market segment. Companies may consider the "upward stretch" for a number of reasons. They may be well entrenched at the lower end of the market segment but desire greater unit margins by moving upward in the market (for instance, the Japanese automotive companies implemented an upward stretch by successfully introducing luxury cars only after becoming well established in the lower end of the market with compact cars). The company may also be interested in experiencing a faster growth rate at the upper end of the market when those conditions exist.

What is two-way market stretching?

Two-way market stretching applies to companies in the middle of a market that want to expand their product line upward and downward. The basic objective is to become competitive in markets not previously served by introducing products into those respective markets.

3.9 NEW-PRODUCT DEVELOPMENT AND MARKETING STRATEGIES

New-product development is essential for a company to remain competitive in today's rapidly changing markets. Marketing plays an important role in new-product development. Analyses of the selected market segments and the targeted consumer groups are performed, and decisions are made regarding the development of appropriate products. Still, the introduction of new products is extremely risky. New product failures are estimated at 80 percent of all new-product launches in certain markets. There are various levels of failure. A complete product failure is a dead loss and provides no cost recovery. Partial product failures allow the recovery of some variable and fixed costs, while a comparative product failure actually provides some profit but is relatively less profitable when compared with other products.

Why is there such a high failure rate with new products?

New-product failures occur for a number of reasons:

- *New products may not have significant advantages.* Certain markets may be saturated, and it is very difficult to develop truly innovative product ideas (for example, the chocolate candy bar market is fairly well saturated, and it is difficult to improve upon the offerings already provided by the chocolate-bar market leaders).

- *Divided markets.* Intense international competition is fragmenting markets into smaller segments. Focusing on smaller market segments increases the risks of failure.

- *Increasing product development costs.* As the technology becomes more complex, the cost of developing new products increases.

- *Shorter product life cycles and product development times.* Technological change is occurring at exponentially increasing rates, which significantly reduces product life cycles as well as mandating shorter product-development times. The risk of failure increases because of greater likelihood of product-development mistakes and misjudgments. Shorter product life cycles also mean a shorter period of time in which to recoup product-development costs.

What are the major stages in new product development?

- *Idea generation.* New-product ideas come from many sources. Customers are one of the best sources of new ideas (software companies rely extensively on their installed user base to provide feedback about how products should be improved). Consumers can be surveyed to identify needs and problems that are otherwise unknown to management. Competitors often introduce new product and service innovations that provide a rich area of product improvement. Employees who work closely with products can also provide significant insight into new product innovations and improvements. Brainstorming can be used by a marketing team whose members give ideas in a free-flow manner. In the final analysis, new-product ideas are the result of inspiration, imagination, and deep experience.

- *Idea screening.* After numerous ideas have been generated, screening is utilized to evaluate the ideas in terms of practicality, cost, profit potential, and strategic fit. Not only must new products have significant profit potential, they must also be consistent with the firm's marketing plan and strategy. Most companies have product evaluation forms in which the products are described and rated according to market potential. Subsequently, these forms are screened by a new-product organizational structure.

  There are two significant risks in the idea-screening stage. One risk is that a product is rejected because management underestimates its market and profit potential. The other risk is that a firm will approve a product not having good market potential or strategic fit because it received inadequate idea screening.

- *Concept development and testing.* If a product idea survives the idea-screening stage, it is developed into a product concept. A product concept is an idea that is developed into an expression of the advantages offered by a new product or service, and the target market to which it will be offered. This is termed a product category concept.

Example 3.5

A company wants to develop a line of nutritional snacks. It converts this product idea into several product concepts within the product category. One product concept consists of a candy made from dried fruit. Another concept is an all-natural cracker using dried fruit to add taste. A third product concept is a dried-meat-flavored product made from prepared soy beans.

- *Business analysis.* Having developed the product concept, a preliminary marketing strategy is developed. This will enable management to evaluate the product concept's business potential. In order to do this, management must perform an extensive cost analysis on product development costs, including research and design, marketing, and production. Product demand estimates are then combined with cost estimates to develop short- to intermediate-term profit estimates.

- *Product development.* Assuming the business analysis determines the product is worthwhile, it then goes to the product development stage, where research and development (R&D) develops a prototype. Normally, product development represents a substantial financial investment over an extended period of time. Additionally, product development must be sensitive to expressed consumer desires. The use of technology, particularly computer-aided design and computer-aided manufacturing (CAD/CAM), can help to shorten development time. When the prototype is actually developed, it must be subjected to rigorous functional testing to ensure the product is viable, safe, and meets expectations. Assuming the product passes the functional testing stage of the product development process, it must then be subjected to consumer testing to determine whether the product would be appropriate for the target market.

- *Market testing.* The market-testing process subjects the developed product to actual target-market conditions. The product is packaged, branded, and introduced using a controlled marketing program. The purpose of market testing is to determine consumer acceptance, the success of various marketing strategies, how large the market actually is, and how competitive it will be. There are several methods used in the market testing process:

  - *Traditional test marketing.* In traditional test marketing, the product is introduced to a selected group of cities. When determining the test-market strategy, management must determine in how many and in which cities the test marketing should be performed, the length of the test marketing process, and what factors should be evaluated. Traditional test marketing also allows a variety of promotional methods to be used to introduce the product in order to determine which method works most effectively. The negative side of the traditional test-marketing process is that it is costly and time consuming.

  - *Research firm test marketing.* The firm introducing a new product may decide to conduct test marketing by contracting with a research firm that directs market research in a group of commercial outlets. Various marketing strategies are carefully controlled and evaluated. Product sales are monitored using scanners and bar codes. Research firm test marketing is performed more quickly and cheaply than traditional test marketing.

  - *Simulated test marketing.* In simulated test marketing, a selected group of shoppers is exposed to advertising for the new product as well as to advertising for competitive products. They are then given a predetermined amount of money and allowed to shop in a simulated store that carries both the new product and existing competitive products. Observations and measures are made of the products purchased, and the consumers are then asked why they purchased their chosen products. Follow-up questions are also asked of the selected consumers after a period of time has elapsed. Simulated test marketing can be conducted quickly and much more economically than either traditional test marketing or research firm test marketing.

- *Commercialization.* If the product successfully passes the market-testing process, the marketer is ready to implement a full commercial introduction. The firm must now make its greatest investment in the entire product development process: manufacturing facilities have to be acquired, a promotional advertising program needs to be developed, sales personnel have to be employed and trained, and administrative support systems have to be put in place. Many activities have to be coordinated. Additionally, evaluations have to be performed concerning the timing, the geographical selection of launch sites, and the targeting of product launch prospects.

3.10 MARKETING-CHANNEL DESIGN DECISIONS

Marketing-channel (also termed channels of distribution) design decisions are critical for successful product distribution. Marketing channels consist of intermediaries who contribute to the product distribution process according to consumer demand. They consist of merchant middlemen, agent middlemen, and facilitators. Companies rely on market intermediaries because of their effectiveness in distributing products and because of their capitalization. A company's chosen channel members develop long-term relationships built on trust and directly affect the marketing process, including price. Marketing channels always have a producer and a final consumer.

Who are merchant middlemen?

Merchant middlemen consist of wholesalers and retailers who actually purchase the product and resell it. Wholesalers buy in large lots and sell in smaller quantities to retailers, who in turn sell individual units to consumers. Wholesalers and retailers assume the risk of ownership in return for a profit markup when selling the merchandise to others.

Who are agent middlemen?

Agent middlemen are sales intermediaries such as brokers, product representatives, and sales representatives who seek others to purchase merchandise. They do not actually purchase any merchandise, and are compensated on the basis of a percentage of sales and/or salary, depending on whether they are independent businesspeople or employees of companies wishing to sell products.

Who are facilitators?

Facilitators are intermediaries who directly assist in the distribution function without taking title to the goods. They consist of a range of organizations including advertising agencies, financial lending organizations, shipping companies, and storage warehouses.

What is channel length?

Channel length describes the number of intermediary levels existing between the producer and the consumer. A direct, or zero, channel is one where there is a direct relationship between the producer and the consumer (for example, a neighborhood bakery may be considered a direct channel because the retail consumer purchases the finished baked goods directly, with no intermediaries). A one-level channel has one intermediary, which is usually a retailer (for instance, a regional bakery-goods operation utilizes local food stores to distribute the product to the consumer). A two-level channel has two intermediaries to distribute products to the consumer (for example, a candy manufacturer sells the product to a wholesaler, who in turn sells to the retailer). A three-level channel has three intermediaries, usually consisting of an agent middleman who sells to a wholesaler, who then sells to a retailer.

How are channels developed?

Developing channels of distribution requires many decisions. Channel distribution needs grow and develop as companies grow and markets change. Increased channel utilization increases costs, which are passed on to the consumer. The design of channel development begins by studying the buying patterns of the target customers.

What are consumer buying patterns?

Consumer buying patterns affect a channel's characteristics and are classified in the following ways:

- *Units purchased.* Different customers have different purchasing needs. Commercial customers normally purchase larger lot sizes than do household consumers. Channel modifications have to be made to meet these different needs.

- *Turnaround times.* Some industries, such as fast foods, use rapid turnaround times as an inherent part of the business, while other businesses may have longer turnaround times. Industries that have customers who need rapid turnaround times require more direct channels of distribution than those with slower turnaround times.

- *Product assortment.* Industries, particularly retail, that offer large product assortments have a need for deeper channels of distribution in order to provide product variety.
- *Services.* High levels of services, including repair, delivery, installation, and others, require more intensive channel utilization.

How many intermediaries should be used in a channel?

Determining the number of intermediaries will affect the marketing of a product. Longer channels have more intermediaries and higher costs. On the other hand, intermediary expertise may be essential to successfully market a particular product. Thus, a manufacturer may try to limit the number of intermediaries in order to contain costs. The trade-off in having fewer intermediaries is limited distribution.

As manufacturers continue to penetrate markets, greater distribution is desired, involving more intermediaries. While this will increase distribution, it will also increase costs while sacrificing some degree of marketing control. This may result in the product being incorrectly positioned.

Finally, not all intermediaries are the same. The marketer wants only those intermediaries who most effectively work with the company to distribute the product.

How do company characteristics affect channel development?

Generally, the companies with the largest array of retail products, particularly product consumables, have the least need for intermediaries. They are well-enough positioned in the market to deal directly with retail outlets. Smaller companies with smaller product lines have a greater need for the market distribution strengths of intermediaries.

How do product characteristics affect channel development?

Products that are perishable, time sensitive (such as fashions), heavy and bulky, or highly unique in nature (such as those requiring specialized training) generally have short channels of distribution. On the other hand, standardized products often move through several intermediaries in the distribution process.

How are channel alternatives evaluated?

There are several issues in evaluating channel alternatives. One issue is choosing the most economically effective channel alternative. Companies must evaluate channel intermediaries based on those that have the largest level of sales per unit of selling cost. Other issues concern the extent to which marketing management control will be lost by including a sales agency or other sales broker in the marketing channel. A final variable is choosing a channel intermediary that will still allow the producer to maintain maximum marketing flexibility in fast-moving markets.

What are the challenges in managing market-channel intermediaries?

Several issues are important in channel management:

- *Choosing the most effective channel alternatives.* Management must determine what the characteristics are for the most effective channel intermediaries. Having done this, management must develop strategies for attracting these channel intermediaries to the marketing channel.

- *Maximizing channel member effectiveness.* Management must motivate channel members to create the most cost-effective market distribution system for the company.

- *Evaluating the effectiveness of intermediaries.* Management must develop channel-member evaluation systems. While seeking the cooperation of channel members, management must determine what profit standards must be used as the basis for evaluation.

3.11 DEVELOPING THE PROMOTION BUDGET

One of the most challenging marketing management functions is developing the company's promotion budget. Promotional advertising is extremely expensive, and establishing an acceptable figure is difficult at best. Companies use many different methods; following are four widely used methods:

- *Funds-available method.* This is the simplest promotion budget allocation method. The marketing manager simply establishes the budget as the amount established by the company's management. It does not require any research and makes long-term planning impractical.

- *Percentage of current sales method.* This method is calculated based on the previous year's or the current year's forecasted sales for various product or service categories. It can be justified in that the promotion budget will increase or decrease proportionally to sales, and it establishes linkage between the sales of a product or service category and the amount budgeted for its promotion. However, this method encourages more spending during growth periods when less may be indicated, and less spending during periods of contraction when more may be appropriate.

- *Matching the competition.* A firm allocates an amount to its promotion budget that matches the competition's. This allows a product or service to maintain an amount of advertising equal to that of its competitors. It can also be claimed that this level of promotion represents an industry consensus. However, it assumes that other companies know the appropriate amount to allocate to the promotion budget, when in fact there may be no justification for this assumption.

- *Objective and task method.* The promotion budget is established based on clear marketing goals, defined tasks needed to achieve the stated goals, and defined expenditure estimates. This method relies on estimating the promotional productivity of the resources allocated in each category. However, developing accurate estimates of the effectiveness of promotional expenditures is difficult at best.

3.12 THE PROMOTIONAL MIX

The promotional mix is the blending of the five promotional areas of advertising, sales promotion, public relations, direct marketing, and personal selling.

- *Advertising.* Advertising is any form of paid public and impersonal communication utilizing the mass media. The purpose of advertising is to emphasize the benefits and characteristics of products or services, often using special effects, including graphics, color, sound, music, famous personalities, testimonials, and related methods.

- *Sales promotion.* Sales promotions consist of various types of incentives, including discounts, rebates, contests, and so on, intended to produce a positive response from consumers. Although they are short-term in nature, promotions are designed to induce a rapid increase in sales.

- *Public relations.* Public relations is communication to an organization's publics that extends beyond its immediate target market. The purpose of public relations is to create a positive image of the organization by providing and explaining information. One of the outcomes of public relations is the creation of publicity for all forms of the mass media. Publicity is advantageous because it usually appears as a news story, so there is no cost to the organization.

- *Direct marketing.* Direct marketing consists of various types of marketing intended to solicit a direct consumer response. Forms of direct marketing include direct mail, telemarketing, and electronic marketing. Direct marketing is aimed at specific individuals in the target market rather than broadly disseminated.

- *Personal selling.* Personal selling is the oldest and most successful form of sales promotion. Personal selling is contingent on developing personal, long-term, one-on-one relationships. Personal selling depends on the development of an organizational sales force.

3.13 ADVERTISING

Advertising is any form of paid nonpersonal communication of messages designed to promote products and services to target markets utilizing the mass media.

What are the objectives of advertising?

The objectives of advertising are to educate, convince, and remind target markets.

- *Educate.* Educational advertising is essential in the early stages of product or service introduction. Educational advertising informs the target consumer about the advantages of a particular product or service and how it can be useful.

- *Convince.* In competitive markets it becomes essential to convince consumers why one product or service is more advantageous than another in terms of features, services, price, or status.

- *Remind.* In mature markets, it is necessary to continuously remind consumers to use a particular brand or service. It is also useful for overcoming buyer's remorse and consumer second thoughts about a purchase by reminding them of the strengths of a particular product or service.

How is the advertising message developed?

Developing advertising is a creative process. The basic purpose of an advertising message is to stress the positive aspects of a product or service. This is done by collecting and analyzing consumer responses and consumer data. Several advertising variations should be developed and tested; however, the reality is that the costs for doing this are prohibitive.

Nonetheless, an advertisement serves several functions. First, it catches the consumer's attention by using a catchy introduction or headline. Here is where effective headlines make a difference: once the advertisement has the consumer's attention, the copy should make its message clear.

Which media should be chosen?

The major media markets include newspapers, television, radio, direct response, magazines, and outdoor media including billboards, buildings, buses, and other outside advertising space. The marketing manager seeks the best fit between the media and the target market. The basic objective is to get the maximum impact for each advertising dollar. This is based on the effectiveness of the ad and the audience size provided by the media for the products and services. Impact can be given a numerical value to rate the specific exposures in a particular medium. Additionally, outcomes have to be continuously evaluated to determine if effectiveness is changing over time.

Other variables include the media's effectiveness in targeting specific geographic areas. The reach of the media is the number of consumers who are exposed to the advertising; the frequency is the number of times the audience is exposed to the advertising message. The total number of exposures can be calculated as follows:

$$\text{Total Number of Exposures (E)} = \text{Reach (R)} \times \text{Frequency (F)}$$

The total number of exposures is known as the gross rating points (GRP), which is used as a measure for rating the media. This figure is usually calculated for an estimate of the percent of the target market that a specific medium actually reaches.

Example 3.6

A marketing manager wants to know what the gross rating points will be for a television ad when its reach is 75 percent of the target market, with an average frequency of five.

$$\text{GRP} = 75 \times 5$$
$$\text{GRP} = 375$$

What is the cost-per-thousand media index?

The cost-per-thousand (CPM) index is a method of evaluating the cost effectiveness of the medium, based on its reach in thousands and the cost of an exposure. The formula for calculating the cost-per-thousand index is

$$\text{Cost Per Thousand (CPM)} = \frac{\text{Exposure Cost} \times 1{,}000}{\text{Reach}}$$

Example 3.7

A marketing manager wants to compare the CPM for a thirty-second advertisement of instant decaffeinated coffee in two different non–prime-time TV network shows serving the same target market.

Network Show A has 3,825,000 viewers who regularly drink decaffeinated coffee, and charges $45,500 for the advertisement. Network Show B has 2,785,000 viewers who regularly drink decaffeinated coffee, and charges $37,500 for the advertisement.

$$\text{Network Show A CPM} = \frac{\$45{,}500 \times 1000}{3{,}825{,}000} = \$11.90$$

$$\text{Network Show B CPM} = \frac{\$37.500 \times 1000}{2{,}785{,}000} = \$13.46$$

In this example, Network Show B charges a higher price per thousand viewers for the advertisement.

How is media timing decided?

Marketing managers have to decide between long-term and short-term media timing schedules. In long-term timing the marketer considers such things as seasonally competitive factors and product characteristics, including repeat buying patterns. Short-term timing considers such factors as the availability of financial resources, the launching of a new product or service, and unique market situations requiring rapid response advertising.

How is advertising impact measured?

Because of its extremely expensive nature, advertising's impact must be measured to ascertain its effectiveness. Advertising effectiveness is measured using pre- and post-testing methodologies.

What is advertising pre-testing?

Pre-testing is an extremely cost-effective method to measure the ability of advertising to get its message to the target market group prior to actually launching a full campaign. Direct consumer group evaluations are a pre-testing method in which consumers rate various types of advertisements. Other types of pre-testing methods are evaluation scales that measure consumer responses, including their ability to recall information from advertisements. Laboratory tests measure physiological responses such as pulse, blood pressure, respiration, and so on, as a result of using different types of advertisements.

What is advertising post-testing?

Post-testing is normally used to measure the changes in brand familiarity and preference. Advertisers hope to have a substantial increase in brand awareness as the result of advertising, and post-testing attempts to measure the extent to which the advertiser has been successful. In post-testing, the consumer market is tested to determine what advertisements were actually read, while recall tests are performed to determine what respondents recall about advertisements they read or saw.

CHAPTER 4

Business Law

Business executives need to be familiar with the legal concepts that impact their business operations and decisions. This chapter provides an overview of the areas of business law that managers and owners are most likely to encounter in the business environment. The law discussed in this chapter consists of basic principles which are generally uniform throughout the states; however, for specific provisions or variations within a particular state, consult an attorney.

4.1 CONTRACT LAW

4.1.1 The Importance of Contracts

Contracts are the basis for commercial activities. A contract is essentially a promise that is enforceable by law, thereby ensuring that society can rely on the promises of others in the conduct of its business.

What constitutes a legally binding contract?

The following are the essential elements of a contract:

- Agreement
- Consideration
- Contractual capacity
- Legality of purpose
- Genuine assent
- Compliance with law as to contract form

How do we know if there is agreement?

An agreement is manifested by an offer, followed by an acceptance that "mirrors" the terms of the offer (prior to revocation). If the acceptance varies any terms of the offer, the acceptance becomes a counteroffer, which in turn must be accepted by the original offeror.

Example 4.1

X offers to sell Y 400 units of product at $100/unit. For there to be an acceptance, Y must agree to pay $100/unit. If Y agrees to purchase 400 units at $99/unit, Y has made a counteroffer, and there is no agreement unless X accepts Y's counteroffer, agreeing to sell at $99/unit.

Unilateral offers may be accepted by performing in accordance with the terms of the offer prior to its revocation.

What is consideration?

Consideration is the fair exchange of something of value to induce the other party to enter into a legally binding contract. Consideration must be bargained for; that is, it must be sought by the parties to the contract. To be legally sufficient to support an enforceable contract, consideration must be beneficial to the promisor (party making the promise) or detrimental to the promisee (party receiving the promise). If something is beneficial to one party, it is usually detrimental to the other.

Example 4.2

X pays Y $400 for Y's promise to deliver goods. The payment of $400 is to X's detriment and to Y's benefit.

What form can consideration take?

Consideration can be

- Money, property, or rights
- Undertaking an act or performance of an act that a party was not previously obligated to undertake
- Forbearance, or refraining from doing something one is legally entitled to do, such as starting legal action to collect a debt
- Creating a legal relationship that did not previously exist; modifying or terminating a legal relationship.

Agreeing to comply with a preexisting duty is not legally sufficient consideration because doing what one is already obligated to do creates no legal benefit received or detriment given.

What if one side thinks the consideration is unfair?

The law requires that the consideration be "adequate," or fair, in order to make a contract enforceable. Courts generally do not question the adequacy of consideration where there is no question of the capacity of the parties or unfair circumstances indicating that one of the parties was not free to bargain.

What if there are disputes as to consideration due?

Sometimes, a party agrees to pay—and the other party agrees to accept—something less than what one of them might have thought the proper consideration should be. This is especially so when the parties settle claims. The following are the most common forms of settling claims or resolving disputes:

- *Accord and satisfaction.* The parties make an agreement (the accord) where the amount necessary to satisfy an unliquidated debt—that is, one in which the amount due is disputed—is usually less than the amount claimed. There can be no accord and satisfaction if the claim is fixed (liquidated).

- *Creditor's composition agreement.* A debtor agrees to forego the right to file a bankruptcy petition in return for the agreement of two or more creditors to accept partial payment.

- *Release.* A release is given and obtained in good faith, in writing, and there is consideration; the releasor cannot recover more than the amount set forth in the release.

Are there any types of agreements that are enforceable without consideration?

The following types of contracts are enforceable even where no consideration is given:

- Promises to pay a debt that has been barred by the Statute of Limitations

- Promises to pay debts that have been legally discharged in bankruptcy

- Detrimental reliance or estoppel; where one party has reasonably relied on the promise to his detriment, the promisor may not deny the contract.

What is legal capacity?

Legal capacity is the ability in the eyes of the law of a party to enter into a binding contract. It is not the same as actual capacity.

Who has legal capacity?

The law generally assumes that the parties to a contract have the capacity to enter into a contract; this includes legal entities such as corporations, partnerships, estates, and trusts, as well as individuals. However, certain individuals may have no legal capacity or limited legal capacity to enter into a binding contract. Many cases turn on the ability of the individual to understand the nature and subject matter of the contract and its consequences. This will determine whether the contract is void or voidable. The most common instances are cases of incompetent persons, intoxicated persons, and minors.

What is a void contract?

A void contract is one with no force and effect, and which is not enforceable from the outset.

What is a voidable contract?

A voidable contract is one that is valid until voided, usually based on the inability of one of the contracting parties to actually, or in the eyes of the law, understand the nature, substance, and consequences of a contract.

Generally, a party may be released from a voidable contract that has not been executed if he is able to make restitution by restoring or returning the money or goods. A voidable contract may also be ratified under certain circumstances, making the contract accepted and legally binding.

Who is considered incompetent and under what circumstances might a contract be binding on him?

Generally, an individual who is declared incompetent by a court and for whom a guardian has been appointed is considered without legal capacity to enter into a contract, rendering the contract null and void.

If an individual is actually incompetent, but there has been no court declaration of incompetence, the contract is voidable once it is shown that the individual lacked the ability to comprehend the nature, subject matter, and consequences of the contract at the time he entered into it.

If a contract is voidable, the contract can be ratified by the appointed guardian of the incompetent, or by the incompetent himself, once he is no longer adjudged incompetent.

Who is considered an intoxicated person, and under what circumstances might a contract be binding on him?

A contract entered into by an intoxicated person is usually voidable. The courts generally try to use objective criteria to determine whether the party was intoxicated instead of delving into the subjective question of the ability to comprehend.

What is the law relating to contracts entered into by minors?

Contracts entered into by minors—persons who have not reached legal maturity—are voidable, and can be disaffirmed at any time during the party's minority or within a reasonable time after reaching adulthood, provided that the minor can make restitution. However, in the case of "necessaries" (food, clothing), even though the minor may disaffirm the contract, he is obligated to pay the value of the goods received. If parents or a guardian are responsible for providing for the minor, there are states in which the parent or guardian may be liable. This is to discourage parties from turning away a person who is in need because of the ability to disaffirm the agreement if he is a minor.

What is meant by legality of purpose?

The subject matter or transaction contracted for must not violate any laws (such as the purchase and sale of contraband) or public policy (such as an agreement not to sell based on race, color, or creed).

Example 4.3

A contract for the purchase and sale of contraband is void and not enforceable.

What factors establish genuineness of assent?

Genuine assent exists where there has been a true "meeting of the minds." The decision to enter into the agreement cannot be based on mistakes, misrepresentation, undue influence, or duress.

What types of mistakes evidence the lack of genuine assent?

Generally, a unilateral mistake as to a material fact will not release the mistaken party from the contract. However, if there is a mutual mistake of fact, the contract may be rescinded.

Where there is a mistake as to value, there is no ground to rescind the contract. The parties are each deemed to assume the risk that the value will change. This, however, must be distinguished from a mistake in fact that affects the value.

Example 4.4

X agrees to sell, and Y agrees to pay one million dollars for, a painting they both believe to be an authentic Picasso. If the painting is a counterfeit, the issue is not one of value; it is one of material fact.

When will a misrepresentation result in lack of genuine assent?

Fraudulent misrepresentation, in which there is an intentional misrepresentation of material fact by one party, will allow the innocent party to rescind. If the innocent party has reasonably relied on the misrepresentation and has been injured, he may also elect to enforce the contract and sue for damages.

Can silence constitute misrepresentation?

Generally, silence is not misrepresentation because there is no legal duty to disclose unless there is a fiduciary relationship.

What if the misrepresentation is innocent or made negligently?

The majority of jurisdictions permit rescission of a contract where there is a misrepresentation of a material fact made innocently or negligently (failure to exercise reasonable care).

What is the difference between undue influence and duress?

Undue influence generally involves a fiduciary relationship in which there is trust placed in the other party to the extent that his own free will can be overcome (such as a client executing a contract on his attorney's advice, which is not beneficial). Where a contract is entered into because of undue influence, the contract is voidable.

Duress requires coercion based upon threatening of the innocent party with a wrongful or illegal act such as blackmail or physical harm. Threatening to exercise a legal right to sue does not constitute duress because the act threatened is not wrongful. A contract entered into under legal duress is void.

4.1.2 Establishing the Contract

How is a contract formed?

An express contract exists if the terms are set forth either orally or in writing. The Statute of Frauds requires that some types of contracts be in writing in order to be enforceable. A contract can also be implied by the conduct of the parties.

What types of contracts must be in writing?

- Contracts creating or transferring an interest in land including property affixed to the land, for instance, contracts to sell land, or to mortgage
- Contracts which by their terms cannot be performed within one year, such as a contract calling for a two-year shipping contract
- Contracts involving the sale of goods in excess of $500
- Promises to pay the debt of another
- Promises in consideration of marriage

Are there exceptions to the Statute of Frauds?

Yes, even though the subject matter of a contract may fall within the Statute of Frauds, it may still be enforceable, although not in writing in the following situations:

- Goods made specifically to the buyer's order that cannot be easily resold
- Admissions in court that a contract was made
- Where performance is complete; problems arise where there is partial performance

4.1.3 Violation of a Contract

What remedies are available if there is a breach of contract?

A breach of contract occurs when a party fails to perform in accordance with the contract. The non-breaching party is entitled to damages.

- *Compensatory damages.* Compensation for the amount the nonbreaching party would have made if there was no breach—for example, the contract price

- *Consequential damages.* Reasonably foreseeable damages that flow directly from the breach (for example, lost profits from resale of goods)

- *Punitive damages.* Rarely awarded in a breach of contract action; punitive damages are meant as a penalty or deterrent to wrongdoing

- *Nominal damages.* Where there is no significant loss or damage; nominal damages may be awarded simply to indicate that the breaching party was wrong

- *Specific performance.* A breaching party may be required to specifically perform pursuant to the terms of the contract where money damages would not adequately compensate or substitute (for example, a contract to sell a Picasso painting)

4.2 SECURED TRANSACTIONS

The area of secured transactions is important because it provides the means by which credit can be extended to businesses by securing the party extending credit of payment. Secured transactions are governed primarily by Article 9 of the Uniform Commercial Code (UCC).

4.2.1 Security Interest

What is a security interest?

Under the UCC, a security interest is an interest "in personal property or fixtures which secure payment or performance of an obligation." The property that secures the interest is the collateral (tangible/physical property and nontangible/nonphysical property, such as trademarks, copyrights).

How is a security interest created?

- By taking possession of the collateral, or by an agreement in writing
- The creditor must give something of value to the debtor
- The debtor has to have rights in the collateral

How can a creditor protect against claims of other creditors to the same property?

Generally, a secured creditor takes priority over unsecured creditors and judgment creditors who have not begun to execute on the judgment. To establish priority, a creditor must "perfect" his security interest. The methods of perfection are

- Filing of a financing statement—signed by the debtor, stating the debtor's and creditor's names and addresses and describing the collateral—with the secretary of state, a local official (for instance, county clerk), or both, depending on the type of collateral
- A "pledge" whereby the secured creditor takes possession of the collateral
- Automatic perfection that attaches when the secured interest is created—that is, purchase-money security interest where the creditor provided funds to the debtor to secure the collateral (mortgage) or retains or takes an interest in the collateral to secure the purchase price; assignment of accounts receivable to a collection agent under certain circumstances

What are the secured creditor's rights if the debtor defaults?

A creditor may repossess the collateral if he can do so without a "breach of the peace" (for example, towing a vehicle without confrontation); otherwise, he must seek a court order. The creditor may retain the collateral in full satisfaction of the debt (upon notice to the debtor) or dispose of it in a reasonable commercial manner (provided notice of time, place, and manner of sale is given). The debtor is entitled to notice except where the goods are fungible.

Where consumer goods are the collateral for a purchase-money security interest, and the debtor has paid 60 percent of the cash price or loan, the creditor must dispose of the collateral within ninety days.

What rights, if any, does the debtor have?

The proceeds from the disposition are first applied to expenses incurred in the disposition, then to the balance of the debt. If there is still a surplus, subordinate secured parties who have served written notice before all proceeds are distributed will be paid, and any further surplus will be given to the debtor. If the proceeds are insufficient to pay the costs of disposition and balance due, the creditor may enter and collect a deficiency judgment.

At any time prior to the creditor disposing of the collateral or declaring the debt satisfied by his retention of the collateral, the debtor may "redeem" the collateral by paying the balance due and the reasonable costs of repossession.

4.3 BANKRUPTCY

4.3.1 The Mechanics of Bankruptcy

What is bankruptcy and how does it work?

Bankruptcy is a procedure under federal and state law allowing an honest debtor to "discharge" (to be relieved of) certain debts so that a fresh start can be made. The federal bankruptcy law preempts (takes priority over) state bankruptcy laws. Upon filing the bankruptcy petition in the United States Bankruptcy Court, an automatic stay is imposed, prohibiting the continuation of collection activities by creditors. The stay preserves the status quo until a court-appointed trustee can begin a procedure supervised by the court, or the debtor can devise a plan that attempts to pay as much as possible to the creditors. The rights of creditors often depend on whether they are secured or unsecured.

What debts can be discharged?

The bankruptcy law provides for the release of the debtor from most unpaid portions of debt balances. Some items—such as alimony, child support, and the taxes that are held by the debtor as a "trustee" (that is, sales taxes and employment withholding taxes that the debtor has failed to pay to the relevant government entities)—may not be discharged.

Among the debts that cannot be discharged are those that may involve fraud or wrongful conduct on the part of the debtor. The law will not allow the debtor to use the law for protection against claims arising from this conduct. Among these claims are

- Claims out of money or property obtained by false pretenses
- Claims based on willful or malicious conduct against another
- Claims based on embezzlement, larceny, misappropriation, or breach of a fiduciary duty

The debtor must be careful to list all creditors so that they will be notified. A creditor who is not listed on the schedules and receives no notice of the bankruptcy will not have his debt discharged.

How are the creditors paid?

This depends on the specific section of the bankruptcy law under which the debtor seeks protection.

What are the various provisions for protection under the bankruptcy law?

The provisions available to individuals and businesses under the bankruptcy law are

- *Chapter 7:* This is sometimes known as a "liquidation plan." The bankruptcy trustee under this section marshals and liquidates all nonexempt assets and pays off the debts. Certain property of the debtor is exempt from liquidation so that the debtor will not be destitute after liquidation.

- *Chapter 11:* This is known also as a "reorganization" or "debtor-in-possession plan." This section is available to a viable business, provided that it is given enough breathing room to devise a plan for the payment of the business's debt. This may include renegotiating installments, interest rates, and sale of some assets. The debtor stays in possession of the business and continues its operations; the debts accrued prior to the filing of the bankruptcy petition are generally stayed. Post-bankruptcy petition debts must generally be paid as accrued. If the debtor cannot come up with a plan to pay off the pre-petition debt in a manner acceptable to the creditors, and provide for the likelihood that the business will survive, the court may order that the business be liquidated.

- *Chapter 13:* This section is available for individuals who have a regular source of income, including sole proprietors whose unsecured debts are less than $100,000, and whose secured debts do not exceed $350,000. The court will allow the debtor to devise a plan for the full or partial payment of creditors over a three- to five-year period. The plan will normally be approved by the court if the creditors will get at least what they would if the debtor had filed Chapter 7.

What typically happens in a Chapter 7 bankruptcy?

The first step is usually the filing of a petition by the debtor. The filing triggers the automatic stay against collections by creditors of pre-petition debts. The debtor normally files a list of its creditors and amounts owed, along with a schedule of the debtor's assets. However, the debtor has up to ten days after the filing of the petition to submit these schedules, along with income and expense information.

The clerk of the court will mail out notices of the bankruptcy filing to the creditors and the debtor, along with the notice of a Section 341 meeting of creditors. The debtor will generally contact and notify the creditors prior to the court notification. Once on notice, a creditor may be held in contempt of court if it makes an attempt to collect its debt.

An interim trustee is appointed until the Section 341 meeting, when the interim trustee will be confirmed or a new one voted on by the creditors. The debtor must be present at this meeting to answer (under oath) any questions from the creditors and the trustee about assets or recent transfers of assets, and material contained in the petition or schedules.

The creditors have 180 days after the first Section 341 meeting to file their "proof of claim," which states the amount of debt owed by the debtor. Failure to file a proof of claim may result in a waiver of any right to share in the proceeds from the liquidation of the debtor's assets.

How does the treatment of a secured creditor differ from that of an unsecured creditor?

A secured creditor will normally be permitted to apply to the court for a "lift" of the automatic stay so that it can proceed to liquidate the security (collateral) by, for example, foreclosing on the property securing a mortgage. Any deficiency not covered by the liquidation of the collateral is treated as unsecured debt. Unsecured creditors must generally wait to share in a portion of the proceeds from the liquidation of the debtor's assets.

What if the debtor has transferred assets prior to the filing of his bankruptcy petition?

The bankruptcy laws seek to ensure that creditors are treated equally, and will not allow a debtor to favor a specific creditor. The trustee is vested with the power to void certain transfers. Among them are

- Preferential transfers made within ninety days of the filing that are in excess of $600

- Preferential liens obtained within ninety days prior to filing based on a pre-petition debt; a lien by an insider (party related to the debtor) within one year can be voided by the trustee

- Fraudulent transfers made within a year prior to the filing of the petition where it can be shown that the transfer was to hinder, to delay, to hide assets, or to defraud creditors, where the transfer was made without adequate consideration, or left the debtor with little or no assets to pay creditors

The creditors and trustee will normally consult on the assets of the debtor. The creditors will assist the trustee by informing him of any known assets of the debtor, and may even go so far as taking action to uncover the assets.

What is the procedure in a Chapter 11 bankruptcy?

After a petition is filed, the court will appoint one or more committees of unsecured creditors to examine records and financial structure, and to assist the debtor in formulating a plan. The committee is authorized to engage accountants, attorneys, and other professionals. A trustee may also be appointed if there are assets to be sold, if there are allegations of gross mismanagement in the operation, or if the court deems it in the best interest of the debtor's estate.

Within 120 days after the court enters an order granting relief, the debtor must submit a plan. The plan will contain the following:

- The classes of claims and interests of the creditors
- How each class is to be treated
- Provisions for the execution of the plan

If the debtor fails to file the plan or to get creditor approval within 180 days after the court's order of relief, the creditors may submit a plan.

The plan is submitted to each class of creditors and requires the approval of two-thirds of the total claim of each class. The approval of the plan by a class is not necessary where the court deems the plan not adverse to that class's interests. In fact, if one class approves, the court may "cram down" the plan and confirm it. Once a plan is confirmed by the court, all creditors are bound.

How does a Chapter 13 bankruptcy work?

After the debtor files his petition, a trustee is appointed. The automatic stay, however, applies only to consumer debt and not to business debt (of a sole proprietor).

The debtor submits a plan in which he will pay all or part of the debt over not more than three years. The court in its discretion may extend the period to up to five years. The essential elements of the plan are

- Statement of the amount of the debtor's future income to be turned over to the trustee at regular intervals
- Provision for the full payment of priority claims in installments
- Provision that all members of each class of creditors be treated the same

The court will confirm the plan if the secured creditors accept it, if creditors' liens are retained, and if the amount creditors receive under the plan equals at least the secured portion of their claim or the debtor surrenders the collateral to the secured creditors.

Prior to the full execution of the plan, the court may allow it to be modified at the request of the trustee, debtor, or creditor.

What happens at the end of these procedures?

When the debtor is discharged in bankruptcy, all pre-petition judgments are voided, and all rights to collect those debts are enjoined. In Chapter 7, a debtor maybe discharged before all of the distributions are made to the creditors from the liquidated assets. In Chapters 11 and 13, the discharge takes place when the plans are executed.

Can creditors force a debtor into bankruptcy?

Yes. The filing of a petition may be voluntary (by the debtor) or involuntary. Creditors will normally file an involuntary petition to force the debtor into bankruptcy in order to have its assets distributed.

What are the requirements for filing an involuntary petition?

If the debtor has twelve or more creditors, at least three, having unsecured debt totaling $5,000, must join the petition. In the event that there are fewer than twelve creditors, one creditor with a debt of $5,000 may file.

The court will generally allow the involuntary petition to go forward over the debtor's objection if

- The debtor is not paying debts when due
- 120 days prior to the filing, a receiver, assignee, or custodian has taken control of all of the debtor's assets

How often can a debtor file for bankruptcy?

In Chapter 7, a debtor may be discharged only once every six years.

4.4 CONSUMER LAWS

There is a great deal of government regulation regarding the protection of consumers, who can generally be described as individuals acquiring goods, services, credit, or land for personal or family use. There are a number of federal statutes dealing with each of these areas, as well as health and safety issues.

4.4.1 Consumer Relationships

What are some of the major laws concerning the purchase and sale of goods to consumers?

There are several major laws concerning advertising, labeling, and packaging; sales tactics in general; and sales of specific items such as real estate.

What controls are there on advertising?

The Federal Trade Commission (FTC) Act prohibits unfair and deceptive advertising that may mislead or deceive a consumer when it goes beyond mere "puffing" (obvious exaggerations or generalizations) about a product.

The law prohibits the practice of "bait and switch," in which a less expensive item is advertised but is not made available to the consumer, who is then encouraged to buy another, more expensive product. This unlawful tactic may be evidenced by the seller's refusal to make the advertised item available, understocking the item, encouraging employees to sell the more expensive item, or inability to deliver the goods advertised within a reasonable time.

In cases of established deceptive advertising, the Federal Trade Commission may issue a cease and desist order, or require affirmative steps on the part of the advertiser to use accurate advertising, or to create an advertisement admitting the prior misleading ads, or it may seek penalties.

What labeling and packaging regulations govern consumer goods?

There are a number of labeling and packaging requirements to inform consumers about contents and safety concerns. The Fair Packaging and Labeling Act requires that labels specifically state the product name, quantity, number of servings, and the names of the manufacturer and distributor. This law also gives the agency the right to impose further requirements with respect to claims made by a company as to nutritional content, packing standards, and the like.

What provisions govern sales tactics to consumers?

Most of the regulations governing sales are supervised by the FTC. In the case of door-to-door sales where the selling entity is not located in the community and there is a greater likelihood of pressure tactics, the law gives consumers the right to rescind their decision to purchase for up to three days ("cooling off period"), and longer if the state law provides for a longer period to reconsider. The seller is required to inform the consumer of this right.

With respect to mail-order or telephone sales, the regulation is primarily through the laws against mail and wire fraud.

What laws apply to the sale of land?

There are two major laws governing the sale of land. The Interstate Land Sales Full Disclosure Act requires that sellers or lessors of one hundred or more lots of vacant land as part of a common promotion file a "statement of record" and obtain approval of the Department of Housing and Urban Development before beginning sales or leases. This also applies where land is sold interstate, and imposes civil and criminal penalties for fraud or other violations of the statute. Under the law, the consumer has a right of rescission similar to the "cooling off period."

The other major statute is the Real Estate Settlement Procedures Act (RESPA). This law informs the consumer of the costs of settlement for the purchase of real estate when a lender is involved. Within three days of the application for a loan, the lender must send a copy of an HUD booklet that explains the settlement procedures and the costs involved (for instance, appraisal fees, title insurance, lender's charges, and attorneys' fees). The lender must, within those three days, provide an estimate of the costs, clearly identify the parties the lender will require the borrower to use, and provide a truth-in-lending statement when the loan is approved.

RESPA expressly prohibits the taking of kickbacks for referrals by the lender or others in the transaction.

What consumer credit protections are available?

Consumer credit is an area in which the consumer is especially vulnerable to unfair practices. Therefore, the law requires certain disclosures and heavily regulates collection practices on both the federal and state levels.

The Truth-in-Lending Act (TILA) requires disclosure of credit or loan terms by sellers and lenders who arrange or extend credit in the ordinary course of their businesses. Individuals are covered under this act, but corporations are not.

The Fair Credit Billing Act is a part of TILA that allows a consumer to refuse payment of a credit-card charge where the purchased product is defective, provided that the consumer has tried to resolve the matter with the seller in good faith. The debtor may also challenge an error in billing by the credit-card company. The company is required to resolve the matter within ninety days of the complaint without additional finance charges or cancellation of the account.

TILA provides that a consumer is responsible only to the extent of $50 for unauthorized credit-card purchases on a lost or stolen card prior to notification of the theft or loss.

The Equal Credit Opportunity Act prohibits the denial of credit because of a person's race, religion, color, sex, marital status, or age.

Under the Fair Credit Reporting Act, consumers are given the right to correct any information on their credit reports. The law requires that the consumer be notified when a party extending credit will obtain credit reports, and they must be given the opportunity to correct any information that might affect their ability to get credit, insurance, or employment.

With respect to collection practices, the Fair Debt Collection Practices Act prohibits a collection agency from

- Contacting the debtor at his place of employment when the employer objects
- Calling the debtor at inconvenient times
- Contacting the debtor directly when he is represented by an attorney
- Contacting third parties about the debt without court authorization (except spouse, parents, or financial counselor)
- Harassing or intimidating the debtor
- Continuing to communicate with the debtor once the debtor has stated his refusal to pay the debt (except to notify debtor of further action being taken)

There are specific provisions regarding the collection of a debt by the garnishing of wages (based on state law), in which the creditor seizes part of the debtor's wages. State law dictates the percentage of the wages that may be garnished (usually not more than 25 percent of after-tax wages) and provides for notice and an opportunity for the debtor to object.

4.5 SALES

Contracts involving the sale of goods is governed by Article 2 of the Uniform Commercial Code (UCC), although common law contracts apply. The rights of the parties in a sale under the UCC is determined by whether either or both are merchants.

4.5.1 Selling Goods or Services

What is a sale?

The UCC defines a sale as "the passing of title from the seller to the buyer for a price." The price may be paid in the form of money, goods, services, or real estate.

What are goods?

Goods are tangible and movable property (for instance, clothing, furniture, appliances). They do not include intangible property (for example, bonds, copyrights, trademarks), nor real estate or fixtures.

Who qualifies as a merchant?

According to the UCC a merchant is

- A person who deals in goods of the kind involved in the contract (for example, retailer, wholesaler, or manufacturer)
- A person who by occupation holds himself out as having skill or knowledge peculiar to the practices or goods involved
- A person who employs a merchant, broker, agent, or other intermediary who holds himself out as having the skill or knowledge peculiar to the goods

When does title pass from the seller to the buyer?

Goods must exist and be identified as those covered by the contract before title can pass to the buyer. When title actually passes is determined by the agreement of the parties or, if not specified, at the time and place that the seller makes delivery.

How do rules under the UCC differ from common law?

There are numerous differences between the rules as set forth under the UCC and common law. Among them are the areas of offer and acceptance, consideration, and the Statute of Frauds. This section will cover only some of the salient points. The reader is referred to UCC Article 2 for more thorough coverage.

How are offers dealt with under the UCC?

The terms of an offer under common law must be definite and certain at the time of its acceptance. Under the UCC, an offer may be accepted and bind the offeror, even where certain terms are left out, as long as a court can establish that the parties intended to enter into a contract and that there is a reasonably certain basis for filling in the missing terms. The following are common situations:

- *Failure to state a price.* The court may set a reasonable price at the time of delivery unless the failure to set the price is the fault of either party, in which case the contract may be rescinded or the parties may set the price.
- *Failure to state shipping arrangements.* The shipper must exercise good faith and use a commercially reasonable manner of shipment.

- *Failure to state quantity.* A court will generally have no basis to grant relief, and the contract will generally not be viable.

How is an acceptance dealt with under the UCC?

Unlike with common law, where an acceptance must be by the means specified or, if by an unauthorized method, must be received before the expiration of the offer, the UCC permits any form of acceptance that is "reasonable under the circumstances" if no method of acceptance is specified.

Under common law, delivery of conforming goods to a carrier constitutes acceptance. Under the UCC, acceptance is effective if there is prompt shipment of the goods or a promise to ship (sent in a commercially reasonable manner).

Under common law, a unilateral offer may be accepted by performance without notification to the offeror of the acceptance. The UCC provides that if notice of acceptance is not given within a reasonable time, the offeror may treat the offer as expired.

An acceptance must "mirror" the terms of the offer under common law; otherwise, it is a counteroffer. The UCC states that if there are different or additional terms in the acceptance, the acceptance is binding unless the acceptance is conditional on the offeror agreeing to the different or additional terms. However, whether the additional or different terms become part of the contract will depend on whether the parties are merchants. If one of the parties is not a merchant, the terms are merely proposals. If both parties are merchants, the terms are included if

- They do not materially alter the terms (for example, present hardships).
- The offer had stated that no terms except those stated in the offer are acceptable.
- The additional or different terms are objected to within a reasonable time.

How does the UCC differ from common law on consideration?

No consideration is required under the UCC for modification of a contract sought in good faith. However, the parties may provide that no modification may be permitted under the contract unless it is made in writing.

What does the UCC say about the Statute of Frauds?

Sales of goods priced at $500 or more must be in writing to be enforceable, and must be signed by the party against whom enforcement is sought. A written confirmation between merchants is sufficient to enforce a contract against the merchant receiving the confirmation if it contains the terms, he fails to object within ten days of receipt, and he knew or had reason to know of the contents of the confirmation.

Other exceptions to the Statute of Frauds are included in the section on contract law.

What other areas are covered under Article 2 of the UCC?

Article 2 also deals with the issues of risk of loss, when an interest is created so that a party has an insurable interest in goods; the obligations of the seller and buyer with respect to delivery and payment; remedies in case of breach of contract; and warranties related to the goods. The subject matter is too voluminous to cover here, so the reader is referred to Article 2 for more thorough coverage. The following are a few additional concepts that may be helpful to the reader.

What are the rules on risk of loss where there is no specific contract provision?

Risk of loss does not always pass with the title to the goods, but may vary depending on manner of shipment or delivery.

- *Free on Board (F.O.B.).* The goods are delivered at the seller's expense to a specific location. Once the goods are put into the hands of the carrier or party at the designated location, risk of loss passes to the buyer.

- *Free Along Side (F.A.S.).* The goods are transported by the seller at his expense and risk until the goods are delivered alongside the ship that will carry the goods, at which time the risk of loss passes to the buyer.

- *Cost, Insurance & Freight (C.I.F., or C. & F. for Cost and Freight).* The risk of loss passes to the buyer once the goods are "put in possession of a carrier."

- *Delivery Ex-Ship.* Risk of loss passes when the goods leave the carrier or are properly unloaded.

What warranties are made about goods under Article 2?

Under the UCC, there are several types of warranties made regarding goods sold; they include warranties of title, express warranties, and implied warranties.

What are the warranties of title?

- *Warranty of good title.* The seller represents that he has good title to the goods and can rightfully transfer the goods.
- *Warranty of no liens.* The seller represents that there are no encumbrances (for instance, claims, security interests) at the time of delivery that have not been disclosed to the buyer.
- *Warranty of no infringements.* This applies to a merchant who represents that the goods sold do not infringe upon any copyrights, trademarks, or patents of third parties. No warranty is made if the goods are manufactured according to specifications provided by the buyer.

A breach of these warranties will result in liability against the seller.

What are express warranties made under Article 2?

Representations about quality, condition, description, or performance of goods are express warranties. These warranties are made by specific statements of facts, providing a sample or model, or on the basis of labeling information.

What are implied warranties made under Article 2?

Representations that the goods are "reasonably fit for the ordinary purposes for which such goods are used" are implied warranties. The goods must be of average, fair, or medium grade, without objection within the trade or market for said types of goods; be properly and adequately labeled; conform to the representations made on the label or container; and represent an even quality and quantity among all such units.

4.6 NEGOTIABLE INSTRUMENTS

Negotiable instruments are part of commercial paper that allow transactions to be facilitated conveniently by acting as cash substitutes or credit instruments.

Commercial paper can be negotiable (governed by Article 3 of the UCC) or nonnegotiable (governed by contract law on assignments). This section covers negotiable instruments.

4.6.1 Issues Surrounding Negotiable Instruments

What is a negotiable instrument?

A negotiable instrument is commercial paper that can be assigned or negotiated. It is defined as an instrument that is

- Signed by the maker or drawer
- Contains an unconditional promise or order to pay a sum certain in money, and no other promise
- Payable on demand or at a time certain
- Payable to order or bearer

Who are the maker and the drawer?

A maker issues a promissory note or a certificate of deposit promising to pay a certain sum to a specific payee or to the bearer of the instrument. To be liable, the maker's signature must appear on the face of the instrument.

The drawer is the one who issues a draft or check, and who writes and signs the instrument.

What does "payable to order" mean?

The instrument specifies a payee (party to receive payment), or as the payee directs (by endorsing and delivering the instrument to another).

Who is a bearer?

A bearer is one in possession of an instrument that does not have a specific payee, or one that has been endorsed by a specific payee "in blank" (payee's signature only).

What are the most common negotiable instruments?

The most common instruments are

- *Draft.* An order by one person (drawer) to another (drawee) to pay money to a third party (payee) or to the bearer
- *Check.* A special type of draft drawn on a bank and payable on demand

- *Promissory note.* A promise by one person (maker) to pay money to another (payee) or to the bearer
- *Certificate of deposit.* A note made by a bank acknowledging that funds were deposited and made payable to the holder of the note

What is negotiation?

Negotiation is the process in which an instrument is transferred to another (transferee) in such a way that the transferee becomes a "holder."

Order paper on which there is a named payee can be transferred by the payee through endorsement (writing "pay to the order of X" and signing it). Bearer paper, on which the payee is "bearer" or which was endorsed by a specific payee without an "order," can be negotiated by delivering the instrument to another party.

What is the significance of being a holder?

Whether a party is a holder and how he became a holder determines his right to collect the payments represented by the instrument, even though there may be certain defenses that would defeat the collection efforts of an ordinary "holder." There is a specific category of "holder" who is given special protection by the UCC, known as the "holder in due course" (HDC). An HDC is one who acquires an instrument for value (consideration), in good faith, and without notice that the instrument is defective or overdue or that a person may have a claim or defense against the collection under that instrument.

For the specific defenses good against an HDC, see Article 3 of the UCC.

4.7 AGENCY LAW

In the operation of a business, one is not able to perform all tasks and must have the ability to delegate. The law of agency allows a principal (one who authorizes another) to appoint an agent to act on his behalf. A third party may deal with the agent as if he is dealing with the principal himself, and hold the principal liable.

Whether a party is liable for the acts of another often turns on whether the party acting is an agent or an independent contractor.

4.7.1 How Agencies Work

How is an agency created?

An agency is created when a principal authorizes another, called the agent, to act on his behalf, and the agent consents to do so.

What is the extent of the agent's authority?

The scope of the agent's authority is based on express authority (oral or written) given by the principal, or implied in law (for instance, based on the position of the agent, those acts reasonably necessary to carry out the principal's instructions).

The Equal Dignity Rule requires that where the underlying subject matter of the agency is required to be in writing to be enforceable under the Statute of Frauds (for example, authorizing an agent to transfer an interest in land), the agency agreement must also be in writing.

What are the duties of the agent?

The duties of an agent are to

- Perform the authorized duties in a reasonable and diligent manner based on the skills and the knowledge he possesses (that is, the agent can be liable for negligence).
- Notify the principal of all material developments. Since the principal will be bound by the agent's acts, he must be informed as to the points on which he may be liable.
- Act with loyalty by acting solely for the principal's benefit, and not in his own or another party's interest.
- Follow instructions that are lawful and clearly stated.
- Account to the principal for all money or property received or paid on behalf of the principal in carrying out his duties as agent. A constructive trust may be imposed on an agent who retains or takes benefits that belong to the principal.

What are the duties of the principal to the agent?

The principal owes certain duties to the agent, provided the agent acts within the scope of the authority granted. The principal may not be obligated to fulfill these duties if the agent has violated one of the duties owed to the principal (breach of contract). Among the duties owed by the principal to the agent are to

- Cooperate so as to allow the agent to carry out his duties.
- Compensate the agent for work done when the parties have agreed upon compensation.
- Reimburse the agent for authorized expenses or reasonable expenses necessary to carry out his duties as agent.
- Indemnify the agent against claims that arise from his carrying out his duties as agent.
- Provide a safe workplace or to warn the agent of possible dangers.

Distinguishing between an independent contractor and an agent

An independent contractor is one who is asked to perform a task for the "employer," but over whom the employer has no control as to how the contractor physically performs the task (for example, a plumber who is asked to repair a pipe). Among the parameters used to determine whether a party is an independent contractor are

- The employer does not exercise control over work details.
- The contractor has an occupation, skills, or a business operation separate from the employer's.
- The work is not supervised by the employer or is executed based on the skills and knowledge of the contractor.
- The contractor supplies the tools, facilities, or means of accomplishing the work.
- The period of hire is short-term or based on the completion of a particular project.
- Method of payment is based on completion.
- The contractor has special skills (is a specialist).
- The greater the number of parameters, the more likely that the party will be deemed an independent contractor.

What is the significance of being an agent or an independent contractor?

An independent contractor is responsible for his own acts, and the employer will not be held liable in the event of negligence or intentional wrongdoing on the part of the independent contractor. The employer (principal), however, may be liable for the acts of its agents (including that of an employee) within the scope of his employment.

4.8 PROPERTY LAW

Property law deals with the legally protected rights and interests in anything that has an ascertainable value. Property is classified as personal property or real property.

4.8.1 How Property Is Treated

What is personal property?

Personal property is either tangible or intangible. Tangible property has physical substance, such as furniture, equipment, and vehicles. Intangible property has no physical substance but represents rights and interest in property (for example, stock certificates represent the percentage interest of a shareholder in a corporation and all of the rights flowing from ownership).

How is ownership of personal property acquired?

Ownership in personal property is acquired by

- *Purchase.* Transfer of title from a seller to a buyer for a price (consideration).
- *Possession.* Taking possession of something that is not owned by anyone (for instance, capture of a wild animal not in violation of any laws).
- *Production.* Made through the labor of a party (for example, painting or writing or manufacture of furniture from raw materials).
- *Gift.* Voluntary transfer of title to property by a donor (giver) exhibiting delivery, donative intent, and acceptance by the donee (recipient).
- *Will or inheritance.* Title to property transferred at the death of another by will or under state law governing estates of decedents.

Can title be acquired in personal property that has not been transferred?

Title can be acquired in some instances where the property is found as set forth below:

- *Abandoned property.* The owner has intentionally discarded the property (for instance, throwing a chair away). The finder who takes possession with an intent to claim ownership becomes the owner (rights are superior to the original owner).

- *Lost property.* The owner did not intentionally part with the property (for example, unbeknownst to the owner, a book falls out of his bag). The true owner can reclaim the property from the finder. If the finder knows the true owner's identity, he must return the property.

- *Mislaid property.* The true owner intentionally places property in a place and, without intent to relinquish title, leaves it. The finder has no rights in the property and is deemed to hold the property for the true owner.

Can there be a transfer of possession without transfer of title?

Transfer of possession of personal property without transfer of title is known as bailment.

Bailments are common in the business world and include such activities as leaving a car at a repair shop or a parking garage, or leaving clothes at the cleaners. A bailment is created when

- The bailor owns or has possessory right to property (for example, is the owner of a car).

- The bailor delivers possession of the property to the bailee (for instance, brings his car to the mechanic for repair).

- The bailee accepts the property knowing that he has a duty to return the property at the bailor's direction (for example, the mechanic must return the car to the owner when the repairs are complete and the bill is paid).

What if the property is damaged while in the bailee's possession?

The rights and liabilities of a bailee are determined by the nature of the bailment created:

- *Bailment for the sole benefit of the bailor.* The bailee receives no benefit (for instance, the bailor is permitted to store goods without charge). The bailee is liable only if he is grossly negligent and has a duty to return the goods at the bailor's direction.

- *Bailment for the sole benefit of the bailee.* The bailor receives no benefit (for example, the bailor lends the bailee his book so the bailee can study). The bailee must exercise great care, and must compensate the bailor if the property is lost or damaged.

- *Bailment for mutual benefit.* Both the bailor and bailee receive benefits (for example, the bailor's clothing is cleaned and the cleaner is paid for the task). The bailee must exercise reasonable care of the property and return the property as directed. The bailor has a duty to disclose known defects that cannot be easily discovered on inspection.

What is real property?

Real property is land or anything permanently attached to it (called fixtures), which includes crops and minerals. Once the crops are harvested or the minerals are mined, they become personal property. Personal property that becomes affixed to the land becomes a fixture (for example, an unattached sink is personal property, but once it is affixed to the structure on the land, it becomes real property).

What rights does a party have in real property?

Rights in real property can generally be described as possessory and non-possessory. Following is a list of some types of rights in real estate, beginning with the most complete.

- *Fee simple absolute.* The most comprehensive form of ownership, in which the owner may use or transfer all or part of his rights to the property. Upon the owner's death, the property will pass to his successors by will or by the inheritance laws of the state.

- *Fee simple defeasible.* Ownership is conditioned upon a state of facts and can be terminated if the facts change (for instance, X continues to own the property "so long as it is used for charity").

- *Life estate.* The party has ownership of the property for his life. Upon death, the property reverts (returns) to the original owner or passes to another if so directed by the owner.

- *Easement.* A non-possessory right in which a party has the right to use real property for a specific purpose (for example, the right to drive through part of a neighbor's property in a common driveway).

- *Profit.* Non-possessory right to enter upon the land of another to remove products of the land (for example, the right to harvest timber).

- *License.* Non-possessory right to enter another property for a specific purpose that can be revoked (as in the right to enter a theater for a show).
- *Leasehold estates.* The conveyance by the owner of property (landlord) to another (tenant) of a right to use and possess property for a specified period of time (lease/tenancy). The tenancy may be
  - *"For years":* for the time expressly stated in the lease contract
  - *Periodic:* for a period based on the frequency of rent payments (rent paid on a monthly basis creates a month-to-month tenancy)
  - *At will:* for as long as both parties agree
  - *At sufferance:* continued possession of property without the landlord's consent

How are rights in real property acquired?

Except for leasehold estates, all rights listed above are generally acquired by deed. The rights under a leasehold estate are acquired by lease (that is, by a contract that may be written or oral, express or implied. See section on Contracts for Statute of Frauds).

Sometimes rights in real property may be acquired without delivery of a deed when a party openly and notoriously occupies or uses land for a period specified by law, without challenge by the real owner (called adverse possession).

What is a deed?

A deed is a document used to transfer possession and title to land. The deed must contain the following:

- Names of the grantor (transferor) and the grantee (transferee)
- Words evidencing intent to transfer
- Legally sufficient description of the land
- The signature of the grantor that has been witnessed and acknowledged before a notary or commissioner of deeds

The deed must be delivered to the grantee. For his protection, the grantee should make sure the deed is recorded.

4.9 INSURANCE

Insurance is a risk-management tool in which an insurance company (insurer) agrees to compensate another (the insured) for a loss or injury. Sometimes the compensation is paid to a third party (beneficiary). The agreement between the insurer and insured is the insurance policy. Insurance covers loss of life, injury, damage to property, liability to others, loss of profits, and many other business interests.

4.9.1 Insurance Protection for the Business

Who is entitled to obtain insurance?

Insurance may be obtained by a party who has an insurable interest, which is an interest in the well-being or life of a person (including himself), or a substantial interest in real or personal property. Without this insurable interest, the purchase of insurance amounts to wagering and may result in acts that violate public policy or encourage unsavory acts. For example, a spouse may buy insurance on the life of a spouse and is generally interested in the well-being of the spouse. However, one has no interest in the well-being of a stranger, and the desire to collect insurance proceeds may result in acts that endanger the life of the stranger.

To be compensated under a policy for loss or injury of another person, an insurable interest must exist at the time the policy is obtained. Compensation for the loss or damage of property will be paid only if the insured has an insurable interest at the time of the loss or damage.

What is "key person" insurance?

This is a policy covering the life of a person important to the enterprise or organization. The enterprise is usually the beneficiary because it expects to suffer a loss in the event of the death or injury of the key person, whose contributions to the business are crucial.

When is the insurance effective?

The effective date of insurance is usually when the "binder" (a temporary contract) is issued, when the actual policy is issued, or when a certain time has passed, indicating that the insurer has accepted the offer of the party desiring to obtain the insurance.

For an insurance contract to be valid and binding, there must be

- An offer to purchase insurance
- An acceptance by the insurer
- Consideration paid for the policy
- Legal purpose for insurance
- Capacity on the part of the parties making the contract

What would allow an insurer to cancel a policy?

Some of the reasons an insurer may cancel a policy are

- Insurance premiums are not paid after proper notice of intent to cancel is given to the insured.
- Discovery of fraud or misstatements by the insured on an application.
- Gross negligence on the part of the insured.
- The insured no longer has an insurable interest (he has sold the insured property).

In the case of life insurance, certain representations made by an applicant may become incontestable, and the policy may not be canceled after the requisite time has passed.

4.10 LABOR AND EMPLOYMENT LAWS

Businesses must be aware of federal and state laws governing their interactions with and responsibilities toward workers and the workplace. Laws in the labor/employment field generally deal with protections against employee injuries, maintenance of income or benefits after employment termination, fair wages, hours and terms of employment, preventing discrimination, employee privacy, and enhancing job security.

4.10.1 Employee Relationships

What legislation governs safety and injury to workers?

Many states have enacted statutes mandating workplace safety and compensation for workers who are injured on the job (workers' compensation). The federal government enacted the Occupational Safety and Health Act of 1970.

What is workers' compensation?

Workers' compensation provides for benefits to be paid to an employee in "work-related" injuries, which arise out of and during the course of employment. Adjudication of the claim and administration of payments are handled by the state. Funding is provided by requiring employers to buy private insurance, to self-insure (maintaining an adequate fund), or to contribute to a state insurance fund.

The worker does not have to prove negligence on the part of the employer; the award is based on "strict liability," or liability regardless of fault. However, the workers' compensation award is exclusive, and the employee may not seek other tort recovery against the employer. The employee is not limited in seeking recovery against a third party.

What may an employee recover under workers' compensation?

- Hospital and medical expenses
- Certain vocational rehabilitation
- Disability benefits
- Set recoveries for loss of body parts
- Survivor/dependent death benefits

How does OSHA work?

The act is administered by the Occupational Safety and Health Administration (OSHA), and mandates that employers provide workers with employment and workplaces free of conditions likely to cause death or serious physical injury.

OSHA may inspect workplaces and issue citations for violations. The employer is required to remedy the violation with "reasonable promptness," not to exceed six months. Failure to comply may result in civil, criminal, and injunctive relief.

Employers are required to maintain records and submit periodic reports of work-related deaths, serious injuries, and exposure to certain toxic and hazardous substances. Employees are protected against employer retaliation for reporting violations to OSHA.

What rights does an employee have after employment is terminated?

There are a number of state and federal provisions for workers after employment is terminated or after retirement.

What is unemployment compensation?

Where employment is terminated due to layoffs, plant closings, and the like, a worker may be entitled to unemployment compensation administered on the federal and state levels. An employee who voluntarily terminates his employment, is terminated for cause (such as bad conduct), or refuses to seek new employment or accept new employment may not be entitled to benefits. Funding is provided by subjecting employers to unemployment-tax payments. The payments received by the employee are usually based on his salary during employment and are for a limited period.

What about health insurance coverage?

The continuation of health insurance coverage after employment termination is a major concern for employees and their families. Under the Consolidated Omnibus Budget Reconciliation Act (COBRA), employers with twenty or more employees must continue group insurance coverage for terminated employees and their families for eighteen to thirty-six months. However, the employee must pay the entire premium. Protection is effective when there is a "qualifying event," such as termination of employment, reduction of work hours, death of an employee, Medicare coverage for the employee, divorce or separation from the covered employee, end of a child's dependent status, or bankruptcy of the employer, which makes an employee, spouse, or dependent no longer eligible for coverage under the employer's group plan.

COBRA sets up specific requirements for notice to the affected parties and guidelines as to time of payments and rates.

What entitlements are there for retired employees?

Retirees are generally entitled to Social Security, which provides income benefits, certain insurance coverage (Medicare), and survivor and death benefits to those who have contributed under the Federal Insurance Contributions Act (RCA) during their working years. Under RCA, a mandatory percentage of an employee's income (up to a maximum set by the regulations) is paid into the system and matched by the employer.

Under the Employee Retirement Security Act of 1974 (ERISA), employers who voluntarily set up retirement systems for their employees are subject to certain rules in order to protect the plan that the employees have come to rely on as part of their retirement, and which was perhaps an inducement to their employment to begin with.

Under ERISA, stringent requirements are set up to ensure the solvency of the plan, such as diversification of investments of the pension funds, imposing certain fiduciary duties (loyalty, no self-interest, disclosure) on the pension fund managers, setting time frames for employees' participation, and providing for the enforcement of rights by the participants in the plan.

What protections are there with respect to ongoing employer/employee relationships?

There are a number of provisions that govern the exercise of the rights of workers to organize and negotiate with their employers.

Among the major pieces of legislation are

- *Norris-LaGuardia Act of 1932.* This protects the rights of workers to peacefully strike, boycott, and picket, and limits the interference of federal courts in the peaceful exercise of these rights.

- *National Labor Relations Act of 1935 (NLRA).* This act was created by the National Labor Relations Board (NLRB), whose function is to curb unfair labor practices, such as interfering with the right of workers to organize or participate in a union, controlling or manipulating a labor organization, making contributions to the union, discrimination against union members or members who file charges with the NLRB, and refusing to bargain with the chosen representative of employees ("collective bargaining").

- *Labor Management Relations Act of 1947.* Also called the Taft-Hartley Act, this act curbs certain powers of unions by making it illegal for the offer of employment to be conditioned upon union membership ("closed shop"). Although union membership may be required after the employee has worked for a prescribed period ("union shop"), state laws may make it illegal to do so. The act permits the president of the United States to seek and obtain an injunction against a strike for eighty days where a strike may cause a national emergency.

- *Labor Management Reporting and Disclosure Act of 1959.* Also known as the Landrum-Griffin Act, this sets forth the rights of union members to attend meetings and nominate and vote for officers, and regulates the business operations of unions by requiring reports and disclosure. It also provides for accountability by union officials for union funds and property, and makes it illegal for ex-convicts or communists to hold union office. The act makes it illegal for unions to require that employers deal only with union-produced goods.

What expectations may employees have with respect to privacy?

In this age of concerns over societal problems—such as crime and substance abuse in the workforce—which affect performance and subject the employer to liabilities (for instance, for accidental injuries), monitoring by employers and the expectations of privacy of the employee have become major issues.

There are laws that prohibit certain employers from requiring, suggesting, or causing employees to take lie-detector tests and drawing conclusions from such tests or from the refusal to take them. However, employers are often permitted to use lie-detector tests when a theft has occurred.

Drug testing is generally considered an invasion of privacy, except in government positions where there is reason to suspect drug use, or where there are health, safety, and welfare issues. Drug testing, however, may be permitted or prohibited by union negotiations or agreement.

If an employer is monitoring employees' telephone calls, he may be in violation of a federal or state statute unless the employee is informed that he is subject to monitoring. The law must often balance the employer's need for surveillance against the employee's right to privacy, and will often examine whether less-intrusive methods were available to the employer.

What constitutes employment discrimination?

Title VII of the Civil Rights Act of 1964 bans discrimination by employers and unions based on race, color, national origin, religion, nationality, age, or sex. The Equal Employment Opportunity Commission (EEOC) is charged with investigating and resolving complaints filed by employees. If the matter cannot be resolved, the EEOC may bring legal action; if it does not, the employee may do so for reinstatement, back pay, retroactive promotions, or even an injunction to prevent future violations once discrimination is proven.

Among the actions that would constitute discrimination are

- *Disparate treatment.* An employer continued to seek candidates or filled a position with someone who was not a member of a protected class when the plaintiff/applicant was a qualified member of the protected class. If the employer can show a legitimate reason for not hiring the applicant (such as lack of experience), the employer will not be liable.

- *Disparate impact.* An employer's practices result in a workforce that does not reflect the composition of protected classes in the local labor market; proof of intent to discriminate is not needed.

- *Sexual harassment.* Promotions, raises, or assignments are given out for sexual favors, or workers are subjected to sexually offensive conduct or comments in the workplace. An employer may be liable for the acts of a worker where the employer knew or should have known of the conduct and failed to correct the action. The act of a supervisory employee may be imputed to the employer and result in liability.

- *Affirmative action.* Preferential treatment is given to minorities and women to make up for past discriminatory actions. This area is presently under intense court and legislative review, and has been heavily criticized for creating "reverse discrimination," in which otherwise qualified applicants who are not women or members of minorities are effectively excluded from obtaining the offered positions.

- *Pregnancy discrimination.* Pregnant women must be treated in the same manner as others with similar ability to work. Equal treatment is required with respect to disability benefits and leave.

- *Age discrimination.* Individuals who are forty years or older are protected by the Age Discrimination in Employment Act of 1967 (ADEA) from discrimination on the basis of age where the employer has twenty or more employees and whose businesses have an impact on interstate commerce. Among the provisions is a prohibition of a mandatory retirement age for non-managerial workers.

- *Disabilities.* Under the Americans with Disabilities Act of 1990 (ADA), an employer may not discriminate against "differently abled" persons whose physical or mental impairments (including blindness, AIDS, cancer, and learning disabilities) substantially limits "one or more major life activities," if a "reasonable accommodation" (without "undue hardship" as assessed by the size of the company, finances, and the like) could be made to enable the person to do his job (for example, installing a ramp for wheelchairs).

What right does an employer have to discharge an employee?

Generally, employers can discharge an employee "at will" (that is, without cause), as long as it is not based upon discrimination or unfair employment practices.

However, there may be protections under state or federal law if the employee is a "whistleblower" who has reported hazardous or illegal practices of the employer to the government or the media. In addition, an implied employment contract may exist where there are employee handbooks, personnel materials, or representations made that the employee will be discharged only "for cause."

Examples: Unacceptable reasons for firing (thus constituting an abusive discharge)

1. A worker asks his superiors to obey securities or environmental laws.

2. An employee is about to become entitled to a bonus.

3. A worker exercises a statutory right (for instance, files a workers' compensation claim).

4. An employee refuses to participate in antirust violations.

5. A worker seeks to have his/her employer comply with consumer protection laws.

6. An employee reports criminal activity by his/her employer (the whistleblower exception to at-will employment).

Thus, while many employment relationships remain at-will, with the employee always free to quit and the employer usually free to fire, there are now some exceptions to the employer's freedom—broad statutory schemes and case-law requirements that employers obey the law and common notions of public policy. (Apart from this tort doctrine, at-will employment has also been restricted by finding implied contracts of good faith and fair dealing—for example, implied or even express contracts based on statements in a company's employee handbook.)

4.11 BUSINESS TORTS, WHITE-COLLAR CRIMES, AND ETHICS

Substantial civil and criminal liability can arise out of business transactions because of tortious conduct (intentional or unintentional wrongs), criminal acts, or violations of ethical duties.

4.11.1 Criminal Acts and Ethical Violations

What kinds of acts constitute business torts?

Business torts are civil wrongs committed within the business context. They include

- *Interference with a contractual relationship.* Intentionally and knowingly inducing a party to breach a valid and enforceable contract and entering into a contract with the inducing party (Mr. X induces a buyer to breach a contract to purchase from another supplier and to purchase from Mr. X instead).

- *Interference with a business relationship.* Soliciting customers who specifically already have a relationship or interest in a competitor's product. This exceeds normal, competitive attempts to attract customers.

- *Appropriation.* Unauthorized use of another's name or likeness for the user's benefit.

- *Defamation.* Making a false statement injuring another's reputation. In business, a defamatory statement is one that injures a party in his credit, professional, business, or trade reputation.

- *Disparagement of product.* Making false statements about the quality or nature of another's product.

What are some common white-collar crimes?

Crimes related to business are often referred to as white-collar crimes. Among them are

- *Bribery.* Tendering something of value to a public official in return for a favor.

- *Money laundering.* Processing illegally earned money through a legitimate business enterprise. In an attempt to prevent this, the law imposes reporting requirements for currency (cash) in excess of $10,000.

- *Insider trading.* Violation of certain Securities and Exchange laws by "insiders" (officers, directors, or parties related to them). This involves making a profit from information not generally available to the public.

- *RICO.* The Racketeer-Influenced and Corrupt Organizations Act prevents participation by organized crime in legitimate enterprises by prohibiting using funds from racketeering to acquire, maintain, or participate in legitimate businesses.

Why is ethics important in business?

Ethics has to do with fairness, duty owed to others, and honesty in one's business. Ethical conduct generally results in better business in that it promotes good will. However, there are legal mandates in the area of ethics, the violation of which can lead to liability. This is especially the case where there is a breach of a fiduciary duty in which there is a relationship based on trust with another party (for example, a doctor, lawyer, or accountant has a relationship based on the trust and confidence of their clients). In a fiduciary relationship, there is a duty to act in the interest of the beneficiary and not for one's own interest, and to perform in a diligent and careful manner in carrying out tasks on behalf of the beneficiary.

PART TWO

Accounting Tools
and Guidelines

CHAPTER 5

Financial Statements, the Sarbanes-Oxley Act, and Corporate Governance

Knowing the financial health of your company is important. Such knowledge can help you allocate resources and pinpoint areas requiring development and problems needing correction. Do you know how your company is doing financially? Is it growing or contracting? Will it be around for a long time? How profitable is your department, and what can be done to improve the profitability picture? These questions and others can be answered if you understand corporate financial statements. On the other hand, if you do not know how your company is doing financially, you cannot provide the necessary financial leadership.

The new century has already included a number of high-profile corporate scandals: Enron, Tyco International, Global Crossing, and WorldCom (now MCI). While these are the most glaring, there are many more companies whose shareholders and employees have suffered as stock prices have fallen, such as Cisco, Nokia, Lucent Technologies, and most Internet-related businesses. A series of corporate accounting scandals on the heels of the Enron debacle have led to new, sweeping accounting guidelines, proposals, and legislation, notably the Sarbanes-Oxley (SOX) Act.

This chapter looks at the key financial statements from an external viewpoint. The Sarbanes-Oxley (SOX) Act is also summarized.

5.1 WHAT AND WHY OF FINANCIAL STATEMENTS

What are financial statements?
What is their significance?

Financial decisions are typically based on information generated from the accounting system. Financial management, stockholders, potential investors, and creditors are concerned with how well the company is doing. The three reports generated by the accounting system and included in the company's annual report are the balance sheet, income statement, and statement of cash flows. Although the form of these financial statements may vary among different businesses or other economic units, their basic purposes do not change.

The balance sheet portrays the financial position of the organization at a particular point in time. It shows what is owned (assets), how much is owed to vendors and lenders (liabilities), and what is left (assets minus liabilities, known as equity or net worth). A balance sheet is a snapshot of the company's financial position as of a certain date. The balance sheet equation can be stated as:

$$\text{Assets} - \text{Liabilities} = \text{Stockholders' Equity.}$$

The income statement, on the other hand, measures the operating performance for a specified period of time (for instance, for the year ended December 31, 20X1). If the balance sheet is a snapshot, the income statement is a motion picture. The income statement serves as the bridge between two consecutive balance sheets. Simply put, the balance sheet indicates the wealth of the company, and the income statement shows how the company did the previous year.

The balance sheet and the income statement tell different things about the company. For example, the fact the company made a big profit last year does not necessarily mean it is liquid (has the ability to pay current liabilities using current assets) or solvent (noncurrent assets are enough to meet noncurrent liabilities). A company may have reported a significant net income but still have a deficient net worth. In other words, to find out how the organization is doing, both statements are needed. The income statement summarizes the company's operating results for the accounting period; these results are reflected in the equity (net worth) on the balance sheet. This relationship is shown in Figure 5.1.

The third basic financial statement is the statement of cash flows. This statement provides useful information about the inflows and outflows of cash that cannot be found in the balance sheet and the income statement.

Figure 5.1 The Balance Sheet and Income Statement

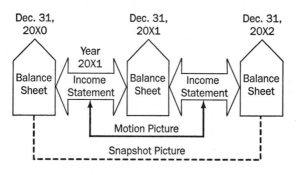

Figure 5.2 shows how these statements, including the statement of retained earnings (to be discussed later), tie together with numerical figures. *Note:* The beginning amount of cash ($50 million) from the 20X1 balance sheet is added to the net increase or decrease in cash (from the statement of cash flows) to derive the cash balance ($111 million), as reported on the 20X2 balance sheet. Similarly, the retained earnings balance as reported on the 20X2 balance sheet comes from the beginning retained earnings balance (20X1 balance sheet) plus net income for the period (from the income statement) less dividends paid. As you study financial statements, these relationships will become clearer, and you will understand the concept of articulation better.

What does the income statement tell you?

The income statement (profit and loss statement) shows the revenue, expenses, and net income (or net loss) for a period of time. A definition of each element follows.

Revenue is the increase in capital arising from the sale of merchandise or the performance of services. When revenue is earned, it results in an increase in cash (money received) or accounts receivable (amounts owed by customers).

Expenses decrease capital and result from performing activities necessary to generate revenue. Expenses that reduce revenue can be categorized as the cost of goods sold and selling and general administrative

Figure 5.2 How the Financial Statements Tie Together

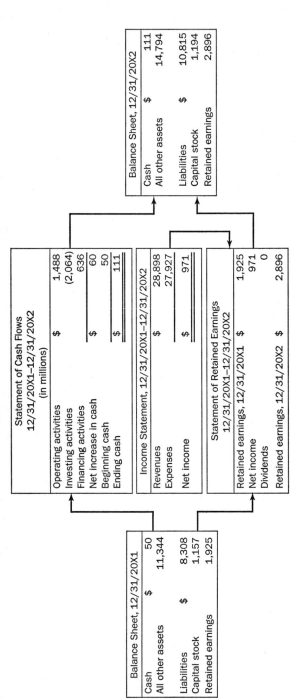

Balance Sheet, 12/31/20X1

Cash	$	50
All other assets		11,344
Liabilities	$	8,308
Capital stock		1,157
Retained earnings		1,925

Statement of Cash Flows
12/31/20X1–12/31/20X2
(in millions)

Operating activities	$	1,488
Investing activities		(2,064)
Financing activities		636
Net increase in cash	$	60
Beginning cash		50
Ending cash	$	111

Income Statement, 12/31/20X1–12/31/20X2

Revenues	$	28,898
Expenses		27,927
Net income	$	971

Statement of Retained Earnings
12/31/20X1–12/31/20X2

Retained earnings, 12/31/20X1	$	1,925
Net income		971
Dividends		0
Retained earnings, 12/31/20X2	$	2,896

Balance Sheet, 12/31/20X2

Cash	$	111
All other assets		14,794
Liabilities	$	10,815
Capital stock		1,194
Retained earnings		2,896

expenditures necessary to conduct business operations (for instance, rent expense, salary expense, depreciation expense) during the period.

Net income is the amount by which total revenue exceeds total expenses. The resulting profit is added to the retained earnings account (accumulated earnings of a company since its inception, less dividends). If total expenses are greater than total revenue, a net loss results, decreasing retained earnings.

Revenue does not necessarily mean receipt of cash, and expense does not automatically imply a cash payment. Net income and net cash flow (cash receipts less cash payments) are different. For example, taking out a bank loan generates cash, but this cash is not revenue, as no merchandise has been sold and no services have been provided. Further, owners' equity does not change, as the loan represents a liability rather than a stockholders' investment, and must be repaid.

Each revenue and expense item has its own account. Such a system enables management to better evaluate and control revenue and expense sources and to examine the relationships among account categories.

5.2 CLASSIFIED FINANCIAL STATEMENTS

Although companies differ in nature, and therefore the specific transactions and accounts differ from business to business, it is useful to classify the entries in financial statements into major categories. Financial statements organized in such a fashion are called classified financial statements.

How detailed is a classified income statement?

In a classified income statement, each major revenue and expense function is listed separately to facilitate analysis. The entries in an income statement are usually classified into four major functions: revenue, cost of goods sold (cost of inventory sold), operating expenses, and other revenue or expenses. The entries in classified income statements covering different time periods are easily compared; the comparison over time of revenue sources, expense items, and the relationship between them can reveal areas that require attention and corrective action. For example, if revenue from services has been sharply declining over the past several months, management will want to know why and then take action to reverse the trend.

Revenue comprises the gross income generated by selling goods (sales) or performing services (professional fees, commission income). To determine net sales, gross sales are reduced by sales returns, allowances (discounts given for defective merchandise), and sales discounts.

Cost of goods sold is the cost of the merchandise or services sold. In a retail business, the cost of goods sold is the beginning inventory plus the cost of buying goods from the manufacturer minus ending inventory; in a service business, it is the cost of the employee services rendered. For a manufacturing company, cost of goods sold is the cost of goods manufactured plus the beginning finished-goods inventory minus the ending finished-goods inventory.

Operating expenses are expenses incurred or resources used in generating revenue. Two types of operating expenses are selling expenses and general and administrative expenses. Selling expenses are costs incurred in the sale of goods or services (for example, advertising, salesperson salaries) and in distributing the merchandise (for instance, freight paid on shipments); they relate solely to the selling function. If a sales manager is responsible for generating sales, his or her performance is judged on the relationship between promotion costs and sales obtained. General and administrative expenses are the costs of running the business as a whole. The salaries of the office clerical staff, administrative executive salaries, and depreciation on office equipment are examples of general and administrative expenses.

Other revenue (expenses) covers incidental sources of revenue and expense that are nonoperating in nature, and that do not relate to the major purpose of the business. Examples are interest income, dividend income, and interest expense.

Figure 5.3 shows a classified income statement.

What is a classified balance sheet?

The balance sheet is classified into major groups of assets, liabilities, and owners' equity. An asset is something owned, such as land or an automobile. A liability is something owed, such as loans payable and mortgage payable. Owners' equity is the residual interest remaining after assets have been reduced by liabilities.

Assets. A classified balance sheet generally breaks assets down into five categories: current assets; long-term investments; property, plant, and equipment (fixed assets); intangible assets; and deferred charges. This

Figure 5.3 A Classified Income Statement

X Company
Income Statement
for the Year Ended December 31, 20XX

Revenue			
Gross Sales		$40,000	
Less: Sales Returns			
and Allowances	$1,000		
Sales Discounts	500	1,500	
Net Sales			$38,500
Cost of Goods Sold			
Inventory, January 1		$1,000	
Add: Purchases		15,000	
Cost of Goods Available for Sale		$16,000	
Less: Inventory, December 31		5,000	
Cost of Goods Sold			11,000
Gross Profit			$27,500
Operating Expenses			
Selling Expenses			
Advertising	$3,000		
Salespeople's Salaries	2,000		
Travel and Entertainment	1,000		
Depreciation on Delivery Truck	500	6,500	
General and Administrative Expenses			
Officers' Salaries	$4,000		
Depreciation	1,000		
Rent	2,000		
Insurance	1,000	8,000	
Total Operating Expenses			14,500
Operating Income			$13,000
Other Expenses (net)			
Interest Expense		$2,000	
Less: Interest Income	$ 500		
Divided Income	1,000	1,500	
Other Expenses (net)			500
Net income			$12,500

breakdown aids in analyzing the type and liquidity of the assets held.

Current assets are assets that are expected to be converted into cash or used up within one year or the normal operating cycle of the business, whichever is greater. (The operating cycle is the time period between the purchase of inventory merchandise for resale and the transfer of inventory through sales, listed as accounts receivable, or receipt of cash. In effect, the operating cycle goes from paying cash to receiving it.) Examples of current assets are cash, short-term investments (investments with a maturity of more than ninety days but intended to be held only until cash is needed for current operations), accounts receivable, inventory, and prepaid expenses (expenditures that will expire within one year from the balance-sheet date and that represent a prepayment for an expense that has not yet been incurred.)

Long-term investments refer to investments in other companies' stocks (common or preferred) or bonds where the intent is to hold them for a period greater than one year. Securities that may be held as short-term or long-term investments fall into three categories: held-to-maturity securities, trading securities, and available-for-sale securities. Trading securities are classified as short-term investments. Available-for-sale securities, depending on the company's intent to hold them, may be classified as either short-term or long-term investments. However, in almost all cases, they are noncurrent. Held-to-maturity securities are always classified as long-term investments.

Property, plant, and equipment (often called fixed assets) are assets employed in the production of goods or services that have a life greater than one year. They are tangible, meaning they have physical substance (you can physically see and touch them), and are actually being used in the course of business. Examples are land, buildings, machinery, and automobiles. Unlike inventory, these assets are not held for sale in the normal course of business.

Intangible assets are assets with a long-term life that lack physical substance and that arise from a right granted by the government, such as patents, copyrights, and trademarks, or by another company, such as a franchise license. An example of the latter is the right (acquired by paying a fee) to open a fast-food franchise and use the name McDonald's.

Deferred charges are certain expenditures that have already been incurred but that are deferred to the future either because they are expected to benefit future revenues or because they represent an appropriate allocation of costs to future operations. In other words, deferred charges are costs charged to an asset because future benefit exists; they are amortized as an expense in the year the related revenue is recognized, and the benefit is consumed in conformity with the accounting principle requiring matching of expense to revenue. Examples are plant rearrangement costs and moving costs. No cash can be realized from such assets; for example, you cannot sell deferred moving costs to anyone because no one will buy them.

Liabilities and stockholders' equity. Liabilities are classified as either current or noncurrent. Current liabilities (those due in one year or less) will be satisfied from current assets. Examples are accounts payable (amounts owed to creditors), short-term notes payable (written evidence of loans due within one year), and accrued expense liabilities (for instance, salaries payable).

Examples of long-term liabilities, which have a maturity of greater than one year, are bonds payable and mortgages payable. The current portion of a long-term liability (the part that is to be paid within one year) is shown under current liabilities. For example, if $1,000 of a $10,000 mortgage is to be paid within the year, that $1,000 is listed as a current liability; the remaining $9,000 is shown under noncurrent liabilities. The stockholders' equity section of the balance sheet consists of capital stock, paid-in-capital, retained earnings, and total stockholders' equity. These are defined below.

Capital stock describes the ownership of the corporation in terms of the number of shares outstanding. Each share is assigned a par value when it is first authorized by the state in which the business is incorporated. Capital stock is presented on the balance sheet at total par value. Therefore, the capital stock account, which is at par value, agrees with the stock certificates (imprinted with the par value) held by stockholders. Preferred stock is listed before common stock because it receives preference should the company be liquidated.

Paid-in capital shows the amount received by the company over the par value for the stock issued. This helps keep track of the par value of issued shares, and the excess over par value paid for it.

Retained earnings represent the accumulated earnings of the company since its inception, less dividends declared and paid to stockholders. There is usually a surplus in this account, but a deficit may occur if the business has been operating at a loss.

Total stockholders' equity is the sum of capital stock, paid-in capital, and retained earnings. In a corporation, owners' equity is referred to as stockholders' equity; in a sole proprietorship or partnership, owners' equity is referred to as capital.

A classified balance sheet is presented in Figure 5.4.

Figure 5.4 A Classified Balance Sheet

X Company
Balance Sheet
December 31, 20XX

Assets		
Current Assets		
Cash	$3,000	
Marketable Securities	1,000	
Accounts Receivable	6,000	
Inventory	5,000	
Total Current Assets		$15,000
Long-Term Investments		
Investment in Y Company Stock		2,000
Property, Plant, and Equipment		
Land	$20,000	
Building (less accumulated depreciation)	30,000	
Machinery (less accumulated depreciation)	7,000	
Delivery Trucks (less accumulated depreciation)	5,000	
Total Property, Plant, and Equipment		62,000
Intangible Assets		
Patents (less accumulated amortization)		3,000
Deferred Charges		
Deferred Moving Costs		1,000
Total Assets		$83,000
Liabilities and Stockholders' Equity		
Current Liabilities		
Accounts Payable	$8,000	
Notes Payable (9 months)	4,000	
Accrued Expense Liabilities	2,000	
Total Current Liabilities		$14,000
Noncurrent Liabilities		
Bonds Payable		30,000
Total Liabilities		$44,000
Stockholders' Equity		
Capital Stock	$20,000	
Paid-in Capital	4,000	
Retained Earnings*	15,000	
Total Stockholders' Equity		39,000
Total Liabilities and Stockholders' Equity		$83,000

*A schedule of retained earnings follows:

Retained earnings—January 1	$10,000
Net income	12,500
Dividends	(7,500)
Retained earnings—December 31	$15,000

5.3 STATEMENT OF CASH FLOWS

Why is the statement of cash flows so important?

It is important to know about cash flow in order to adequately plan expenditures. Should there be a cutback on payments because of a cash problem? Is the organization getting most of the cash? What products or projects are cash drains or cash cows? Is there enough money to pay bills and buy needed machinery?

A company is required to prepare a statement of cash flows in its annual report. This statement contains useful information for external users, such as lenders and investors, who make economic decisions about a company. The statement presents the sources and uses of cash and is a basis for cash-flow analysis. In this section, we discuss what the statement of cash flows is, how it looks, and how to analyze it.

What are the specific contents of the statement of cash flows?

The statement of cash flows classifies cash receipts and cash payments arising from investing activities, financing activities, and operating activities.

Investing activities. Investing activities include the results of the purchase or sale of debt and equity securities of other entities and fixed assets. Cash inflows from investing activities are comprised of (1) receipts from sales of equity and debt securities of other companies and (2) amounts received from the sale of fixed assets. Cash outflows for investing activities include (1) payments to buy equity or debt securities of other companies and (2) payments to buy fixed assets.

Financing activities. Financing activities include the issuance of stock and the reacquisition of previously issued shares (treasury stock), as well as the payment of dividends to stockholders. Also included are debt financing and repayment. Cash inflows from financing activities are comprised of funds received from the sale of stock and the incurrence of debt. Cash outflows for financing activities include (1) repaying debt, (2) repurchasing of stock, and (3) issuing dividend payments.

Operating activities. Operating activities are connected to the manufacture and sale of goods or the rendering of services. Cash inflows from operating activities include (1) cash sales or collections on accounts receivable arising from the initial sale of merchandise or rendering of service and (2) cash receipts from debt securities (for example, interest income) or equity securities (for example, dividend income) of other entities. Cash outflows for operating activities include (1) cash paid for raw material or merchandise intended for resale, (2) payments on accounts payable arising from the initial purchase of goods, (3) payments to suppliers of operating expense items (for instance, office supplies, advertising, insurance), and (4) wages. Figure 5.5 shows an outline of the statement of cash flows.

Figure 5.5 The Statement of Cash Flows

Format of the Statement of Cash Flows
(Indirect Method)

Net cash flow from operating activities:		
Net income	$980,000	
Adjustments for noncash expenses, revenues, losses, and gains included in income:		
Depreciation	20,000	
Net cash flow from operating activities		$1,000,000
Cash flows from investing activities:		
Purchase machinery	$(630,000)	
Investments in other companies' stocks	(70,000)	
Sale of land	200,000	
Net cash flows provided (used) by investing activities:		(500,000)
Cash flows from financing activities:		
Issuance of common stock	$400,000	
Issuance of bonds payable	100,000	
Payment on long-term mortgage payable	(160,000)	
Payment of dividends	(40,000)	
Net cash provided (used) by financing activities		300,000
Net increase (decrease) in cash		$800,000
Schedule of noncash investing and financing activities:		
Issuance of preferred stock for building		$180,000
Conversion of bonds payable to common stock		100,000

5.4 CASH-FLOW ANALYSIS

How do you analyze the cash-flow position of a company?

Along with financial ratio analysis, cash-flow analysis is a valuable tool. The cash flow statement provides information on how the company generated and used cash—that is, why cash flow increased or decreased. An analysis of the statement is helpful in appraising past performance, projecting the company's future direction, forecasting liquidity trends, and evaluating the company's ability to satisfy its debts at maturity.

CHECKLIST FOR CASH–FLOW ANALYSIS QUESTIONS

Because the statement lists the specific sources and uses of cash during the period, it can be used to answer the following questions:

- How was the expansion in plant and equipment financed?
- What use was made of net income?
- Where did funds come from?
- How much required capital is generated internally?
- Is the dividend policy in balance with its operating policy?
- How much debt was paid off?
- How much was received from the issuance of stock?
- How much debt financing was taken out?

The cash flow per share equals net cash flow divided by the number of shares. A high ratio is desirable because it indicates a liquid position—that is, the company has ample cash on hand.

Operating section. An analysis of the operating section of the statement of cash flows determines the adequacy of cash flow from operating activities. For example, an operating cash outlay for refunds given to customers for deficient goods indicates a quality problem with the merchandise, while payments of penalties, fines, and lawsuit damages reveal poor management practices that result in nonbeneficial expenditures.

Investing section. An analysis of the investing section can identify investments in other companies. These investments may lead to an attempt to assume control of another company for purposes of diversification. The analysis may also indicate a change in future direction or a change in business philosophy.

An increase in fixed assets indicates capital expansion and future growth. A contraction in business arising from the sale of fixed assets without adequate replacement is a negative sign.

Financing section. An evaluation of the financing section reveals the company's ability to obtain financing in the money and capital markets, as well as its ability to meet obligations. The financial mixture of bonds, long-term loans from banks, and equity instruments affects risk and the cost of financing. Debt financing carries greater risk because the company must generate adequate funds to pay the interest costs and to retire the obligation at maturity; thus, a very high percent of debt to equity is generally not advisable. The problem is acute if earnings and cash flow are declining. On the other hand, reducing long-term debt is desirable because it points to lowered risk.

The ability to obtain financing through the issuance of common stock at attractive terms (high stock price) indicates that the investing public is optimistic about the financial well-being of the business. The issuance of preferred stock may be a negative sign, as it may mean the company is having difficulty selling its common stock. Perhaps investors view the company as very risky and will invest only in preferred stock because preferred stock has a preference over common stock in the event of the company's liquidation. One must evaluate the company's ability to pay dividends. Stockholders who rely on a fixed income (for instance, a retired couple), may be unhappy when dividends are cut or eliminated.

How do you prepare and analyze the statement of cash flows?

This section contains an analysis of a hypothetical statement of cash flows, prepared from sample balance-sheet and income-statement figures.

Example 5.1

X Company provides the following financial statements:

X Company
Comparative Balance Sheets
December 31 (in millions)

Assets	20X1	20X0
Cash	$ 40	$ 47
Accounts receivable	30	35
Prepaid expenses	4	2
Land	50	35
Building	100	80
Accumulated depreciation	(9)	(6)
Equipment	50	42
Accumulated depreciation	(11)	(7)
Total Assets	$254	$228

Liabilities and Stockholders' Equity

Accounts payable	$ 20	$ 16
Long-term notes payable	30	20
Common stock	100	100
Retained earnings	104	92
Total liabilities and stockholders' equity	$254	$228

X Company
Income Statement for the Year Ended December 31, 20X1
(in millions)

Revenue		$300
Operating expenses (excluding depreciation)	$200	
Depreciation	7	207
Income from operations		$ 93
Income tax expense		32
Net income		$ 61

X Company
Statement of Cash Flows for the Year Ended December 31, 20X1
(in millions)

Operating activities:		
Net income		$61
Adjustments to reconcile net income to cash provided by operating activities:		
Depreciation	$ 7	
Changes in operating assets and liabilities:		
Decrease in accounts receivable	5	
Increase in prepaid items	(2)	
Increase in accounts payable	4	
Cash provided by operating activities		75
Cash flow from investing activities		
Purchase of land	($15)	
Purchase of building	(20)	
Purchase of equipment	(8)	(43)
Cash flow from financing activities		
Issuance of long-term notes payable	$10	
Payment of cash dividends	(49)	(39)
Net decrease in cash		$ 7

Assume the company has a policy of paying very high dividends.

Information for 20X0 follows: Net income, $32; cash flow from operations, $20.

A financial analysis of the statement of cash flows reveals that the profitability and operating cash flow of X Company improved from 20X0 to 20X1. The company's earnings performance was good, and the $61 earnings resulted in cash inflow from operations of $75. Thus, compared to 20X0, 20X1 showed better results.

The decrease in accounts receivable may reveal better collection efforts. The increase in accounts payable is a sign that suppliers are confident they will be paid and are willing to give interest-free financing. The acquisition of land, building, and equipment points to a growing business undertaking capital expansion. The issuance of long-term notes payable indicates that the company is financing part of its assets through debt. Stockholders will be happy with the significant dividend payout of 80.3 percent (dividends divided by net income, or $49/$61). Overall, there was a decrease in cash on hand of $7, but this should not cause alarm because of the company's profitability and the fact that cash was used for capital expansion and dividend payments. It is recommended that the dividend payout be reduced from its high level, and that the funds be reinvested in the business; the reduction of dividends by more than $7 would result in a positive net cash flow for the year, which is needed for immediate liquidity.

Example 5.2

Y Company presents the following statement of cash flows.

Y Company
Statement of Cash Flows
for the Year Ended December 31, 20X0

Operating activities:		
Net income		$134,000
Adjustments to reconcile net income to cash provided by operating activities:		
Depreciation	$21,000	
Changes in operating assets and liabilities:		
Decrease in accounts receivable	10,000	
Increase in prepaid items	(6,000)	
Increase in accounts payable	35,000	60,000
Cash provided by operating activities		
Cash flows from investing activities		
Purchase of land	($70,000)	
Purchase of building	(200,000)	
Purchase of equipment	(68,000)	
Cash used by investing activities		(338,000)

Cash flows from financing activities		
Issuance of bonds	150,000	
Payment of cash dividends	(18,000)	
Cash provided by financing activities		132,000
Net decrease in cash		$(12,000)

An analysis of the statement of cash flows reveals that the company is profitable and that cash flow from operating activities exceeds net income, which indicates good internal cash generation. The ratio of cash flow from operating activities to net income is a solid 1.45 ($194,000/$134,000). A high ratio is desirable because it shows that earnings are backed up by cash. The decline in accounts receivable may indicate better collection efforts; the increase in accounts payable shows the company can obtain interest-free financing. The company is definitely in the process of expanding for future growth, as demonstrated by the purchase of land, building, and equipment. The debt position of the company has increased, indicating greater risk for investors. The dividend payout was 13.4 percent ($18,000/$134,000), which is good news for stockholders, who look positively on companies that pay dividends. The decrease of $12,000 in cash flow for the year is a negative sign.

How can you use the statement of cash flows for corporate planning?

Current profitability is only one important factor in predicting corporate success; current and future cash flows are also essential. In fact, it is possible for a profitable company to have a cash crisis; for example, a company with significant credit sales but a very long collection period may show a profit without actually having the cash from those sales.

Financial managers are responsible for planning how and when cash will be used and obtained. When planned expenditures require more cash than planned activities are likely to produce, financial managers must decide what to do. They may decide to obtain debt or equity funds, or to dispose of some fixed assets or even a whole business segment. Alternatively, they may decide to cut back on planned activities by modifying operational plans—such as ending a special advertising campaign or delaying new acquisitions—or to revise planned payments to financing sources such as bondholders or stockholders. Whatever is decided, the financial manager's goal is to balance the cash available and the need for cash over both the short and the long term.

Evaluating the statement of cash flows is essential if one is to accurately appraise an entity's cash flows from operating, investing, and financing activities and its liquidity and solvency positions. Inadequacy in cash flow has possible serious implications, including declining profitability, greater financial risk, and even possible bankruptcy.

5.5 OTHER SECTIONS OF THE ANNUAL REPORT

What other crucial information does the annual report contain?

Other sections in the annual report, in addition to the financial statements, are helpful in understanding the company's financial health. These sections include the highlights, review of operations, footnotes, supplementary schedules, and auditor's report.

Highlights. The highlights section provides comparative financial-statement information and covers important points such as profitability, sales, dividends, market price of stock, and asset acquisitions. At a minimum, the company provides sales, net-income, and earnings-per-share figures for the last two years.

Review of operations. The review of operations section discusses the company's products, services, facilities, and future directions in both numbers and narrative form.

Report of independent public accountants. The independent accountant is a certified public accountant (CPA) in public practice who has no financial or other interest in the client whose financial statements are being examined. In this part of the annual report, the accountant expresses an opinion on the fairness of the financial statement numbers.

CPAs render four types of audit opinions: an unqualified opinion, a qualified opinion, a disclaimer of opinion, and an adverse opinion. The auditor's opinion is heavily relied upon because he or she is knowledgeable, objective, and independent.

Unqualified opinion. An unqualified opinion means the CPA is satisfied that the company's financial statements present fairly its financial position and results of operations, and gives the financial manager confidence that the financial statements are an accurate reflection of the company's financial health and operating performance.

A typical standard report presenting an unqualified opinion follows.

Independent Auditor's Report

We have audited the accompanying balance sheet of ABC Company as of December 31, 20X2, and the related statements of income, retained earnings, and cash flows for the year then ended. These financial statements are the responsibility of the Company's management. Our responsibility is to express an opinion on these financial statements based on our audit.

We conducted our audit in accordance with generally accepted auditing standards. Those standards require that we plan and perform the audit to obtain reasonable assurance about whether the financial statements are free of material misstatement. An audit includes examining, on a test basis, evidence supporting the amounts and disclosures in the financial statements. An audit also includes assessing the accounting principles used and significant estimates made by management, as well as evaluating the overall financial statement presentation. We believe that our audit provides a reasonable basis for our opinion.

In our opinion, the financial statements referred to above present fairly, in all material respects, the financial position of ABC Company as of December 31, 20X2, and the results of its operations and its cash flows for the year then ended in conformity with generally accepted accounting principles.

If the company is facing a situation with an uncertain outcome that may substantially affect its financial health, such as a lawsuit, the CPA may still give an unqualified opinion. However, there will probably be an explanatory paragraph describing the material uncertainty; this uncertainty will undoubtedly affect readers' opinions of the financial-statement information. A financial manager would be well advised to note the contingency (potential problem, such as a dispute with the government) and its possible adverse financial effects on the company.

Qualified opinion. The CPA may issue a qualified opinion if the company has placed a "scope limitation" on his or her work. A scope limitation prevents the independent auditor from doing one or more of the following: (1) gathering enough evidential matter to permit the expression of an unqualified opinion; (2) applying a required auditing procedure; or (3) applying one or more auditing procedures considered necessary under the circumstances.

If the scope limitation is fairly minor, the CPA may issue an "except for" qualified opinion. This may occur, for example, if the auditor is unable to confirm accounts receivable or observe inventory.

Disclaimer of opinion. When a severe scope limitation exists, the auditor may decide to offer a disclaimer of opinion. A disclaimer indicates that the auditor was unable to form an opinion on the fairness of the financial statements.

Adverse opinion. The auditor may issue an adverse opinion when the financial statements do *not* present the company's financial position, results of operations, retained earnings, and cash flows fairly and in conformity with generally accepted accounting principles. By issuing an adverse opinion, the CPA is stating that the financial statements may be misleading.

Obviously, the financial manager wants the independent auditor to render an unqualified opinion. Disclaimers and adverse opinions are viewed very negatively by such readers as investors and creditors, who then put little if any faith in the company's financial statements.

Footnotes. Financial statements themselves are concise and condensed, and any explanatory information that cannot readily be abbreviated is added in greater detail in the footnotes. In such cases, the report contains a statement similar to the following: "The accompanying footnotes are an integral part of the financial statements."

Footnotes provide detailed information on financial statement figures; accounting policies; explanatory data, such as mergers and stock options; and any additional disclosure.

Footnote disclosures usually include accounting methods; estimated figures, such as inventory pricing, pension fund, and profit-sharing arrangements; terms and characteristics of long-term debt; particulars of lease agreements; contingencies, and tax matters.

The footnotes appear at the end of the financial statements and explain the figures in those statements both in narrative form and in numbers. It is essential that the financial manager evaluate footnote information to arrive at an informed opinion about the company's financial stature and earning potential.

Supplementary schedules and tables. Supplementary schedules and tables enhance the financial manager's comprehension of the company's financial position. Some of the more common schedules are five-year summary of operations, two-year quarterly data, and segmental information. This summary provides income statement information for the past five years, including dividends on preferred stock and common stock. It also reveals operating trends. Some companies provide ten-year comparative data.

Two-year quarterly data. This schedule gives a quarterly breakdown of sales, profit, high and low stock price, and the common stock dividend. Quarterly operating information is particularly useful for a seasonal business because it helps readers to more accurately track the business's highs and lows. The quarterly market price reveals fluctuations in the market price of stock, while the dividend quarterly information reveals how regularly the company pays dividends.

Segmental disclosure. This important supplementary schedule presents financial figures for the segments of the business, enabling readers to evaluate each segment's profit potential and risk. Segmental data may be organized by industry, foreign area, major customer, or government contract.

A segment is reportable if any *one* of the following conditions exists:

- Revenue is 10 percent or more of total corporate revenue.
- Operating profit is 10 percent or more of total corporate operating profit.
- Identifiable assets are 10 percent or more of total corporate assets.

The company must also disclose if foreign operations, sales to a major customer, or domestic contract revenue provide 10 percent or more of total sales. The percentage derived and the source of the sales must be stated.

Useful segment information that may be disclosed includes sales, operating profit, total assets, fixed assets, intangible assets, inventory, cost of sales, depreciation, and amortization.

History of market price. Although this information is optional, many companies provide a brief history of the market price of stock, such as quarterly highs and lows. This information reveals the variability and direction in the market price of stock.

5.6 QUARTERLY REPORT

How do you read a quarterly report?

In addition to the annual report, publicly held companies issue quarterly reports that provide updated information on sales and earnings and describe any material changes that have occurred in the business or its operations. These quarterly reports may provide unaudited financial statements or updates on operating highlights, changes in outstanding shares, compliance with debt restrictions, and pending lawsuits.

At a minimum, quarterly reports must provide data on sales, net income, taxes, nonrecurring revenue and expenses, accounting changes, contingencies (for instance, tax disputes), additions or deletions of business segments, and material changes in financial position.

The company may provide financial figures for the quarter itself (for example, the third quarter, from July 1 to September 30) or cumulatively from the beginning of the year (cumulative up to the third quarter, or January 1 to September 30). Prior-year data must be provided in a form that allows for comparisons. The financial manager should read the quarterly report in conjunction with the annual report.

5.7 MANAGEMENT'S DISCUSSION AND ANALYSIS (MD&A) SECTION OF AN ANNUAL REPORT

What does the management's discussion and analysis (MD&A) section of an annual report address to the user?

The Management's Discussion and Analysis (MD&A) section of an annual report must be included in SEC filings. The content of the MD&A section is required by regulations of the SEC. The MD&A contains standard financial statements and summarized financial data for at least five years. Other matters must be included in annual reports to shareholders, and in Form 10-K, filed with the SEC. The MD&A addresses in a nonquantified manner the prospects of the company. The SEC examines it with care to determine that management has disclosed material information affecting the company's future results. Disclosures about commitments and events that may affect operations or liquidity are mandatory. Thus, the MD&A section pertains to liquidity, capital resources, and results of operations.

5.8 THE SARBANES-OXLEY (SOX) ACT

What sweeping changes in corporate financial reporting are required by the Sarbanes-Oxley (SOX) Act?

President George W. Bush signed the Sarbanes-Oxley Act of 2002 (Public Law 107-204) on Tuesday, July 30, 2002. Congress presented the act (www.whitehouse.gov/infocus/corporateresponsibility/) to the president on July 26, 2002, after passage in the Senate by a 99–0 vote and in the House by a 423–3 margin.

GROUPS IMPACTED BY THE SARBANES-OXLEY ACT

1. CPAs and CPA firms auditing public companies;

2. Publicly traded companies, their employees, officers, and owners—including holders of more than 10 percent of the outstanding common shares. This category would include CPAs employed by publicly traded companies as chief financial officers (CFOs) or in the finance department;

3. Attorneys who work for or have as clients publicly traded companies; and

4. Brokers, dealers, investment bankers, and financial analysts who work for these companies.

The act changes how publicly traded companies are audited, and reshapes the financial reporting system. This act adopts tough new provisions to deter and punish corporate and accounting fraud and corruption, ensures justice for wrongdoers, and protects the interests of workers and shareholders.

This bill improves the quality and transparency of financial reporting, independent audits, and accounting services for public companies. It also

- Creates a Public Company Accounting Oversight Board (www.pcaobus.org) to enforce professional standards, ethics, and competence for the accounting profession;

- Strengthens the independence of firms that audit public companies;

- Increases corporate responsibility and the usefulness of corporate financial disclosure;

- Increases penalties for corporate wrongdoing;

- Protects the objectivity and independence of securities analysts; and

- Increases Securities and Exchange Commission resources.

Remember this: Under this law, CEOs and CFOs must personally vouch for the truth and fairness of their company's disclosures, and those financial disclosures will be broader and better than ever before.

Corporate officials will play by the same rules as their employees. In the periods during which workers are prevented from buying and selling company stock in their pensions or 401(k)s, corporate officials will also be prohibited from any buying or selling.

Corporate misdeeds will be found and punished. This law authorizes new funding for investigators and technology at the SEC to uncover wrongdoing. The SEC will now have the administrative authority to bar dishonest directors and officers from ever again serving in positions of corporate responsibility. The penalties for obstructing justice and shredding documents are greatly increased.

Specifics

NEW PUBLIC COMPANY ACCOUNTING OVERSIGHT BOARD (PCAOB)

- **Oversight Board.** The law establishes a five-member accounting oversight board that is subject to Securities and Exchange Commission (SEC) oversight.

- **CPA.** Though the board oversees accounting firms, only two members of the board may be CPAs.

- **Appointing the Board.** The SEC will appoint the board.

- **Board Duties.** Duties of the board include registering public accounting firms that prepare audit reports and establishing or adopting auditing, quality-control, ethics, and independence standards. The board also inspects, investigates, and disciplines public accounting firms and enforces compliance with the act.

- **Registration with the Board Is Mandatory.** Public accounting firms, foreign or domestic, that participate in the preparation or issuance of any audit report with respect to a public company must register with the board. Registration and annual fees collected from each registered CPA firm will go toward the costs of processing and reviewing applications and annual reports.

- **Seven-Year Record Retention Requirement.** PCAOB must adopt a rule to require registered

CPA firms to prepare and maintain audit work papers and other information related to an audit for at least seven years in sufficient detail to support the conclusions reached in the audit report. (A separate criminal provision requires retention of all audit and review work papers for five years from the end of the fiscal year in which the audit or review was completed.)

- **Cooperation with CPA Groups.** The board will cooperate with professional accountant groups and advisory groups to increase the effectiveness of the standards-setting process. (The PCAOB may cooperate, but authority to set standards rests with the PCAOB, subject to SEC review.)

- **Annual Inspections.** Inspection of registered public accounting firms shall occur annually for every registered public accounting firm that regularly provides audit reports for more than one hundred issuers (at least once every three years for registered firms that audit fewer than one hundred issuers).

- **Investigations.** The board may investigate any act, omission, or practice by a registered firm or an individual associated with a registered firm for any possible violation of the act, the board's rules, professional standards, or provisions of the securities laws relating to the preparation and issuance of audit reports.

  The board may require testimony or documents and information (including audit work papers) from a registered firm or individual associated with a registered firm, or in the possession of any other person.

  Sanctions for violations that the board finds may include

  (a) suspension or revocation of a registration;

  (b) suspension or bar of a person from further associating with any registered public accounting firm;

  (c) limitations on the activities of a firm or person associated with the firm; and

  (d) penalties of up to $2 million per violation, up to a maximum of $15 million. Individuals employed or associated with a registered firm who violate the act can face penalties that range from required additional continuing professional education (CPE) or training, disbarment of the individual from further association with any registered public accounting firm, or even a fine of up to $100,000 for each violation, up to a maximum of $750,000. (A portion of the penalties collected will go to accounting scholarships.)

- **Funding.** The law also provides independent funding for the Financial Accounting Standards Board (FASB). While the SEC and American Institute of CPAs (AICPA) have both recognized FASB as the standard-setting body for accounting principles, federal authority to issue auditing, quality-control, ethics, and independence standards may seriously impact the AICPA's role in official pronouncements.

- **Source.** The budget for the board and FASB will be payable from "annual accounting support fees" set by the board and approved by the SEC. The fees will be collected from publicly traded companies and will be determined by dividing the average monthly equity market capitalization of the company for the preceding fiscal year by the average monthly equity market capitalization of all such companies for that year.

OTHER REQUIREMENTS FOR CPA FIRMS

- **Most Consulting Banned for Audit Clients.** Title II of the act prohibits most "consulting" services outside the scope of practice of auditors.

  (a) **Prohibited Services.** These services are prohibited even if pre-approved by the issuer's audit committee.

    Prohibited services include
    - Bookkeeping and related services,
    - Design and implementation of financial information systems,
    - Appraisal or valuation services (including fairness opinions and contribution-in-kind reports),
    - Actuarial services,
    - Internal audit outsourcing,
    - Services that provide any management or human resources,
    - Investment or broker/dealer services,
    - Legal and "expert services unrelated to the audit," and
    - Any other service that the board determines, by regulation, is impermissible.

(b) **Services Not Prohibited.** Firms, however, may provide tax services (including tax planning and tax compliance) or others that are not listed, provided the firm receives pre-approval from the board. However, certain tax-planning products, such as tax avoidance services, may be considered prohibited nonaudit services.

- **Audit Reports Require Concurring Partner Review.** The act requires a concurring or second partner's review and approval of all audit reports and their issuance.

- **"Revolving Door" Employment of CPAs with Audit Clients Is Banned.** A registered CPA firm is prohibited from auditing any SEC-registered client whose chief executive, CFO, controller, or equivalent was on the audit team of the firm within the past year.

- **Audit Partner Rotation Required.** Audit partners who have performed audit services or who have been responsible for reviewing the audit of a particular client must be rotated every five consecutive years. CPAs should read carefully the requirements for rotation of both the partner-in-charge and the concurring review partner for certain organizational constraints.

  (a) **No Firm Rotation Requirement.** Firm rotation is not required. However, the U.S. Comptroller General will study and review the potential effects of mandatory rotation and will report its findings to the Senate Committee on Banking, Housing, and Urban Affairs and the House Committee on Financial Services.

- **CPA Firms Are Required to Report Directly to the Audit Committee.**

- **CPA Firm Consolidations to Be Studied.** The U.S. Comptroller General will conduct a study analyzing the impact of the merger of CPA firms to determine if consolidation leads to higher costs, lower quality of services, impairment of auditor independence, or lack of choice.

- **Corporate and Criminal Fraud Accountability.** Changes to the securities laws can penalize anyone found to have destroyed, altered, hidden, or falsified records or documents to impede, obstruct, or influence an investigation conducted by any federal agency, or in filing bankruptcy, with fines or up to twenty years imprisonment, or both

- **Current Requirements for Audit Firms.** Accountants are required to maintain all audit or review work papers for a period of five years from the end of the fiscal period in which the audit or review was concluded.

- **Additional Rules.** The law requires the SEC to promulgate rules and regulations on the retention of any and all materials related to an audit, including communications, correspondence, and other documents created, sent, or received in connection with an audit or review.

  (a) **Penalties.** Violating the requirement or the rules that will be developed will result in a fine, or up to ten years imprisonment, or both.

OF NOTE TO INDUSTRY MEMBERS—REQUIREMENTS FOR CORPORATIONS, THEIR OFFICERS, AND BOARD MEMBERS

- **No Lying to the Auditor.** The act makes it unlawful for an officer, director, or anyone acting for a principal to take any action to fraudulently influence, coerce, manipulate, or mislead the auditing CPA firm.

- **Code of Ethics for Financial Officers.** The SEC is mandated to issue rules adopting a code of ethics for senior financial officers.

- **Financial Expert Requirement.** The SEC is required to issue rules requiring a publicly traded company's audit committee to be comprised of at least one member who is a financial expert.

- **Audit Committee Responsible for Public Accounting Firm.** The act vests the audit committee of a publicly traded company with responsibility for the appointment, compensation, and oversight of any registered public accounting firm employed to perform audit services.

- **Audit Committee Independence.** Audit committee members are required to be members of the board of directors of the company, and to be otherwise independent.

- **CEOs and CFOs Required to Affirm Financials.** Chief executive officers (CEOs) and chief financial officers (CFOs) must certify in every annual report that they have reviewed the report, and that it does not contain untrue statements or omissions of material facts.

(a) **Penalty for Violation.** If material noncompliance causes the company to restate its financials, the CEO and CFO forfeit any bonuses and other incentives received during the twelve-month period following the first filing of the erroneous financials.

- **CEOs and CFOs Must Enact Internal Controls.** CEOs and CFOs will be responsible for establishing and maintaining internal controls to ensure they are notified of material information.

- **Penalties for Fraud.** The act also has stiffened penalties for corporate and criminal fraud by company insiders. The law makes it a crime for a company to destroy, alter, or falsify records in a federal investigation or in declaring bankruptcy. The penalty for those found guilty includes fines, or up to twenty years imprisonment, or both.

- **Companies Affected by the Act.** Publicly traded companies affected by the act are those defined as an "issuer" under Section 3 of the Securities Exchange Act of 1934 whose securities are registered under Section 12 of the 1934 act. An issuer also is considered a company that is required to file reports under Section 15(d) of the act, or that files or has filed a registration statement that has not yet become effective under the Securities Act of 1933. The SEC has yet to provide further guidance as to entities covered by the act.

- **Debts Not Dischargeable in Bankruptcy.** The act amends federal bankruptcy law to make non-dischargeable in bankruptcy certain debts that result from a violation relating to federal or state securities law, or of common law fraud pertaining to securities sales or purchases.

- **Expanded Statute of Limitations for Securities Fraud.** A civil action brought by a nongovernment entity or individual, an action involving a claim of securities fraud, deceit, or manipulation may be brought not later than the earlier of two years after discovery, or five years after the violation.

- **No Listing on National Exchanges for Violators.** The SEC will direct national securities exchanges and associations to prohibit the listing of securities of a noncompliant company.

- **No Insider Trading.** No insider trading is permitted during pension-fund blackout periods. The insider must forfeit any profit during this period to the company.

- **SEC Rules on Enhanced Financial Disclosures.**

  (a) *Off-Balance Sheet Transactions:* All quarterly and annual financial reports filed with the SEC must disclose all material off-balance sheet transactions, arrangements, obligations (including contingent obligations), and other relationships of the issuer with unconsolidated entities. Disclosure must be made on significant aspects relating to financial condition, liquidity, capital expenditures, resources, and components of revenue and expenses.

  (b) *Pro Forma Figures:* Pro forma financial information in any report filed with the SEC or in any public release cannot contain false or misleading statements or omit material facts necessary to make the financial information not misleading.

- **No Personal Loans.** The act permits no personal loans or extensions of credit to company executives, either directly or though a subsidiary, except for certain extensions of credit under an open-ended credit plan or charge card, home improvement and manufactured home loans, or extensions of credit by a broker or dealer to its employee to buy, trade, or carry securities.

  (a) The terms of permitted loans cannot be more favorable than those offered to the general public.

Criminal Penalties Enhanced*

Behavior	Sentence
The alteration, destruction, concealment of any records with the intent of obstructing a federal investigation.	Fine and/or up to ten years imprisonment.
Failure to maintain audit or review "work papers" for at least five years.	Fine and/or up to five years imprisonment.
Anyone who "knowingly executes, or attempts to execute, a scheme" to defraud a purchaser of securities.	Fine and/or up to ten years imprisonment.

Any CEO or CFO who "recklessly" violates his or her certification of the company's financial statements.	Fine of up to $1,000,000 and/or up to ten years imprisonment.
If "willfully" violates.	Fine of up to $5 million and/or up to twenty years imprisonment.
Two or more persons who conspire to commit any offense against or to defraud the United States or its agencies.	Fine and/or up to ten years imprisonment.
Any person who "corruptly" alters, destroys, conceals, etc., any records or documents with the intent of impairing the integrity of the record or document for use in an official proceeding.	Fine and/or up to twenty years imprisonment.
Mail and wire fraud.	Increase from five to twenty years imprisonment.
Violating applicable Employee Retirement Income Security Act (ERISA) provisions.	Various lengths, depending on violation.

*Source: Sarbanes-Oxley Act of 2002, and New York City Office of the Comptroller.

ANALYST CONFLICTS OF INTEREST

- **No Retaliation against Analysts.** Brokers and dealers of securities are not allowed to retaliate, or threaten to retaliate, against an analyst employed by the broker or dealer as a result of an adverse, negative, or unfavorable research report on a public company.

- **Conflict of Interest Disclosures.** Securities analysts and brokers or dealers are required to disclose conflicts of interest, such as

  (a) Whether the analyst has investments or debt in the company he or she is reporting on;

  (b) Whether any compensation received by the broker, dealer, or analyst is "appropriate in the public interest and consistent with the protection of investors";

(c) Whether an issuer has been a client of the broker or dealer; and

(d) Whether the analyst received compensation with respect to a research report based on investment banking revenues.

ATTORNEY REQUIREMENTS

- **Requirement of Attorneys to Report Violations.** The SEC is required to issue rules setting forth minimum standards of professional conduct for attorneys appearing and representing a public company in any manner in front of the commission. As part of this ruling, the SEC will be compelled to issue rules on the following:

  (a) Requiring attorneys employed by a public company to report to the chief counsel or CEO of the company evidence of a "material" violation of securities law, breach of fiduciary duty, or similar violation by the company or its agent.

  (b) Once reported, if the counsel or CEO does not appropriately respond to the evidence, the attorney must report the evidence to the board of directors or its audit committee.

CHAPTER 6

How to Evaluate and Improve a Company's Financial Performance

This chapter covers how to analyze a company's financial statements, comprised of the balance sheet and income statement. Financial statement analysis attempts to answer the following basic questions:

1. How well is the business doing?
2. What are its strengths?
3. What are its weaknesses?
4. How does it fare in the industry?
5. Is the business improving or deteriorating?

A complete set of financial statements, as explained in the previous chapter, will include the balance sheet, income statement, and statement of cash flows. The first two are vital in financial-statement analysis. We will discuss the various financial statement analysis tools that you will use in evaluating the firm's present and future financial conditions. These tools include horizontal, vertical, and ratio analysis, which give relative measures of the performance and financial condition of the company. We will also discuss tools that can be used to help improve corporate profitability and shareholder value. These include return on investment (ROI), the Du Pont formula, financial leverage, and return on equity (ROE).

6.1 HOW TO EVALUATE A COMPANY'S FINANCIAL PERFORMANCE

Why analyze financial statements?

The analysis of financial statements means different things to different people. It is essential to creditors, present and prospective investors, and the firm's own management for their respective decisions.

A creditor is primarily interested in the firm's debt-paying ability. A short-term creditor, such as a vendor or supplier, is ultimately concerned with the firm's ability to pay its bills and therefore wants to be assured that the firm is liquid. A long-term creditor, such as a bank or bondholder, on the other hand, is interested in the firm's ability to repay interest and principal on borrowed funds.

An investor is interested in the present and future level of return (earnings) and risk (liquidity, debt, and activity). Investors evaluate a firm's stock based on an examination of its financial statements. This evaluation considers overall financial health, economic and political conditions, industry factors, and future outlook of the company. The analysis attempts to ascertain whether the stock is overpriced, underpriced, or priced in proportion to its market value. A stock is valuable only if the business's future financial performance can be predicted. Financial statement analysis provides much of the data necessary to forecast earnings and dividends.

Management must relate the analysis to all of the questions raised by creditors and investors, because these interested parties must be satisfied for the firm to obtain capital as needed.

6.1.1 Horizontal and Vertical Analysis

How do horizontal and vertical analysis work?

Comparison of two or more years' financial data is known as horizontal analysis. Horizontal analysis concentrates on the trend in the accounts in dollar and percentage terms over the years. It is typically presented in comparative financial statements (see TLC, Inc., financial data in Figures 6.1 and 6.2). In annual reports, comparative financial data are usually shown for five years.

Through horizontal analysis one can pinpoint areas of wide divergence requiring investigation. For example, in the income statement shown in Figure 6.2, the significant rise in sales returns taken with the reduction in sales for 20X0–20X1 should cause concern. One might compare the results with the results of competitors.

It is essential to present both the dollar amount of change and the percentage of change, as the use of one without the other may result in erroneous conclusions. The interest expense from 20X0–20X1 went up by 100.0 percent, but this represented only $1,000 and may not require further investigation. In a similar vein, a large number change might cause a small percentage change and not be of any great importance. Key changes and trends can also be highlighted by

Figure 6.1 TLC, Inc. Comparative Balance Sheet (In Thousands of Dollars) December 31, 20X2, 20X1, 20X0

			Increase/Decrease			% Increase/Decrease	
	20X2	20X1	20X0	20X2–20X1	20X1–20X0	20X2–20X1	20X1–20X0
Assets							
Current Assets:							
Cash	$28	$36	$36	(8.00)	0.00	-22.2%	0.0%
Short-term investments	22	15	7	5.00	6.00	46.7%	114.3%
Accounts receivable	21	16	10	5.00	6.00	31.3%	60.0%
Inventory	53	46	49	7.00	(3.00)	15.2%	-6.1%
Total current assets	124	113	102	11.00	11.00	9.7%	10.8%
Plant and equip.	103	91	83	12.00	8.00	13.2%	9.6%
Total assets	227	204	185	23.00	19.00	11.3%	10.3%
Liabilities							
Current liabilities	56	50	51	6.00	(1.00)	12.0%	-2.0%
Long-term debt	83	74	69	9.00	5.00	12.2%	7.2%
Total liabilities	139	124	120	15.00	4.00	12.1%	3.3%
Stockholders' Equity							
Common stock, $10 par, 4,600 shares	46	46	46	0.00	0.00	0.0%	0.0%
Retained earnings	42	34	19	8.00	15.00	23.5%	78.9%
Total stockholders' equity	88	80	65	8.00	15.00	10.0%	23.1%
Total liab. and stockholders' equity	$227	$204	$185	$23.00	$19.00	11.3%	10.3%

Figure 6.2 TLC, Inc. Comparative Income Statement (In Thousands of Dollars) For the Years Ended December 31, 20X2, 20X4, 20X0

	20X2	20X1	20X0	Increase/Decrease 20X2–20X1	Increase/Decrease 20X1–20X0	% Increase/Decrease 20X2–20X1	% Increase/Decrease 20X1–20X0
Sales	$98.3	$120.0	$56.6	($21.7)	$63.4	–18.1%	112.0%
Sales return & allowances	18.0	10.0	4.0	8.0	6.0	80.0%	150.0%
Net sales	80.3	110.0	52.6	(29.7)	57.4	–27.0%	109.1%
Cost of goods sold	52.0	63.0	28.0	(11.0)	35.0	–17.5%	125.0%
Gross profit	28.3	47.0	24.6	(18.7)	22.4	–39.8%	91.1%
Operating expenses							
Selling expenses	12.0	13.0	11.0	(1.0)	2.0	–7.7%	18.2%
General expenses	5.0	8.0	3.0	(3.0)	5.0	–37.5%	166.7%
Total operating expenses	$17.0	$21.0	$14.0	($4.0)	$7.0	–19.0%	50.0%
Income from operations	$11.3	$26.0	$10.6	($14.7)	$15.4	–56.5%	145.3%
Nonoperating income	4.0	1.0	2.0	3.0	(1.0)	300.0%	–50.0%
Income before interest & taxes	15.3	27.0	12.6	(11.7)	14.4	–43.3%	114.3%
Interest expense	2.0	2.0	1.0	0.0	1.0	0.0%	100.0%
Income before taxes	13.3	25.0	11.6	(11.7)	13.4	–46.8%	115.5%
Income taxes (40%)	5.3	10.0	4.6	(4.7)	5.4	–46.8%	115.5%
Net income	$8.0	$15.0	$7.0	($7.0)	$8.0	–46.8%	115.5%

the use of common-size statements. A common-size statement is one that shows the separate items appearing on it in terms of percentage. Preparation of common-size statements is known as vertical analysis. In vertical analysis, a material financial statement item is used as a base value, and all other accounts on the financial statement are compared to it. In the balance sheet, for example, total assets equal 100 percent. Each asset is stated as a percentage of total assets. Similarly, total liabilities and stockholders' equity is assigned 100 percent, with a given liability or equity account stated as a percentage of the total liabilities and stockholders' equity, respectively. Figure 6.3 shows a common-size income statement based on the data provided in Figure 6.2.

Placing all assets in common-size form clearly shows the relative importance of the current assets as compared to the noncurrent assets. It also shows that significant changes have taken place in the composition of the current assets over the past year. Notice, for example, that receivables have increased in relative importance, and that cash has declined in relative importance.

Figure 6.3 Income Statement and Common Size Analysis TLC, Inc.

(In Thousands of Dollars)
For the Years Ended December 31, 20X2 & 20X1

	20X2 Amount	%	20X1 Amount	%
Sales	$98.30	122.40%	$120.00	109.10%
Sales Return & Allowances	18.00	22.40%	10.00	9.10%
Net Sales	80.30	100.00%	110.00	100.00%
Cost of Goods Sold	52.00	64.80%	63.00	57.30%
Gross Profit	28.30	35.20%	47.00	42.70%
Operating Expenses				
Selling Expenses	12.00	14.90%	13.00	11.80%
General Expenses	5.00	6.20%	8.00	7.30%
Total Operating Expenses	$17.00	21.20%	$21.00	19.10%
Income from Operations	$11.30	14.10%	$26.00	23.60%
Nonoperating Income	4.00	5.00%	1.00	0.90%
Income before Interest & Taxes	15.30	19.10%	27.00	24.50%
Interest Expense	2.00	2.50%	2.00	1.80%
Income before Taxes	13.30	16.60%	25.00	22.70%
Income Taxes (40%)	5.30	6.60%	10.00	9.10%
Net Income	$8.00	9.90%	$15.00	13.60%

The deterioration in the cash position may be a result of inability to collect from customers.

For the income statement, 100 percent is assigned to net sales with all other revenue and expense accounts related to it. It is possible to see at a glance how each dollar of sales is distributed between the various costs, expenses, and profits. For example, notice in Figure 6.3 that 64.8 cents of every dollar of sales was needed to cover cost of goods sold in 20X2, as compared to only 57.3 cents in the prior year; also notice that only 9.9 cents out of every dollar of sales remained for profits in 20X2—down from 13.6 cents in the previous year.

Compare the vertical percentages of the business to those of the competition, and to industry norms. This will determine how the company fares in the industry.

6.1.2 Working with Financial Ratios

What is ratio analysis?

Horizontal and vertical analysis compare one figure to another within the same category. It is also vital to compare two figures applicable to different categories. This is accomplished by ratio analysis. This section discusses how to calculate the various financial ratios, and how to interpret them. The results of the ratio analysis allow one:

1. To appraise the position of a business.
2. To identify trouble spots that need attention.
3. To provide the basis for making projections and forecasts about the course of future operations.

Think of ratios as measures of the relative health or sickness of a business. Just as a doctor takes readings of a patient's temperature, blood pressure, heart rate, and so on, it is important to take readings of a business's liquidity, profitability, leverage, efficiency in using assets, and market value. Where the doctor compares the readings to generally accepted guidelines such as a temperature of 98.6 degrees as normal, we will make some comparisons to the norms.

What are the two major comparisons?

To obtain useful conclusions from the ratios, two comparisons must be made:

- *Industry comparison.* This allows an answer to the question, "How does a business fare in the industry?" To answer this question, compare the company's ratios to those of competing companies in the industry or with industry standards (averages).

Industry norms can be obtained from financial services, such as Value Line, Dun and Bradstreet, the Philadelphia-based Risk Management Association (RMA), and Standard and Poor's. Numerous online services, such as AOL and MSN Money Central, to name a few, also provide these data. For example, RMA has been compiling statistical data on financial statements for more than seventy-five years. The RMA Annual Statement Studies provide statistical data from more than 150,000 actual companies on many key financial ratios, such as gross margin, operating margins, and return on equity and assets. To put real authority into the "industry average" numbers the company is beating, the Statement Studies are the way to go. They're organized by Statistical Industry Codes (SIC), and the financial statement studies for the industry are available for $59.95 in report form or over the Internet (www.rmahq.org).

- *Trend analysis.* To see how the business is doing over time, compare a given ratio for one company over several years to observe the direction of financial health or operational performance.

What are the major categories of financial ratios?

Financial ratios can be grouped into the following types: liquidity, asset utilization (activity), solvency (leverage and debt service), profitability, and market value.

Liquidity Liquidity is the firm's ability to satisfy maturing short-term debt. Liquidity is crucial to carrying out the business, especially during periods of adversity. It relates to the short term—typically a period of one year or less. Poor liquidity might lead to higher cost of financing and inability to pay bills and dividends. The three basic measures of liquidity are (a) net working capital, (b) the current ratio, and (c) the quick (acid-test) ratio.

(Throughout this discussion, refer to Figures 6.1 and 6.2 to ensure an understanding of where the numbers come from.)

Net working capital equals current assets minus current liabilities. Net working capital for 20X2 is:

$$
\begin{aligned}
\text{Net working capital} &= \text{current assets} \\
&\quad - \text{current liabilities} \\
&= \$124 - \$56 \\
&= \$68
\end{aligned}
$$

In 20X1, net working capital was $63. The rise over the year is favorable.

The current ratio equals current assets divided by current liabilities. The ratio reflects the company's ability to satisfy current debt from current assets.

$$\text{Current ratio} = \left(\frac{\text{Current assets}}{\text{Current liabilities}} \right)$$

For 20X2, the current ratio is

$$\left(\frac{\$124}{\$56} \right) = 2.21$$

In 20X1, the current ratio was 2.26. The ratio's decline over the year points to a slight reduction in liquidity.

A more stringent liquidity test can be found in the quick (acid-test) ratio. Inventory and prepaid expenses are excluded from the total of current assets, leaving only the more liquid (or quick) assets to be divided by current liabilities.

$$\text{Acid-test ratio} = \frac{\text{cash} + \text{marketable securities}}{\text{current liabilities}}$$

The quick ratio for 20X2 is

$$\left(\frac{\$28 + \$21 + \$22}{\$56} \right) = 1.27$$

In 20X1, the ratio was 1.34. A small reduction in the ratio over the period points to less liquidity.

The overall liquidity trend shows a slight deterioration, as reflected in the lower current and quick ratios, although it is better than industry norms (see Table 6.4 for industry averages). A mitigating factor is the increase in net working capital.

Asset utilization. Asset utilization (activity, turnover) ratios reflect the ways in which a company uses its assets to obtain revenue and profit. One example is how well receivables are turning into cash. The higher the ratio, the more efficiently the business manages its assets.

Accounts receivable ratios include the accounts receivable turnover and the average collection period.

The accounts receivable turnover indicates the number of times accounts receivable are collected in a year. This is derived by dividing net credit sales by average accounts receivable.

Average accounts receivable can be calculated by the average accounts receivable balance during a certain period:

$$\frac{\text{Accounts}}{\text{receivable turnover}} = \frac{\text{net credit sales}}{\text{average accounts receivable}}$$

For 20X2, the average accounts receivable is

$$\frac{\$21 + \$16}{2} = \$18.5$$

The accounts receivable turnover for 20X2 is

$$\frac{\$80.3}{\$18.5} = 4.34$$

In 20X1, the turnover was 8.46. There is a sharp reduction in the turnover rate, pointing to a collection problem.

The average collection period is the length of time it takes to collect receivables. This represents the number of days receivables are held.

$$\frac{\text{Average}}{\text{collection period}} = \frac{365 \text{ days}}{\text{accounts receivable turnover}}$$

In 20X2, the collection period is

$$\frac{365}{4.34} = 84.1 \text{ days}$$

It takes this firm about 84 days to convert receivables to cash. In 20X1, the collection period was 43.1 days. The significant lengthening of the collection period may be a cause for some concern. The long collection period may be a result of the presence of many doubtful accounts, or it may be a result of poor credit management.

Inventory ratios are especially useful when a buildup in inventory exists. Inventory ties up cash; holding large amounts of inventory can result in lost opportunities for profit, as well as increased storage costs. Before extending credit or lending money, examine the firm's inventory turnover and average age of inventory.

$$\text{Inventory turnover} = \frac{\text{cost of goods sold}}{\text{average inventory}}$$

The inventory turnover for 20X2 is

$$\frac{\$52}{\$49.5} = 1.05$$

For 20X1, the turnover was 1.33.

$$\frac{\text{Average age}}{\text{of inventory}} = \frac{365}{\text{inventory turnover}}$$

In 20X2, the average age is

$$\frac{365}{1.05} = 347.6 \text{ days}$$

In the previous year, the average age was 274.4 days. The reduction in the turnover and increase in inventory age points to a longer holding of inventory. Consider why the inventory is not selling as quickly.

The operating cycle is the number of days it takes to convert inventory and receivables to cash.

$$\text{Operating cycle} = \text{average collection period} + \text{average age of inventory}$$

In 20X2, the operating cycle is

$$84.1 \text{ days} + 347.6 \text{ days} = 431.7 \text{ days}$$

In the previous year, the operating cycle was 317.5 days. An unfavorable direction is indicated because additional funds are tied up in noncash assets. Cash is being collected more slowly.

Calculating the total asset turnover indicates whether the company is efficiently employing its total assets to obtain sales revenue. A low ratio may indicate too high an investment in assets in comparison to the sales revenue generated.

$$\text{Total asset turnover} = \frac{\text{net sales}}{\text{average total assets}}$$

In 20X2, the ratio is

$$\frac{\$80.3}{(\$204 + \$277)/2} = \frac{\$80.3}{\$215.5} = 0.37$$

In 20X1, the ratio was .57 ($110/$194.5). There has been a sharp reduction in asset utilization.

TLC, Inc., has suffered a sharp deterioration in activity ratios, pointing to a need for improved credit and inventory management, even though the 20X2 ratios are not far out of line with the industry averages (see Figure 6.4). It appears that the company's problems are inefficient collection and obsolescence of inventory.

Solvency (leverage and debt service). Solvency is the company's ability to satisfy long-term debt as it becomes due. One should be concerned about the long-term financial and operating structure of any firm in which one might be interested. Another important consideration is the size of debt in the firm's capital structure, which is referred to as financial leverage. (Capital structure is the mix of the long-term sources of funds used by the firm).

Solvency also depends on earning power; in the long run, a company will not satisfy its debts unless it earns profit. A leveraged capital structure subjects the company to fixed interest charges, which contributes to earnings instability. Excessive debt may also make it

Figure 6.4 TLC, Inc. Summary of Financial Ratios—Trend and Industry Comparisons

Ratios	Definitions	20X1	20X2	Industry[a]	Ind.	Evaluation[b] Trend	Overall
Liquidity							
Net working capital	Current assets − current liabilities	63	68	56	good	good	good
Current Ratio	Current assets/current liabilities	2.26	2.21	2.05	OK	OK	OK
Quick (acid-test) ratio	(Cash + short-term investments + accounts receivable)/current liabilities	1.34	1.27	1.11	OK	OK	OK
Asset Utilization							
Accounts receivable turnover	Net credit sales/average accounts receivable	8.46	4.34	5.5	OK	poor	poor
Average collection period	365 days/accounts receivable turnover (days)	43.1	84.1	66.4	OK	poor	poor
Inventory turnover	Cost of goods sold/average inventory	1.33	1.05	1.2	OK	poor	poor
Average age of inventory	365 days/inventory turnover (days)	274.4	347.6	N/A	N/A	poor	poor
Operating cycle	Average collection period + average age of inventory (days)	317.5	431.7	N/A	N/A	poor	poor
Total asset turnover	Net sales/average total assets	0.57	0.37	0.44	OK	poor	poor
Solvency							
Debt ratio	Total liabilities/total assets	0.61	0.61	N/A	N/A	OK	OK
Debt-equity ratio	Total liabilities/stockholders' equity	1.55	1.58	1.3	poor	poor	poor
Times interest earned	Income before interest and taxes/interest expense (times)	13.5	7.65	10	OK	poor	poor

Figure 6.4 (continued)

Ratios	Definitions	20X1	20X2	Industry[a]	Evaluation[b]		
					Ind.	Trend	Overall
Profitability							
Gross profit margin	Gross profit/net sales	0.43	0.35	0.48	poor	poor	poor
Profit margin	Net income/net sales	0.14	0.1	0.15	poor	poor	poor
Return on total assets	Net income/average total assets	0.077	0.037	0.1	poor	poor	poor
Return on equity(ROE)	Earnings available to common stockholders/avg. stockholders' equity	0.207	0.095	0.27	poor	poor	poor
Market Value							
Earnings per share(EPS)	(Net income − preferred dividend)/common shares outstanding	3.26	1.74	4.51	poor	poor	poor
Price/earnings (P/E) ratio	Market price per share/EPS	7.98	6.9	7.12	OK	poor	poor
Book value per share	(Total stockholders' equity − Preferred stock)/ common shares outstanding	17.39	19.13	N/A	N/A	good	good
Price/book value ratio	Market price per share/book value per share	1.5	0.63	N/A	N/A	poor	poor
Dividend yield	Dividends per share/market price per share						
Dividend payout	Dividends per share/EPS						

(a) Obtained from sources not included in this chapter.
(b) Represents subjective evaluation.

difficult for the firm to borrow funds at reasonable rates during tight money markets.

The debt ratio reveals the amount of money a company owes to its creditors. Excessive debt means greater risk to the investor. (Note that equity holders come after creditors in bankruptcy.) *Note:* How much debt is too much? The rule of thumb is this: the debt portion should be less than 50 percent. All bankruptcies arise from a company's inability to meet its debt obligations, according to www.BankruptcyData.com.

The debt ratio is

$$\text{Debt ratio} = \frac{\text{Total liabilities}}{\text{Total assets}}$$

In 20X2, the ratio is

$$\frac{\$139}{\$227} = 0.61$$

Table 6.1 shows the debt ratios for selected companies.

Table 6.1 Debt Ratios 2003

Best Buy	9.0%
Pfizer	6.5
Johnson & Johnson	9.8
Wal-Mart Stores	34.0
Harley-Davidson	20.2
Sysco	30.9
Lowes	35.9

Source: *The Business Week 50,* by Business Week, McGraw-Hill, Spring 2003, p. 130.

The debt-equity ratio will indicate if the firm has a great amount of debt in its capital structure. Large debts mean that the borrower has to pay significant periodic interest and principal. Also, a heavily indebted firm incurs a greater risk of running out of cash in difficult times. The interpretation of this ratio depends on several variables, including the ratios of other firms in the industry, the degree of access to additional debt financing, and stability of operations.

$$\text{Debt-equity ratio} = \frac{\text{Total liabilities}}{\text{Stockholders' equity}}$$

In 20X2, the ratio is

$$\frac{\$139}{\$88} = 1.58$$

In the previous year, the ratio was 1.55. The trend is relatively static.

Times interest earned (interest coverage ratio) tells you how many times the firm's before-tax earnings would cover interest. This is a safety margin indicator, in that it reflects how much of a reduction in earnings a company can tolerate.

$$\frac{\text{Times interest}}{\text{earned}} = \frac{\text{Income before interest and taxes}}{\text{interest expenses}}$$

For 20X2, the ratio is

$$\frac{\$15.3}{\$2.0} = 7.65$$

In 20X1, interest was covered 13.5 times. The reduction in coverage during the period is a bad sign. It means that less earnings are available to satisfy interest charges.

Also, note liabilities that have not yet been reported in the balance sheet by closely examining footnote disclosure. For example, find out about lawsuits, noncapitalized leases, and future guarantees.

As shown in Figure 6.3, the company's overall solvency is poor relative to the industry averages, even though it has remained fairly constant. There has been no significant change in its ability to satisfy long-term debt. Note that significantly less profit is available to cover interest payments.

Profitability. A company's ability to earn a good profit and return on investment is an indicator of its financial well-being and the efficiency with which it is managed. Poor earnings have detrimental effects on market price of stock and dividends. Total dollar net income has little meaning unless it is compared to the input in getting that profit.

The gross profit margin shows the percentage of each dollar remaining once the company has paid for acquired goods. A high margin reflects good earning potential.

$$\text{Gross profit margin} = \frac{\text{gross profit}}{\text{net sales}}$$

In 20X2, the ratio is

$$\frac{\$28.3}{\$80.3} = 0.35$$

The ratio was .43 in 20X1. The reduction shows that the company now receives less profit on each dollar sale.

Perhaps higher relative cost of merchandise sold is at fault.

Profit margin shows the earnings generated form revenue, and is a key indicator of operating performance. Profit margin provides an idea of the firm's pricing, cost structure, and production efficiency.

$$\text{Profit margin} = \frac{\text{net income}}{\text{net sales}}$$

The ratio in 20X2 is

$$\frac{\$8}{\$80.3} = 0.10$$

For the previous year, profit margin was .14. The decline in the ratio shows a downward trend in earning power. (Note that these percentages are available in the common-size income statement, as given in Figure 6.2).

Return on investment is a prime indicator because it allows one to evaluate the profit to be earned if one invests in the business. Two key ratios are the return on total assets and the return on equity.

The return on total assets shows whether management is efficient in using available resources to get profit.

$$\text{Return on total assets} = \frac{\text{net income}}{\text{average total assets}}$$

In 20X2, the return is

$$\frac{\$8}{(\$227 + \$204)/2} = 0.037$$

In 20X1, the return was .077. There has been a deterioration in the productivity of assets in generating earnings.

The return on equity (ROE) reflects the rate of return earned on the stockholders' investment.

$$\frac{\text{Return on}}{\text{common equity}} = \frac{\text{net income available to stockholder}}{\text{average stockholders' equity}}$$

The return in 20X2 is

$$\frac{\$8}{(\$88 + \$80)/2} = 0.095$$

In 20X1, the return was .207. There has been a significant drop in return to the owners.

The overall profitability of the company has decreased considerably, causing a decline in both return on assets and return on equity. Perhaps lower earnings were due in part to higher costs of short-term financing arising from the decline in liquidity and activity ratios. Moreover, as turnover rates in assets go down, profit will similarly decline because of a lack of sales and higher costs of carrying higher current asset balances. As indicated in Figure 6.4, industry comparisons reveal that the company is faring very poorly in the industry.

Table 6.2 shows industries with high return on equity (in excess of 20 percent).

Table 6.2 Industries with High Return on Equity (ROE) Rates (in Excess of 20%) 2003

Consumer Products	29.5%
Conglomerates	18.6
Food	20.4
Fuel	16.6
Health Care	22.3

Source: *The Business Week 50,* by Business Week, McGraw-Hill, Spring 2003, pp. 87–113.

Market value. Market value ratios relate the company's stock price to its earnings (or book value) per share. Also included are dividend-related ratios.

Earnings per share (EPS) is the ratio most widely watched by investors. EPS shows the net income per common share owned. To obtain the net income available to common stockholders, reduce net income by the preferred dividends. Where preferred stock is not in the capital structure, EPS is determined by dividing net income by common shares outstanding. EPS is a gauge of corporate operating performance, and of expected future dividends.

$$\text{EPS} = \frac{\text{net income} - \text{preferred dividend}}{\text{common shares outstanding}}$$

EPS in 20X2 is

$$\frac{\$8}{4,600 \text{ shares}} = \$1.74$$

For 20X1, EPS was $3.26. The sharp reduction over the year should cause alarm among investors. As shown in Figure 6.4, the industry average EPS in 20X2 is much higher than that of TLC, Inc. ($4.51 per share vs. $1.74 per share).

Table 6.3 provides a list of highly profitable companies in terms of EPS.

Table 6.3 Highly Profitable Companies (in Terms of EPS) 2003

General Dynamics	4.65
Bank of America	4.18
Dupont	4.15
Phillips Petroleum	5.57
Amerada Hess	10.25
UST	5.51

Source: *The Business Week 50,* by Business Week, McGraw-Hill, Spring 2003, pp. 87–113.

The price/earnings (P/E) ratio, also called earnings multiple, reflects the company's relationship to its stockholders. The P/E ratio represents the amount investors are willing to pay for each dollar of the firm's earnings. A high multiple (cost per dollar of earnings) is favored because it shows that investors view the firm positively. On the other hand, investors looking for value would prefer a relatively lower multiple (cost per dollar of earnings), as compared with companies of similar risk and return.

$$\text{Price/earnings ratio} = \frac{\text{market price per share}}{\text{earnings per share}}$$

Assume a market price per share of $12 on December 31, 20X2, and $26 on December 31, 20X1. The P/E ratios are

$$20X2: \frac{\$12}{\$1.74} = 6.9$$

$$20X1: \frac{\$26}{\$3.26} = 7.98$$

From the lower P/E multiple, you can infer that the stock market now has a lower opinion of the business. However, some investors argue that a low P/E ratio can mean that the stock is undervalued. Nevertheless, the decline over the year in stock price was 54 percent ($14/$26), which should cause deep investor concern.

Table 6.4 shows price-earnings ratios of certain companies.

Table 6.4 P/E Ratios

Company	Industry	2003
Boeing	Aerospace	13
General Motors	Cars & Trucks	30
Phillip Morris	Consumer Products	14
Nordstrom	Retailing	27
Intel	Semiconductor	150
Safeway	Food	17

Source: *The Business Week 50,* by Business Week, McGraw-Hill, Spring 2003, pp. 87–113.

Book value per share equals the net assets available to common stockholders divided by shares outstanding. Comparing book value per share to market price per share provides another view of how investors feel about the business.

The book value per share in 20X2 is

$$\text{Book value per share} = \frac{\text{Total stockholders' equity} - \text{preferred stock}}{\text{common shares outstanding}}$$

$$= \frac{\$88,000 - 0}{4,600} = \$19.13$$

In 20X1, book value per share was $17.39

The increased book value per share is a favorable sign because it indicates that each share now has a higher book value. However, in 20X2, market price is much less than book value, which means that the stock market does not value the security highly. In 20X1, market price *did* exceed book value, but there is now some doubt in the minds of stockholders concerning the company. However, some analysts may argue that the stock is underpriced.

The price/book value ratio shows the market value of the company in comparison to its historical accounting value. A company with old assets may have a high ratio, whereas one with new assets may have a low ratio. Thus, the changes in the ratio should be noted in an effort to appraise the corporate assets.

The ratio equals

$$\text{Price/book value} = \frac{\text{Market prices per share}}{\text{Book value per share}}$$

In 20X2, the ratio is

$$\frac{\$12}{\$19.13} = 0.63$$

In 20X1, the ratio was 1.5. The significant drop in the ratio may indicate a lower opinion of the company in the eyes of investors. Market price of stock may have dropped because of a deterioration in liquidity, activity, and profitability ratios. The major indicators of a company's performance are intertwined (that is, one affects the other), so problems in one area may spill over into another. This appears to have happened to the company in this example.

Dividend ratios help determine the current income from an investment. Two relevant ratios are

$$\text{Dividend yield} = \frac{\text{dividends per share}}{\text{market price share}}$$

$$\text{Dividend payout} = \frac{\text{dividends per share}}{\text{earnings per share}}$$

Table 6.5 shows the dividend yield ratios of some companies.

Table 6.5 Dividend Yield Ratios 2003

Boeing	1.48
General Motors	3.78
Wells Fargo	2.22
General Electric	1.87
Coca-Cola	1.69
Procter & Gamble	1.79

Source: *The Business Week 50,* by Business Week, McGraw-Hill, Spring 2003, pp. 87–113; MSN Money Central Investor (http://investor.msn.com).

There is no such thing as a "right" payout ratio. Stockholders look unfavorably upon reduced dividends, a sign of possible deteriorating financial health. However, it should be noted that companies with ample opportunities for growth at high rates of return on assets tend to have low payout ratios.

An overall evaluation—summary of financial ratios. As indicated in this chapter, a single ratio or a single group of ratios is not adequate for assessing all aspects of a firm's financial condition. Figure 6.4 summarizes the 20X1 and 20X2 ratios calculated in the previous sections, along with the industry average ratios for 20X2. Figure 6.4 also shows the formula used to calculate each ratio. The last three columns of the figure contain subjective assessments of TLC's financial condition based on trend analysis and 20X2 comparisons to the industry norms. (Note, however, that five-year ratios are generally needed for trend analysis to be more meaningful.)

By appraising the trend in the company's ratios from 20X1 to 20X2, we see from the drop in the current and quick ratios that there has been a slight detraction in short-term liquidity, although the company has been above the industry averages. Working capital has improved. A material deterioration in the activity ratios has occurred, indicating that improved credit and inventory policies are required. This is not terribly alarming, however, because these ratios are not way out of line with industry averages. Also, total utilization of assets, as indicated by the total asset turnover, shows a deteriorating trend.

Leverage (amount of debt) has been constant. However, there is less profit available to satisfy interest charges. TLC's profitability has deteriorated over the year. In 20X2, it is consistently below the industry average in every measure of profitability. Consequently, the return on the owner's investment and the return on total assets have gone down. The earnings decrease may be partly due to the firm's high cost of short-term financing, and partly due to operating inefficiency. The higher costs may be due to receivable and inventory difficulties that forced a decline in the liquidity and activity ratios. Furthermore, as receivables and inventory turn over less, profit will fall off from a lack of sales and from the costs of carrying more in current asset balances.

The firm's market value, as measured by the price/earnings (P/E) ratio, is respectable as compared with the industry. But it shows a declining trend.

In summary, it appears that the company is doing satisfactorily in the industry in many categories. The 20X1–20X2 period, however, seems to indicate that the company is heading for financial trouble in terms of earnings, activity, and short-term liquidity. The business needs to concentrate on increasing operating efficiency and asset utilization.

Is ratio analysis a panacea?

While ratio analysis is an effective tool for assessing a business's financial condition, the following limitations must be noted:

1. Accounting policies vary among companies and can inhibit useful comparisons. For example, the use of different depreciation methods (straight-line vs. double-declining balance) will affect profitability and return ratios.

2. Management may "fool around" with (or "window-dress") the figures. For example, necessary research expense can be reduced just to bolster net income. This practice, however, will almost always hurt the company in the long run.

3. A ratio is static and does not reveal future flows. For example, it will not answer such questions as, "How much cash do you have in your pocket now?" or "Is that sufficient, considering expenses and income over the next month?"

4. A ratio does not indicate the quality of its components. For example, a high quick ratio may contain receivables that may not be collected.

5. Reported liabilities may be undervalued. An example is a lawsuit on which the company is contingently liable.

6. The company may have multiple lines of business, making it difficult to identify the industry group of which the company is a part.

7. Industry averages cited by financial advisory services are only approximations. Hence, a company's ratios may have to be compared to those of competing companies in the industry.

6.2 HOW TO ANALYZE AND IMPROVE CORPORATE PROFITABILITY AND SHAREHOLDER VALUE

How are managerial performance and the return to stockholders measured?

The ability to measure performance is essential in developing incentives and controlling operations toward the achievement of organizational goals. Perhaps the most widely used single measure of profitability of an organization is the rate of return on investment (ROI). Related is the return to stockholders, known as the return on equity (ROE). This section will discuss and define the relationship between ROI and ROE. The ability to measure managerial performance is essential in controlling operations toward the achievement of organizational goals. As companies grow or their activities become more complex, they attempt to decentralize decision making as much as possible. They do this by restructuring the firm into several divisions and treating each as an independent business. The managers of these subunits or segments are then evaluated on the basis of the effectiveness with which they use the assets entrusted to them.

6.2.1 Return on Investment (ROI) and the Du Pont Formula

What is return on investment (ROI)?

ROI relates net income to invested capital (total assets). ROI provides a standard for evaluating how efficiently management employs the average dollar invested in a firm's assets, whether that dollar came from owners or creditors. Furthermore, a better ROI can also translate directly into a higher return on the stockholders' equity.

ROI is calculated as

$$\text{ROI} = \frac{\text{Net profit after taxes}}{\text{Total assets}}$$

Example 6.1

Consider the following financial data:

$$\text{Total assets} = \$100,000$$
$$\text{Net profit after taxes} = \$18,000$$
$$\text{ROI} = \frac{\text{Net profit after taxes}}{\text{Total assets}} = \frac{\$18,000}{\$100,000} = 18\%$$

The problem with this formula is that it only indicates how a company did and how well it fared in the industry; it has very little value from the standpoint of profit planning.

What is ROI made up of—Du Pont formula?

ROI can be broken down into two factors—profit margin and asset turnover. In the past, managers have tended to focus only on the profit margin earned and have ignored the turnover of assets. It is important to realize that excessive funds tied up in assets can be just as much of a drag on profitability as excessive expenses can. The Du Pont Corporation was the first major company to recognize the importance of looking at both net profit margin and total asset turnover in assessing the performance of an organization. The ROI breakdown, known as the Du Pont formula, is expressed as a product of these two factors, as shown below.

$$\text{ROI} = \frac{\text{Net profit after taxes}}{\text{Total assets}} = \frac{\text{Net profit after taxes}}{\text{Sales}}$$
$$\times \frac{\text{Sales}}{\text{Total assets}}$$
$$= \text{Net profit} \times \text{Total asset turnover}$$

The Du Pont formula combines the income statement and balance sheet into this otherwise static measure of performance. Net profit margin is a measure of profitability or operating efficiency; it is the percentage of profit earned on sales. This percentage shows how many cents attach to each dollar of sales. On the other hand, total asset turnover measures how well a company manages its assets. This is the number of times by which the investment in assets turn over each year to generate sales.

The breakdown of ROI is based on the thesis that the profitability of a firm is directly related to management's ability to manage assets efficiently and to control expenses effectively.

Example 6.2

Assume the same data as in Example 6.1. Also assume sales of $200,000.

$$\text{ROI} = \frac{\text{Net profit after taxes}}{\text{Total assets}} = \frac{\$18,000}{\$100,000} = 18\%$$

Alternatively,

$$\text{Net profit margin} = \frac{\text{Net profit after taxes}}{\text{Total assets}}$$

$$= \frac{\$18,000}{\$200,000} = 9\%$$

$$\text{Total asset turnover} = \frac{\text{Sales}}{\text{Total assets}}$$

$$= \frac{\$200,000}{\$100,000} = 2 \text{ times}$$

Therefore,

$$\text{ROI} = \text{Net profit margin} \times \text{Total asset turnover}$$
$$= 9\% \times 2 \text{ times} = 18\%$$

The breakdown provides much insight to financial managers regarding how to improve profitability of the company and investment strategy. (Note that net profit margin and total asset turnover are hereafter called margin and turnover, respectively, for short). Specifically, this breakdown has several advantages over the original formula (that is, net profit after taxes divided by total assets) for profit planning. They are

1. The importance of turnover as a key to overall return on investment is emphasized in the breakdown. In fact, turnover is just as important as profit margin in enhancing overall return.

2. The importance of sales is explicitly recognized, unlike in the original formula.

3. The breakdown stresses the possibility of trading one for the other in an attempt to improve the overall performance of a company. The margin and turnover complement each other. In other words, a low turnover can be made up by a high margin, and vice versa.

Example 6.3

The breakdown of ROI into its two components shows that a number of combinations of margin and turnover can yield the same rate of return, as shown below:

	Margin	×	**Turnover**	=	**ROI**
(1)	9%	×	2 times	=	18%
(2)	6	×	3	=	18
(3)	3	×	6	=	18
(4)	2	×	9	=	18

The turnover-margin relationship and its resulting ROI are depicted in Figure 6.5.

Figure 6.5 Turnover-Margin Relationship

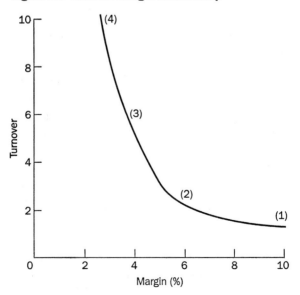

Is there an optimal ROI?

Figure 6.1 can also be looked at as showing four companies that performed equally well (in terms of ROI), but with varying income statements and balance sheets. There is no ROI that is satisfactory for all companies. Sound and successful operation must point toward the optimum combination of profits, sales, and capital employed. The combination will necessarily vary, depending on the nature of the business and the characteristics of the product. An industry with products tailor-made to customers' specifications will have different margins and turnover ratios than industries that mass-produce highly competitive consumer goods. For example, the combination (4) may describe a supermarket operation that inherently works with low margin and high turnover, while the combination (1) may be a jewelry store that typically has a low turnover and high margin.

How do you use the Du Pont formula for profit planning?

The breakdown of ROI into margin and turnover gives management insight into planning for profit improvement by revealing where weaknesses exist: margin, or turnover, or both. Various actions can be taken to enhance ROI. Generally, management can

1. Improve margin.
2. Improve turnover.
3. Improve both.

Alternative 1 demonstrates a popular way of improving performance. Margins may be increased by reducing expenses, raising selling prices, or increasing sales faster than expenses. Some of the ways to reduce expenses are

1. Use less costly inputs of materials. (Note, though, that this can be dangerous in today's quality-oriented environment.)
2. Automate processes as much as possible to increase labor productivity. (But note that this will probably increase assets, thereby reducing turnover.)
3. Bring the discretionary fixed costs under scrutiny, with various programs either curtailed or eliminated. Discretionary fixed costs arise from annual budgeting decisions by management. Examples include advertising, research and development, and management development programs. The cost-benefit analysis is called for in order to justify the budgeted amount of each discretionary program.

A company with pricing power can raise selling prices and retain profitability without losing business. Pricing power is the ability to raise prices even in poor economic times when unit sales volume may be flat and capacity may not be fully utilized. It is also the ability to pass on cost increases to consumers without attracting domestic and import competition, political opposition, regulation, new entrants, or threats of product substitution. The company with pricing power must have a unique economic position. Companies that offer unique, high-quality goods and services (where the service is more important than the cost) hold this economic position.

Alternative 2 may be achieved by increasing sales while holding the investment in assets relatively constant, or by reducing assets. Some of the strategies to reduce assets are

1. Dispose of obsolete and redundant inventory. The computer has been extremely helpful in this regard, making continuous monitoring of inventory for better control more feasible.

2. Devise various methods of speeding up the collection of receivables, and also evaluate credit terms and policies.

3. See if there are unused fixed assets.

4. Use the converted assets (primarily cash) obtained from the use of the previous methods to repay outstanding debts or repurchase outstanding issues of stock. Those funds may be used elsewhere to get more profit, which will improve margin as well as turnover.

Alternative 3 may be achieved by increasing sales, or by any combination of alternatives 1 and 2.

Figure 6.6 shows complete details of the relationship of ROI to the underlying ratios—margin and turnover—and their components. This will help identify more detailed strategies to improve margin, turnover, or both.

Example 6.4

Assume that management sets a 20 percent ROI as a profit target. The company is currently making an 18 percent return on its investment.

$$\text{ROI} = \frac{\text{Net profit after taxes}}{\text{Total assets}}$$

$$= \frac{\text{Net profit after taxes}}{\text{Sales}}$$

$$\times \frac{\text{Sales}}{\text{Total assets}}$$

Present situation:

$$18\% = \frac{18,000}{200,000} \times \frac{200,000}{100,000}$$

The following are illustrative of the strategies that might be used to improve margin or turnover. (Each strategy is independent of the others.)

Figure 6.6 Relationships of Factors Influencing ROI

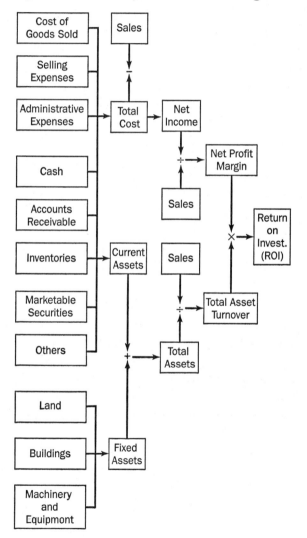

Alternative 1: Increase the margin while holding turnover constant. Pursuing this strategy would involve leaving selling prices as they are and making every effort to increase efficiency to reduce expenses. By doing so, expenses might be reduced by $2,000, without affecting sales and investment, to yield a 20 percent target ROI, as follows:

$$20\% = \frac{20,000}{200,000} \times \frac{200,000}{100,000}$$

Alternative 2: Increase turnover by reducing investment in assets while holding net profit and sales constant. Working capital might be reduced or some land might be sold, reducing investment in assets by $10,000, without affecting sales and net income, to yield the 20 percent target ROI, as follows:

$$20\% = \frac{18,000}{200,000} \times \frac{200,000}{90,000}$$

Alternative 3: Increase both margin and turnover by disposing of obsolete and redundant inventories, or through an active advertising campaign. For example, trimming down $5,000 worth of investment in inventories would also reduce the inventory holding charge by $1,000. This strategy would increase ROI to 20 percent, as follows:

$$20\% = \frac{19,000}{200,000} \times \frac{200,000}{95,000}$$

Excessive investment in assets is just as much of a drag on profitability as excessive expenses are. In this case, cutting unnecessary inventories also helps cut down expenses of carrying those inventories, so that both margin and turnover are improved at the same time. In practice, Alternative 3 is much more common than Alternatives 1 and 2.

6.2.2 Return on Equity (ROE) and the Modified Du Pont Formula

What is the relationship between ROI and return on equity (ROE)? Can return to stockholders be improved through financial leverage?

Generally, a better management performance (that is, a high or above-average ROI) produces a higher return to equity holders. However, even a poorly managed company that suffers from below-average performance can generate an above-average return on the stockholders' equity, simply called the return on equity (ROE). This is because borrowed funds can magnify the returns a company's profits represent to its stockholders.

Another version of the Du Pont formula, called the modified Du Pont formula, reflects this effect. The formula ties together the ROI and the degree of financial leverage (use of borrowed funds). The financial leverage is measured by the equity multiplier, which is the ratio of a company's total asset base to its equity investment, or, stated another way, the ratio of how many dollars of assets held per dollar of stockholders' equity. Financial leverage is calculated by dividing total assets by stockholders' equity. This measurement gives an indication of how much of a company's assets are financed by stockholders' equity, and how much with borrowed funds.

The return on equity (ROE) is calculated as follows

$$
\begin{aligned}
\text{ROI} &= \frac{\text{Net profit after taxes}}{\text{Stockholders' equity}} \\
&= \frac{\text{Net profit after taxes}}{\text{Total assets}} \times \frac{\text{Total assets}}{\text{Stockholders' equity}} \\
&= \text{ROI} \quad\quad\quad\quad \times \text{Equity multiplier}
\end{aligned}
$$

ROE measures the returns earned on the owners' (both preferred and common stockholders') investment. The use of the equity multiplier to convert the ROI to the ROE reflects the impact of the leverage (use of debt) on the stockholders' return.

$$
\begin{aligned}
\text{The equity multiplier} &= \frac{\text{Total assets}}{\text{Stockholders' equity}} \\
&= \frac{\text{Total assets}}{\text{Total assets} - \text{Total liabilities}} \\
&= \frac{1}{1 - \dfrac{\text{Total liabilities}}{\text{Total assets}}} \\
&= \frac{1}{(1 - \text{debt ratio})}
\end{aligned}
$$

Figure 6.7 shows the relationship among ROI, ROE, and financial leverage.

Example 6.5

In Example 6.1, assume stockholders' equity of $45,000.
Then,

$$\text{equity multiplier} = \frac{\text{Total assets}}{\text{Stockholders' equity}}$$

$$= \frac{\$100,000}{\$45,000} = 2.22$$

$$= \frac{1}{1 - \text{debt ratio}} = \frac{1}{1 - 0.55} = \frac{1}{0.45} = 2.22$$

$$\text{ROE} = \frac{\text{Net profit after taxes}}{\text{Stockholders' equity}} = \frac{\$18,000}{\$45,000} = 40\%$$

Figure 6.7 ROI, ROE, and Financial Leverage

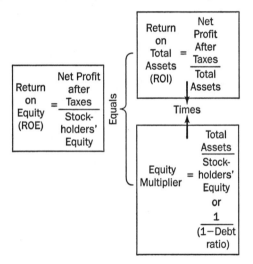

$$\text{ROE} = \text{ROI} \times \text{equity multiplier} = 18\% \times 2.22 = 40\%$$

If the company used only equity, the 18 percent ROI would equal ROE. However, 55 percent of the firm's capital is supplied by creditors ($45,000/$100,000 = 45% is the equity-to-asset ratio; $55,000/$100,000 = 55% is the debt ratio). Since the 18 percent ROI all goes to stockholders, who put up only 45 percent of the capital, the ROE is higher than 18 percent. This example indicates the company was using leverage (debt) favorably.

Example 6.6

To further demonstrate the interrelationship between a firm's financial structure and the return it
generates on the stockholders' investments, here is a
comparison of two firms that generate $300,000 in
operating income. Both firms employ $800,000 in
total assets, but they have different capital structures. One firm employs no debt, whereas the other
uses $400,000 in borrowed funds. The comparative
capital structures are shown as

	A	B
Total assets	$800,000	$800,000
Total liabilities	—	400,000
Stockholders' equity(a)	800,000	400,000
Total liabilities and stockholders' equity	$800,000	$800,000

Firm B pays 10 percent interest for borrowed funds.
The comparative income statements and ROEs for
firms A and B would look like this:

Operating income	$300,000	$300,000
Interest expense	—	(40,000)
Profit before taxes	$300,000	$260,000
Taxes (30% assumed)	(90,000)	(78,000)
Net profit after taxes (b)	$210,000	$182,000
ROE [(b)/(a)]	26.25%	45.5%

The absence of debt allows firm A to register higher
profits after taxes. But the owners of firm B enjoy a
significantly higher return on their investments. This
provides an important view of the positive contribution debt can make to a business—within a certain
limit. Too much debt can increase the firm's financial
risk, and thus the cost of financing.

What is the role of financial leverage in enhancing shareholder value?

If the assets in which the funds are invested are able
to earn a return greater than the fixed rate of return required by the creditors, the leverage is positive, and the
common stockholders benefit. The advantage of this
formula is that it enables the company to break its

ROE into a profit margin portion (net profit margin), an efficiency-of-asset-utilization portion (total asset turnover), and a use-of-leverage portion (equity multiplier). This shows that the company can raise shareholder return by employing leverage—taking on larger amounts of debt to help finance growth.

Because financial leverage affects net profit margin through added interest costs, management must look at the various pieces of this ROE equation, within the context of the whole, to earn the highest return for stockholders. Financial managers have the task of determining just what combination of asset return and leverage will work best in their competitive environment. Most companies try to keep at least a level equal to what is considered to be "normal" within the industry.

A word of caution: Unfortunately, leverage is a double-edged sword. If assets are unable to earn a high enough rate to cover fixed finance charges, the stockholder suffers. This happens because part of the profits from the assets the stockholder has provided to the firm will have to go to make up the shortfall to the long-term creditors, and he or she will be left with a smaller return than might otherwise have been earned.

CHAPTER 7

Internal Accounting Applications for Your Company

In this chapter, you will find measures and guidelines for internally evaluating your company's performance. There are discussions of

- Divisional and departmental performance analysis
- Selling-price formulation and strategy
- Product-line evaluation techniques
- Budgeting process and budget types
- Variance analysis for highlighting and correcting problem performance areas
- Cost management and activity-based costing (ABC)
- Life-cycle costs and target costing
- Balanced scorecards

As a management executive, your goals should be many. Among them include profitability, high market share, product leadership, personnel development, productivity, and employee satisfaction. The guidelines set forth in this chapter will help you to realize your company's potential in all these areas.

7.1 HOW TO ANALYZE DIVISIONAL AND DEPARTMENTAL PERFORMANCE

What criteria are used for measuring performance?

In evaluating how well a business segment is doing, use the following criteria:

- Budgeted versus actual cost
- Profitability—in order to arrive at the profit of a division, prices for internal transfers may have to be established

- Return on investment
- Residual income

For managerial accountants: Evaluate administrative functions by preparing performance reports. Look at such dollar indicators as executive salaries and service department costs, as well as nondollar measures such as number of files handled, phone calls taken, and invoices processed. *Note:* It's more difficult to evaluate the performance of a marketing department than a manufacturing department. Why? The former depends more on external factors, which are more difficult to control than internal ones.

When evaluating a division manager, look at controllable profit—that is, controllable revenue less controllable costs. *Remember:* The manager should not be held accountable for factors (costs, for example) beyond his or her control.

What is the cost-center approach?

The cost-center approach is an efficiency evaluation in which budgeted cost is compared to actual cost. A cost center is most often the smallest segment of activity or area of responsibility for which costs are accumulated. This approach is typically used by departments rather than divisions. Departmental profit is difficult to derive because of problems with revenue and cost allocations.

What is divisional profit?

Divisional profit equals a division's revenue less direct and indirect costs. Because it is possible to determine divisional earnings, profit is the method of evaluation used most often. The divisional profit concept allows for decentralization, as each division is treated as a separate business entity with responsibility for making its own profit.

How do I use transfer pricing?

In determining divisional profit, a transfer price may be necessary. This is the price charged among divisions for the transfer of an assembled product or service. *Managerial Accountants:* Possible transfer prices include

- *Actual cost plus profit markup.* This allows cost inefficiencies to be passed on from the selling division to the buying division.

- *Negotiated market price.* This equals the outside market price less the amount saved (for instance, for transportation, salesperson salaries, and commissions) by working from within the organization. The negotiated market value for services may be based on a per-hour rate or a flat rate. If a negotiated price cannot be agreed upon, the transfer price would be established arbitrarily by a higher authority. This is the best price to use because it reflects the true value of the item.

- *Budgeted cost plus profit markup.* This should be used when a negotiated market price is not available, say for a new product. Here, the selling division has an incentive to control its cost because credit will be applied on the basis of budgeted cost only.

Example 7.1

Division A wants to transfer an assembled item to Division B. Division A can sell the item to an outside company for $100. Cost savings of transferring the item internally are $20 (that is, shipping costs, insurance on delivery, sales commission). Thus, the transfer price should be $80.

Suggestion: Do not use a temporarily high or low market price. Rather, use the average market price for the given period.

Rule of thumb: The maximum transfer price is the price that the buying division can purchase the item for outside. Do not allow the selling division to charge a higher price. In fact, if the buying division can get the item from the outside for less than it can from the inside, the selling division is probably quite inefficient.

Example 7.2

The selling division wants to charge $50 for an internal transfer. The buying division can acquire the same item from outside for $45. The transfer price should be $45.

Something to think about: If the buying division can get the item at less than the selling division price, should the buying division be forced to buy inside (at the outside price, of course), or should it be permitted to buy outside? The answer depends on what would be best for overall corporate profitability.

Example 7.3

The selling division wants to charge $70 for one hundred assembled units. Current statistics for the selling division follow:

Units sold	10,000
Variable cost per unit	$50
Fixed cost	$100,000

Therefore, the selling division's fixed cost per unit is currently

$10 ($100,000/10,000)

Idle capacity (underutilization of facilities) exists. The buying division can buy the item outside for $55, so this should be the maximum transfer price. The buying division should buy from inside because it would be best for overall corporate profitability. Following is evidence.

Savings to selling division: (variable cost × units): $50 × 100	$5,000
Cost to buying division: (outside price × units): $55 × 100	$5,500
Disadvantage to company if buying division goes outside:	$500

Conclusion: There is no saving in fixed cost to the selling division if the buying division goes outside. Why? When idle capacity exists, fixed cost remains constant regardless of units produced.

How is divisional profit determined?

With an understanding transfer pricing, the divisional profit can be determined.

Example 7.4

XYZ Corporation has two production divisions (assembling and finishing), and one service division (maintenance). The assembling division assembles 800 units, 200 of which are sold to an outside concern for $40 each. The other 600 units are transferred to the finishing division, which in turn sells the units at $80 each. The negotiated market value is $35 each. The maintenance division earns revenue of $3,000 rendering services to the public. This division also renders repair services to the assembling division at a fair market value of $6,000, and to the finishing division at a fair market value of $8,000. The costs applicable to the divisions are

	Assembling	Finishing	Maintenance
Direct	$4,000	$5,000	$4,300
Indirect (allocated)	$6,000	$7,000	$5,000

Managerial accountants: You can now determine the profit of each division as shown in Figure 7.1. The total profit of XYZ Corporation equals the aggregate of its divisions, or $27,700 ($13,000 + $7,000 + $7,700), excluding nonallocated central costs. This is verified as follows:

Revenue to outside ($8,000 + $48,000 + $3,000)		$59,000
Less cost		
Direct ($4,000 + $5,000 + $4,300)	$13,300	
Indirect ($6,000 + $7,000 + $5,000)	18,000	
Total costs		(31,300)
Profit (before nonallocated costs)		$27,700

Note: Certain corporate costs are not allocated to any division. Examples of these include interest expense on corporate debt and the president's salary.

How does one measure return on investment (ROI)?

Return on investment equals net income divided by total assets.

This performance measure is superior to profit because it accounts not only for earnings, but also for the assets to get those earnings.

Example 7.5

Compare the following data for Divisions X and Y:

	Division X	Division Y
Net income	$ 100	$ 1,000
Assets	$1,000	$100,000
Return on investment	10%	1%

Division X is clearly the better division. Why? It earns a higher rate on assets employed.

Managerial accountants: In deriving ROI for a division, assign revenue, expenses, and assets (including direct

Figure 7.1

Assembling (A)		Finishing (F)		Maintenance (M)	
Revenue 200 × $40	$8,000	Revenue: 600 × $80	$48,000	Revenue	$3,000
Transfer price (F):				Transfer price (A)	6,000
600 × $35	21,000				
Total revenue	$29,000			Transfer price (F)	8,000
				Total revenue	$17,000
Costs		Costs		Costs	
Direct	$4,000	Direct	$5,000	Direct	$4,300
Indirect	6,000	Indirect	7,000	Indirect	5,000
Transfer price (M)	6,000	Transfer price (A)	21,000	Total costs	$ 9,300
Total costs	$16,000	Transfer price(M)	8,000	Profit	$ 7,700
Profit	$13,000	Total costs	$41,000		
		Profit	$ 7,000		

and indirect), for each division. Those belonging to the corporation are allocated to each division by some predetermined basis.

In using ROI, value total assets at replacement cost or CPI-adjusted value. Using book value or gross cost causes ROI to go up artificially over time because total assets (the denominator) decrease.

When is residual income used to evaluate divisional performance?

Another approach to measuring divisional performance is residual income (RI). RI is the operating income, which a division is able to earn above some minimum rate of return on its operating assets. RI, unlike ROI, is an absolute amount of income rather than a specific rate of return. When RI is used to evaluate divisional performance, the objective is to maximize the total amount of residual income, not to maximize the overall ROI figure. RI is regarded as a better measure of performance than ROI because it encourages investment in projects that would be rejected under ROI. A major disadvantage of RI, however, is that it cannot be used to compare divisions of different sizes. RI tends to favor the larger divisions due to the larger amount of dollars involved.

Why is economic value added (EVA) gaining popularity as a financial metric?

Residual income is more widely known as economic value added (EVA). Many firms are addressing the issue of aligning division managers' incentives with those of the firm by using EVA as a measure of performance. EVA encourages managers to focus on increasing the value of the company to shareholders because EVA is the value created by a company in excess of the cost of capital for the investment base. Improving EVA can be achieved in three ways:

1. Invest capital in high-performing projects.
2. Use less capital.
3. Increase profit without using more capital.

Here are a number of well-known companies that use EVA:

Bausch & Lomb	Georgia-Pacific	Toys "R" Us
Briggs & Stratton	Herman Miller	Tupperware
Coca-Cola	JC Penney	Whirlpool
Eli Lilly	Sprint	

Internal auditors: Consider the following advantages of residual income as a measure of divisional performance:

- It incorporates risk. The riskier the division, the higher the minimum required rate of return assigned to it.
- It uses different rates of return for different types of assets.
- It assigns different rates of return to different divisions, depending on risk.
- It is expressed in dollars rather than as a percent. This leads to goal consistency between the corporation and the division.

Warning: Because the assignment of risk is subjective, residual income will always have this basic limitation.

How should I weigh controllability?

When evaluating a divisional manager, look at the controllable profit for which he or she is responsible. *Warning:* Allocating uncontrollable costs to the manager breeds resentment.

7.2 CONTRIBUTION MARGIN ANALYSES

What is the contribution margin?

The contribution margin equals sales less variable costs. A detailed contribution margin income statement has the following components:

Sales

Less: Variable cost of sales
Manufacturing contribution margin

Less: Variable selling and administrative expenses
Contribution margin

Less: Fixed costs
Net income

Example 7.6

The selling price of an item is $6; unit sales total 520,000; beginning inventory is 40,000; ending inventory is 60,000; unit variable manufacturing cost is $4; variable selling cost per unit is $1.20; fixed manufacturing overhead totals $200,000; and selling and administrative expenses come to $80,000.

With this information, the units produced for the period can be calculated as follows:

Sales	520,000
Ending inventory	60,000
Merchandise needed	580,000
Less beginning inventory	(40,000)
Production	540,000

The contribution margin income statement would be as follows:

Sales (520,000 × $6)		$3,120,000
Less variable cost of sales		
Beginning inventory (40,000 × $4)	$ 160,000	
Variable cost of goods manufactured (540,000 × $4)	2,160,000	
Variable cost of goods available	2,320,000	
Less ending inventory (60,000 × $4)	(240.000)	
Total		(2,080,000)
Manufacturing contribution margin		$1,040,000
Less variable selling and administrative expenses (520,000 × $1.20)		(624,000)
Contribution margin		$ 416,000
Less fixed costs		
Overhead	200,000	
Selling and administrative	80,000	
Total		(280,000)
Net income		$ 136,000

Management executives: Use contribution margin analysis to appraise the performance of your manager and program. *Caution:* This approach is acceptable only for internal reporting!

When should I sell a product below normal selling price?

A company should accept an order at below-normal selling price when idle capacity exists (since fixed cost remains constant), as long as there is a contribution margin on that order.

Example 7.7

Ten thousand units are currently sold at $30 per unit. Variable cost per unit is $18, and fixed costs total $100,000. Therefore, the fixed cost per unit equals $10 ($100,000/10,000). Idle capacity exists. A prospective customer is willing to buy one hundred units at a selling price of only $20 per unit.

Ignoring market considerations (for example, unfavorable reaction by customers paying $30 per unit), you should recommend the sale of the additional one hundred units. Why? Because it results in a positive additional (marginal) profitability of $200, as indicated in the following example:

Sales (100 × $20)	$2,000
Less variable cost (100 × $18)	(1,800)
Contribution margin	200
Less fixed cost	0[a]
Net income	$ 200
Sales (100 × $20)	$2,000
Less variable cost (100 × $18)	(1,800)
Contribution margin	200
Less fixed cost	(50)
Net income	$ 150

Example 7.8

Financial data for T Corporation are given as follows:

	Per Unit
Selling price	$5.40
Direct material cost	1.50
Direct labor	1.70
Variable overhead	0.40
Fixed overhead ($100,000/40,000 units)	2.50

Selling and administrative expenses are fixed, except for sales commissions, which are 12 percent of the selling price. Idle capacity exists.

---

[a]Because of idle capacity, there is no additional fixed cost. If the order were to increase fixed cost by $50, say, because it required a special tool, it would still be financially advantageous to sell the item at $20. The additional profit would be $150, as illustrated in the next example.

An additional order has been received for six hundred units from a prospective customer at a selling price of $4.50. Accept the order; because fixed costs stay the same at idle capacity, a net profit results, as illustrated in this example:

Sales (600 × $4.50)	$2,700
Less variable manufacturing costs (600 × $3.60[a])	(2,160)
Manufacturing contribution margin	$ 540
Less variable selling and administrative expenses (12% × $2,700)	(324)
Contribution margin	216
Less fixed cost	(0)
Net income	$ 216

[a]Variable manufacturing cost equals variable manufacturing cost per unit times number of units produced.

Example 7.9

The marketing manager has decided that for Product A he wants a markup of 30 percent over cost. Particulars concerning a unit of Product A are as follows:

Direct material cost	$ 4,000
Direct labor	10,000
Overhead	2,500
Total cost	$16,500
Markup on cost (30 percent)	4,950
Selling price	$21,450

Total direct labor for the year equals $1,200,000. Total overhead for the year equals 25 percent of direct labor ($300,000), of which 40 percent is fixed and 60 percent is variable. The customer offers to buy a unit of Product A for $18,000. Idle capacity exists. Accept the extra order because it provides a marginal profit, as indicated in this example:

Selling price	$18,000
Less variable cost	
Direct material	$ 4,000
Direct labor	10,000

Variable overhead ($10,000 × 15%)[a]	1,500	(15,500)
Contribution margin		$2,500
Less fixed overhead		(0)
Net income		$2,500

Management executives: Employ contribution analysis to see the optimum way of utilizing capacity.

Example 7.10

A company produces a raw metal that can either be sold at this stage or processed further and sold as an alloy. Information on the raw metal and alloy follows:

	Raw Metal	Alloy
Selling price	$150	$230
Variable cost	$ 80	$110

Total fixed cost is $300,000; the raw metal, the alloy, or both can be manufactured; 800,000 hours of capacity are available; unlimited demand exists for both the raw metal and the alloy; two hours are required to make one ton of raw metal and three hours are needed to produce one ton of alloy.

The contribution margin per hour is computed as follows:

	Raw Metal	Alloy
Selling price	$150	$230
Less variable cost	(80)	(110)
Contribution margin	70	120
Hours per ton	2	3
Contribution margin per hour	$35	$40

Produce only the alloy; it results in a higher contribution margin per hour. Fixed costs do not enter into the calculation because they are constant regardless of whether the raw metal or the alloy is manufactured.

For managerial accountants: Use contribution-margin analysis to determine the bid price on a contract.

[a]Variable overhead equals 15 percent of direct labor, calculated as follows:

$$\frac{\text{Variable overhead}}{\text{Direct labor}} = \frac{60 \times \$300,000}{\$1,200,000}$$

$$= \frac{\$180,000}{\$1,200,000} = 15\% \text{ of direct labor}$$

Example 7.11

Travis Company has received an order for six thousand units. The management executive wants to know the minimum bid price that would produce a $14,000 increase in profit. The current income statement follows:

Income Statement

Sales (30,000 units × $20)		$600,000
Less cost of sales		
Direct material	$60,000	
Direct labor	150,000	
Variable overhead ($150,000 × 40%)	60,000	
Fixed overhead	80,000	(350,000)
Gross margin		$250,000
Less selling and administrative expenses		
Variable (includes transportation costs of $0.20 per unit)	15,000	
Fixed	85,000	(100,000)
Net income		$150,000

If the contract is taken, the cost patterns for the extra order will remain the same, with these exceptions:

- Transportation costs will be paid by the customer.
- Special tools costing $6,000 will be required for just this order and will not be reusable.
- Direct labor time for each unit under the order will be 10 percent longer.

What to do: Derive the bid price in this manner:

Current Cost Per Unit

Selling price	$20	($600,000/30,000)
Direct material	2	($60,000/30,000)
Direct labor	5	($150,000/30,000)
Variable overhead	40%	of direct labor cost ($60,000/$150,000)
Variable selling and administrative expense	$0.50	($15,000/30,000)

See Figure 7.2.

Figure 7.2 Income Statement

	Income Statement		
Units	30,000	36,000	
	Current	Projected[d]	Computed last
Sales	$600,000	$680,000[d]	
Cost of sales			
Direct material	$ 60,000	$ 72,000	($2 × 36,000)
Direct labor	150,000	183,000	($150,000 + [6,000 × $5.50[a]])
Variable overhead	60,000	73,200	($183,000 × 40%)
Fixed overhead	80,000	86,000	($80,000 + $6,000)
Total	$350,000	$414,200	
Variable selling and administrative costs	$ 15,000	$ 16,800	($15,000 + [6,000 × $.30])
Fixed selling and administrative costs	85,000	85,000	
Total	$150,000	$101,800	
Net income	$150,000	$164,000[c]	

[a] $5 × 1.10 = $5.50   [b] $0.50 − $0.20 = $0.30   [c] $150,000 + $14,000 = $164,000

[d] Net income + selling and administrative expenses + cost of sales = sales

$164,000 + $101,800 + $414,200 = $680,000

The contract price for the six thousand units should be $80,000 ($680,000 − $600,000), or $13.33 per unit ($80,000/6,000).

The contract price per unit of $13.33 is less than the $20 current selling price per unit. Remember, by accepting the order, total fixed cost will remain the same, except for the $6,000 cost of special tools.

Management executives: The contribution-margin income statement approach can be used to evaluate the performance of department managers as well as their divisions.

Example 7.12

Let's assume a three-division company. Relevant data are displayed in Figure 7.3. It can be concluded from Figure 7.3 that Division X shows the highest profit.

7.3 PRICING TOOLS

What pricing method should I use?

Product pricing is a matter of concern to management executives, accountants, and marketing managers. Use either of the following two methodologies:

- Absorption costing approach. Here, pricing equals total cost plus profit markup. This approach covers all costs and should be employed when pricing new products and current business.

- Contribution margin approach. When a new order comes in and the prospective customer will buy only at a lower price, use the contribution margin approach, particularly when idle capacity exists. Here, the price is set at the variable cost plus profit markup. Remember, at idle capacity, fixed cost is constant. The order should only be accepted when selling price is greater than variable cost.

How do I analyze pricing policies if I am a managerial accountant?

Analyze the impact that economies of scale have on the costs and required production time. Evaluate the degree to which increased worker experience (that is, the learning curve) will lower the per-unit cost with increased production.

Figure 7.3

| | Total | Divisions | | |
		X	Y	Z
Sales	$500,000	$300,000	$150,000	$50,000
Less variable manufacturing costs[a]	(200,000)	(100,000)	(70,000)	(30,000)
Manufacturing contribution margin	$300,000	$200,000	$ 80,000	$20,000
Less variable selling and administrative expenses[b]	60,000	(25,000)	(30,000)	(5,000)
Contribution margin	$240,000	$175,000	$ 50,000	$15,000
Less controllable fixed costs[c]	(40,000)	(20,000)	(18,000)	(2,000)
Short-run performance margin[d]	$200,000	$155,000	$ 32,000	$13,000
Less uncontrollable fixed costs[e]	(60,000)	(50,000)	(9,000)	(1,000)
Segment margin[f]	$140,000	$105,000	$ 23,000	$12,000
Joint fixed costs[g]	(60,000)			
Net income	$110,000			

[a]Variable manufacturing costs equal direct material, direct labor, and variable overhead. The variable manufacturing costs are derived by multiplying the variable manufacturing cost per unit by the number of units produced.

[b]Variable selling and administrative costs equal variable selling and administrative cost per unit times number of units sold.

[c]Controllable fixed costs are controllable by the division manager, if, for instance, he or she is responsible for advertising.

[d]Short-run performance margin equals the profitability figure used to evaluate the division manager's performance.

[e]Uncontrollable fixed costs equal costs for which the division manager has no responsibility, such as property taxes and insurance.

[f]Segment margin is the profitability figure used to evaluate divisional performance. This is the last earnings figure shown for each division. The segment margin of all divisions is equal to the total segment margin of the company.

[g]Joint fixed costs are not allocated to divisions because it is not rational to do so since joint costs do not apply to divisions. These might include professional fees, president's salary, and interest expense on corporate debt.

Determine different prices based on the segment involved, whether manufacturer, wholesaler, retailer, or consumer. The price to each segment will differ depending on the applicable marketing costs, such as advertising and distribution.

What price methods should I use if I am a marketing manager?

When you establish a price, take the following factors into account:

- Return on sales
- Share of market
- Age categorization
- Economic breakdown
- Regional location
- Social aspects
- Ethnic wants

Also, consider the customer's perception of prestige— higher pricing may suggest a "quality" image to the consumer.

To attract further business for other products or service contracts, contribution margin pricing is preferable full costing. However, do not use this approach if selling at a lower price might bring a negative reaction from existing customers.

Caution: When increasing the price, do so only to the point that it does not cause a disproportionate decrease in volume. For instance, a 14 percent price increase may result in a 20 percent reduction in volume, thereby effecting overall lower earnings.

Set target rates of return for products that depend on risk, stage in the life cycle, and whether the initial sale generates subsequent business for other products or services. Ask to what extent the product line is affected by the learning curve (see Section 8.4).

7.4 EVALUATING THE PRODUCT LINES

What factors do I consider when evaluating a product line?

Management executives: Appraise introduction of a new product according to its synergistic effects— that is, how the new product fits into the whole product line.

Financial managers: Decide whether to discontinue products that show losses. In making a decision, consider the following factors:

- Eliminating a product would reduce volume and sales commissions but would necessitate higher base salaries for salespeople.

- Fixed costs must still be recovered.

Consider keeping products that show a net loss based on full costing but show a contribution margin.

Inventory stockouts should be recorded along with lost sales. Back-order costs should likewise be determined (see also Section 8.5).

Suggestion: Finance risky product lines with less risky funding, thereby reducing overall business risk. For example, a fad item should be financed with equity.

Marketing managers: Appraise the riskiness of product lines by computing the probability distribution in price, volume, and cost for products.

How should I prepare marketing analysis reports?

To make reports clear, you should express them not only in dollars but in percentages, ratios, and graphs. Also provide reasons for any problems, along with appropriate recommendations.

7.5 HOW TO MEASURE MARKETING EFFECTIVENESS

How do I measure marketing effectiveness?

Here's what can be done within each job function:

- *Management executives:* Examine product warranty complaints and their disposition.

- *Managerial accountants:* Determine revenue, cost, and earnings by product line, customer, industry segment, geographic area, distribution channel, type of marketing effort, and average order size.

- *Financial managers:* Prepare new product evaluations in terms of risk and profitability.

- *Marketing managers:* Appraise strengths and weaknesses of the competition, as well as promotional effectiveness. Evaluate revenue, marketing costs, and profits before, during, and after promotion efforts. Also, know the competitor's reaction. Identify advertising costs by media, including newspaper, journal, direct mail, television, and radio.

How do I measure the effectiveness of the sales force?

Guide for managerial accountants: Gauge sales force effectiveness by looking at income generated by salespeople, call frequency, sales incentives, sales personnel costs (for instance, salary, auto, hotel), and dollar value of orders obtained per hour spent.

Financial managers: To gauge performance of marketing employees, compute the following ratios:

- Revenue and/or net income per employee
- Marketing costs to sales

Doing so will determine a proper selling price, identify poor marketing activities, and establish a proper discount.

For marketing managers: In determining salesperson profitability, subtract variable product costs and selling expenses from sales. Also, determine the profitability by type of sales solicitation (phone, mail, or personal visit). Find out the break-even point for each salesperson.

Establish an optimal commission plan for salespeople by incorporating the following strategies:

- Give a higher commission for original business than for repeat business.
- Vary commission rates depending on the territory and type of product being sold (for example, a slow-moving item could have a higher commission).
- Base the commission on the product's profitability rather than on the selling price.
- Use a graduated commission rate on product sales that exceed the established quota.

Suggestion: Do not evaluate sales performance on actual sales generated but on profitability.

What financial measures should I use to evaluate success?

Financial measures of marketing success include

- Market share
- Sales
- Trend in inventory at wholesalers and retailers
- Profit margin

Management executives: Look at marketing costs in terms of physical distribution, including inventory management, order processing, packaging, warehousing, shipping vehicle, and customer services.

Financial managers: Evaluate marketing costs according to the means of distribution, whether retailer, direct mail, or wholesaler. Examine the trend in the percentage of marketing cost to revenue as a basis for ascertaining the selling price.

7.6 BUDGETING TECHNIQUES

What is a budget?

A budget is a plan that quantifies the company's goals in terms of specific financial and operating objectives. Follow these steps in the budgeting process:

- Establish goals.
- Develop strategies.
- Formulate plans of action.
- Evaluate the market.
- Look at economic and political conditions.
- Analyze competition.
- Identify the life cycle of the product.
- Appraise the company's financial strength.
- Take corrective action.

How do I formulate a budget?

Budgets may cover a long- or short-term period. The first step in budgeting is to estimate future sales; then, production costs are based upon these estimates.

A flexible budget employs budgeted figures at different capacity levels. Choose the best expected (normal) capacity level (100 percent) and assign pessimistic (80 percent), optimistic (110 percent), and full (150 percent) capacity levels.

Management executives: Formulating a budget shows how the company's performance is at varying capacity levels. Fixed costs remain constant as long as the firm operates below full capacity.

What types of budgets must I prepare?

Many types of budgets should be prepared, including production, cash, sales, costs, profit, purchases, and forecasted financial statements.

Production budgets. This type of budget tells how many units will be produced, and their cost, for a given period. This budget will help financial managers to find out cash needs. *Managerial accountants:* This budget is necessary for proper planning.

Example 7.13

A company has a sales budget of 30,000 finished units. Beginning inventory is 6,000 units, and the expected ending inventory is 18,000 units. The cost per unit is $8. Budgeted production cost is estimated as follows:

Budgeted sales	30,000
Desired ending inventory	18,000
Need	48,000
Beginning inventory	(6,000)
Budgeted production	42,000
Budget cost of production (42,000 × $8)	$336,000

Assume three pieces of raw material are needed to produce one unit. There are 65,000 pieces on hand at the beginning of the period. Desired ending inventory is 80,000 pieces. Budgeted purchases of needed pieces are as follows:

Needed for production (42,000 × 3)	126,000
Desired ending inventory	80,000
Need	206,000
Beginning inventory	(65,000)
Budgeted purchases	141,000

If each piece costs $1.50, the budgeted cost of purchases is $211,500 (141,000 × $1.50).

Cash budgets. In preparing a cash budget, start with beginning cash, add cash receipts, and subtract cash payments to arrive at ending cash. Cash receipts include anything that yields cash, like borrowing money or selling assets. *Caution:* Cash receipts are not necessarily the same as revenue (for example, credit sales). Cash payments consist of cash disbursements, like buying assets or paying off debt. Not all expenses are cash payments (for example, depreciation).

Of special note: In many cases, cash collections will have to be predicted when a cash discount is given for early collection.

Example 7.14

A company sells on terms of 3%/10 days, net/30 days. The following collection pattern has been observed:

- 60 percent of credit sales are collected within the discount period.
- 30 percent are collected at the end of thirty days.

- The balance is collected at the end of sixty days.
- At the end of any month, 25 percent of sales on which cash discounts will be taken are still uncollected.

Estimated sales are

	Oct.	Nov.	Dec.
Cash sales	$ 50,000	$40,000	$ 80,000
Credit sales	$100,000	$90,000	$120,000

September credit sales are $110,000 and August credit sales are $85,000.

Figure 7.4 is a table of collections on sales.

Internal auditors: To appraise performance of managers and programs, make a comparison between budgeted and actual revenue, cost, and time.

Zero-Base Budgeting (ZBB). With ZBB, each year's expected expenditure must be justified. Existing and new programs must have value and contribute to overall objectives of the firm. Each project is reexamined at the beginning of the period. When a project does not meet established criteria, it is dropped.

STEPS FOR FINANCIAL MANAGERS IN USING ZBB

- Appraise the activity of a division, department, or operation.
- Analyze each activity from a cost-benefit perspective.
- Formulate a decision package that accomplishes the specified goal.
- Rank the decision packages in order of priority.
- Assign limited funds to competing activities on the basis of merit.

What should the decision package include?

The decision package describes the activity to be performed and consists of various ways (in time and money) to meet the objective. The manager indicates a recommended path as well as alternative possibilities. Then upper management decides which path to fund, assuming it wishes to accept the activity.

A decision package may be rejected, accepted at a minimal funding level, accepted at the minimal funding level plus an increment, or approved at the requested funding level.

Figure 7.4

Month	Collections on Current Month's Sales		Collections from Previous Month's Sales		Collections from Credit Sales Made Two Months Ago[d]	Total
	Cash	*Credit[a]*	*Discount[b]*	*No Discount[c]*		*Total*
October	$50,000	$43,650	$16,005	$33,000	$ 8,500	$151,155
November	40,000	39,285	14,550	30,000	11,000	134,835
December	80,000	52,380	13,095	27,000	10,000	182,475

[a] $0.6 \times 0.97 \times 0.75 \times$ current sales

[b] $0.6 \times 0.97 \times 0.25 \times$ credit sales from previous month

[c] $0.3 \times$ credit sales from previous month

[d] $0.1 \times$ credit sales from two months earlier

7.7 HIGHLIGHTING PROBLEM AREAS WITH VARIANCE ANALYSIS

What is a variance analysis?

Variance analysis is a comparison between standard and actual performance. Variance analysis is useful to managerial accountants, financial managers, production managers, and those in marketing.

Use variance analysis to

- Control costs.
- "Red flag" present and prospective problems (thus following the "management by exception" principle).
- Identify responsibility; know whom to "call on the carpet."
- Formulate corporate objectives.
- Aid in decision making.
- Provide a vehicle for better communication within the organization.

Prepare performance reports that focus on the difference between budgeted and actual figures. Look at the following items:

- Production (cost, quantity, and quality), to gauge the foremen's performance
- Sales and market share, to evaluate marketing managers
- Profit, to appraise overall operations
- Return on investment, to evaluate asset utilization

How do marketing managers compute sales variances?

Example 7.15

Budgeted sales for 20X1

Product A: 8,000 units at $5.50 per unit	$ 44,000
Product B: 24,000 units at $7.50 per unit	180,000
Expected sales revenue	$224,000

Actual sales for the year

Product A: 6,000 units at $6.00 per unit	$ 36,000
Product B: 28,000 units at $7.00 per unit	196,000
Actual sales revenue	$232,000

A positive sales variance of $8,000 is composed of sales price and volume variances. The sales-price variance equals actual selling price versus (minus) budgeted selling price times actual units sold.

Product A ($6.00 vs. $5.50 × 6,000)	$ 3,000 F[a]
Product B ($7.00 vs. $7.50 × 28,000)	14,000 U[b]
Sales price variance	$11,000 U

[a]Favorable.
[b]Unfavorable.

The sales-volume variance equals actual quantity versus budgeted quantity times budgeted selling price.

Product A (6,000 vs. 8,000 × $5.50)	$11,000 U
Product B (28,000 vs. 24,000 × $7.50)	30,000 F
Sales volume variance	$19,000 F

Proof

Sales price variance	$11,000 U
Sales volume variance	19,000 F
Sales variance	$ 8,000 F

How do I apply standards and cost variances?

When actual cost exceeds standard cost, variance is unfavorable. Be sure to determine the reason behind the variance in order to facilitate appropriate corrective action.

Set standards according to their application as follows:

Job Function	Situation	Standard
Financial managers	Cost reduction	Stringent
Managerial accountants	Inventory valuation	Fair
Marketing managers	Pricing decision	Realistic
Buyers	Expensive purchases	Perfection

When should I do a variance analysis?

Standard prices (material price, wage rate) are determined at the beginning of the period.

Variance analysis can be performed by year, quarter, month, day, or hour, depending on the importance of identifying a problem quickly.

Managerial accountants: Because the number of units produced or services rendered are unknown until the end of the period, such variances cannot be arrived at until then.

How do I interpret a variance analysis?

Immaterial variance percentages (that is, variance divided by standard cost) not exceeding 5 percent need not be investigated further unless they occur consistently and show a potential problem.

Managerial accountants: When a product is made or a service is rendered, compute the following three measures:

- Actual cost equals actual price times actual quantity, where actual quantity equals actual quantity per unit of work times actual units of work produced.

- Standard cost equals standard price times standard quantity, where standard quantity equals standard quantity per unit of work times actual units of work produced.

- Control variance equals actual cost minus standard cost.

Control variance consists of the following components:

- Price (rate, cost) variance (standard price versus actual price times actual quantity)
- Quantity (usage, efficiency) variance (standard quantity versus actual quantity times standard price)

Compute these for both material and labor.

Material variances. *Managerial accountants:* The material price variance allows for the appraisal of the purchasing department function and examination of the effect of raw material cost changes on overall corporate earnings. The material quantity variance is the responsibility of the production supervisor.

Example 7.16

The standard cost of one unit of output (product or service) was $15: three pieces at $5 per piece. During the period, 8,000 units were produced. Actual cost was $14 per unit: two pieces at $7 per piece.

Material control variance

Standard quantity times standard price (24,000 × $5)	$120,000
Actual quantity times actual price (16,000 × $7)	112,000
	$ 8,000 F

Material price variance

Standard price versus actual price times actual quantity ($5 vs. $7 × 16,000)	$32,000 U

Material quantity variance

Standard quantity versus actual quantity times standard price (24,000 vs. 16,000 × $5)	$40,000 F

Management executives: Material price variances cannot be controlled when higher prices arise from inflation or shortage situations, or when rush orders are required by the customer who will bear the ultimate cost increase.

Look for possible causes of unfavorable material variances.

**Checklist of Unfavorable
Material Variance**

Cause	*Responsible Entity*
Unnecessarily high prices paid	Purchasing
Purchased material differed from specifications	Purchasing
Inspection did not reveal defective goods	Receiving
Workers' incompetency	Foremen
Poor supervision	Foremen
Deficient mix in material	Production manager
Immediate delivery of materials by plane	Traffic
Unfavorable quantity variance	Foremen
Forced acquisitions	Purchasing
Unanticipated change in production volume	Sales manager

Solutions for management executives: After examining the nature and degree of the material price variance, it may be necessary to

- Increase prices
- Substitute cheaper materials
- Change a production method or specification
- Implement a cost-reduction plan

Labor variances. The standard labor rate should be based on the contracted hourly wage rate. Where wage rates are set by union contract, the labor rate variance will typically be minimal. Labor efficiency standards are normally established by engineers on the basis of an analysis of the manufacturing operation. Labor variance is determined exactly as material variance is determined.

Example 7.17

The standard cost for labor is four hours times $9 per hour, or $36 per unit. During the period, 7,000 units were manufactured. The actual cost is six hours times $8 per hour, or $48 per unit.

Labor-control variance

Standard quantity times standard price (28,000 × $9)	$252,000
Actual quantity times actual price (42,000 × $8)	336,000
	$ 84,000 U

Labor-price variance

Standard price versus actual price times actual quantity ($9 vs. $8 × 42,000)	$ 42,000 F

Labor-quantity variance

Standard quantity versus actual quantity × standard price (28,000 vs. 42,000)	$126,000 U

Internal auditors: Examine reasons for an unfavorable labor-price variance. Some examples are:

Cause	Responsible entity
Use of overqualified or an excessive number of workers	Production manager or union contract
Improper work assignments from poor job descriptions	Personnel
Overtime	Production planning

Note: An unfavorable labor-price variance may be unavoidable when experienced workers are in short supply.

Determine reasons for an unfavorable labor-efficiency variance, including

Cause	Responsible entity
Improper supervision	Factory foremen
Deficient machinery	Maintenance
Poor-quality material	Purchasing
Inadequate material supply	Purchasing

Overhead variances. The overhead variance consists of the controllable and volume variances. The necessary computations are

- Overhead control variance equals actual overhead versus standard overhead (standard hours times standard overhead rate).

- Controllable variance equals actual overhead versus budget adjusted to standard hours. *Note:* Budget adjusted to standard hours equals fixed overhead plus variable overhead (standard hours times standard variable overhead rate).

- Volume variance equals standard overhead versus budget adjusted to standard hours.

Example 7.18

The following information is provided by Company M:

Budgeted overhead (includes fixed overhead of $7,500 and variable overhead of $10,000)	$17,500
Budgeted hours	10,000
Actual overhead	$ 8,000

Actual units produced	800
Standard hours per unit of production	5

Preliminary calculations

Budgeted fixed overhead ($7,500/10,000 hr)	$0.75
Budgeted variable overhead ($10,000/10,000 hr)	1.00
Total budgeted overhead ($17,500/10,000 hr)	$1.75
Standard hours (800 units × 5 hr per unit)	4,000

Overhead control variance

Actual overhead		$ 8,000
Standard overhead		
Standard hours	4,000 hr	
Standard overhead rate	$1.75	(7,000)
		$ 1,000 U

Controllable variance

Actual overhead		$ 8,000
Budget adjusted to standard hours		
Fixed overhead	$7,500	
Variable overhead (standard hours × standard variable overhead rate − 4,000 × $1)	4,000	11,500
		3,500 F

Volume variance

Standard overhead	$ 7,000
Budget adjusted to standard hours	11,500
	$ 4,500 U

Factory foremen are responsible for the controllable variance and thus influence actual overhead incurred. The volume variance looks at plant utilization and thus is controllable by management executives and production managers.

Management executives: Variable-overhead variance data are useful in formulating output level and output mix decisions. They also help in appraising decisions regarding variable inputs. *Warning:* Fixed-overhead variance data do not generate useful information for operating decisions, but they do furnish information regarding decision-making astuteness when buying some combination of fixed plant size and variable production inputs.

A consistently unfavorable overhead volume variance may arise from purchasing the wrong size plant, deficient scheduling, insufficient orders, material shortages, equipment failure, long operating time, or poorly trained employees. Idle capacity may indicate long-run operating planning problems.

Raw material costs. Examine the variability in raw material costs. *Managerial accountants:* Look at price instability as discussed in trade publications. *Hint to management executives:* Emphasize vertical integration to reduce the price and supply risk of raw materials.

Variances for selling expenses. Cost variances for the selling function may pertain to the territory, product, or personnel. *Marketing managers:* Evaluate your sales force within a territory, including time spent and expenses incurred.

Example 7.19

Company O provided the following sales data:

Standard cost	$240,000
Standard salesperson days	2,000
Standard rate per salesperson day	$ 120
Actual cost	$238,000
Actual salesperson days	1,700
Actual rate per salesperson day	$ 140

Total cost variance

Actual cost	$238,000
Standard cost	240,000
	$ 2,000 F

Categorize the total favorable variance of $2,000 into salesperson days and salesperson costs.

Variance in salesperson days

Actual days versus standard days times standard rate per day (1,700 vs. 2,000 × $120)	$36,000 F

Because fewer days than expected were required to handle the sales territory, the variance is favorable.

Variance in salesperson costs

Actual rate versus standard rate times
actual days ($140 vs. $120 × 1,700) $34,000 U

Because the actual rate per day exceeded the standard rate per day, the variance is unfavorable.

7.8 ACTIVITY-BASED COSTING (ABC)

What is wrong with traditional cost systems?

Many companies use a traditional cost system, such as job-order costing or process costing, or some hybrid of the two. This traditional system may provide distorted product-cost information. In fact, companies selling multiple products are making critical decisions about product pricing, making bids, or product mix based on inaccurate cost data. In all likelihood, the problem is not with assigning the costs of direct labor or direct materials. These prime costs are traceable to individual products, and most conventional cost systems are designed to ensure that this tracing takes place.

However, the assignment of overhead costs to individual products is another matter. Using the traditional methods of assigning overhead costs to products, using a single predetermined overhead rate based on any single activity measure can produce distorted product costs. Activity-based costing (ABC) attempts to get around this problem. An ABC system assigns costs to products based on the product's use of activities, not product volume. This system has been proven to produce more accurate product costing results in an environment where there is diversity in product line and services coming out of the same shop. A recent survey by the Institute of Management Accounting shows that more than 30 percent of the companies that responded are using ABC systems to replace their existing traditional cost systems.

Overhead costing: A single-product situation. The accuracy of overhead cost assignment becomes an issue only when multiple products are manufactured in a single facility. If only a single product is produced, all overhead costs are caused by that product, and traceable to it. The overhead cost per unit is simply the total overhead for the year divided by the number of hours or units produced.

The cost calculation for a single-product setting is illustrated in Table 7.1. There is no question that the cost of manufacturing the product illustrated in Table 7.1 is $ 28.00 per unit. All manufacturing costs were incurred specifically to make this product. Thus, one way to ensure product-costing accuracy is to focus on producing one product. For this reason, some multiple-product firms choose to dedicate entire plants to the manufacture of a single product.

By focusing on only one or two products, small manufacturers are able to calculate the cost of manufacturing high-volume products more accurately, and to price them more effectively.

Table 7.1 Unit Cost Computation: Single Product

	Manufacturing Costs	Produced Units	Unit Cost
Direct materials	$800,000	50,000	$16.00
Direct labor	200,000	50,000	4.00
Factory overhead	400,000	50,000	8.00
Total	$1,400,000	50,000	$28.00

Overhead costing: A multiple-product situation. In a multiple-product or multi-job situation, manufacturing overhead costs are caused jointly by all products. The problem is one of trying to identify the amount of overhead caused or consumed by each. This is accomplished by searching for cost drivers, or activity measures that cause costs to be incurred.

In a traditional setting, it is normally assumed that overhead consumption is highly correlated with the volume of production activity, measured in terms of direct labor hours, machine hours, or direct labor dollars. These volume-related cost drivers are used to assign overhead to products to develop plant-wide or departmental rates.

Example 7.20

To illustrate the limitation of this traditional approach, and of ABC, assume that Global Metals, Inc., has established the following overhead cost pools and cost drivers for their product:

Overhead Cost Pool	Budgeted Overhead Cost	Cost Driver	Predicted Level for Cost Driver	Predetermined Overhead Rate
Machine setups	$100,000	Number of setups	100	$1,000 per setup
Material handling	100,000	Weight of raw material	50,000 pounds	$2.00 per pound

Overhead Cost Pool	Budgeted Overhead Cost	Cost Driver	Predicted Level for Cost Driver	Predetermined Overhead Rate
Waste control	50,000	Weight of hazardous chemical used	10,000 pounds	$5.00 per pound
Inspection	75,000	Number of inspections	1,000	$75 per inspection
Other overhead costs	$200,000	Machine hours	20,000	$10 per machine hour
	$525,000			

Job No. 107 consists of 2,000 special-purpose machine tools with the following requirements:

Machine set-ups	2 setups
Raw material required	10,000 pounds
Waste material required	2,000 pounds
Inspections	10 inspections
Machine hours	500 machine hours

The overhead assigned to Job No. 107 is computed as:

Overhead Cost Pool	Predetermined Overhead Rate	Level of Cost Driver	Assigned Overhead Cost
Machine setups	$1,000 per setup	2 setups	$2,000
Material handling	$2.00 per pound	10,000 pounds	20,000
Waste control	$5.00 per pound	2,000 pounds	10,000
Inspection	$75 per inspection	10 inspections	750
Other overhead cost	$10 per machine hour	500 machine hours	5,000
Total			$37,750

The total overhead cost assigned to Job No. 107 is $37,750, or $18.88 per tool ($37,750/2,000).

Compare this with the overhead cost that is assigned to the job if the firm uses a single predetermined overhead rate based on machine hours:

Total budgeted overhead cost / Total predicted machine hours

= $525,000/20,000

= $26.25 per machine hour

Under this approach, the total overhead cost assigned to Job No. 107 is $13,125 ($26.25 per machine hour × 500 machine hours). This is only $6.56 per tool ($13,125/2,000), which is about one-third of the overhead cost per tool computed when multiple cost drivers are used.

To summarize,

	ABC	*Traditional*
Total factory overhead assigned	$37,750	$13,125
Per tool	$18.88	$6.56

The reason for this wide discrepancy is that these special-purpose tools require a relatively large number of machine setups, a sizable amount of waste materials, and several inspections. Thus, they are relatively costly in terms of driving overhead costs. Use of a single predetermined overhead rate obscures that fact.

Inaccurately calculating the overhead cost per unit to the extent illustrated above can have serious adverse consequences for the firm. For example, it can lead to poor decisions about pricing, product mix, or contract bidding.

Cost accountants: The cost accountant needs to weigh carefully such considerations in designing a product-costing system. A costing system using multiple cost drivers is more costly to implement and use, but it may save millions through improved decisions.

Remember: An ABC approach is expensive to implement and keep. Companies considering ABC should perform a cost-benefit test. The benefits are most significant when a company has

1. different products or services that make different demands on resources.

2. stiff competition, where knowledge of costs and cost control is critical.

ABC forces management to think in terms of simplifying operations (activities). Once activities that are consumed by a product are identified, the process can be evaluated with a view to cutting costs.

Checklist for Cost Drivers

Manufacturing:

Machine hour	Miles driven
Direct labor hour or dollars	Computer time
Number of setups	Square footage
Weight of materials handled	Number of vendors
Number of units reworked	Asset value
Number of orders placed	Number of labor transactions
Number of orders received	Number of units scrapped
Number of inspections	Number of parts
Number of material handling operations	Replacement cost
Number of orders shipped	Design time
Hours of testing time	

Nonmanufacturing

Number of hospital beds occupied
Number of surgeries
Number of take-offs and landings for an airline
Flight hours
Number of rooms occupied in a hotel

Selling

Number of sales calls
Number of orders obtained
Volume of sales

Warehousing

Number of items stored
Volume of items stored

Credit and collection

Number of customer orders
Dollar amount of customer orders on account

7.9 LIFE-CYCLE COSTS AND TARGET COSTING

What is life-cycle costing?

Life-cycle costing tracks and accumulates all product costs in the value chain from research and development and design of products and processes through production, marketing, distribution, and customer service. The value chain is the set of activities required to design, develop, produce, market, and service a product (or service). The terms "cradle-to-grave costing" and "womb-to-tomb costing" convey the sense of fully capturing all costs associated with the product.

Life-cycle costing focuses on minimizing locked-in costs—for example, by reducing the number of parts, promoting standardization of parts, and using equipment that can make more than one kind of product. Product life cycle is simply the time a product exists—from conception to abandonment. Life-cycle costs are all costs associated with the product for its entire life cycle. These costs include development (planning, design, and testing), manufacturing (conversion activities), and logistics support (advertising, distribution, warranty, and so on).

Can you achieve cost reduction through life-cycle costing?

Because total customer satisfaction has become a vital issue in the new business setting, whole-life cost has emerged as the central focus of life-cycle cost management. Whole-life cost is the life-cycle cost of a product, plus after-purchase (or post-purchase) costs that consumers incur, including operation, support, maintenance, and disposal. Since the costs a purchaser incurs after buying a product can be a significant percentage of whole-life costs and, thus, an important consideration in the purchase decision, managing activities so that whole-life costs are reduced can provide an important competitive advantage. *Note:* Cost reduction, not cost control, is the emphasis. Moreover, cost reduction is achieved by judicious analysis and management of activities.

Studies show that 90 percent or more of a product's costs are committed during the development stage. Thus, it makes sense to emphasize management of activities during this phase of a product's existence. Every dollar spent on premanufacturing activities is known to save eight to ten dollars on manufacturing and post-manufacturing activities. The real opportunities for cost reduction occur before manufacturing begins. Managers need to invest more in premanufacturing assets and dedicate more resources to activities in the early phases of the product life cycle so that overall whole-life costs can be reduced.

What is the role of target costing?
How does it differ from cost-plus pricing?

Life-cycle and whole-life cost concepts are associated with target costing and target pricing. A firm may determine that market conditions require that a product sell at a given target price. Hence, target cost can be determined by subtracting the desired unit profit margin from the target price. The cost reduction objectives of life-cycle and whole-life cost management can therefore be determined using target costing.

Thus, target costing becomes a particularly useful tool for establishing cost-reduction goals. Toyota, for example, calculates the lifetime target profit for a new car model by multiplying a target profit ratio times the target sales. The estimated profit is then calculated by subtracting the estimated costs from target sales. Usually at this point, target profit is greater than estimated profit. The cost reduction goal is defined by the difference between the target profit and the estimated profit. Toyota then searches for cost-reduction opportunities through better design of the new model. Toyota's management recognizes that more opportunities exist for cost reduction during product planning than in actual development and production.

The Japanese developed target costing to enhance their ability to compete in the global marketplace. This approach to product pricing differs significantly from the cost-based methods just described. Instead of first determining the cost of a product or service and then adding a profit factor to arrive at its price, target costing reverses the procedure. Target costing is a pricing method that involves (1) identifying the price at which a product will be competitive in the marketplace, (2) defining the desired profit to be made on the product, and (3) computing the target cost for the product by subtracting the desired profit from the competitive market price. The formula is

Target Price − Desired Profit = Target Cost

Target cost is then communicated to the engineers and product designers, who use it as the maximum cost to be incurred for the materials and other resources needed to design and manufacture the product. It is their responsibility to create the product at or below its target cost.

Figure 7.5 compares the cost-plus philosophy with the target-costing philosophy.

Figure 7.5 Cost-Plus Pricing versus Target Costing

	Formula	*Implications*
Cost-plus pricing	Cost base + markup = selling price	• Cost is the base (given) • Markup is added (given) • The firm puts the product on the market and hopes the selling price is accepted
Pricing based on target costing	Target selling price − Desired profit = Target cost	• Markets determine prices (given) • Desired profit must be sustained for survival (given) • Target cost is the residual, the variable to be managed

Example 7.21

A salesperson at Milmool Products Company has reported that a customer is seeking price quotations for two electronic components: a special-purpose battery charger (Product X101) and a small, transistorized machine computer (Product Y101). Competing for the customer's order are one French company and two Japanese companies. The current market price ranges for the two products are as follows:

Product X101	$310–$370 per unit
Product Y101	$720–$820 per unit

The salesperson feels that if Milmool could quote prices of $325 for Product X101 and $700 for Product Y101, the company would get the order and gain a significant share of the global market for those goods. Milmool's usual profit markup is 25 percent of total unit cost.

The company's design engineers and cost accountants put together the following specifications and costs for the new products:

Activity-based cost rates:

Materials handling activity	$1.30 per dollar of raw materials and purchased parts cost
Production activity	$3.50 per machine hour
Product delivery activity	$24.00 per unit of X101; $30.00 per unit of Y101

	Product X101	Product Y101
Projected unit demand	26,000	18,000
Per unit data:		
Raw materials cost	$30.00	$65.00
Purchased parts cost	$15.00	$45.00
Manufacturing labor		
Hours	2.6	4.8
Hourly labor rate	$12.00	$15.00
Assembly labor		
Hours	3.4	8.2
Hourly labor rate	$14.00	$16.00
Machine hours	12.8	28.4

The company wants to address the following three questions:

1. What is the target cost for each product?
2. What is the projected total unit cost of production and delivery?
3. Using the target costing approach, should the company produce the products?

1. Target cost for each product

Product X101 = $325.00 ÷ 1.25 = $260.00*
Product Y101 = $700.00 ÷ 1.25 = $560.00

*Target Price − Desired Profit = Target Cost

$$325.00 - .25X = X$$
$$325.00 = 1.25X$$
$$X = \frac{\$325.000}{1.25} = \$260.00$$

2. Projected total unit cost of production and delivery:

	Product X101	Product Y101
Raw materials cost	$ 30.00	$ 65.00
Purchased parts cost	15.00	45.00
Total cost of raw materials and parts	$ 45.00	$110.00
Manufacturing labor X101 (2.6 hours × $12.00) Y101 (4.8 hours × $15.00)	31.20	72.00
Assembly labor X101 (3.4 hours × $14.00) Y101 (8.2 hours × $16.00)	47.60	131.20
Activity-based costs		
Materials handling activity X101 ($45.00 × $1.30) Y101 ($110.00 × $1.30)	58.50	143.00
Production activity		
X101 (12.8 machine hours × $3.50) Y101 (28.4 machine hours × $3.50)	44.80	99.40
Product delivery activity		
X101	24.00	
Y101		30.00
Projected total unit cost	$251.10	$585.60

3. Production decision

	Product X101	Product Y101
Target unit cost	$260.00	$560.00
Less: projected unit cost	251.10	(585.60
Difference	$8.90	($25.60)

Product X101 can be produced below its target cost, so it should be produced. As currently designed, Product Y101 cannot be produced at or below its target cost; either it needs to be redesigned, or the company should drop plans to make it.

7.10 BALANCED SCORECARD

How does a balanced scorecard evaluate performance work?

A problem with assessing performance with such financial measures as profit, ROI, and Economic Value Added (EVA) only is that the financial measures are "backward-looking." In other words, today's financial measures illuminate the accomplishments and failures of the past. An approach to performance measurement that also focuses on what managers are doing today to create future shareholder value is the balanced scorecard.

Essentially, a balanced scorecard is a set of performance measures constructed for four dimensions of performance. As indicated in Figure 7.6, the dimensions are financial, customer, internal processes, and learning and growth. Having financial measures is critical, even if they are backward-looking. After all, these measures have a great effect on the evaluation of the company by shareholders and creditors. Customer measures examine the company's success in meeting customer expectations; internal process measures examine the company's success in improving critical business processes; and learning and growth measures examine the company's success in improving its ability to adapt, innovate, and grow. The customer, internal processes, and learning and growth measures are generally thought to be predictive of *future* success (that is, they are not backward-looking).

How is balance achieved in a balanced scorecard?

A variety of potential measures for each dimension of a balanced scorecard are indicated in Figure 7.6. After reviewing these measures, note how "balance" is achieved:

- Performance is assessed across a balanced set of dimensions (financial, customer, internal processes, and innovation).
- Quantitative measures (for instance, number of defects) are balanced with qualitative measures (for example, ratings of customer satisfaction).
- There is a balance of backward-looking measures (for instance, financial measures such as growth in sales) and forward-looking measures (for example, number of new patents as an innovation measure).

Figure 7.6 Balanced Scorecard

		Measures
Financial	Is the company achieving its financial goals?	Operating income
		Return on assets
		Sales growth
		Cash flow from operations
		Reduction of administrative expense
Customer	Is the company meeting customer expectations?	Customer satisfaction
		Customer retention
		New customer acquisition
		Market share
		On-time delivery
		Time to fill orders
Internal Processes	Is the company improving critical internal processes?	Defect rate
		Lead time
		Number of suppliers
		Material turnover
		Percent of practical capacity
Learning and Growth	Is the company improving its ability to innovate?	Amount spent on employee training
		Employee satisfaction
		Employee retention
		Number of new products
		New product sales as a percent of total sales
		Number of patents

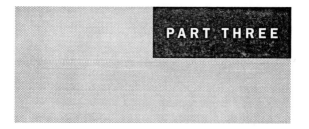

PART THREE

Financial Analysis, Metrics, Assessment Management, and Financing

CHAPTER 8

Cost-Volume-Profit Analysis, Operating Leverage, and Discounting Analysis

Break-even analysis lies at the heart of your company's success. Whether you're a management executive, managerial accountant, financial manager, or financial analyst, understanding this technique is a must.

As its basis, break-even analysis draws upon contribution margin analysis, discussed in Chapter 7. Operating leverage follows directly from break-even analysis. The third component, discounting analysis (present and future value analysis), completes the spectrum of analytic techniques found in this chapter. Together, they will help you keep your company afloat and turn a profit.

8.1 COST-VOLUME-PROFIT (CVP) ANALYSIS

What is cost-volume-profit analysis?

Cost-volume-profit (CVP) analysis, together with cost-behavior information, helps MBAs perform many useful analyses. CVP analysis deals with how profit and costs change with a change in volume. More specifically, CVP looks at the effects on profits of changes in such factors as variable costs, fixed costs, selling prices, volume, and mix of products sold. By studying the relationships of costs, sales, and net income, management is better able to cope with many planning decisions. Closely related is the concept of *leverage*, which is that portion of the fixed costs that represents a risk to the firm.

What is break-even analysis?

Break-even analysis, a branch of CVP analysis, determines the break-even sales level. Break-even point—the financial crossover point when revenues exactly match costs does not show up in corporate earnings reports, but CFOs find it an extremely useful measurement in a variety of ways.

How can I use CVP analysis in solving business problems?

CVP analysis tries to answer the following questions:

- What sales volume is required to break even?
- What sales volume is necessary to earn a desired profit?
- What profit can be expected on a given sales volume?
- How would changes in selling price, variable costs, fixed costs, and output affect profits?
- How would a change in the mix of products sold affect the break-even and target-income volume and profit potential?

What are the uses of break-even analysis?

Use break-even analysis to organize your thinking on important broad features of your business. This is especially pertinent when beginning a new activity, such as starting a new business, expanding an already existing business, or introducing a new product or service.

Many managers within a company will find uses for break-even analysis. It answers these important questions:

- *Management executives:* Have the company's break-even possibilities been improving, or have they been deteriorating over time? What will be the impact of major labor negotiations?
- *Marketing managers:* Will a major marketing campaign generate sufficient sales to justify the cost of the campaign? Would introduction of a new product add or detract from the company's profitability?
- *Production managers:* Would modernization of production facilities pay for itself?

Accountants are responsible for providing data for the break-even analysis. Financial analysts or investors might want to know about efforts a company makes to reduce its break-even point.

CHECKLIST OF USES FOR BREAK-EVEN ANALYSIS

- *Economic analysis of new product.* Based on demand forecasts and estimates of production costs (variable and fixed), the economic impact of a new product can be estimated.

- *Labor contract negotiations.* The effect of increased variable costs resulting from higher wages on the break-even level of output can be analyzed.

- *Choice of production process.* The choice of reducing variable costs at the expense of incurring higher fixed costs can be evaluated. Management might decide to become more capital-intensive by performing tasks in the production process through use of equipment rather than labor. Application of the CVP model can indicate what the effects of this trade-off will be on the break-even output for the given product.

- *Pricing policy.* The sales price of a new product can be set to achieve a target income level. Furthermore, should market penetration be a prime objective, the price could be set that would cover slightly more than the variable costs of production and provide only a partial contribution to the recovery of fixed costs. The negative income at several possible sales prices can then be studied.

- *Location selection.* Some of the costs of having a facility in a location will be fixed, and some will vary with the volume of business. The cost structure and the volume of sales will probably be different for each location being considered. It is important to realize that the lowest-cost location will always be the maximum-profit location.

- *Financing decisions.* Analysis of the firm's cost structure will reveal the proportion that fixed operating costs bear to sales. If this proportion is high, the firm might reasonably decide not to add any fixed financing costs on top of the high fixed operating costs.

- *Make or buy decision.* Break-even analysis can often be used to determine volume requirements in deciding whether to purchase from suppliers or to manufacture in-house a certain component part.

- *Capital budgeting analysis.* As a complementary technique to discounted cash flow (DCF) techniques, the CVP model locates, in a rough way, the sales volume needed to make a project economically beneficial to the firm. CVP should not be used to replace the DCF methodology.

What are the key factors in break-even analysis?

The break-even point depends on three factors:

- The product's selling price
- The variable costs of production, selling, and administration
- The fixed costs of production, selling, and administration

The stability of the selling price during a given income period depends on several factors, including the general market conditions and the behavior of the economy overall.

Break-even analysis, if used properly, will enable an in-depth evaluation of production and administrative activities. *What to do*: Forecast production, selling, and administrative costs, and then exclude those that are fixed or variable.

8.2 CONTRIBUTION MARGIN

What does contribution margin mean?

For accurate CVP analysis, a distinction must be made between costs: they are either variable or fixed. Mixed costs must be separated into their variable and fixed components.

In order to compute the break-even point and perform various CVP analyses, note the following important concepts.

The contribution margin is the excess of sales (S) over the variable costs (VC) of the product or service. The contribution margin (CM) is the amount of money available to cover fixed costs (FC) and to generate profit. Symbolically, CM = S − VC.

Unit CM. The unit CM is the excess of the unit-selling price (p) over the unit variable cost (v). Symbolically, unit CM = $p - v$.

CM ratio. The CM ratio is the contribution margin as a percentage of sales, that is,

$$\text{CM Ratio} = \frac{\text{CM}}{\text{S}} = \frac{(\text{S} - \text{VC})}{\text{S}} = 1 - \frac{\text{VC}}{\text{S}}$$

The CM ratio can also be computed using per-unit data as follows:

$$\text{CM Ratio} = \frac{\text{Unit CM}}{p} = \frac{(p - v)}{p} = 1 - \frac{v}{p}$$

Note that the CM ratio is 1 minus the variable cost ratio. For example, if variable costs are 40 percent of sales, the variable cost ratio is 40 percent and the CM ratio is 60 percent.

Example 8.1

To illustrate the various concepts of CM, consider the following data for Porter Toy Store:

	Total	Per Unit	Percentage
Sales (1,500 units)	$37,500	$25	100%
Less: Variable costs	15,000	10	40
Contribution margin	$22,500	$15	60%
Less: Fixed costs	15,000		
Net income	$7,500		

From the data listed above, CM, unit CM, and the CM ratio are computed as follows:

$$CM = S - VC = \$37,500 - \$15,000 = \$22,500$$

$$\text{Unit CM} = p - v = \$25 - \$10 = \$15$$

$$\text{CM Ratio} = CM / S = \$22,500 / \$37,500$$

$$= 1 - (\$15,000 / \$37,500) = 1 - 0.4 = 0.6 = 60\%$$

or

$$= \text{Unit CM} / p = \$15 / \$25 = 0.6 = 60\%$$

How can the break-even sales be computed?

The break-even point represents the level of sales revenue that equals the total of the variable and fixed costs for a given volume of output at a particular capacity use rate. For example, one might want to ask the break-even occupancy rate (or vacancy rate) for a hotel, or the break-even load rate for an airliner.

Generally, the lower the break-even point, the higher the profit and the less the operating risk, other things being equal. The break-even point also provides managerial accountants with insights into profit planning.

The break-even point can be computed in two different ways: the equation approach and the graphical approach. The equation approach is based on the cost-volume-profit equation, which shows the relationships among sales, variable and fixed costs, and net income:

$$S = VC + FC + \text{Net Income}$$

At the break-even volume, $S = VC + FC + 0$. Defining x = volume in units, the above relationship can be written in terms of x:

$$px = vx + FC$$
$$(p - v)x = FC$$

Solving for x yields the following formula for break-even sales volume:

$$x = \frac{FC}{(p - v)} = \frac{\text{Fixed costs}}{\text{Unit CM}}$$

or

$$\text{Break-even point in dollars (S)} = \frac{\text{Fixed costs}}{\text{CM ratio}}$$

Note: The sales revenue needed to break even is that point at which the company covers all costs but generates no income.

$$S = VC + FC + 0$$
$$S = (VC/S)S + FC$$
$$(1 - VC/S)S = FC$$
$$S = \frac{FC}{(1 - VC/S)}$$
$$= \frac{\text{Fixed costs}}{(1 - \text{Variable cost ratio})} = \frac{\text{Fixed costs}}{\text{CM ratio}}$$

Example 8.2

Using the same data given in Example 8.1, where unit CM = \$25 − \$10 = \$15 and CM ratio = 60%, we get the following:

$$\text{Break-even point in units} = \$15{,}000/\$15$$
$$= 1{,}000 \text{ units}$$
$$\text{Break-even point in dollars} = \$15{,}000/0.6$$
$$= \$25{,}000$$

Or, alternatively,

$$1{,}000 \text{ units} \times \$25 = \$25{,}000$$

Can I express break-even graphically?

The graphical approach to obtaining the break-even point is based on the so-called break-even (B-E) chart, as shown in Figure 8.1. Sales revenue, variable costs, and fixed costs are plotted on the vertical axis, while volume (x) is plotted on the horizontal axis. The break-even point is the point where the total sales revenue line intersects the total cost line. The chart can also effectively report profit potentials over a wide range of activity, and can therefore be used as a tool for discussion and presentation.

The profit-volume (P-V) chart, as shown in Figure 8.2, focuses directly on how profits vary with changes in volume. Profits are plotted on the vertical axis, while units of output are shown on the horizontal axis. The P-V chart provides a quick, condensed comparison of how alternative pricing, variable costs, or fixed costs may affect net income as volume changes. The P-V chart can be easily constructed from the B-E chart. *Note:* The slope of the chart is the unit CM.

Figure 8.1 Break-Even Chart

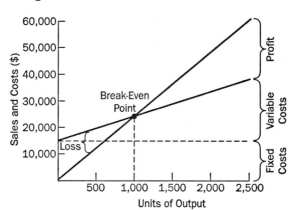

Figure 8.2 Profit-Volume (P-V) Chart

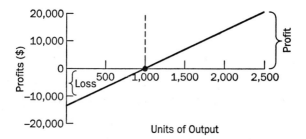

8.3   FROM BREAKEVEN TO TARGET PROFITS

How can I determine desired profit levels?

The objective of a business is not simply to break even, but to make a profit. Break-even analysis can be easily extended to focus on a target level of profits.

There are two ways in which target net income can be expressed:

    Case 1: As a specific dollar amount
    Case 2: As a percentage of sales

Case 1
As a specific dollar amount, the formula is

$$\frac{\text{Target income}}{\text{sales volume}} = \frac{\text{Fixed costs} + \text{Target income}}{\text{Unit CM}}$$

Case 2
Specifying target income as a percentage of sales, the cost-volume equation is

$$px = vx + FC + \%(px)$$

Solving this for x yields:

$$\frac{FC}{p - v - \%(p)}$$

In words, the equation reads as follows:

$$\text{Target income sales volume} = \frac{\text{Fixed costs}}{\text{Unit CM} - (\% \text{ of unit of sales price})}$$

Example 8.3

Using the same data given in Example 8.1, assume that Porter Toy Store wishes to attain

Case 1: A target income of $15,000 before tax
Case 2: A target income of 20 percent of sales

In Case 1, the target income volume would be

$$(\$15,000 + \$15,000) / (\$25 - \$10)$$
$$= \$30,000 / \$15 = 2,000 \text{ units}$$

In Case 2, the target income volume required is

$$\$15,000/[(\$25 - \$10) - (20\%)(\$25)]$$
$$= \$15,000/(\$15 - \$5) = 1,500 \text{ units}$$

What is the impact of income taxes on target income volume?

If target income (expressed as a specific dollar amount) is given on an after-tax basis, an adjustment is necessary before the previous formula can be used. The reason is that the profit target is expressed in before-tax terms. Therefore, the after-tax target income must be first converted to a before-tax target, as follows:

$$\text{Before-tax target income} = \frac{\text{After-tax target income}}{(1 - \text{tax rate})}$$

Example 8.4

Assume in Example 8.1 that Porter Toy Store wants to achieve an after-tax income of $6,000. The tax rate is 40 percent. The first step is

$$\frac{\$6,000}{(1 - 0.4)} = \$10,000$$

The second step is to plug this figure into the regular formula, as follows:

Target income volume = ($15,000 + $10,000) / 15
$$= 1,667 \text{ units}$$

Example 8.5

Using the same data given in Example 8.1, assume that Porter Toy Store wants to attain a target income of $15,000 before tax.

The target income volume would be

($15,000 + $15,000) / ($25 − $10)
$$= \$30,000 / \$15 = 2,000 \text{ units}$$

What is the cash break-even point?

If a company has a minimum of available cash, or if the opportunity cost of holding excess cash is too high, management may want to know the volume of sales that will cover all cash expenses during a period. This is known as the cash break-even point. Not all fixed operating costs involve cash payments. For example, depreciation expenses are non-cash fixed charges. Another example is prepaid expenses, such as prepaid insurance and prepaid rent. The time period for which the break-even analysis is being performed might not involve an actual cash outlay for insurance coverage. To find the cash break-even point, the non-cash charges must be subtracted from fixed costs. Therefore, the cash break-even point is lower than the usual break-even point. The formula is

Cash break-even point

= (Fixed costs − Non-cash expenses) / Unit CM

Example 8.6

Assume in Example 8.1 that the total fixed costs of $15,000 include depreciation of $1,500. Then the cash break-even point is

$$(\$15,000 - \$1,500) / (\$25 - \$10)$$
$$= \$13,500 / \$15 = 900 \text{ units}$$

Porter Toy Store has to sell 900 units to cover only the fixed costs involving cash payments of $13,500, and to break even.

What is the use of margin of safety?

The margin of safety is a measure of difference between the actual sales and the break-even sales. It is the amount by which sales revenue may drop before losses begin, and is expressed as a percentage of expected sales:

Margin of safety = (Expected sales

– Break-even sales)/Expected sales

The margin of safety is used as a measure of operating risk. The larger the ratio, the safer the situation, since there is less risk of reaching the break-even point.

Example 8.7

Assume Porter Toy Store projects sales of $35,000, with a break-even sales level of $25,000. The projected margin of safety is

$$(\$35,000 - \$25,000) / \$35,000 = 28.57\%$$

8.4 "WHAT-IF" ANALYSIS

How is CVP analysis used in solving "what-if" scenarios?

The concepts of contribution margin and the contribution income statement have many applications in profit planning and short-term decision making. Many "what-if" scenarios can be evaluated using these as planning tools—and especially when utilizing a spreadsheet program such as Excel. Some applications are illustrated in Examples 8 through 12, using the same data as in Example 8.1.

Example 8.8

Recall from Example 8.1 that Porter Toy Store has a CM of 60 percent and fixed costs of $15,000 per period. Assume that the store expects sales to go up by

$10,000 for the next period. How much will income increase?

Using the CM concepts, the impact of a change in sales on profits can be quickly computed. The formula for computing the impact is

Change in net income = Dollar change in sales
$$\times \text{ CM ratio}$$

Thus

Increase in net income = $10,000 × 60% = $6,000

Therefore, the income will go up by $6,000, assuming there is no change in fixed costs. If given a change in unit sales instead of dollars, the formula becomes

Change in net income = Change in unit sales
$$\times \text{ Unit CM}$$

Example 8.9

Assume that the store expects sales to go up by 400 units. How much will income increase? In Example 8.1, the store's unit CM is $15. Again, assuming there is no change in fixed costs, the income will increase by $6,000.

$$400 \text{ units} \times \$15 = \$6,000$$

Example 8.10

What net income is expected on sales of $47,500?

The answer is the difference between the CM and the fixed costs:

CM: $47,500 × 60%	$28,500
Less: Fixed costs	15,000
Net income	$13,500

Example 8.11

Porter Toy Store is considering increasing the advertising budget by $5,000, which would increase sales revenue by $8,000. Should the advertising budget be increased?

The answer is no, because the increase in the CM is less than the increased cost:

Increase in CM: $8,000 × 60%	$4,800
Increase in advertising	5,000
Decrease in net income	($200)

Example 8.12

Consider the original data. Assume again that Porter Toy Store is currently selling 1,500 units per period. In an effort to increase sales, management is considering cutting its unit price by $5 and increasing the advertising budget by $1,000.

If these two steps are taken, management feels that unit sales will go up by 60 percent. Should the two steps be taken?

A $5 reduction in the selling price will cause the unit CM to decrease from $15 to $10. Thus,

Proposed CM: 2,400 units × $10	$24,000
Present CM: 1,500 units × $15	22,500
Increase in CM	$1,500
Increase in advertising outlay	1,000
Increase in net income	$500

The answer, therefore, is yes. Alternatively, the same answer can be obtained by developing comparative income statements in a contribution format:

	(A) Present (1,500 units)	(B) Proposed (2,400 units)	Difference (B–A)
Sales	$37,500 (@$25)	$48,000 (@$20)	$10,500
Less: Variable cost	15,000 (@$10)	24,000 (@$10)	9,000
CM	$22,500	$24,000	$ 1,500
Less: Fixed costs	15,000	16,000	1,000
Net income	$ 7,500	$ 8,000	$ 500

8.5 SALES-MIX ANALYSIS

What effect does the sales mix have?

Break-even and cost-volume-profit analyses require some additional computations and assumptions when a company produces and sells more than one product. In multi-product firms, sales mix is an important factor in calculating an overall company break-even point.

Different selling prices and different variable costs result in different unit CM and CM ratios. As a result, the break-even points and cost-volume-profit relationships vary with the relative proportions of the products sold, called the *sales mix*.

In break-even and CVP analyses, it is necessary to predetermine the sales mix and then compute a weighted average unit CM. It is also necessary to assume that the sales mix does not change for a specified period. The break-even formula for the company as a whole is

$$\text{Break-even sales in units (or in dollars)} = \frac{\text{Fixed costs}}{\text{Weighted average unit CM (or CM ratio)}}$$

Example 8.13

Assume that Knibex, Inc., produces cutlery sets of high-quality wood and steel. The company makes a deluxe cutlery set and a standard set that have the following unit CM data:

	Deluxe	*Standard*
Selling price	$15	$10
Variable cost per unit	12	5
Unit CM	$ 3	$ 5
Sales mix	60%	40%
	(based on sales volume)	
Fixed costs	$76,000	

The weighted average unit CM = ($3)(0.6) + ($5)(0.4) = $3.80. Therefore, the company's break-even point in units is

$$\$76{,}000/\$3.80 = 20{,}000 \text{ units}$$

which is divided as follows:

Deluxe: 20,000 units × 60% = 12,000 units
Standard: 20,000 units × 40% = 8,000
                                20,000 units

Note: An alternative is to build a package containing three deluxe models and two economy models (3:2 ratio). By defining the product as a package, the multiple-product problem is converted into a single-product problem. Then use the following three steps:

Step 1
Computer analyze the package CM as follows:

	Deluxe	*Standard*
Selling price	$15	$10
Variable cost per unit	12	5
Unit CM	$ 3	$ 5
Sales mix	3	2
Package CM	$ 9	$10
	$19 package total	

Step 2
Determine the number of packages that need to be sold to break even, as follows:

$76,000/$19 per package = 4,000 packages

Step 3
Multiply this number by their respective mix units:

Deluxe: 4,000 packages $\times$ 3 units = 12,000 units
Standard: 4,000 packages $\times$ 2 units = <u> 8,000 units</u>
                                                    20,000 units

Example 8.14

Assume that Dante, Inc., is a producer of recreational equipment. Dante expects to produce and sell three types of sleeping bags—the Economy, the Regular, and the Backpacker. Information on the bags is given below:

	Budgeted			
	Economy	*Regular*	*Back-packer*	*Total*
Sales	$30,000	$60,000	$10,000	$100,000
Sales mix	30%	60%	10%	100%
Less VC	24,000	40,000	5,000	69,000
	(80%)	(66⅔%)	(50%)	
CM	$ 6,000	$20,000	$ 5,000	$ 31,000
CM ratio	20%	33⅓%	50%	31%
Fixed costs				$ 18,600
Net income				$ 12,400

The CM ratio for Dante, Inc., is

$31,000/$100,000 = 31 percent.

Therefore, the break-even point in dollars is

$18,600/0.31 = $60,000

which will be split in the mix ratio of 3:6:1 to give us the following break-even points for the individual products:

Economy:	$60,000 × 30% =	$18,000
Regular:	$60,000 × 60% =	36,000
Backpacker:	$60,000 × 10% =	6,000
		$60,000

One of the most important assumptions underlying CVP analysis in a multi-product firm is that the sales mix will not change during the planning period. But if the sales mix changes, the break-even point will also change.

Example 8.15

Assume that total sales from Example 8.14 was achieved at $100,000, but that the actual mix came out differently from the budgeted mix (that is, for Economy, 30 percent to 55 percent, for Regular, 60 percent to 40 percent, and for Backpacker, 10 percent to 5 percent).

	Actual			
	Economy	*Regular*	*Back-packer*	*Total*
Sales	$55,000	$40,000	$5,000	$100,000
Sales mix	55%	40%	5%	100%
Less: VC	44,000	26,667*	2,500**	73,167
CM	$11,000	$13,333	$2,500	$ 26,833
CM ratio	20%	33⅓%	50%	26.83%
Fixed costs				$ 18,600
Net income				$ 8,233

*$26,667 = $40,000 × (100% − 33⅓%) = $40,000 × 66⅔%
**$2,500 = $5,000 × (100% − 50%) = $5,000 × 50%

Note: The shift in sales mix toward the less profitable line, Economy, has caused the CM ratio for the company as a whole to drop from 31 percent to 26.83 percent.

The new break-even point will be

$$\$18,600/0.2683 = \$69,325$$

The break-even dollar volume has increased from $60,000 to $69,325.

The deterioration (improvement) in the mix caused net income to go down (up). It is important to note that, generally, the shift of emphasis from low-margin products to high-margin ones will increase the overall profits of the company.

What are the limitations of break-even analysis?

In its simplest form, break-even analysis makes a number of assumptions about which one must be very clear. One such assumption treats the unit selling price as a constant. This, in turn, rests on two further assumptions: (1) the elasticity of demand must be very high for the unit selling price to remain constant as sales volume expands, and (2) the selling price must remain relatively stable over the income period. In truth, neither assumption is likely to hold in actual practice, and this makes forecasting the unit selling price much more difficult.

The second major assumption holds that unit variable costs are also constant, and that fixed and variable costs have been properly separated, identified, and quantified. However, separating variable from fixed costs is an ongoing problem.

Once the unit variable cost has been determined, make certain it remains constant over the income period. If it does not, a series of breakdown calculations incorporating the most probable unit variable costs must be computed.

Likewise, examine the likelihood that total fixed costs will remain constant. Do this at every level of analysis. If there are factors that will cause fixed costs to vary, compute a series of break-even analyses using the most probable values of total fixed costs.

A rule for management executives: One major objective should be to keep a tight grip on the company's break-even volume. This means constant efforts to keep break-even from increasing as a result of adverse conditions that lower unit selling price and raise unit variable costs and total fixed costs.

CHECKLIST OF QUESTIONS CONCERNING BREAK-EVEN ANALYSIS

- Is demand sufficiently elastic that rises in sales volume would have no appreciable effect on unit selling price?
- Is unit selling price expected to be relatively stable over the income period to which the break-even analysis applies?
- Have costs been measured properly? Have historical costs been adjusted appropriately to reflect

future costs during the income period (or income periods) under study?

- Are total fixed costs expected to remain constant over the income period under study?
- Does the break-even analysis assume organizational slack? That is, are costs assumed to have been appropriately minimized?
- Is unit variable cost assumed to be constant?
- Is the probable range of break-even volumes estimated in terms of a particular future period or periods?
- Does the break-even analysis provide probability estimates as to whether or not breakeven can be achieved?

8.6 OPERATING LEVERAGE

What is leverage, and what are the types?

Companies want to know where they are with respect to the break-even point. If they are operating around break-even point sales, management may be more conservative in its approach to implementing changes and mapping out new strategies. On the other hand, if they are operating well away from the break-even point, management will be more liberal because the downside risk is not as great. A measure that relates to this distance between break-even sales and current or planned sales volume is leverage.

Leverage is that portion of the fixed costs that represents a risk to the firm. Operating leverage, a measure of operating risk, refers to the fixed operating costs found in the firm's income statement. Financial leverage, a measure of financial risk, refers to financing a portion of the firm's assets, bearing fixed financing charges in hopes of increasing the return to the common stockholders. The higher the financial leverage, the higher the financial risk, and the higher the cost of capital. (Cost of capital rises because it costs more to raise funds for a risky business.) Total leverage is a measure of total risk.

How do I measure operating leverage?

Operating leverage is a measure of operating risk and arises from fixed operating costs. A simple indication of operating leverage is the effect that a change in sales has on earnings.

The formula is

Operating leverage at a given level of sales (x)

$$= \frac{\text{Percentage change in operating income}}{\text{Percentage change in sales}}$$

$$= \frac{(p - v)x}{(p - v)x - \text{FC}}$$

where operating income $= (p - v)x - \text{FC}$

Example 8.16

The Wayne Company manufactures and sells doors to home builders. The doors are sold for $25 each. Variable costs are $15 per door, and fixed operating costs total $50,000. Assume that the Wayne Company is currently selling 6,000 doors per year. Its operating leverage is

$$\frac{(p - v)}{(p - v)x - \text{FC}} = \frac{(\$25 - \$15)(6,000)}{(\$25 - \$15)(6,000) - \$50,000}$$

$$= \frac{\$60,000}{\$10,000} = 6$$

This means that if sales increase (decrease) by 1 percent, the company can expect its net income to increase (decrease) by six times that amount, or 6 percent.

8.7 TIME VALUE OF MONEY—FUTURE AND PRESENT VALUES

Often, today's and tomorrow's dollars are treated the same when, in fact, they are not the same. A dollar now is worth more than a dollar to be received later. This statement sums up an important principle: money has a time value. The truth of this principle is not that inflation might make the dollar received at a later time worth less in buying power; the truth is that a company could invest the dollar now, and have more than a dollar at the specified later date.

Time value of money is a critical consideration in financial and investment decisions. For example, compound interest calculations are needed to determine future sums of money resulting from an investment. Discounting, or the calculation of present value, which is inversely related to compounding, is used to evaluate the future cash flow associated with capital budgeting projects. There are plenty of applications of time value of money in finance.

What is the importance of present (discount) and future (compound) value calculations?

Management executives, planners, financial or investment analysts, and investors should know that present and compound value calculations lie at the very heart of their decisions.

Use present and compound value techniques when estimating the present values of items reported in a statement of financial condition. *Be aware:* Every statement is composed of present values of asset, liability, and ownership interest. In reality, accountants do not report most items appearing on the statement in terms of present values, but rather in terms of historical costs or some modification thereof. The longer an item appears on a statement, the less likely it is that these cost values relate to present values. Be aware of this limitation, and use the statement properly.

Present and compound value techniques are essential for planning purposes, particularly when estimating

- Present values used in investment and capital budget decisions
- Effects of inflation on organizational activities
- Present values of loans, bonds, annual installments to a sinking fund, and so on

What is money worth in the future?

A dollar in hand today is worth more than a dollar to be received tomorrow because of the interest to be earned from putting it in a savings account or placing it in an investment account. Compounding interest means that interest earns interest. For the discussion of the concepts of compounding and time value, let us define the following:

$$F_n = \text{future value} = \text{the amount of money at the end of year } n$$
$$P = \text{principal}$$
$$i = \text{annual interest rate}$$
$$n = \text{number of years}$$

Then,

$$F_1 = \text{the amount of money at the end of year 1} = \text{principal and interest} = P + iP = P(1 + i)$$
$$F_2 = \text{the amount of money at the end of year 2} = F_1(1 + i) = P(1 + i)(1 + i) = P(1 + i)^2$$

The future value of an investment compounded annually at rate i for n years is

$$F_n = P(1 + i)^n = P \cdot T_1(i,n)$$

where $T_1(i,n)$ is the compound amount of $1 (this can be found in Table 8.1, at the end of the chapter).

Example 8.17

If $1,000 is placed in a savings account earning 8 percent interest compounded annually, how much money will be in the account at the end of four years?

$$F_n = P(1 + i)^n$$

$$F_4 = \$1,000 (1 + 0.08)^4 = \$1,000\,T_1(8\%, 4 \text{ years})$$

In Table 8.1, the T_1 for four years at 8 percent is 1.361. Therefore,

$$F_4 = \$1,000 (1.361) = \$1,361$$

Example 8.18

A large sum of money is invested in the stock of PWU Corporation. The company paid a $3 dividend per share. The dividend is expected to increase by 20 percent per year for the next three years. Project the dividends for years one through three.

$$F_n = P(1 + i)^n$$

$$F_1 = \$3(1 + 0.2)^1 = \$3\,T_1(20\%, 1) = \$3 (1.200) = \$3.60$$

$$F_2 = \$3(1 + 0.2)^2 = \$3\,T_1(20\%, 2) = \$3 (1.440) = \$4.32$$

$$F_3 = \$3(1 + 0.2)^3 = \$3\,T_1(20\%, 3) = \$3 (1.728) = \$5.18$$

How does intrayear compounding affect future values?

Interest is often compounded more frequently than once a year. Banks, for example, compound interest quarterly, daily, and even continuously. If interest is compounded m times a year, the general formula for solving the future value becomes

$$F_n = P\left(1 + \frac{i}{m}\right)^{n \cdot m} = P \cdot T_1(i/m, n \cdot m)$$

The formula reflects more frequent compounding (n · m) at a smaller interest rate per period (i/m). For example, in the case of semiannual compounding (m = 2), the preceding formula becomes

$$F_n = P(1 + i/2)^{n \cdot 2} = P \cdot T_1(i/2, n \cdot 2)$$

Example 8.19

A deposit of $10,000 is made to an account offering an annual interest rate of 20 percent. The money will be kept on deposit for five years. The interest rate is compounded quarterly. The accumulated amount at the end of the fifth year is calculated as follows:

$$F_n = P\left(1 + \frac{i}{m}\right)^{n \cdot m} = P \cdot T_1(i/m, n \cdot m)$$

where

$$P = \$10,000$$
$$i/m = 20\%/4 = 5\%$$
$$n \cdot m = 5 \times 4 = 20$$

Therefore,

$$F_5 = \$10,000(1 + .05)^{20} = \$10,000 \, T_1(5\%, 20)$$
$$= \$10,000 \,(2.653) = \$26,530$$

Example 8.20

Assume that $P = \$1,000$, $i = 8\%$, and $n = 2$ years. Then, for annual compounding ($m = 1$),

$$F_2 = \$1,000(1 + 0.08)^2 = \$1,000 \, T_1(8\%, 2)$$
$$= \$1,000(1.166) = \$1,166.00$$

semiannual compounding ($m = 2$),

$$F_2 = \$1,000\left(1 + \frac{0.08}{2}\right)^{2 \cdot 2}$$
$$= \$1,000(1 + .04)^4 = \$1,000 \, T_1(4\%, 4)$$
$$= \$1,000(1.170)$$
$$= \$1,170.00$$

quarterly compounding ($m = 4$),

$$F_2 = \$1,000\left(1 + \frac{0.08}{4}\right)^{2 \cdot 4}$$
$$= \$1,000(1 + .02)^8 = \$1,000 \, T_1(2\%, 8)$$
$$= \$1,000(1.172)$$
$$= \$1,172.00$$

As the example shows, the more frequently interest is compounded, the greater the amount accumulated. This is true for any interest, for any period of time.

How do I determine future value of an ordinary annuity?

An annuity is defined as a series of payments (or receipts) of a fixed amount for a specified number of periods. Each payment is assumed to occur at the end of the period. The future value of an annuity is a compound annuity that involves depositing or investing an equal sum of money at the end of each year for a certain number of years and allowing it to grow.

Let S_n = the future value on an n-year annuity. A = the amount of an annuity.

Then,

$$S_n = A(1 + i)^{n-1} + A(1 + i)^{n-2} + \cdots + A(1 + i)^0$$
$$= A[(1 + i)^{n-1} + (1 + i)^{n-2} + \cdots + (1 + i)^0]$$
$$= A \cdot \sum_{t=0}^{n-1}(1 + i)^t = A\left[\frac{(1 + i)^n - 1}{i}\right] = A \cdot T_2(i,n)$$

$T_2(i,n)$ represents the future value of an annuity of $1, for n years, compounded at i percent. (This can be found in Table 8.2 at the end of this chapter.)

Example 8.21

Determine the sum of money you will have in a savings account at the end of six years if you deposit $1,000 at the end of each year for the next six years. The annual interest rate is 8 percent. The $T_2(8\%, 6$ years) is given in Table 8.2 as 7.336. Therefore,

$$S_6 = \$1,000\, T_2(8\%, 6) = \$1,000\,(7.336) = \$7,336$$

Example 8.22

If $30,000 is deposited semiannually into a fund for ten years, and the annual interest rate is 8 percent, the amount accumulated at the end of the tenth year is calculated as follows:

$$S_n = A \cdot T_2(i, n)$$

where

$$A = \$30,000$$
$$i = 8\%/2 = 4\%$$
$$n = 10 \times 2 = 20$$

Therefore,

$$S_n = \$30,000\, T_2(4\%, 20)$$
$$= \$30,000\,(29.778)\, 5\, \$893,340$$

What is present value?

Present value is the present worth of future sums of money. The process of calculating present values, or discounting, is the opposite of finding the compounded future value. In connection with present value calculations, the interest rate i is called the discount rate. The discount rate used is more commonly called the cost of capital, which is the minimum rate of return required by the investor.

Recall that

$$F_n = P (1 + i)^n$$

Therefore,

$$P = \frac{F_n}{(1 + i)^n} = F_n\left[\frac{1}{(1 + i)^n}\right] F_n \cdot T_3(i,n)$$

$T_3(i,n)$ represents the present value of $1, and this is given in Table 8.3, at the end of this chapter.

Example 8.23

You have been given an opportunity to receive $20,000 six years from now. If you can earn 10 percent on your investments, what is the most you should pay for this opportunity? To answer this question, compute the present value of $20,000 to be received six years from now at a 10 percent rate of discount. F_6 is $20,000, i is 10 percent, and n is six years. $T_3(10\%, 6)$ from Table 8.3 is 0.565.

$$P = \$2,000\left[\frac{1}{(1 + 0.1)^6}\right] = \$20,000\, T_3(10\%, 6)$$
$$= \$20,000(0.565) = \$11,300$$

This means that the investment can earn 10 percent, and you would be indifferent to receiving $11,300 now or $20,000 six years from today, since the amounts are time-equivalent. In other words, you could invest $11,300 today at 10 percent and have $20,000 in six years.

How do I compute mixed streams of cash flows?

The present value of a series of mixed payments (or receipts) is the sum of the present value of each individual payment. The present value of each individual payment is the payment times the appropriate T_3 value.

Example 8.24

Management is thinking of starting a new product line that initially costs $32,000. The annual projected cash inflows are:

Year 1	$10,000
Year 2	$20,000
Year 3	$ 5,000

If the investment must earn a minimum of 10 percent, should this new product line be undertaken?

The present value of this series of mixed streams of cash inflows is calculated as follows:

Year	Cash inflows	$\times T_3(10\%, n)$	Present Value
1	$10,000	0.909	$ 9,090
2	$20,000	0.826	$16,520
3	$ 5,000	0.751	$ 3,755
			$29,365

Since the present value of the projected cash inflows is less than the initial investment, this project should not be undertaken.

What is the present value of an annuity?

Interest received from bonds, pension funds, and insurance obligations all involve annuities. To compare these financial instruments, we need to know the present value of each. The present value of an annuity (P_n) can be found by using the following equation:

$$P_n = A \cdot \left[\frac{1}{(1+i)^1} \right] + A \cdot \left[\frac{1}{(1+i)^2} \right]$$

$$+ \cdots + A \cdot \left[\frac{1}{(1+i)^n} \right]$$

$$= A \cdot \left[\frac{1}{(1+i)^n} + \frac{1}{(1+i)^2} + \cdots + \frac{1}{(1+i)^n} \right]$$

$$= A \cdot \sum_{t=1}^{n} \frac{1}{(1+i)^t} = A \cdot \frac{1}{i} \left[1 - \frac{1}{(1+i)} \right]$$

$$= A \cdot T_4(i,n)$$

$T_4(i,n)$ represents the present value of an annuity of $1, discounted at i percent for n years. (This is found in Table 8.4 at the end of this chapter.)

Example 8.25

Assume that the cash inflows in Example 8.24 form an annuity of $10,000 for three years. The present value is

$$P_n = A \cdot T_4(i,n)$$
$$P_3 = \$10,000 \, T_4(10\%, 3 \text{ years}) = \$10,000 \, (2.487)$$
$$= \$24,870$$

What are perpetuities?

Some annuities go on forever; these are called perpetuities. An example of a perpetuity is preferred stock that yields a constant dollar dividend indefinitely. The present value of a perpetuity is found as follows:

$$\text{Present value of a perpetuity} = \frac{\text{receipt}}{\text{discount rate}} = \frac{A}{i}$$

Example 8.26

Assume that a perpetual bond has an $80-per-year interest payment, and that the discount rate is 10 percent. The present value of this perpetuity is

$$P = \frac{A}{i} = \frac{\$80}{0.10} = \$800$$

What are the uses of present and compound values?

Future and present values have numerous applications in financial and investment decisions. Six of these applications are presented below.

Deposits to accumulate a future sum (or sinking fund). A financial manager might want to find the annual deposit (or payment) that is necessary to accumulate a future sum. To find this future amount (or sinking fund), the formula for finding the future value of an annuity can be used.

$$S_n = A \cdot T_2(i,n)$$

Solving for A, we obtain

$$\text{Annual deposit amount} = A = \frac{S_n}{T_2(i,n)}$$

Example 8.27

Determine the equal annual end-of-year deposits required to accumulate $5,000 at the end of five years in a fund. The interest rate is 10 percent. The annual deposit is

$$S_5 = \$5,000$$
$$T_2(10\%, 5 \text{ years}) = 6.105 \text{ (from Table 8.2)}$$
$$A = \frac{\$5,000}{6.105} = \$819$$

In other words, if $819 is deposited at the end of each year for five years at 10 percent interest, $5,000 will have accumulated at the end of the fifth year.

Example 8.28

For a sinking fund for the retirement of a bond thirty years from now, at an interest rate of 10 percent, the annual year-end contribution needed to accumulate $1,000,000 is

$$S_{30} = \$1,000,000$$
$$T_2(10\%, 30 \text{ years}) = 164.49$$
$$A = \frac{\$1,000,000}{164.49} = \$6,079.40$$

Amortized loans. If a loan is to be repaid in equal periodic amounts, it is an amortized loan. Examples of amortized loans include auto loans, mortgage loans, and most commercial loans. The periodic payment can be computed as follows:

$$P_n = A \cdot T_4(i,n)$$

Solving for A, we obtain

$$\text{Amount of loan} = A = \frac{P_n}{T_4(i,n)}$$

Example 8.29

If $200,000 if borrowed for five years at an interest rate of 14 percent, the annual year-end payment on the loan is calculated as follows (see also Table 8.4):

$$P_5 = \$200,000$$
$$T_4(14\%, 5 \text{ years}) = 3.433$$
$$\text{Amount of loan} = A = \frac{P_5}{T_4(14\%, 5 \text{ years})} = \frac{\$200,000}{3.433}$$
$$= \$58,258.08$$

Example 8.30

A forty-month bank loan of $5,000 is taken out at a 12 percent annual interest rate. Following is the equations to find out the monthly loan payment:

$$i = 12\% / 12 \text{ months} = 1\%$$
$$P_{40} = \$5,000$$
$$T_4(1\%, 40 \text{ months}) = 32.835 \text{ (from Table 8.4)}$$

Therefore,

$$A = \frac{\$5,000}{32.835} = \$152.28$$

So, repaying the principal and interest on a $5,000, 12 percent, forty-month loan, requires payments of $152.28 a month for the next forty months.

Example 8.31

Assume that a firm borrows $2,000, to be repaid in three equal installments at the end of each of the next three years. The bank charges 12 percent interest. The amount of each payment is

$$P_3 = \$2,000$$
$$T_4(12\%, 3 \text{ years}) = 2.402$$

Therefore,

$$A = \frac{\$2,000}{2.402} = \$832.64$$

How to develop loan amortization schedule. Each loan payment consists partly of interest and partly of principal. The breakdown is often displayed in a loan amortization schedule. The interest component of the payment is largest in the first period (because the principal balance is the highest) and subsequently declines, whereas the principal portion is smallest in the first period (because of the high interest) and increases thereafter, as shown in the following example.

Example 8.32

Using the same data as in Example 8.31, we set up the following amortization schedule:

Year	Payment	Interest	Repayment of Principal	Remaining Balance
0				$2,000.00
1	$832.64	$240.00(a)	$592.64(b)	$1,407.36
2	$832.64	$168.88	$663.76	$743.60
3	$832.64	$89.23	$743.41(c)	

(a) Interest is computed by multiplying the loan balance at the beginning of the year by the interest rate. Therefore, interest in year 1 is $2,000(0.12) = $240; in year 2 interest is $1,407.36(0.12) = $168.88; and in year 3 interest is $743.60(0.12) = $89.23. All figures are rounded.

(b) The reduction in principal equals the payment less the interest portion ($832.64 − $240.00 = $592.64).

(c) Not exact because of accumulated rounding errors.

Annual Percentage Rate (APR). Different types of investments use different compounding periods. For example, most bonds pay interest semiannually; banks generally pay interest quarterly. If a financial manager wants to compare investments with different compounding periods, he or she needs to put them on a common basis. The annual percentage rate (APR), or effective annual rate, is used for this purpose and is computed as follows:

$$APR = \left(1 + \frac{i}{m}\right)^m - 1.0$$

Here i = the stated, nominal or quoted rate, and m = the number of compounding periods per year.

Example 8.33

If the nominal rate is 6 percent, compounded quarterly, the APR is

$$APR = \left(1 + \frac{i}{m}\right)^m - 1.0 = \left(1\,1\,\frac{0.006}{4}\right)^4 - 1.0$$

$$= (1.015)^4 - 1.0 = 1.0614 - 1.0 = 0.0614 = 6.14\%$$

This means that if one bank offered 6 percent with quarterly compounding while another offered 6.14 percent with annual compounding, they would be paying the same effective rate of interest.

Annual percentage rate (APR) also is a measure of the cost of credit expressed as a yearly rate. It includes interest as well as other financial charges, such as loan origination and certain closing fees. The lender is required to disclose the APR. This provides a good basis for comparing the cost of loans, including mortgage plans.

Rates of growth. In finance, it is necessary to calculate the compound annual rate of growth, associated with a stream of earnings. The compound annual growth rate in earnings per share is computed as follows:

$$F_n = P \cdot T_1(i,n)$$

Solving this for T_1, we obtain

$$T_1(i,n) = \frac{F_n}{P}$$

Example 8.34

Assume that a company has earnings per share of $2.50 in 19X1, and ten years later the earnings per share has increased to $3.70. The compound annual rate of growth in earnings per share is computed as follows:

$$F_{10} = \$3.70 \text{ and } P = \$2.50$$

Therefore,

$$T_1(i,10) = \frac{\$3.70}{\$2.50} = 1.48$$

In Table 8.1 (at the end of this chapter), a T_1 of 1.48 at ten years is at $i = 4\%$. The compound annual rate of growth is therefore 4 percent.

Bond values. Bonds call for the payment of a specific amount of interest for a stated number of years, and the repayment of the face value at the maturity date. Thus, a bond represents an annuity plus a lump sum. Its value is found as the present value of the payment stream. The interest is usually paid semiannually.

$$V = \sum_{t=1}^{n} \frac{I}{(1+i)^t} + \frac{M}{(1+i)^n}$$
$$= I \cdot T_4(i,n) + M \cdot T_3(i,n)$$

where

I = interest payment per period

M = par value, or maturity value, usually \$1,000

i = investor's required rate of return

n = number of periods

Example 8.35

Assume there is a ten-year bond with a 10 percent coupon, paying interest semiannually and having a face value of \$1,000. Since interest is paid semiannually, the number of periods involved is twenty, and the semiannual cash inflow is \$100/2 = \$50.

Assume that there is a required rate of return of 12 percent for this type of bond. The present value (V) of this bond is

$$V = \$50 \cdot T_4(6\%, 20) + \$1,000 \cdot T_3(6\%, 20)$$
$$= \$50(11.470) + \$1,000(0.312)$$
$$= \$573.50 + \$312.00 = \$885.50$$

Note: The required rate of return (12 percent) is higher than the coupon rate of interest (10 percent), so the bond value (or the price investors are willing to pay for this particular bond) is less than its \$1,000 face value.

Can a computer help?

Besides manual calculations using the future and present value tables discussed so far, these calculations also can be done using:

Financial calculators

Spreadsheet software, such as Excel.

Note: Depending on the method used, rounding errors in answers are unavoidable. Computer software can be extremely helpful in making these calculations. For example, Excel's PV (rate, nper, pmt, fv, type) determines the present value of an investment, based on a series of equal payments, discounted at a periodic interest rate over the number of periods. To calculate the present value of an annuity due, use the following formula:

PV (rate,nper,pmt,fv,type)*(1 + rate).

What are limitations of present- and compound-value techniques?

What are some assumptions that underlie the present- and compound-value techniques? First, all the ingredients (or variables) used in the calculation of present or compound value (amounts being discounted or subject to growth, the interest rates used, and the discount or growth periods) are known with certainty. Second, the interest rate used for discounting or growth is constant over the given time period. Third, all amounts in a series are equal to each other. The second and third assumptions can be dropped, but doing so leads to an entirely new realm, replete with difficulties. If the first assumption is dropped, various statistical estimation techniques will be necessary, and present and compound values become subject to statistical estimation rather than arithmetic calculation.

In the real world, there is always uncertainty. This means that appropriate statistical techniques should be used to determine best estimates for each variable.

Table 8.1 The Future Value of $1
(Compound Amount of $1.00) $= (1 + i)^n = T_1(I, n)$

Periods	4%	6%	8%	10%	12%	14%	20%
1	1.040	1.060	1.080	1.100	1.120	1.140	1.200
2	1.082	1.124	1.166	1.210	1.254	1.300	1.440
3	1.125	1.191	1.260	1.331	1.405	1.482	1.728
4	1.170	1.263	1.361	1.464	1.574	1.689	2.074
5	1.217	1.338	1.469	1.611	1.762	1.925	2.488
6	1.265	1.419	1.587	1.772	1.974	2.195	2.986
7	1.316	1.504	1.714	1.949	2.211	2.502	3.583
8	1.369	1.594	1.851	2.144	2.476	2.853	4.300
9	1.423	1.690	1.999	2.359	2.773	3.252	5.160
10	1.480	1.791	2.159	2.594	3.106	3.707	6.192
11	1.540	1.898	2.332	2.853	3.479	4.226	7.430
12	1.601	2.012	2.518	3.139	3.896	4.818	8.916
13	1.665	2.133	2.720	3.452	4.364	5.492	10.699
14	1.732	2.261	2.937	3.798	4.887	6.261	12.839
15	1.801	2.397	3.172	4.177	5.474	7.138	15.407
16	1.873	2.540	3.426	4.595	6.130	8.137	18.488
17	1.948	2.693	3.700	5.055	6.866	9.277	22.186
18	2.026	2.854	3.996	5.560	7.690	10.575	26.623
19	2.107	3.026	4.316	6.116	8.613	12.056	31.948
20	2.191	3.207	4.661	5.728	9.646	13.743	38.338
30	3.243	5.744	10.063	17.450	29.960	50.950	237.380
40	4.801	10.286	21.725	45.260	93.051	188.880	1469.800

Table 8.2 The Future Value of an Annuity of $1
(Compound Amount of an Annuity of $1) $= T_2(i,n)$

Periods	4%	6%	8%	10%	12%	14%	20%
1	1.000	1.000	1.000	1.000	1.000	1.000	1.000
2	2.040	2.060	2.080	2.100	2.120	2.140	2.200
3	3.122	3.184	3.246	3.310	3.374	3.440	3.640
4	4.247	4.375	4.506	4.641	4.779	4.921	5.368
5	5.416	5.637	5.867	6.105	6.353	6.610	7.442
6	6.633	6.975	7.336	7.716	8.115	8.536	9.930
7	7.898	8.394	8.923	9.487	10.289	10.730	12.916
8	9.214	9.898	10.637	11.436	12.300	13.233	16.499
9	10.583	11.491	12.488	13.580	14.776	16.085	20.799
10	12.006	13.181	14.487	15.938	17.549	19.337	25.959
11	13.486	14.972	16.646	18.531	20.655	23.045	32.150
12	15.026	16.870	18.977	21.385	24.133	37.271	39.580
13	16.627	18.882	21.495	24.523	28.029	32.089	48.497
14	18.292	21.015	24.215	27.976	32.393	37.581	59.196
15	20.024	23.276	27.152	31.773	37.280	43.842	72.035
16	21.825	25.673	30.324	35.950	42.759	50.980	87.442
17	23.698	28.213	33.750	40.546	48.884	59.118	105.930
18	25.645	30.906	37.450	45.600	55.750	68.394	128.120
19	27.671	33.760	41.446	51.160	63.440	78.969	154.740
20	29.778	36.778	45.762	57.276	75.052	91.025	186.690
30	56.085	79.058	113.283	164.496	241.330	356.790	1181.900
40	95.026	154.762	259.057	442.597	767.090	1342.000	7343.900

*Payments (or receipts) at the *end* of each period.

Table 8.3 The Present Value of $1 = T₃ (I,n)

Periods	4%	6%	8%	10%	12%	14%	16%	18%	20%	22%	24%	26%	28%	30%	40%
1	.962	.943	.926	.909	.893	.877	.862	.847	.833	.820	.806	.794	.781	.769	.714
2	.925	.890	.857	.826	.797	.769	.743	.718	.694	.672	.650	.630	.610	.592	.510
3	.889	.840	.794	.751	.712	.675	.641	.609	.579	.551	.524	.500	.477	.455	.364
4	.855	.792	.735	.683	.636	.592	.552	.516	.482	.451	.423	.397	.373	.350	.260
5	.822	.747	.681	.621	.567	.519	.476	.437	.402	.370	.341	.315	.291	.269	.186
6	.790	.705	.630	.564	.507	.456	.410	.370	.335	.303	.275	.250	.227	.207	.133
7	.760	.665	.583	.513	.452	.400	.354	.314	.279	.249	.222	.198	.178	.159	.095
8	.731	.627	.540	.467	.404	.351	.305	.266	.233	.204	.179	.157	.139	.123	.068
9	.703	.592	.500	.424	.361	.308	.263	.225	.194	.167	.144	.125	.108	.094	.048
10	.676	.558	.463	.386	.322	.270	.227	.191	.162	.137	.116	.099	.085	.073	.035
11	.650	.527	.429	.350	.287	.237	.195	.162	.135	.112	.094	.079	.066	.056	.025
12	.625	.497	.397	.319	.257	.208	.168	.137	.112	.092	.076	.062	.052	.043	.018
13	.601	.469	.368	.290	.229	.182	.145	.116	.093	.075	.061	.050	.040	.033	.013
14	.577	.442	.340	.263	.205	.160	.125	.099	.078	.062	.049	.039	.032	.025	.009
15	.555	.417	.315	.239	.183	.140	.108	.084	.065	.051	.040	.031	.025	.020	.006

16	.534	.394	.292	.218	.163	.123	.093	.071	.054	.042	.032	.025	.019	.015	.005
17	.513	.371	.270	.198	.146	.108	.080	.060	.045	.034	.026	.020	.015	.012	.003
18	.494	.350	.250	.180	.130	.095	.069	.051	.038	.028	.021	.016	.012	.009	.002
19	.475	.331	.232	.164	.116	.083	.060	.043	.031	.023	.017	.012	.009	.007	.002
20	.456	.312	.215	.149	.104	.073	.051	.037	.026	.019	.014	.010	.007	.005	.001
21	.439	.294	.199	.135	.093	.064	.044	.031	.022	.015	.011	.008	.006	.004	.001
22	.422	.278	.184	.123	.083	.056	.038	.026	.018	.013	.009	.006	.004	.003	.001
23	.406	.262	.170	.112	.074	.049	.033	.022	.015	.010	.007	.005	.003	.002	
24	.390	.247	.158	.102	.066	.043	.028	.019	.013	.008	.006	.004	.003	.002	
25	.375	.233	.146	.092	.059	.038	.024	.016	.010	.007	.005	.003	.002	.001	
26	.361	.220	.135	.084	.053	.033	.021	.014	.009	.006	.004	.002	.002	.001	
27	.347	.207	.125	.076	.047	.029	.018	.011	.007	.005	.003	.002	.001	.001	
28	.333	.196	.116	.069	.042	.026	.016	.010	.006	.004	.002	.002	.001	.001	
29	.321	.185	.107	.063	.037	.022	.014	.008	.005	.003	.002	.001	.001	.001	
30	.308	.174	.099	.057	.033	.020	.012	.007	.004	.003	.002	.001	.001		
40	.208	.097	.046	.022	.011	.005	.003	.001	.001						

Table 8.4 The Present Value of an Annuity of $1 = T₄(I,n)

Per-iods	3%	4%	5%	6%	7%	8%	10%	12%	14%	16%	18%	20%	22%	24%
1	.9709	.9615	.9524	.9434	.9346	.9259	.9091	.8929	.8772	.8621	.8475	.8333	.8197	.8065
2	1.9135	1.8861	1.8594	1.8334	1.8080	1.7833	1.7355	1.6901	1.6467	1.6052	1.5656	1.5278	1.4915	1.4568
3	2.8286	2.7751	2.7232	2.6730	2.6243	2.5771	2.4869	2.4018	2.3216	2.2459	2.1743	2.1065	2.0422	1.9813
4	3.7171	3.6299	3.5460	3.4651	3.3872	3.3121	3.1699	3.0373	2.9137	2.7982	2.6901	2.5887	2.4936	2.4043
5	4.5797	4.4518	4.3295	4.2124	4.1002	3.9927	3.7908	3.6048	3.4331	3.2743	3.1272	2.9906	2.8636	3.7454
6	5.4172	5.2421	5.0757	4.9173	4.7665	4.6229	4.3553	4.1114	3.8887	3.6847	3.4976	3.3255	3.1669	3.0205
7	6.2303	6.0021	5.7864	5.5824	5.3893	5.2064	4.8684	4.5638	4.2883	4.0386	3.8115	3.6046	3.4155	3.2423
8	7.0197	6.7327	6.4632	6.2098	5.9713	5.7466	5.3349	4.9676	4.6389	4.3436	4.0776	3.8372	3.6193	3.4212
9	7.7861	7.4353	7.1078	6.8017	6.5152	6.2469	5.7590	5.3282	4.9464	4.6065	4.3030	4.0310	3.7863	3.5655
10	8.5302	8.1109	7.7217	7.3601	7.0236	6.7101	6.1446	5.6502	5.2161	4.8332	4.4941	4.1925	3.9232	3.6819
11	9.2526	8.7605	8.3064	7.8869	7.4987	7.1390	6.4951	5.9377	5.4527	5.0286	4.6560	4.3271	4.0354	3.7757
12	9.9540	9.3851	8.8633	8.3838	7.9427	7.5361	6.8137	6.1944	5.6603	5.1971	4.7932	4.4392	4.1274	3.8514
13	10.6350	9.9856	9.3936	8.8527	8.3577	7.9038	7.1034	6.4235	5.8424	5.3423	4.9095	4.5327	4.2028	3.9124
14	11.2961	10.5631	9.8986	9.2950	8.7455	8.2442	7.3667	6.6282	6.0021	5.4675	5.0081	4.6106	4.2646	3.9616
15	11.9379	11.1184	10.3797	9.7122	9.1079	8.5595	7.6061	6.8109	6.1422	5.5755	5.0916	4.6755	4.3152	4.0013

16	12.5611	11.6523	10.8378	10.1059	9.4466	8.8514	7.8237	6.9740	6.2651	5.6685	5.1624	4.7296	4.3567	4.0333
17	13.1661	12.1657	11.2741	10.4773	9.7632	9.1216	8.0216	7.1196	6.3729	5.7487	5.2223	4.7746	4.3908	4.0591
18	13.7535	12.6593	11.6896	10.8276	10.0591	9.3719	8.2014	7.2497	6.4674	5.8178	5.2732	4.8122	4.4187	4.0799
19	14.3238	13.1339	12.0853	11.1581	10.3356	9.6036	8.3649	7.3658	6.5504	5.8775	5.3162	4.8435	4.4415	4.0967
20	14.8775	13.5903	12.4622	11.4699	10.5940	9.8181	8.5136	7.4694	6.6231	5.9288	5.3527	4.8696	4.4603	4.1103
21	15.4150	14.0292	12.8212	11.7641	10.8355	10.0168	8.6487	7.5620	6.6870	5.9731	5.3837	4.8913	4.4756	4.1212
22	15.9369	14.4511	13.1630	12.0416	11.0612	10.2007	8.7715	7.6446	6.7429	6.0113	5.4099	4.9094	4.4882	4.1300
23	16.4436	14.8568	13.4886	12.3034	11.2722	10.3711	8.8832	7.7184	6.7921	6.0442	5.4321	4.9245	4.4985	4.1371
24	16.9355	15.2470	13.7986	12.5504	11.4693	10.5288	8.9847	7.7843	6.8351	6.0726	5.4509	4.9371	4.5070	4.1428
25	17.4131	15.6221	14.0939	12.7834	11.6536	10.6536	9.0770	7.8431	6.8729	6.0971	5.4669	4.9476	4.5139	4.1474
26	17.8768	15.9828	14.3752	13.0032	11.8258	10.8100	9.1609	7.8957	6.9061	6.1182	5.4804	4.9563	4.5196	4.1511
27	18.3270	16.3296	14.6430	13.2105	11.9867	10.9352	9.2372	7.9426	6.9352	6.1364	5.4919	4.9636	4.5243	4.1542
28	18.7641	16.6631	14.8981	13.4062	12.1371	11.0511	9.3066	7.9844	6.9607	6.1520	5.5016	4.9697	4.5281	4.1566
29	19.1885	16.9837	15.1411	13.5907	12.2777	11.1584	9.3696	8.0218	6.9830	6.1656	5.5098	4.9747	4.5312	4.1585
30	19.6004	17.2920	15.3725	13.7648	12.4090	11.2578	9.4269	8.0552	7.0027	6.1772	5.5168	4.9789	4.5338	4.1601
40	23.1148	19.7928	17.1591	15.0463	13.3317	11.9246	9.7791	8.2438	7.1050	6.2335	5.5482	4.9966	4.5439	4.1659

CHAPTER 9

Capital Budgeting

Capital budgeting involves planning for the best selections and financing of long-term investments. In this chapter, the following six techniques are described to help you select the best long-term investment proposals:

- Payback period
- Discounted payback period
- Accounting (simple) rate of return (ARR)
- Net present value (NPV)
- Internal rate of return (IRR) (or time-adjusted rate of return)
- Profitability index (or present-value index)

Your selection will necessarily involve judgments about future events about which you have no direct knowledge. Your task will be to minimize your chances of being wrong. The risk-return trade-off method shown in this chapter is one way to help you come to grips with uncertainty.

9.1 CAPITAL BUDGETING

What is capital budgeting?

Capital budgeting is a selection technique used to evaluate long-term investment proposals. It can be done in a number of ways, four of which are described in this chapter. Understanding these techniques is important for managerial accountants and management executives in both for-profit and nonprofit industries. Mid-level managers should also be familiar with capital budgeting because they are, to some degree, concerned with investment and management of resources.

What are the uses of capital budgeting?

Whenever there is a decision regarding how to invest major chunks of resources, there is a capital budgeting problem. Ask the following questions:

- Should I replace certain equipment?
- Should I expand facilities by renting additional space, buying an existing building, or constructing a new building?
- Should I invest in high-tech information technology (IT)?
- Should I launch new product development?
- Do I have an opportunity to refinance an outstanding debt issue? Should I do it?
- I've been contemplating a merger. Should I go ahead with it?
- I've been thinking about adding a new product to our line. Should I?
- I'm considering a new major advertising campaign. Should I hold off?

What are the features of investment projects?

Long-term investments have three important features:

1. They typically involve a large amount of initial cash outlay, which tends to have a long-term impact on the firm's future profitability. Therefore, this initial cash outlay needs to be justified on a cost-benefit basis.

2. There are expected recurring cash inflows (for example, increased revenues, savings in cash operating expenses, and so on) over the life of the investment project. This frequently requires considering the time value of money. Depreciation expense is a consideration only to the extent that it affects the cash flows for taxes. Otherwise, depreciation is excluded from the analysis because it is a non-cash expense.

3. Income taxes could make a difference in the accept or reject decision. Therefore, income tax factors must be taken into account in every capital budgeting decision.

9.2   TECHNIQUES FOR EVALUATING INVESTMENT PROPOSALS

What are the popular evaluation techniques?

Several methods of evaluating investment projects follow:

- Payback period
- Discounted payback period
- Accounting (simple) rate of return (ARR)
- Net present value (NPV)
- Internal rate of return (IRR) (or time-adjusted rate of return)
- Profitability index (or present-value index)

The NPV method and the IRR method are called discounted cash-flow (DCF) methods. Each of these methods is discussed below.

How is the payback period determined?

The payback period measures the length of time required to recover the amount of initial investment. When the annual cash flows are constant and of equal amounts, the payback period can be calculated by dividing the initial investment by the cash inflows through increased revenues or cost savings.

Example 9.1

Assume:

Cost of investment	$18,000
Annual after-tax cash savings	$3,000

Then, the payback period is

$$\text{Payback period} = \frac{\text{initial investment}}{\text{cost savings}}$$

$$= \frac{\$18,000}{\$3,000} = 6 \text{ years}$$

Decision rule: Choose the project with the shorter payback period. The rationale behind this choice is this: the shorter the payback period, the less risky the project, and the greater the liquidity. *Note*: When periodic cash flows are not equal, calculation of the payback period is more complex.

Example 9.2

Consider two projects whose after-tax cash inflows are not even. Assume each project costs $1,000.

	Cash	*Inflow*
Year	A($)	B($)
1	100	500
2	200	400
3	300	300
4	400	100
5	500	
6	600	

When cash inflows are not even, the payback period has to be found by trial and error. The payback period of project A is 4 years ($1,000 = $100 + $200 + $300 + $400). The payback period of project B is 2⅓ years ($1,000 = $500 + $400 + $100):

$$2 \text{ years} + \frac{\$100}{\$300} = 2\tfrac{1}{3} \text{ years}$$

Project B is the project of choice in this case, since it has the shorter payback period.

What are the pros and cons of the payback period method?

The advantages of using the payback period method of evaluating an investment project are that (1) it is simple to compute and easy to understand, and (2) it handles investment risk effectively. The shortcomings of this method are that (1) it does not recognize the time value of money, and (2) it ignores the impact of cash inflow received after the payback period; essentially, cash flows after the payback period determine the profitability of an investment.

How is the discounted payback period determined?

Take into account the time value of money by using the discounted payback period. The payback period will be longer using the discounted method because money is worth less over time. Discounted payback is computed by adding the present value of each year's cash inflows until they equal the initial investment.

$$\text{Discounted payback} = \frac{\text{Initial cash outlays}}{\text{Discounted annual cash inflows}}$$

Example 9.3

An investment of $40,000 is made and receives the following cash inflows. The discounted payback period is calculated as follows:

Year	Cash Inflows	T1 Factor	Present Value	Accumulated Present Value
1	$15,000	.9091	$13,637	$13,637
2	20,000	.8264	16,528	30,165
3	28,000	.7513	21,036	51,201

Thus,

$$\$30,165 + \frac{\$40,000 - \$30,165}{\$21,036} = 2 \text{ years} + .47$$

$$= 2.47 \text{ years}$$

What is the accounting rate of return?

Accounting rate of return (ARR) measures profitability from the conventional accounting standpoint by relating the required investment—or sometimes the average investment—to the future annual net income.

Decision rule: Under the ARR method, choose the project with the higher rate of return.

Example 9.4

Consider the following investment:

Initial investment	$6,500
Estimated life	20 years
Cash inflows per year	$1,000
Depreciation per year (using straight-line method)	$325

$$\text{ARR} = \frac{\text{Project's average annual income}}{\text{Initial (or average) investment}}$$

Average investment is defined as follows:

$$\text{Average investment} = \frac{(I - S)}{2} + S$$

where I = initial (original) investment and S = salvage value. When there is no salvage value, the average investment = I/2

Decision rule: Under the ARR method, choose the project with the higher rate of return.

What are the benefits and drawbacks of the ARR method?

The advantages of this method are that it is understandable, is simple to compute, and recognizes the profitability factor.

The shortcomings of this method are that it fails to recognize the time value of money, and it uses accounting instead of cash-flow data.

What is internal rate of return?

Internal rate of return (IRR) is defined as the rate of interest that equates I with the PV of future cash inflows. In other words, at IRR,

$$I = PV$$

or

$$NPV = 0$$

Decision rule: Accept the project if the IRR exceeds the cost of capital. Otherwise, reject it.

Example 9.5

Consider the following investment:

Initial investment	$37,910
Estimated life	5 years
Annual cash inflows after taxes	$10,000
Cost of capital (minimum required rate of return)	8%

We set the following equality (I = PV):

$$\$37,910 = \$10,000. \; T_4(i, 5 \text{ years})$$
$$T_4(i, 5 \text{ years}) = \frac{\$37,910}{\$10,000} = 3.791$$

which is right on 10 percent in the five-year line of Table 8.4.

Since the IRR of the investment is greater than the cost of capital (8 percent), accept the project.

What are the benefits and drawbacks of the IRR method?

The advantage of using the IRR method is that it considers the time value of money, and therefore is more exact and realistic than the ARR method. The shortcomings of this method are that (1) it is time-consuming to compute, especially when the cash inflows are not even, although most business calculators and spreadsheet software programs can calculate IRR, and (2) it fails to recognize the varying sizes of investment in competing projects.

Note: When cash inflows are not even, IRR is computed by the trial-and-error method, which is not discussed here. Financial calculators such as those made by Texas Instruments and Sharp have a key for IRR calculations.

What is net present value?

Net present value (NPV) is the excess of the present value (PV) of cash inflows generated by the project over the amount of the initial investment (I):

$$NPV = PV - I$$

The present value of future cash flows is computed using the so-called cost of capital (or minimum required rate of return) as the discount rate. In the case of an annuity, the present value would be

$$PV = A \cdot T_4 (i, n)$$

where A is the amount of the annuity. The value of T_4 is found in Table 8.4 in Chapter 8.

Decision rule: If NPV is positive, accept the project. Otherwise, reject it.

Example 9.6

Assume the same data given in Example 9.5, and the net present value of the cash inflows is as follows:

$$
\begin{aligned}
PV = A \cdot T_4 (i, n) \\
= \$10{,}000\ T_4(8\%, 5\ \text{years}) \\
= \$10{,}000\ (3.993) \qquad \$39{,}930 \\
\text{Initial investment (I)} \qquad \underline{37{,}910} \\
\text{Net present value (NPV} = PV - I) \qquad \underline{\$\ 2{,}020}
\end{aligned}
$$

Because the NPV of the investment is positive, the investment should be accepted.

What are the pros and cons of the NPV method?

The advantages of the NPV method are that it obviously recognizes the time value of money, and it is easy to compute whether the cash flows are in the form of an annuity or vary from period to period.

Can a computer help?

Spreadsheet programs can be used in making IRR calculations. For example, Excel has a function IRR (values, guess). Excel considers negative numbers, such as the initial investment, as cash outflows, and positive numbers as cash inflows. Many financial calculators have similar features.

As in Example 9.3, calculate the IRR of a $37,910 investment (the value −37910, entered in year 0, followed by five monthly cash inflows of $10,000). Using a guess of 8 percent (the value of 0.08), which is in effect the cost of capital, the formula would be @IRR (values, 0.08) and Excel would return 10 percent as shown below.

Year 0	1	2	3	4	5
−37910	10000	10000	10000	10000	10000
IRR =	10%				
NPV =	$2,017.10				

Note: The Excel formula for NPV is NPV (discount rate, cash inflow values) + I, where I is given as a negative number.

How does the profitability index work?

The profitability index uses the same variables as NPV but combines them differently. Profitability index (PI) is defined as the ratio of the total PV of future cash inflows to the initial investment; that is, PV/I. This index is used as a means of ranking projects in descending order of attractiveness. Normally, when comparing more than one project, the one with the higher PI is the more profitable. *Caution:* A higher PI does not always coincide with the project with the highest NPV.

Decision rule: If PI is greater than 1, the project is a good candidate for investment.

Example 9.7

Using the data in Example 9.5, the profitability index is

$$\frac{PV}{I} = \frac{\$39,930}{\$37,910} = 1.05$$

Because this project generates $1.05 for each dollar invested (that is, its profitability index is greater than 1), the project should be accepted.

The profitability index has the advantage of putting all projects on the same relative basis, regardless of size.

What is capital rationing?

Capital rationing occurs when a company cannot or will not undertake all investment projects with NPV greater than or equal to zero. Usually the company has set an upper limit to its capital budget, thereby preventing it from undertaking all projects.

How do I select the best mix of projects with a limited budget?

Many firms specify a limit on the overall budget for capital spending. Capital rationing is concerned with the problem of selecting the mix of acceptable projects that provides the highest overall NPV. The profitability index is used widely in ranking projects competing for limited funds.

Example 9.8

A company with a fixed budget of $250,000 needs to select a mix of acceptable projects from the following:

Pro-jects	I($)	PV($)	NPV($)	Profitability Index	Rank-ing
A	70,000	112,000	42,000	1.60	1
B	100,000	145,000	45,000	1.45	2
C	110,000	126,500	16,500	1.15	5
D	60,000	79,000	19,000	1.32	3
E	40,000	38,000	−2,000	0.95	6
F	80,000	95,000	15,000	1.19	4

The ranking resulting from the profitability index shows that the company should select projects A, B, and D.

	I	PV
A	$70,000	$112,000
B	100,000	145,000
D	60,000	79,000
	$230,000	$336,000

Therefore,

$$NPV = \$336,000 - \$230,000 = \$106,000$$

How do the projects relate to each other?

Investment projects are either independent or mutually exclusive. They are independent if both can be undertaken simultaneously. When this occurs, there's no need to rank one project over another. Projects are mutually exclusive when only one project can be carried out. In such a case, it is necessary to rank the projects to determine which is more attractive.

How do you choose between mutually exclusive investments?

A project is said to be mutually exclusive if the acceptance of one project automatically excludes the acceptance of one or more other projects (for example, two alternative uses of a single plot of land). In the case in which one must choose between mutually exclusive investments, the NPV and IRR methods may result in contradictory indications. The conditions under which contradictory rankings can occur are

1. Projects that have different life expectancies.
2. Projects that have different sizes of investment.
3. Projects whose cash flows differ over time (for example, the cash flows of one project increase over time, while those of another decrease).

The contradictions result from different assumptions with respect to the reinvestment rate on cash flows from the projects.

1. The NPV method discounts all cash flows at the cost of capital, thus implicitly assuming that these cash flows can be reinvested at this rate.
2. The IRR method assumes that cash flows are reinvested at the often unrealistic rate specified by the project's internal rate of return. Thus, the implied reinvestment rate will differ from project to project.

Thus, the relative desirability of mutually exclusive projects depends on what rate of return the subsequent cash flows can earn. The NPV method generally gives correct ranking, since the cost of capital is a more realistic reinvestment rate. The cost of capital tends to give a close approximation for the market rate of return.

Example 9.9

Assume the following:

| | \multicolumn{6}{c}{Cash Flows} |
	0	1	2	3	4	5
A	(100)	120				
B	(100)				201.14	

Computing IRR and NPV at 10 percent gives the following different rankings:

	IRR	NPV at 10%
A	20%	9.01
B	15%	24.90

The difference in ranking between the two methods is caused by the methods' reinvestment rate assumptions. The IRR method assumes Project A's cash inflow of $120 is reinvested at 20 percent for the subsequent four years, and the NPV method assumes $120 is reinvested at 10 percent. The correct decision is to select the project with the higher NPV (that is, Project B), because the NPV method assumes a more realistic reinvestment rate—that is, the cost of capital (10 percent in this example).

The net present values plotted against various discount rates (costs of capital) results in the NPV profiles for projects A and B (see Figure 9.1). An analysis of Figure 9.1 indicates that at a discount rate larger than 14 percent, A has a higher NPV than B. Therefore, A should be selected. At a discount rate less than 14 percent, B has the higher NPV than A, and thus should be selected.

Figure 9.1 The NPV Graph

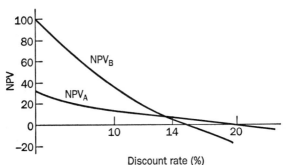

The correct decision is to select the project with the higher NPV, since the NPV method assumes a more realistic reinvestment rate—that is, the cost of capital.

Which is the preferable project if NPV and IRR do not give consistent signals?

In order to resolve this conflict, know the interest rate or rates at which the company will be able to reinvest net cash inflows from the projects as these funds are generated. In other words, there exists a need to forecast future or compound values of the net cash inflows as of the end of the expected life of the projects.

What is the use of modified internal rate of return?

The modified internal rate of return (MIRR) is defined as the discount rate that forces the initial cash outlay to equal to the present value of terminal (future) value compounded at the cost of capital.

The MIRR forces cash-flow reinvestment at the cost of capital rather than at the project's own IRR, which was the problem with the IRR. MIRR avoids the problem of multiple IRRs. However, conflicts can still occur in ranking mutually exclusive projects of different sizes. NPV should again be used when this occurs.

Example 9.10

Refer to Example 9.9, where computing IRR and NPV at 10 percent gives the following different rankings:

Project	IRR	NPV at 10%
A	20%	$ 9.01
B	15%	24.90

As previously noted, the correct decision is to select the project with the higher NPV (Project B), since the NPV method assumes a more realistic reinvestment rate—that is, the cost of capital (10 percent in this example). The MIRR overcomes this problem.

Project A's MIRR
First, compute the project's terminal value at a 10 percent cost of capital.

$$120 \times T_1(10\%, 4 \text{ years}) = 120 \times 1.4641 = 175.69$$

Next, find the IRR by setting

$$100 = 175.69 \, T_3(\text{MIRR}, 5 \text{ years})$$
$$T_3 = 100/175.69 = 0.5692, \text{ which gives MIRR}$$
$$= \text{about } 12\%$$

Now we see the consistent ranking from both the NPV and MIRR methods.

	MIRR	NPV at 10%
A	12%	$ 9.01
B	15%	24.90

Note: Microsoft Excel has a function MIRR (values, finance_rate, reinvest_rate).

9.3 EFFECT OF INCOME TAXES ON CAPITAL BUDGETING DECISIONS

How do income-tax factors affect investment decisions?

Income taxes make a difference in many capital budgeting decisions. In other words, the project that seems attractive on a before-tax basis may have to be rejected on an after-tax basis. Income taxes typically affect both the amount and the timing of cash flows. Because net income—not cash inflows—is subject to tax, after-tax cash inflows are not usually the same as after-tax net income.

Let us define

$$S = \text{Sales}$$
$$E = \text{Cash operating expenses}$$
$$d = \text{Depreciation}$$
$$t = \text{Tax rate}$$

Then, before-tax cash inflows (or before-tax cash savings) $= S - E$ and net income $= S - E - d$. By definition,

After-tax cash inflows = Before-tax cash inflows − Taxes
$$= (S - E) - (S - E - d)(t)$$

Rearranging gives the short-cut formula:

After-tax cash inflows $= (S - E)(1 - t) + (d)(t)$

As can be seen here, the deductibility of depreciation from sales in arriving at net income subject to taxes reduces income tax payments, and thus serves as a tax shield.

Tax shield = Tax savings on depreciation $= (d)(t)$

Example 9.11

Assume

$S = \$12,000$

$E = \$10,000$

$d = \$500$ per year using the straight-line method

$t = 30\%$

Then,

After-tax cash inflow $= (\$12,000 - \$10,000)(1 - 0.3)$
$$+ (\$500)(0.3)$$
$$= (\$2,000)(.7) + (\$500)(0.3)$$
$$= \$1,400 + \$150 = \$1,550$$

Note that a tax shield = tax savings on deprecia-tion = (d)(t)

$$= (\$500)(.3) = \$150$$

Since the tax shield is dt, the higher the deprecia-tion deduction, the higher the tax savings on depre-ciation. Therefore, an accelerated depreciation method (such as double-declining balance) pro-duces higher tax savings than the straight-line method. Accelerated methods produce higher pre-sent values for the tax savings, which may make a given investment more attractive.

Example 9.12

The Shalimar Company estimates that it can save $2,500 a year in cash operating costs for the next ten years if it buys a special-purpose machine at a cost of $10,000. No salvage value is expected. Assume that the income tax rate is 30 percent, and the after-tax cost of capital (minimum required rate of re-turn) is 10 percent. After-tax cash savings can be calculated as follows.

Note that depreciation by straight-line is $10,000/10 = $1,000 per year. Here, before-tax cash savings = (S − E) = $2,500. Thus,

$$\text{After-tax cash savings} = (S − E)(1 − t) + (d)(t)$$
$$= \$2,500(1 − 0.3) + \$1,000(0.3)$$
$$= \$1,750 + \$300 = \$2,050$$

To see if this machine should be purchased, the net present value can be calculated.

$$PV = \$2,050 \, T_4(10\%, 10 \text{ years})$$
$$= \$2,050 \, (6.145) = \$12,597.25$$

Thus,

$$NPV = PV − I = \$12,597.25 − \$10,000 = \$2,597.25$$

Since NPV is positive, the machine should be pur-chased.

What is the effect of ACRS on investment decisions?

Although traditional depreciation methods still can be used to compute depreciation for book pur-poses, 1981 saw a new method of computing deprecia-tion deductions for tax purposes. The rule is called the Modified Accelerated Cost Recovery System (MACRS) rule, as enacted by Congress in 1981 and then modified somewhat in 1986 under the Tax Reform Act of 1986. This rule is characterized as follows:

1. It abandons the concept of useful life and accelerates depreciation deductions by placing all depreciable assets into one of eight age-property classes. It calculates deductions based on an allowable percentage of the asset's original cost (see Tables 9.1 and 9.2). With a shorter life than useful life, the company would be able to deduct depreciation more quickly and save more in income taxes in the earlier years, thereby making an investment more attractive. The rationale behind the system is that this way the government encourages the company to invest in facilities and increase its productive capacity and efficiency. (Remember that the higher d, the larger the tax shield (d)(t)).

Table 9.1 Modified Accelerated Cost Recovery System Classification of Assets

	Property Class					
Year	3-year	5-year	7-year	10-year	15-year	20-year
1	33.3%	20.0%	14.3%	10.0%	5.0%	3.8%
2	44.5	32.0	24.5	18.0	9.5	7.2
3	14.8[a]	19.2	17.5	14.4	8.6	6.7
4	7.4	11.5[a]	12.5	11.5	7.7	6.2
5		11.5	8.9[a]	9.2	6.9	5.7
6		5.8	8.9	7.4	6.2	5.3
7			8.9	6.6[a]	5.9[a]	4.9
8			4.5	6.6	5.9	4.5[a]
9				6.5	5.9	4.5
10				6.5	5.9	4.5
11				3.3	5.9	4.5
12					5.9	4.5
13					5.9	4.5
14					5.9	4.5
15					5.9	4.5
16					3.0	4.4
17						4.4
18						4.4
19						4.4
20						4.4
21						2.2
Total	100%	100%	100%	100%	100%	100%

[a] Denotes the year of changeover to straight-line depreciation.

Table 9.2 MACRS Tables by Property Class

Property Class & Depreciation Method	Useful Life (ADR Midpoint Life)[a]	Examples of Assets
3-year property 200% declining balance	4 years or less	Most small tools are included; the law specifically excludes autos and light trucks from this property class.
5-year property 200% declining balance	More than 4 years to less than 10 years	Autos and light trucks, typewriters, copiers, duplicating equipment, heavy computers, general-purpose trucks, and research and experimentation equipment are included.
7-year property 200% declining balance	10 years or more to less than 16 years	Office furniture and fixtures, most machinery, and equipment used in production are included.
10-year property 200% declining balance	16 years or more to less than 20 years	Various machinery and equipment, such as that used in petroleum distilling and refining and in the milling of grain, are included.
15-year property 150% declining balance	20 years or more to less than 25 years	Sewage treatment plants, telephone and electrical distribution facilities, and land improvements are included.
20-year property 150% declining balance	25 years or more	Service stations and other real property with an ADR midpoint life of less than 27.5 years are included.
27.5-year property straight-line	Not applicable	All residential rental property is included.
31.5-year property straight-line	Not applicable	All nonresidential property is included.

[a] The term ADR midpoint life means the "useful life" of an asset in a business sense; the appropriate ADR midpoint lives for assets are designated in the tax regulations.

2. Because the allowable percentages in Table 9.2 add up to 100 percent, there is no need to consider the salvage value of an asset in computing depreciation.

3. The company may elect to use the straight-line method. The straight-line convention must follow what is called the half-year convention. This means that the company can deduct only half of the regular straight-line depreciation amount in the first year. The reason for electing to use the MACRS optional straight-line method is that some firms may prefer to stretch out depreciation deductions using the straight-line method rather than to accelerate them. Those firms are the ones just starting out or that have little or no income and wish to show more income on their income statements.

Example 9.13

Assume that a machine falls under a three-year property class and costs $3,000 initially. The straight-line option under MACRS differs from the traditional straight-line method in that under this method, the company would deduct only $500 depreciation in the first year and the fourth year ($3,000/3 years = $1,000; $1,000/2 = $500). The following table compares the straight-line half-year convention with the MACRS.

Year	Straight-line (half-year) depreciation	Cost		MACRS %	MACRS deduction
1	$500	$3,000	×	33.3%	$999
2	1,000	3,000	×	44.5	1,335
3	1,000	3,000	×	14.8	444
4	500	3,000	×	7.4	222
	$3,000				$3,000

Example 9.14

A machine costs $10,000. Annual cash inflows are expected to be $5,000. The machine will be depreciated using the MACRS rule, and will fall under the three-year property class. The cost of capital after taxes is 10 percent. The estimated life of the machine is four years. The tax rate is 30 percent. The salvage value of the machine at the end of the fifth year is expected to be $1,200. The tax rate is 30 percent. Should the machine be purchased? Use the NPV method.

The formula for computation of after-tax cash inflows $(S - E)(1 - t) + (d)(t)$ needs to be computed separately. The NPV analysis can be performed as follows:

		Present value factor @ 10%	Present value
(S – E) (1 – t):			
$5,000 $5,000 (1 – .3) = **$3,500**			
For 5 years for **5** years	**$3,500**	3.791(a)	$13,268.50

(d)(t):		MACRS			
Year	Cost	% d	(d)(t)		
1	$10,000 × 33.3%	$3,330	**$999**	.909(b)	908.09
2	$10,000 × 44.5	4,450	**1,335**	.826(b)	1,102.71
3	$10,000 × 14.8	1,480	**444**	.751(b)	333.44
4	$10,000 × 7.4	740	**222**	.683(b)	151.63

Salvage value:					
$1,200 in	$1,200				
year 5:	(1 – .3)	**$840**	.621(b)		521.64
	$840(c)				
	in year **5**				
	Present				
	value (PV)				$16,286.01

(a) T_4 (10%, 4 years) = 3.170 (see Table 8.4 in Chapter 8).

(b) T_3 values (year 1, 2, 3, 4, 5) obtained from Table 8.3 in Chapter 8.

(c) Any salvage value received under the MACRS rules is a taxable gain (the excess of the selling price over book value, in this example $1,200), because the book value will be zero at the end of the life of the machine.

Since NPV = PV – I = $16,286.01 – $10,000 = $6,286.01 is positive, the machine should be purchased.

9.4 THE LEASE-PURCHASE DECISION

What is the lease-purchase decision?

Firms considering the acquisition of new assets commonly confront the lease-purchase decision. This is a hybrid capital-budgeting decision that forces a company to compare the leasing and financing (purchasing) alternatives.

Can you describe some of the leasing benefits?

There are tax benefits from leasing equipment rather than financing it with a term loan. Depending upon one's needs and the nature of one's business, the entire lease payment may be fully deductible as a business expense, thereby reducing one's taxable income. With a loan, only the interest and depreciation can be deducted. Another benefit a lease offers is 100 percent financing, plus additional amounts on the equipment's costs to cover "soft costs" such as taxes, shipping, and installation. Some term loans offer 100 percent financing but, typically, they cover the cost of equipment only.

A lease can help one manage cash flow. The payments are usually lower than for a term loan. Because a lease payment often requires no down payment or deposit, one can get the necessary equipment without depleting reserve capital. The types of business that most often lease equipment to generate revenue are manufacturing, transportation, printing, and professional corporations, such as medical, law, or accounting firms. Leasing works well for such companies because they can keep their equipment current without having to dip into capital to do it. Since the business's capital is not being used for equipment, it can be used for business development and expansion.

What are loan benefits?

A loan is the best choice, however, if a company wants to keep the equipment and build equity quickly. Loans can be structured so the equipment can be owned outright at the end of the term.

Note: If one wants to retain equipment beyond the lease term and prefers to know the full cost of the financing up front, one may choose a lease purchase option. As its name implies, this option requires no additional payment to own the equipment at the end of the lease.

Can you prepare a present-value comparison?

To make an intelligent financial decision on a lease-purchase, an after-tax cash outflow, present-value comparison is needed. There are special steps to take when making this comparison.

When considering a lease, take the following steps:

1. Determine the annual lease payment. Because the annual lease payment is typically made in advance, the formula used is:

   Amount of lease $= A + A . T_4(i, n - 1)$ or A

   $$= \frac{\text{Amount of lease}}{1 + T_4 (i, n - 1)}$$

   Notice that $n - 1$ is used, rather than n.

2. Find the after-tax cash outflows.

3. Find the present value of the after-tax cash outflows.

When considering a purchase, take the following steps:

1. Find the annual loan amortization by using

$$A = \frac{\text{Amount of loan for the purchase}}{T_4\,(i, n - 1)}$$

The step may not be necessary since this amount is usually available.

2. Calculate the interest. The interest is segregated from the principal in each of the annual loan payments because only the interest is tax-deductible.

3. Find the cash outflows by adding interest and depreciation (plus any maintenance costs), and then compute the after-tax outflows.

4. Find the present value of the after-tax cash outflows using Table 8.3 in Chapter 8.

Example 9.15

A firm has decided to acquire a computer system, costing $100,000, with an expected life of five years, after which the system is not expected to have any residual value. The system can be purchased by borrowing, or it can be leased. If leasing is chosen, the lessor requires a 12 percent return. As is customary, lease payments are made in advance; that is, at the end of the year prior to each of the ten years. The tax rate is 50 percent and the firm's cost of capital, or after-tax cost of borrowing, is 8 percent.

First, compute the present value of the after-tax cash outflows associated with the leasing alternative.

Step 1 is to find the annual lease payment:

$$A = \frac{\text{Amount of lease}}{1 + T_4\,(i, n - 1)}$$

$$= \frac{\$100,000}{1 + T_4\,(12\%, 4\ \text{years})} = \frac{\$100,000}{1 + 3.3073}$$

$$= \frac{\$100,000}{4.3073} = \$23,216\ (\text{rounded})$$

Steps 2 and 3 can be done in the same schedule, as follows:

Year	(1) Lease Pay-ment($)	(2) Tax Savings ($)	(3)= (1)−(2) After-Tax Cash Outflow($)	(4) PV at 8%	(5)= (3) × (4) PV of Cash Outflow ($, rounded)
0	23,216		23,216	1.000	23,216
1–4	23,216	11,608[a]	11,608	3.3121[b]	38,447
5		11,608	(11,608)	0.6806[a]	(7,900)
					53,763

[a] $23,216 × 50%
[b] From Table 8.4 in Chapter 8.
[c] From Table 8.3 in Chapter 8.

If the asset is purchased, the firm is expected to finance it entirely with a 10 percent unsecured term loan. Straight-line depreciation is used, with no salvage value. There-fore, the annual depreciation is $20,000 ($100,000/5 years).

1. In this alternative, first find the annual loan pay-ment by using

$$A = \frac{\text{Amount of loan}}{T_4\,(i,\,n)}$$

$$A = \frac{\$100,000}{T_4(10\%,\,5\text{ years})}$$

$$= \frac{\$100,000}{3.7906} = \$26,381 \text{ (rounded)}$$

2. Calculate the interest by setting up a loan amorti-zation schedule.

Yr	(1) Loan Pay-ment($)	(2) Beginning-of-Yr Principal($)	(3)= (2)(10%) Interest($)	(4)= (1)−(3) Principal($)	(5)= (2)−(4) End-of-Yr Principal
1	26,381	100,000	10,000	16,381	83,619
2	26,381	83,619	8,362	18,019	65,600
3	26,381	65,600	6,560	19,821	45,779
4	26,381	45,779	4,578	21,803	23,976
5	26,381	23,976[a]	2,398	23,983[a]	

[a] Because of rounding errors, there is a slight difference between (2) and (4)

Steps 3 (cash outflows) and 4 (present values of those outflows) can be done as follows:

The sum of the present values of the cash outflows for leasing and purchasing by borrowing shows that purchasing is preferable because the PV of borrow-ing is less than the PV of leasing ($52,087 versus $53,761). The incremental savings are $1,674. *Note:* The slight discrepancy is due to rounding errors.

Lease versus Purchase Evaluation Report

| | Leasing | | Purchase/Borrow | | | | | Discounted Cash Flow | |
| | | Net After Tax Cash | Loan | Interest | Depreciation | Net After-Tax Cash | Present Value | | |
Year	Lease Payments	Flow	Payments	Expense	Expense	Flow	Factor	Leasing	Purchase
0	$ 23,216	$ 23,216					1	$23,216	
1	23,216	11,608	$ 26,381	$10,000	$ 20,000	$11,381	0.9259	10,748	10,538
2	23,216	11,608	26,381	8,362	20,000	12,200	0.8573	9,952	10,459
3	23,216	11,608	26,381	6,560	20,000	13,101	0.7938	9,214	10,400
4	23,216	11,608	26,381	4,578	20,000	14,092	0.735	8,532	10,358
5		(11,608)	26,381	2,398	20,000	15,182	0.6806	(7,900)	10,333
	$116,080	$58,040	$131,905	$31,898	$100,000	$65,956		$53,761	$52,087

	Lease Proposal	Purchase Proposal
Cost of machine	$ 100,000	$ 100,000
Terms of payment	5 years	5 years
Interest rate	12%	10%
Down payment		
Monthly lease payment at the end of the year	$ 23,216	
Monthly loan payment		$ 26,381
Depreciation		Straight-line
Residual purchase price	0%	0
Corporate tax bracket	50%	50%
After-tax cost of capital	8%	8%

9.5 CAPITAL BUDGETING AND INFLATION

How does inflation impact capital budgeting?

The accuracy of capital budgeting decisions depends on the accuracy of the data regarding cash inflows and outflows. For example, failure to incorporate price-level changes due to inflation in capital budgeting situations can result in errors in the predicting of cash flows and, therefore, in incorrect decisions.

What are the ways in which to incorporate price-level changes into capital budgeting decisions?

Typically, an analyst has two options when dealing with a capital budgeting situation with inflation: (1) restate the cash flows in nominal terms and discount them at a nominal cost of capital (minimum required rate of return), or (2) restate both the cash flows and cost of capital in constant terms and discount the constant cash flows at a constant cost of capital. The two methods are basically equivalent.

Example 9.16

A company has the following projected cash flows estimated in real terms:

	Real Cash Flows (000s)			
Period	0	1	2	3
	−100	35	50	30

The nominal cost of capital is 15 percent. Assume that inflation is projected at 10 percent a year. Then the first cash flow for Year 1, which is $35,000 in current dollars, will be 35,000 × 1.10 = $38,500 in Year 1 dollars. Similarly, the cash flow for Year 2 will be 50,000 × $(1.10)^2$ = $60,500 in Year 2 dollars, and so on. If these nominal cash flows are discounted at the 15 percent nominal cost of capital, the result is the following net present value (NPV) in thousands of dollars:

Period	Cash Flows	T_3 (Table 8.3)	Present Values
0	−100	1.000	−100.00
1	38.5	.870	33.50
2	60.5	.756	45.74
3	39.9	.658	26.25
		NPV =	_5.49_ or $5,490

Instead of converting the cash-flow forecasts into nominal terms, the cost of capital could be converted into real terms using the following formula:

$$\text{Real cost of capital} = \frac{1 + \text{nominal cost of capital}}{1 + \text{inflation rate}} - 1$$

In the example, this gives

$$
\begin{aligned}
\text{Real cost of capital} &= (1 + .15)/(1 + .10) - 1 \\
&= 1.15/1.10 - 1 \\
&= 1.045 - 1 \\
&= .045 \text{ or } 4.5\%
\end{aligned}
$$

The same answer will result, except for rounding errors ($5,490 vs. $5,580).

Period	Cash Flows	$T_3 = 1/(1 + .045)^n$	Present Values
0	−100	1.000	−100.00
1	35	$1/(1 + .045)$ = .957	33.50
2	50	$1/(1.045)2$ = .916	45.80
3	30	$1/(1.045)3$ = .876	26.28
		NPV =	5.58 or $5,580

9.6 CAPITAL BUDGETING SOFTWARE

What are some popular capital budgeting software programs?

There are many software packages, such as ready-to-use Excel worksheets, called templates. The following are samples of such software.

1. *Investment-Calc PRO 2002 Version 5.0* (www. mlnsoft.com/software/most_popular/index.php): With Investment-Calc PRO Version 5.0 the user can create and manipulate ready-to-use cash-flow Excel worksheets to analyze business, capital, share, lease-purchase, and cash-flow forecasts for internal use, for acquisitions, and for calculating best valuation for sale. The program calculates net present values, internal rate of return, accounting rate of return, share valuation, and economic valuations over any forecast period— fifteen, twenty, thirty or fifty years. Investment-Calc incorporates self-generating tables that calculate yearly asset depreciation values for any yearly capital purchase program; prepares tax calculations; calculates annual lease and loan finance costs and repayments; compounds money values; and transfers all values automatically into the user's spreadsheets to help save time.

2. *Budget-Calc PRO 2002* (www.mlnsoft.com/software/most_popular/index.php): Budget-Calc PRO provides ten budgeting templates, plus dynamic (self-adjusting) Excel tables for depreciation and loan amortization for preparing investment forecasts, profit/loss budgets, cash-flow forecasts, capital budgets, sales, ninety-one-day AP/AR forecasts, and annual employee productivity plans quickly and accurately (FASB 141 and 142 goodwill and intangible variable depreciation tables included).

CHAPTER 10

Assets Management, Financing Techniques, and Portfolio Theory

In this chapter, you will learn how to manage your company's assets and liabilities in order to generate the highest return at the lowest possible risk. Whether you are a financial manager, managerial accountant, or investment analyst, you should be concerned with

- Determining the proper mixture of assets in the total asset structure
- Receiving cash promptly while delaying its payment
- Selling to the right customers
- Formulating a sound investment strategy
- How to diversify to reduce risk

This chapter also helps you develop techniques for obtaining financing. If you're a financial manager, you'll learn how to go about raising funds on a short-, intermediate-, or long-term basis. Or, if you're an executive, the following factors will be very much your concern:

- The cost of capital for examining financing alternatives
- The appropriateness of your company's dividend policy
- The effects of inflation
- The effects of the business cycle
- Diversification

Economists and financial managers: You'll learn how to use economic indicators of performance for the purpose of evaluating your own company's financial health. All these techniques will help you cope with everyday situations as they arise.

10.1 MANAGING WORKING CAPITAL

What is working capital?

Working capital equals current assets less current liabilities; it is a measure of liquidity. *Caution to financial managers:* A higher balance in total current assets means greater ability to meet the debt, but it also means less return earned on total assets. *Remember:* Fixed assets generate a higher rate of return than current assets.

What is the risk-return trade-off in current versus fixed assets?

Fixed assets comprise the basic structure of a business, representing plant and manufacturing equipment. Assuming a viable business, a higher return is expected on machinery than on marketable securities, which, in fact, usually amount to less than the overall cost of capital. There is a risk-return trade-off here, since current assets represent less risk but lower return. Similarly, financing with current liabilities rather than long-term debt typically involves lower-cost but greater-liquidity risk. The greater the debt maturity, the more uncertainty, and hence generally the greater the cost.

What approach should I use for financing assets?

For management executives: It's probably best to use a hedging approach whereby assets are financed by liabilities of similar maturity. This will ensure that adequate funds are available to meet the debt when it is due.

10.2 MAXIMIZING YOUR RETURN ON CASH

What is necessary for good cash management?

For financial managers or management executives, cash management is important. If a company is holding on to cash unnecessarily, it is losing a return that could be earned by investing. The cash balance held should depend on forecasted cash flows, probability of running out of cash, maturity of debt, and ability to borrow. Forecasting information is needed to determine (1) the best time to incur and pay back debt and (2) the amount to transfer daily between accounts. Use such techniques as accounting budgets, zero-base budgeting, and quantitative models such as time series and probabilities.

Management executives use this rule: Required cash balance equals transaction balances (required for normal business activity), plus precautionary balances (needed for emergencies), plus compensating balances (needed for financing commitments).

How can I accelerate cash receipts?

Use the following techniques.

CHECKLIST OF WAYS TO ACCELERATE CASH RECEIPTS

- *Lockbox.* This is a location where customer payments are mailed, usually a strategic post-office box. Payments are then picked up several times during the day by the bank.
- *Concentration banking.* Funds are collected in local banks and transferred to a main concentration account.
- *Immediate transfer of funds between banks.* Transfers are accomplished through depository transfer checks or via wire.
- *Cash discounts for early payment.*
- *Accelerated billing practices.*
- *Personal collection efforts.*
- *Cash-on-delivery.*
- *Postdated customer checks.*
- *Depositing checks promptly.*
- *Obtaining cash tied up unnecessarily in other accounts* (for example, loans to company officers).

What to do: Compare the return earned from the newly acquired cash to the cost of implementing an accelerated cash-management system. Lockbox services are primarily good for collecting large-dollar, low-volume receipts. Because of its high per-item cost, a lockbox does not always provide net savings.

Example 10.1

Akel Corporation is considering a lockbox arrangement that would cost $350,000 per year. Daily collections average $1 million. Mailing and processing time will be reduced by four days with the arrangement. The rate of return is 10 percent. The cost-benefit analysis is shown as follows:

Annual return on freed cash	
10% × 4 × $1,000,000	$400,000
Annual cost	350,000
Savings	**$ 50,000**

Conclusion: The lockbox arrangement is profitable.

Example 10.2

Loft Corporation presently has a lockbox with Colt Bank. The bank handles $1.5 million per day for a $300,000 compensating balance. Loft is considering canceling this arrangement and instead dividing its western region through arrangements with two other banks. Most Bank will handle $1 million per day, with a compensating balance of $225,000, and Davis Bank will handle $500,000 per day, with a compensating balance of $200,000. In both instances, collections will improve by one half-day. The rate of return is 11 percent. A cost-benefit analysis shows the following:

Accelerated cash receipts of $1.5 million per day × 1/2 day	$750,000
Increased compensating balance	125,000
Increased cash flow	$625,000
Return rate	× 11%
Net annual savings	$ 68,750

Conclusion: The new arrangement is financially feasible.

How can I delay cash payments?

Try these techniques:

CHECKLIST OF WAYS TO DELAY CASH PAYMENTS

- *Centralize the payable operation.* This enables the company to meet obligations at the most profitable time. It also enhances the ability to predict disbursement float in the system.
- *Use drafts.* A draft is given to the bank for collection, which in turn goes to the issuer for acceptance. After that, the funds are deposited to pay the draft.
- *Use a computer terminal to transfer funds between various bank accounts at opportune times.*
- *Draw checks on remote banks.* For example, a New York company could use a California bank.
- *Mail checks from post offices with limited services, or where mail must go through several handling points.*
- *Use probability analysis to determine the expected time for checks to clear.* For example, funds deposited on payday may not equal the entire payroll, since not all checks will be cashed on that day.
- *Make partial payments.*

Suggestion for management executives: Consider "payment float"—that is, the difference between the checkbook balance and the bank balance. When float is used effectively, a company can hold a higher bank balance, even though a lower cash balance appears on the books.

Example 10.3

Company X writes checks averaging $50,000 per day; each check takes three days to clear. The company will have a checkbook balance of $150,000 less than the bank's records.

How much cash do I need on hand?

You can predict the optimum amount of transaction cash needed under conditions of certainty. First, compute the sum of the fixed cost applicable to transactions, and the opportunity cost of holding cash balances as follows:

$$\frac{F(T)}{C} + \frac{i(C)}{2}$$

where

C = given cash balance

F = fixed cost of transaction

T = total cash required for time period

i = interest rate on marketable securities

The following formula was developed by W. Baumol to compute the optimal cash level (K):

$$K = \sqrt{\frac{2FT}{i}}$$

Average cash balance equals

$$\frac{K}{2}$$

and the number of required transactions equals

$$\frac{\text{transaction cash}}{K}$$

Example 10.4

Company B expects a cash need of $4 million over a one-month period, to be paid out at a constant rate. The opportunity interest rate is 0.5 percent for one month. The cost for each transaction is $100. The optimal transaction size is computed as follows:

$$K = \sqrt{\frac{2FT}{i}} = \sqrt{\frac{2(100)(4,000,000)}{0.005}} = \$400,000$$

The average cash balance equals

$$\frac{K}{2} = \frac{\$400,000}{2} = \$200,000$$

The number of transactions required equals

$$\frac{\$400,000}{400,000} = 1$$

Suggestion for financial managers: Use a stochastic model for cash management when major uncertainty regarding cash payments exists. The Miller-Orr model places an upper ceiling (referred to as *d* dollars) and lower limit ("zero" dollars) for cash balances. When the upper limit is reached, a transfer takes place from securities to cash. The transaction will not occur as long as the cash balance falls within the limits of the model.

Take the following factors into account when using the Miller-Orr model:

- Fixed costs of a securities transaction (F)
- The daily interest rate on marketable securities (t)
- The deviation in daily net cash flows (σ^2)

The objective is to meet cash requirements at the lowest possible cost. When the cash balance reaches *d*, this amount less the cost of securities bought (z) reduces the balance to *z* dollars. When the cash balance equals zero, *z* dollars are sold and the new balance again reaches *z*. *Note to management executives:* The minimum cash balance is established at an amount greater than zero to act as a safety buffer (as, for example, delays in transfer).

Use these formulas for optimal and average cash balance:

$$\text{Optimal cash balance } (z) = \sqrt[3]{\frac{3F\sigma^2}{4i}}$$

$$\text{Optimal upper limit } (d) = 3z$$

$$\text{Average cash balance} = \frac{(z + d)}{3}$$

Example 10.5

Company J wishes to use the Miller-Orr model. The following data are given:

Fixed cost of a securities transaction	$10
Deviation in daily net cash flows	$50
Daily interest rate on securities $\left(\dfrac{10\%}{360}\right)$	0.0003

The optimal cash balance, the upper limit of cash needed, and the average cash balance are computed as follows:

$$z = \sqrt[3]{\frac{3(10)(50)}{4(0.0003)}} = \sqrt[3]{\frac{3(10)(50)}{0.0012}}$$

$$= \sqrt[3]{\frac{1,500}{0.0012}} = \sqrt[3]{1,250,000} = \$102$$

The optimal cash balance (z) = $102

The upper limit (*d*) = 3 × $102 = $306

The average cash balance = $\dfrac{\$102 + \$106}{3}$ = $136

Discussion: When the upper limit ($306) is reached, $204 of securities ($306 − $102) will be purchased, thereby obtaining the optimal cash balance of $102. When the lower limit of $0 dollars is reached, $102 of securities will be sold, again bringing the optimal cash balance to $102.

10.3 MANAGING ACCOUNTS RECEIVABLE

What can I do to manage receivables properly?

Financial managers, managerial accountants, and management executives will want to manage receivables in order to maximize return and minimize risk. Following are some of the many things that can be done.

CHECKLIST OF APPROACHES TO THE
MANAGEMENT OF ACCOUNTS RECEIVABLE

- Age accounts receivable for overdue balances and compare them to industry and competitive norms as well as your own prior years.
- Periodically revise credit limits based on your customers' changing financial health.
- When there might be a problem with collection, obtain collateral at least equal in amount to the account balance.
- Use collection agencies when warranted.
- Factor (sell) accounts receivable when net savings occur.

- Bill large sales immediately.
- Employ cycle billing for uniformity in the billing process.
- Mail customer statements within one day of the period's end.
- Offer delayed payment terms to stimulate demand.
- Carefully evaluate customers' financial health before giving credit.
- Obtain credit insurance to guard against abnormal losses from bad debt.
- Avoid typically high-risk receivables—for example, customers in a financially troubled industry or country.

Should I consider cash discounts?

Management executives: Decide whether cash discounts should be given for early payment. *What to do:* Implement discount policy, provided the return on funds obtained from early collection is greater than the cost of the discount.

Example 10.6

Blake Company provides the following data:

Current annual credit sales	$8,000,000
Collection period	2 months
Terms	net/30
Minimum rate of return	15%

The financial manager is considering whether to offer a 2/10, net/30 discount. He anticipates that 25 percent of the customers will take advantage of the discount. The collection period should decline to 1.5 months.

The advantage of the policy is shown as follows.

Return
The average accounts receivable balance prior to the change in policy is

$$\frac{\text{credit sales}}{\text{accounts receivable turnover}} = \frac{\$8,000,000}{6} = \$1,333,333$$

The average accounts receivable balance subsequent to change in policy is:

$$\frac{\$8,000,000}{8} = \underline{1,000,000}$$

Decrease in average accounts receivable	$333,333
Rate of return	× 15%
Return	$ 50,000
Discount	
Cost of discount 0.02 × 0.25 × $8,000,000	$ 40,000
Net advantage of discount policy	$ 10,000

When should I give credit to marginal customers?

Management executives: Management executives are often faced with a decision of whether to give credit to somewhat marginal customers. *What to do:* Give credit when the profitability of the additional sales is greater than the additional cost associated with the discount. When idle capacity exists, this additional profitability equals the contribution margin (sales minus variable cost). But remember to add these costs, too: higher bad debts, opportunity cost of putting funds in receivables for a longer period of time, and increased clerical costs for servicing an additional customer base.

Example 10.7

Long Corporation provides the following data:

Selling price per unit	$5
Variable cost per unit	$2
Fixed cost per unit	$2
Annual credit sales	600,000 units
Collection period	1 month
Minimum return	24%

The financial manager is considering a proposal to liberalize credit. He expects sales to increase by 20 percent. The collection period on total accounts will be two months. Bad debts will increase by $90,000.

The following calculations show that the policy should be implemented:

Additional profit on increased sales

Additional units (600,000 × 20%)		120,000
Contribution margin per unit		
Selling price	$5	
Less variable cost	$2	× $3
Additional profitability		$360,000

Bad debts

Higher bad debts $90,000

Opportunity cost of increased balance in accounts receivable

Current average investment in accounts receivable

$$\text{Average accounts receivable} \times \frac{\text{cost}}{\text{selling price}}$$

$$\frac{\text{credit sales}}{\text{accounts receivable turnover}} \times \frac{\text{cost}}{\text{selling price}}$$

$$\frac{\$3,000,000^a}{12} \times \frac{\$4}{\$5} \qquad\qquad \$200,000$$

The average investment in accounts receivable after change in credit policy is

$$\frac{\$3,600,000^b}{6} \times \frac{\$3.67^c}{\$5} \qquad \$440,000$$

Increased average investment in accounts receivable	$240,000
Minimum rate	× 0.24
Opportunity cost	$ 57,600

Net advantage to policy

Additional profitability		$360,000
Additional cost		
Bad debts	$90,000	
Opportunity cost	57,696	(147,696)
Savings		**$212,304**

Calculations

a) $5 × 600,000 units = $3,000,000

b) $3,000,000 + 0.20 ($3,000,000) = $3,600,000

c) New average unit cost:

	Units	× Unit Cost =	Total Cost
Current volume	600,000	$4	$2,400,000
Additional volume	120,000	2	240,000
After proposal	720,000		$2,640,000

New average unit cost = $2,640,000/720,000 units
$$= \$3.67$$

The new average unit cost went down from $4 to $3.67 because the fixed cost is spread over more units.

How much credit should I give?

Management executives: Sometimes management must decide whether to give full credit to presently limited- or no-credit customers. *Remember this:* Use full credit only when it will lead to a net profit.

Example 10.8

Company D classifies its customers by risk ratings:

Category	Uncollectible Account (%)	Collection Period	Credit Policy	Increase in Annual Sales If Credit Restrictions Are Relaxed
A	1	20 days	Unlimited	$ 50,000
B	4	40	Restricted	500,000
C	18	70	No credit	700,000

Gross profit averages 20 precent of sales. The minimum rate of return is 14 percent. Of course, Category A receives unlimited credit. However, full credit should be extended only to Category B, and not Category C, as indicated in the following table.

	Category B	Category C
Gross profit		
500,000 × 0.2	$100,000	
700,000 × 0.2		$140,000
Less bad debts addition		
500,000 × 0.04	(20,000)	
700,000 × 0.18		(126,000)
Incremental average investment in accounts receivable		
$\frac{40}{360} \times (80\% \times 200,000)$		
	$44,444	
$\frac{70}{360} \times (80\% \times 700,000)$		$108,889
Opportunity cost × .14	(6,222)	× 0.14 (15,244)
Net earnings	**$73,778**	**($1,244)**

10.4 FORMULATING THE BEST INVESTMENT STRATEGY

What factors should I consider when selecting an investment portfolio?

When selecting an investment portfolio, look at these factors:

- Financial
- Risk versus return
- Tax implications

A company's present financial picture governs the magnitude and type of risk that can be undertaken. For example, if liquidity is strong, long-term securities might be the choice. Or, to maintain needed liquidity, short-term bills (for instance, market certificates, treasury bills) might be better. *Remember this:* With greater liquidity there is less return because short-term securities yield less.

What are the various types of investments?

CHECKLIST OF INVESTMENT TYPES

- Direct equity claims
    Common stock
    Options
    Warrants
- Indirect equity claims
    Mutual funds
- Creditor claims
    Savings accounts
    Money market certificates
    Money market funds
    Treasury securities
    Commercial paper
    Bonds
- Preferred stock

How should I manage the investment portfolio?

Financial managers: Stagger the maturity dates of the securities. For example, if all the securities mature on a single date, the reinvestment may be subject to low returns if interest rates are low at that time.

Management executives: Examine the risk. Look at the degree of diversification and stability of the portfolio.

Investment analysts: Consider securities with negative correlations to each other. *Be on guard:* Declines in portfolio market values may not be entirely reflected in the accounts. Use the ratio of revenue (dividend income, interest income, and so on) to the carrying value as a clue. Also, examine the footnotes for subsequent event disclosure regarding any unrealized losses that have taken place in the portfolio.

Financial managers: It may be desirable to adjust downward the extent to which an investment account can be realized in the case of such declines. Also, appraise the riskiness of the portfolio by computing the standard deviation of its rate of return.

Example 10.9

Winston Company reports the following data for year-ends 20X1 and 20X2:

	20X1	*20X2*
Investments	$30,000	$33,000
Income from investments (dividends and interest)	4,000	3,200

The 20X2 annual report has a footnote titled "Subsequent Events," which indicates a $5,000 decline in the portfolio as of March 2, 20X3. The ratio of investment income to total investments went from 0.133 in 20X1 to 0.097 in 19X2, indicating a higher realization risk in the portfolio. Additionally, the post–balance sheet disclosure of a $5,000 decline in value should prompt a downward adjustment of the amount to which the year-end portfolio can be realized.

What kinds of risks are involved in investing?

CHECKLIST OF INVESTING RISKS

- *Business risk.* This relates to factors such as financial condition and product demand.
- *Liquidity risk.* This applies to the possibility that an investment may not be sold on short notice for its market value. A security sold at a high discount may have high liquidity risk.
- *Default risk.* This refers to the borrower's inability to make interest payments or principal repayments on debt. A bond issued by a company with significant financial problems might be a default risk.
- *Market risk.* This relates to changes in the stock price caused by changes in the market itself.

- *Purchasing-power risk*. This applies to the likelihood of decreased purchasing power. Bonds are a good example of this because the issuer pays back in cheaper dollars.

- *Interest rate risk*. This refers to the variability in the value of an investment as interest rates, money market, or capital market conditions change. This factor applies to fixed-income securities such as bonds. As interest rates increase, bond prices decrease.

- *Concentration risk*. This reflects a lack of diversification in the portfolio.

What should 1 know about taxes?

Financial managers: When formulating an optimal investment strategy, tax aspects must be considered. For example, interest income on bonds is fully taxable, whereas dividend income has an 85 percent tax exclusion (only 15 percent of dividends are subject to tax). When securities held for more than one year are sold at a gain, only 15 percent of the profit is taxable. Thus, there is an advantage in holding appreciated securities for longer than one year. *Remember this:* Income from U.S. government securities are taxable for federal purposes, but are exempt from local taxes. Income from municipals is exempt from both federal and local taxes.

What is a technical analysis?

A technical analysis looks at the direction and magnitude of the market in determining when or what to buy or sell. Technical analysts believe stock prices of individual companies tend to move with the market as they react to various supply-and-demand forces. Charts and graphs of internal market data, including prices and volume, are also helpful.

What are the key indicators of stock market performance?

A discussion of six major indicators of market performance follows.

Trading volume. Trading volume points to the health and trend of the market. Market volume of stocks depends on supply-and-demand relationships, which in turn point to market strength or weakness. For instance, expect higher prices can be expected when demand increases.

Upside-downside index. This illustrates the difference between stock volume advancing and decreasing, typically based on a ten-day or thirty-day moving average. The index assists in identifying expected market turning points.

Market breadth. This relates to the dispersion of general price fluctuation and may be useful as an advance indicator of major price declines or advances.

Breadth index. This involves computing, daily, the net advancing or declining issues of a broad range of securities from the New York Stock Exchange. The index is determined by dividing net advances (number of securities with price increases less declines) by the number of securities traded. This index differs from a limited stock-market average (like the Dow Jones Industrial Average of 30 stocks) by virtue of the greater spread between the number advances and declines.

Example 10.10

Assume net declines equal 40, securities traded equal 1,100, and the breadth index equals −3.6. This figure can be related to a base year or combined in a 150-day moving average. The figures obtained are then related to the Dow Jones Industrial Average. When *both* indexes are increasing, this indicates market strength.

The market breadth can also be determined for individual securities by computing net volume (up-ticks less down-ticks).

Example 10.11

Bette Corporation trades 90,000 shares for the day, with 60,000 on the upside; 20,000 on the downside; and 10,000 at no change. The net volume difference at day's end is 40,000 traded on up-ticks.

Financial managers: Look for any sign of divergence between the price trend and net volume. If one occurs, anticipate a reversal in the price trend.

Barron's Confidence Index. This is useful when evaluating the trading patterns of bond investors, and it helps determine when to buy and sell. The index assumes bond traders, are more knowledgeable than stock traders, and that they identify trends more quickly. The index equals

$$\frac{\text{Yield on Barron's 10 top-grade corporate bonds}}{\text{Yield on Dow Jones 40 bond average}}$$

The numerator reflects a lower yield than the denominator because it uses higher-quality bonds. For example, if the Dow Jones yield is 14 percent and the Barron's yield is 11.5 percent, the confidence index is 0.82 1. *Rule of thumb:* When bond investors are bullish, yield differences between high-grade and low-grade bonds will be small.

Odd-lot trading. This refers to transactions of one hundred shares or less and is used as a reflection of popular opinion. *The rule of contrary opinion:* The investment analyst determines what small traders are doing, and then does the opposite. An odd-lot index consists of the ratio of odd-lot purchases to odd-lot sales.

Charts. These are used to appraise market conditions and price behavior of individual securities. By looking at past trends, it is possible to predict the future.

Relative strength analysis. This relates to predicting individual stock prices and consists of computing a ratio of monthly average stock prices to a monthly average "market index" or "industry group index." Or, you can compute the ratios of specific industry group indexes to the total market index. *Observation:* If a stock or industry group outperforms the market, you may view this as a positive sign.

10.5 HOW TO BEST FINANCE YOUR BUSINESS

What financing alternatives are available?

Financial managers and executives should be familiar with three alternative sources of financing: short-term (less than one year), intermediate-term (one to five years), and long-term (longer than five years). To plan the best financing strategy, evaluate the risks and costs applicable to each alternative. Consider these factors:

- The company's financial position (cash flow, debt position, and so on)
- Cost of alternative funding sources
- Availability of future financing
- Risk
- Inflation rate
- Expected money-market trends
- Tax rate
- Stability of operations
- Overall management objectives

What type of financing should I select?

Following are some sources of short- and intermediate-term financing:

- *Trade credit.* Trade credit is easy to get, has no or minimal cost, and requires no collateral. Creditors tend to be more lenient when payment problems occur, too.

- *Bank.* To obtain a bank loan, the company must have a good financial position, with sufficient stockholders' equity. Loans may be secured (collateralized) or unsecured. In a secured loan, the company must pledge an asset to back the security. Or, a line of credit that promises loans up to a maximum amount can be obtained.

- *Finance company.* If a bank loan is unavailable, a finance company may be necessary. There will be a higher interest rate and required collateral.

- *Commercial paper.* This is a short-term, unsecured note issued by the highest-quality companies. Their interest rate is less than the prime rate charged by banks.

- *Receivable financing.* Accounts receivable may be sold outright (factored) or assigned to a bank or finance company in return for immediate cash. There's a high financing cost involved here.

- *Inventory financing.* This typically occurs when receivable financing has been used up. Inventory must be marketable.

- *Leasing.* By leasing property, only a minor cash outlay may be required. Usually, a purchase option accompanies the agreement.

Following are some sources of long-term financing:

- *Mortgages.* These are notes payable to banks that are secured by real property. Mortgages have favorable interest rates, fewer financing restrictions, long payment schedules, and ready availability.

- *Bonds.* These are long-term debt issued to the public. Bonds offer some advantages over stocks. For instance, interest from bonds is tax deductible, whereas stock dividends are not; the payback is in cheaper dollars because of inflation; and equity interests (that is, voting rights) remain intact. Also, call provisions allow for the bonds to be bought back before maturity. On the other hand, certain risks must be accepted, including the inability to meet debt payments as well as indenture restrictions. Indenture refers to the agreement between the bond issuer and the bond investor.

- *Equity securities (preferred and common stock).* Common stock refers to residual equity ownership in the business. Common stockholders have voting power, but come after preferred stockholders in receiving dividends and in liquidation. Equity securities do not involve fixed charges, maturity dates, or sinking-fund requirements. Dividends need not be paid during periods of financial distress. However, dividend payments are not tax deductible and therefore will incur higher costs to the company. And since divided payments also hold greatest risk to common stockholders, the cost of funds will be greater. Common stocks dilute ownership and voting rights as well.

What is the cost of raising funds?

Vital for financial managers: The cost of capital is calculated from a weighted average of debt and equity security costs. Compare these averages under various alternative financing strategies. The financial manager's input will bear heavily when deciding the best source of financing in a given situation. *Remember this:* The alternative with the least overall cost of capital is best.

What is the cost of short-term debt?

The cost of short-term debt applies to the interest rate on bank or finance company loans. *Remember this:* Interest is a tax-deductible expense.

$$\text{Cost of short-term debt} = \frac{\text{Interest}}{\text{Proceeds received}}$$

If a bank discounts a loan, interest is deducted from the face of the loan to get the proceeds. When a compensating balance is required (that is, a percent of the face loan is held by the bank as collateral), proceeds are also reduced. In either case, the effective or real interest rate on the loan is higher than the face interest rate, owing to the proceeds received from the loan being less than the amount (face) of the loan.

Example 10.12

Company A takes a $150,000, one-year, 13 percent loan. The loan is discounted, and a 10 percent compensating balance is required. The effective interest rate is computed as follows:

$$\frac{13\% \times \$150,000}{\$115,500^a} = \frac{\$19,500}{\$115,500} = 16.89\%$$

^aProceeds received =

Face of loan	$150,000
Less interest	(19,500)
Compensating balance (10% × $150,000)	(15,000)
Proceeds	$115,500

Notice how the effective cost of the loan is significantly greater than the stated interest rate.

What is the cost of long-term debt?

The real cost of bonds is obtained by computing two types of yield: simple (face) yield and yield to maturity (effective interest rate). The first involves an easy approximation, but the second is much more accurate.

What you should know: The nominal interest rate equals the interest paid on the face (maturity value) of the bond and is always stated on a per-annum basis. Bonds are always issued in $1,000 denominations, and may be sold above face value (at a premium) or below (at a discount). A bond is sold at a discount when the interest rate is below the going market rate. In this case, the yield will be higher than the nominal interest rate. The opposite holds for bonds issued at a premium.

$$\text{Simple yield} = \frac{\text{nominal interest}}{\text{present value of bond}}$$

$$\text{Yield to maturity} = \frac{\text{nominal interest} + \dfrac{\text{discount}}{\text{years}} \left(\dfrac{\text{or premium}}{\text{years}}\right)}{\dfrac{\text{present value} + \text{maturity value}}{2}}$$

Example 10.13

Prentice Corporation issues a $400,000, 12 percent, ten-year bond for 97 percent of face value. Yield computations follow:

Nominal annual
payment   = 12% × $400,000

                = $48,000

Bond proceeds $\quad$ = 97% × \$400,000
$\qquad\qquad\qquad$ = \$388,000

Bond discount $\quad$ = 3% × \$400,000
$\qquad\qquad\qquad$ = \$12,000 or
$\qquad\qquad\qquad\qquad$ \$400,000 − \$388,000
$\qquad\qquad\qquad$ = \$12,000

Simple yield $\qquad$ =

$$\frac{12\% \times \$400,000}{97\% \times \$400,000} = \frac{\$48,000}{\$388,000} = 12.4\%$$

Yield to maturity $\quad= \dfrac{\$48,000 + \dfrac{\$12,000}{10}}{\dfrac{\$388,000 + \$400,000}{2}}$

$$= \frac{\$48,000 + \$1,200}{\$369,000}$$

$$= \frac{449,200}{\$394,000} = 12.5\%$$

Note: Because the bonds were sold at a discount, the yield exceeds the nominal interest rate (12%).

What is the cost of equity securities?

The cost of equity securities comes in the form of dividends, which are not tax deductible.

The cost of common stock

$$= \frac{\text{dividends per share for current year}}{\text{net proceeds per share}} + \text{growth rate in dividends}$$

where net proceeds per share = market price per share − flotation costs (that is, cost of issuing securities, such as brokerage fees and printing costs). The cost of preferred stock is stated in the dividend rate. If this is not given, the cost of preferred stock would be computed as it is for common stock.

Example 10.14

ABC Company's dividend per share is \$10, net proceeds per share are \$70, and the dividend growth rate is 5 percent.

The cost of the stock $= \dfrac{\$10}{\$10} + 0.05 = 19.3\%$

How do I compute the weighted average cost of capital?

When computing the weighted average cost of capital, consider the percent of the total and after-tax cost of each financing alternative.

Example 10.15

Bloated Company provides the following from its financial statements:

Bonds payable (16%)	$ 4 million
Preferred stock (dividend rate = 13%)	1 million
Common stock	5 million
Total	$10 million

Dividends per share on common stock are $11; net proceeds per share are $80; growth rate on dividends is 4 percent; and tax rate is 40 percent.

The weighted average cost of capital is computed as follows:

	Percent	After-Tax Cost	Weighted Average Cost
Bonds payable	0.40	0.096[a]	0.038
Preferred stock	0.10	0.130	0.013
Common stock	0.50	0.178[b]	0.089
	1.00		0.140

[a]Cost of bonds payable: $16\% \times 60\% = 0.096$

[b]Cost of bonds payable = $\dfrac{\text{dividends per share}}{\text{net proceeds per share}}$ + growth rate in dividends

$$\frac{\$11}{\$80} + .004 = 0.178$$

What is the cost of not taking a discount on accounts payable?

If a discount is not taken on accounts payable by paying earlier, an opportunity cost has been lost, or the return foregone from an alternative use of funds or time. *Take notice:* Financial managers who do not take the discount typically show a lack of financial astuteness. Why? The cost of paying is usually higher than the cost of borrowing money.

The opportunity cost can be computed with this formula:

$$\frac{\text{discount foregone}}{\text{use of proceeds}} \times \frac{360}{\text{days use of money}}$$

Example 10.16

XYZ Company purchases $500,000 of merchandise on credit terms of 2/10, net/30. The company does not pay within ten days and thus loses the discount.

$$\text{Opportunity cost} = \frac{0.02 \times \$500,000}{0.98 \times \$500,000} \times \frac{360}{20}$$

$$= \frac{\$10,000}{\$490,000} \times 180 = 36.7\%$$

Surely management would have been better off to take advantage of the discount by borrowing $490,000 at the prime interest rate.

How do I evaluate a dividend policy?

For financial managers: A dividend policy must be attractive to the investing public by satisfying current stockholders and prompting new investment. Psychologically, investors like to receive stable dividends. If dividends are cut, stockholders may become worried and sell. The result: stock price declines.

On the other hand, from a purely financial perspective, earnings should be retained by the business, rather than distributed to stockholders, because the company typically earns a greater return than the individual stockholder does, and this will result in appreciation in the market price of the stock.

Management executives: If financial problems exist within the company, the distribution will seriously impair the company's health. By distributing earnings, refinancing will be required, and cost of capital will be very high. *Your dilemma:* It's generally best to retain funds rather than distribute them in the form of dividends to the company or individual investor. But, since stockholders are basically unsophisticated in financial analysis, they will demand dividends.

What to do: To satisfy stockholders while retaining as much as possible, there are two options: establish a minimum dividend base and give a bonus dividend during very good times, or create the impression of a growth company that typically retains earnings for expansion purposes.

Financial managers: Look at the trends in these dividend-related ratios:

$$\text{Dividend payout} = \frac{\text{dividends per share}}{\text{earnings per share}}$$

$$\text{Dividend yield} = \frac{\text{dividends per share}}{\text{market price per share}}$$

Investors generally favor increasing trends.

How does the business cycle affect a company?

One company or industry cannot control fundamental economic conditions. To the extent that one can insulate oneself from the effects of a broader economy, corporate stability will be greater. *Hint:* Look for stability in operations because it enhances predictability and planning.

Companies that have product lines with inelastic demand (such as food and medicine) are affected less by the business cycle. Companies with product lines or services correlated positively to changes in real gross domestic product (such as airlines) have greater earnings instability.

10.6 HOW TO REDUCE RISK: DIVERSIFY

Diversification is usually an answer to reduction in risk. "Diversify" means "Don't put all your eggs in one basket." With a diversified portfolio (for instance, stocks, bonds, real estate, and savings accounts), the value of all these investments does not increase or decrease at the same time or in the same magnitude. Thus, the company can be protected against fluctuations. The company may diversify into different lines of businesses that are not subject to the same economic and political influences. Thus, it can protect itself against fluctuations in earnings.

What is portfolio theory?

The central theme of portfolio theory is that rational investors behave in a way that reflects their aversion to taking increased risk without being compensated by an adequate increase in expected return. Also, for any given expected return, most investors will prefer a lower risk, and for any given level of risk, they will prefer a higher return to a lower return. Harry Markowitz showed how to calculate a set of "efficient" portfolios. An investor then will choose from among a set of efficient portfolios the best that is consistent with the risk profile of the investor.

Most financial assets are not held in isolation, but rather as part of a portfolio. Therefore, the risk-return analysis should not be confined to single assets only. It is important to look at portfolios and the gains from diversification. What is important is the return on the portfolio—not just the return on one asset—and the portfolio's risk.

How is portfolio return computed?

The expected return on a portfolio (r_p) is simply the weighted average return of the individual sets in the portfolio, the weights being the fraction of the total funds invested in each asset:

$$r_p = w_1r_1 + w_2r_2 + \cdots + w_nr_n = \sum_{j=1}^{n} w_jr_j$$

where

r_j = expected return on each individual asset

w_j = fraction for each respective asset investment

n = number of assets in the portfolio

$$\sum_{j=1}^{n} w_j = 1.0$$

Example 10.17

A portfolio consists of assets A and B. Asset A makes up one-third of the portfolio and has an expected return of 18 percent. Asset B makes up the other two-thirds of the portfolio and is expected to earn 9 percent. The expected return on the portfolio is

Asset	Return (r_j)	Fraction (w_j)	w_jr_j
A	18%	$\frac{1}{3}$	$\frac{1}{3} \times 18\% = 6\%$
B	9%	$\frac{2}{3}$	$\frac{2}{3} \times 9\% = 6\%$
			$r_p = 12\%$

How do you calculate portfolio risk?

Unlike with returns, the risk of a portfolio (σ_p) is not simply the weighted average of the standard deviations of the individual assets in the contribution; a portfolio's risk is also dependent on the correlation coefficients of its assets. The correlation coefficient (ρ) is a measure of the degree to which two variables "move" together. It has a numerical value that ranges from -1.0 to 1.0. In a two-asset (A and B) portfolio, the portfolio risk is defined as

$$\sigma_p = \sqrt{w_A^2\sigma_A^2 + w_B^2\sigma_B^2 + 2\rho_{AB}w_Aw_B\sigma_A\sigma_B}$$

where

σ_A and σ_B = standard deviations of assets A and B, respectively

w_A and w_B = weights, or fractions, of total funds invested in assets A and B

ρ_{AB} = the correlation coefficient between assets A and B.

Incidentally, the correlation coefficient is the measurement of joint movement between two securities.

How do I diversify?

As can be seen in the preceding formula, the portfolio risk, measured in terms of σ, is not the weighted average of the individual asset risks in the portfolio. Note that in the formula, we have the third term (ρ), which makes a significant contribution to the overall portfolio risk. What the formula basically shows is that portfolio risk can be minimized or completely eliminated by diversification. The degree of reduction in portfolio risk depends upon the correlation between the assets being combined. Generally speaking, by combining two perfectly negatively correlated assets ($\rho = -1.0$), we are able to eliminate the risk completely. In the real world, however, most securities are negatively—but not perfectly—correlated. In fact, most assets are positively correlated. We could still reduce the portfolio risk by combining even positively correlated assets. An example of the latter might be ownership of two automobile stocks or two housing stocks.

Example 10.18

Assume the following:

Asset	σ	w
A	20%	$\frac{1}{3}$
B	10%	$\frac{2}{3}$

The portfolio risk, then, is

$$\sigma_p = \sqrt{w_A^2\sigma_A^2 + w_B^2\sigma_B^2 + 2\rho_{AB}w_Aw_B\sigma_A\sigma_B}$$
$$= [(1/3)^2 (0.2)^2 + (2/3)^2(0.1)^2$$
$$+ 2\rho_{AB} (1/3)(2/3)(0.2)(0.1)]^{1/2}$$
$$= 0.0089 + 0.0089\rho_{AB}$$

(a) Now assume that the correlation coefficient between A and B is $+1$ (a perfectly positive correlation). This means that when the value of asset A increases in response to market conditions, so does the value of asset B, and it does so at exactly the same rate as A. The portfolio risk when $\rho_{AB} = +1$ then becomes

$$\sigma_p = 0.0089 + 0.0089\rho_{AB} = 0.0089 + 0.0089(+1)$$
$$= 0.1334 = 13.34\%$$

(b) If $\rho_{AB} = 0$, the assets lack correlation, and the portfolio risk is simply the risk of the expected returns on the assets—that is, the weighted average of the standard deviations of the individual assets in the portfolio. Therefore, when $\rho_{AB} = 0$, the portfolio risk for this example is

$$\sigma_p = 0.0089 + 0.0089\rho_{AB} = 0.0089 + 0.0089(0)$$
$$= 0.0089 = 8.9\%$$

(c) If $\rho_{AB} = -1$ (a perfectly negative correlation coefficient), as the price of A rises, the price of B declines at the very same rate. In such a case, risk would be completely eliminated. Therefore, when $\rho_{AB} = -1$, the portfolio risk is

$$\sigma_p = 0.0089 + 0.0089\rho_{AB} = 0.0089 + 0.0089(-1)$$
$$= 0.0089 - 0.0089 = 0 = 0$$

When comparing the results of (a), (b), and (c), it is clear that a positive correlation between assets increases a portfolio's risk above the level found at zero correlation, while a perfectly negative correlation eliminates that risk.

Example 10.19

To illustrate the point of diversification, assume data on the following three securities are as follows:

Year	Security X (%)	Security Y (%)	Security Z (%)
20X1	10	50	10
20X2	20	40	20
20X3	30	30	30
20X4	40	20	40
20X5	50	10	50
r_j	30	30	30
σ_j	14.14	14.14	14.14

Note here that securities X and Y have a perfectly negative correlation, and securities X and Z have a perfectly positive correlation. Notice what happens to the portfolio risk when X and Y, and X and Z, are combined. Assume that funds are split equally between the two securities in each portfolio.

Year	Portfolio XY (50%–50%)	Portfolio XZ (50%–50%)
20X1	30	10
20X2	30	20
20X3	30	30
20X4	30	40
20X5	30	50
r_p	30	30
σ_p	0	14.14

Again, see that the two perfectly negative correlated securities (XY) result in a zero overall risk.

10.7 BETA—THE CAPITAL ASSET PRICING MODEL (CAPM)

What is beta?

Many investors hold more than one financial asset. A portion of a security's risk (called unsystematic risk) can be controlled through diversification. This type of risk is unique to a given security. Business, liquidity, and default risks, which were discussed earlier, fall in this category. Non-diversifiable risk, more commonly referred to as systematic risk, results from forces outside the firm's control and are therefore not unique to the given security. Purchasing power, interest rate, and market risks fall into this category. This type of risk is measured by beta.

Beta (β) measures a security's volatility relative to an average security. A particular stock's beta is useful in predicting how much the security will go up or down, provided that it is known which way the market will go. It does help in figuring out risk and expected return.

Most of the unsystematic risk affecting a security can be diversified away in an efficiently constructed portfolio. Therefore, this type of risk does not need to be compensated with a higher level of return. The only relevant risk is systematic risk, or beta risk, for which the investor can expect to receive compensation. Investors, are compensated for taking this type of risk, which cannot be controlled.

Under the capital asset pricing model (CAPM), in general, there is a relationship between a stock's expected (or required) return and its beta. The following formula is very helpful in determining a stock's expected return:

$$r_j = r_f + \beta(r_m - r_f)$$

In words,

Expected return = risk-free rate + beta
$\times$ (market risk premium)

where r_j = the expected (or required) return on security j; r_f = the risk-free rate on a security such as a T-bill; r_m = the expected return on the market portfolio (such as Standard and Poor's 500 Stock Composite Index or Dow Jones 30 Industrials); and β = beta, an index of systematic (non-diversifiable, non-controllable) risk.

The market risk premium ($r_m - r_f$) equals the expected market return (r_m) minus the risk free rate (r_f).

The market risk premium is the additional return above that which could be earned on, say, a T-bill, to compensate for assuming a given level of risk (as measured by beta).

Thus, the formula shows that the required (expected) return on a given security is equal to the return required for securities that have no risk, plus a risk premium required by the investor for assuming a given level of risk. The key idea behind the formula is that the relevant measure of risk is the risk of the individual security, or its beta. The higher the beta for a security, the greater the return expected (or demanded) by the investor.

Example 10.20

Assume that $r_f = 6\%$, and $r_m = 10\%$ If a stock has a beta of 2.0, its risk premium should be 14 percent:

$$r_j = r_f + \beta(r_m - r_f)$$
$$6\% + 2.0\,(10\% - 6\%) = 6\% + 8\% = 14\%$$

This means that an extra 8 percent (risk premium) would be expected (or demanded) on this stock on top of the risk-free return of 6 percent. Therefore, the total expected (required) return on the stock should be 14 percent:

$$6\% + 8\% = 14\%$$

Example 10.21

The higher a stock's beta, the greater the return expected (or demanded) by the investor, as follows:

Stock	Beta	Required Return
Mobil	.85	$6\% + .85(12\% - 6\%) = 11.1\%$
Bristol-Meyers	1.0	$6\% + 1.0(12\% - 6\%) = 12\%$
Neiman-Marcus	1.65	$6\% + 1.65(12\% - 6\%) = 15.9\%$

How is beta read?

Beta (β) measures a security's volatility relative to an average security. Putting it another way, beta is a measure of a security's return over time, compared to that of the overall market. For example, if a company's beta is 2.0, it means that if the stock market goes up 10 percent, the company's common stock goes up 20 percent; if the market goes down 10 percent, the company's stock price goes down 20 percent. Here is how to read betas:

Beta	Meaning
0	The security's return is independent of the market. An example is a risk-free security (for instance, T-Bill).
0.5	The security is half as volatile as the market.
1.0	The security is a volatile or risky as the market (that is, average risk). This is the beta value of the market portfolio (for example, Standard & Poor's 500).
2.0	The security is twice as volatile, or risky, as the market.

Figure 10.1 shows examples of betas for selected stocks.

Figure 10.1 Betas for Some Selected Corporations

Company	Ticker Symbol	Beta
IBM	IBM	1.3
Wal-Mart	WMT	1.0
Microsoft	MSFT	1.7
McDonald's	MCD	0.7
Pfizer	PFE	0.6
Nokia	NOK	2.1

Source: MSN Money Central Investor (moneycentral.msn.com/investor/home.asp), *Company Report*, December 21, 2003.

10.8 THE ARBITRAGE PRICING MODEL (APM)

What is the difference between the CAPM and the arbitrage pricing model (APM)?

The CAPM assumes that required rates of return depend only on one risk factor, the stock's beta. The arbitrage pricing model (APM) disputes this and includes any number of risk factors:

$$r = r_f + \beta_1 RP_1 + \beta_2 RP_2 + \cdots + \beta_n RP_n$$

where

r = the expected return for a given stock or portfolio

r_f = the risk-free rate

β_i = the sensitivity (or reaction) of the returns of the stock to unexpected changes in economic forces i $(i = 1, \ldots n)$

RP_i = the market risk premium associated with an unexpected change in the economic force

n = the number of relevant economic forces

The following five economic forces are often suggested:

1. Changes in expected inflation
2. Unanticipated changes in inflation
3. Unanticipated changes in industrial production
4. Unanticipated changes in the yield differential between low- and high-grade bonds (the default-risk premium)
5. Unanticipated changes in the yield differential between long-term and short-term bonds (the term structure of interest rates)

Some document the importance of industry factors, investor confidence, exchange rates, oil prices, and a host of other variables. It appears, however, that we are still a long way from being able to describe with confidence the underlying reasons for cross-sectional differences in average returns.

Example 10.22

Suppose a three-factor APM holds, and the risk-free rate is 6 percent. Two particular stocks are interesting: A and B. The returns on both stocks are related to factors 1 and 2, as follows:

$$r = 0.06 + \beta_1(0.09) - \beta_2(0.03) + \beta_3(0.04)$$

The sensitivity coefficients for the two stocks are given below.

Stock	β_1	β_2	β_3
A	0.70	0.80	0.20
B	0.50	0.04	1.20

Calculate the expected returns on both stocks as follows:

For stock A: $r = 0.06 + (0.70)(0.09) - (0.80)(0.03) + (0.20)(0.04)$

$= 10.70\%$

For stock B: $r = 0.06 + (0.50)(0.09) - (0.04)(0.03) + (1.20)(0.04)$

$= 14.10\%$

Stock B requires a higher return, indicating it is the riskier of the two. Part of the reason for this is that its return is substantially more sensitive to the third economic force than stock A's is.

PART FOUR

Quantitative
Methods and
Computer
Applications

CHAPTER 11

Decision Making with Statistics and Forecasting

As a decision maker, you'll find yourself in many situations in which large volumes of data need to be analyzed. These data could be sales figures, income, or a multitude of other possibilities. And they could be used for a variety of purposes, including risk analysis, figuring return on investments, or other financial decisions. Effective use of statistics and forecasting techniques will prove necessary as your company grows.

11.1 HOW TO USE BASIC STATISTICS

The most commonly used statistics that describe characteristics of data are the mean and the standard deviation.

What is a mean, and how is it used?

The mean gives an average (or central) value of the data. Three such means are common. They are

- Arithmetic mean
- Weighted mean
- Geometric mean

What is an arithmetic mean?

The arithmetic mean is a simple average. To find it, sum the values of the data and divide by the number of data entries or observations:

$$\bar{x} = \frac{\sum x}{n}$$

where

$$\bar{x} = \text{the arithmetic mean (called x-bar)}$$
$$x = \text{the data values}$$
$$n = \text{number of observations}$$

Example 11.1

John Jay Lamp Company has a revolving credit agreement with a local bank. Last year, the loan showed the following month-end balances:

January	18,500
February	21,000
March	17,600
April	23,200
May	18,600
June	24,500
July	60,000
August	40,000
September	25,850
October	33,100
November	41,000
December	28,400

The mean monthly balance is computed as follows:

$$\frac{\begin{matrix}\$18{,}500 + \$21{,}000 + \$17{,}600 + \$23{,}200 \\ + \$18{,}600 + \$24{,}500 + \$60{,}000 + \$40{,}000 \\ + \$25{,}850 + \$33{,}100 + \$41{,}000 + \$28{,}400\end{matrix}}{12}$$

$$\frac{= \$351{,}750}{12} = \$29{,}312.50$$

What is a weighted mean?

When observations have different degrees of importance or frequency, a weighted mean enables one to account for this. The formula for a weighted mean is

$$\text{Weighted mean} = \sum(w)(x)$$

where

w = weight assigned to each observation, expressed as a percentage or relative frequency

Example 11.2

Company J uses three grades of labor to produce a finished product, as follows:

Grade of Labor	Labor Hours per Unit of Labor	Hourly Wages (x)
Skilled	6	$10.00
Semiskilled	3	8.00
Unskilled	1	6.00

The arithmetic mean (average cost) of labor per hour for this product can be computed as follows:

$$\text{Arithmetic mean} = \frac{\$10.00 + \$8.00 + \$6.00}{3}$$

$$= \$8.00 \text{ per hour}$$

However, this implies that each grade of labor was used in equal amounts, and this is not the case. To calculate the average cost of labor per hour correctly, the weighted average should be computed as follows:

$$\text{Weighted mean} = \$10.00(6/10) + \$8.00(3/10)$$
$$+ \$6.00(1/10) = \$9.00 \text{ per hour}$$

Note: The weights equal the proportion of the total labor required to produce the product.

What is a geometric (compound) mean?

Sometimes quantities change over a period of time; for example, the rate of return on investment or rate of growth in earnings over a period of years. In such cases, it is necessary to know the geometric mean, which uses the average rate or percentage of change. Use the following formula:

Geometric (compound) mean
$$= \sqrt[n]{(1 + x_1)(1 + x_2)\cdots(1 + x_n)} - 1$$

where

x = the rate of change (in percent)
n = number of periods

Example 11.3

A stock doubles during one period, and then depreciates back to the original price, as shown in the following table. Dividend income (current income) is nonexistent.

	Time Periods		
	$t = 0$	$t = 1$	$t = 2$
Price (end of period)	$80	$160	$80
HPR	—	100%	−50%

The rate of return for periods 1 and 2 are computed as follows:

Period 1 (t = 1) = $\dfrac{\$160 - \$80}{\$80} = \dfrac{\$80}{\$160} = 100\%$

Period 2 (t = 2) = $\dfrac{\$80 - \$160}{160} = \dfrac{-\$80}{\$160} = -50\%$

The rate of return is the average of 100 percent and −50 percent, or 25 percent:

$$\frac{100\% + (-50\%)}{2} = 25\%$$

However, the stock bought for $40 and sold for the same price two periods later did not earn 25 percent; it earned zero. This can be illustrated by determining the compound average return.

Note that

$n = 2, x_1 = 100\% = 1$, and $x_2 = -50\% = -0.5$

Then,

Geometric (compound) mean return =

$$\sqrt[2]{(1 + x_1)(1 + x_2)} - 1 = \sqrt{(1 + 1)(1 - 0.5)} - 1$$
$$= \sqrt{(2)(0.5)} - 1$$
$$= \sqrt{1} - 1 = 1 - 1 = 0$$

where

$x_1 = 100\%$ or 1

$x_2 = -50\%$ or −0.5

What is standard deviation?

The standard deviation measures the extent to which data spreads out or disperses. *Managers:* Important inferences can be made from past data with this statistic; for example, when measuring the risk of purchasing a financial asset. The standard deviation, denoted with the Greek letter σ, read as sigma, is defined as follows:

$$\sigma = \sqrt{\frac{\sum(x - \bar{x})^2}{n - 1}}$$

where $\bar{x}$ is the mean (arithmetic average).

What to do: Calculate the standard deviation using these five steps:

1. Subtract the mean from each element of the data.
2. Square each of the differences obtained in Step 1.

3. Add together all the squared differences.
4. Divide the sum of all the squared differences by the number of values, minus one.
5. Take the square root of the quotient obtained in Step 4.

Example 11.4

One and a half years of quarterly returns are listed below for ABC Mutual Fund.

Time period	x	$(x - \bar{x})$	$(x - \bar{x})^2$
1	10%	0	0
2	15	5	25
3	20	10	100
4	5	−5	25
5	−10	−20	400
6	20	10	100
	60		650

The mean return and standard deviation over this period are computed as follows:

$$\bar{x} = 60/6 = 10\%$$

$$\sigma = \sqrt{\frac{\Sigma(x - \bar{x})^2}{n - 1}} = \sqrt{\frac{650}{6 - 1}} = \sqrt{130} = 11.40\%$$

Conclusion: ABC Fund has returned, on the average, 10 percent over the last six quarters, and the variability about its average return was 11.40 percent. The high-standard deviation (11.40 percent) relative to the average return of 10 percent indicates that the fund is very risky.

11.2 USING FORECASTING TECHNIQUES

11.2.1 Moving Averages

How do I use moving averages?

With the moving average, simply take the most recent observations (n) to calculate an average. Then, use this as the forecast for the next period. Moving averages are updated as new data are received. *Note:* The number of periods to use can be chosen on the basis of the relative importance attached to old versus current data.

Example 11.5

Assume that the marketing manager has the following sales data.

Date	Actual Sales (Y_t)
Jan. 1	46
2	54
3	53
4	46
5	58
6	49
7	54

In order for the marketing manager to predict the sales for the seventh and eighth days of January, she must pick the number of observations to be averaged. She used two possibilities: a six-day and a three-day period.

Case 1

$$Y'_7 = \frac{46 + 54 + 53 + 46 + 58 + 49}{6} = 51$$

$$Y'_8 = \frac{54 + 53 + 46 + 58 + 49 + 54}{6} = 52.3$$

where Y' = predicted

Case 2

$$Y'_7 = \frac{46 + 58 + 49}{3} = 51$$

$$Y'_8 = \frac{58 + 49 + 54}{3} = 53.6$$

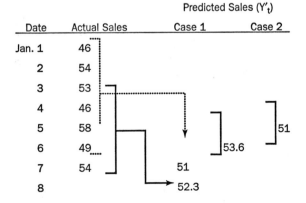

		Predicted Sales (Y'_t)	
Date	Actual Sales	Case 1	Case 2
Jan. 1	46		
2	54		
3	53		
4	46		
5	58		51
6	49	53.6	
7	54	51	
8		52.3	

In terms of the relative importance of new versus old data, in Case 1, the old data received a weight of 5/6, and current data of 1/6. In Case 2, the old data received a weight of only 2/3, while current observation received a weight of 1/3. Thus, the marketing manager's choice of the number of periods to use in a moving average is a measure of the relative importance attached to old versus current data.

What are the advantages and disadvantages of moving averages?

The moving average is simple to use, and easy to understand. However, there are two shortcomings:

- It requires that a great deal of data be retained and carried along from forecast period to forecast period.
- All data in the sample are weighted equally. If more recent data are more valid than older data, why not give recent data greater weight?

The forecasting method known as exponential smoothing gets around these disadvantages.

11.2.2 Exponential Smoothing

What is the basis of exponential smoothing?

Exponential smoothing is a popular technique for short-run forecasting. It uses a weighted average of past data as the basis of the forecast. The procedure assumes the future is more dependent upon the recent past than on the distant past, and thus gives the heaviest weight to more recent data, and smaller weights to those of the more distant past. *When to use it:* The method is most effective when randomness and no seasonal fluctuations are present. *Caution:* The method does not include industrial or economic factors, such as market conditions, prices, or competitors' actions.

What is the model?

The formula for exponential smoothing is

$$Y'_{t+1} = \alpha Y_t + (1 - \alpha)Y'_t$$

or, in words,

$$Y'_{new} = \alpha Y_{old} + (1 - \alpha)Y'_{old}$$

where

Y'_{new} = Exponentially smoothed average to be used as the forecast

Y_{old} = Most recent actual data

Y'_{old} = Most recent smoothed forecast

α = Smoothing constant

Remember this: The higher the α, the higher the weight given to the more recent data.

Example 11.6

YSY provides the following sales data:

Time Period (t)	Actual Sales (1000)(Y_t)
1	$60.0
2	64.0
3	58.0
4	66.0
5	70.0
6	60.0
7	70.0
8	74.0
9	62.0
10	74.0
11	68.0
12	66.0
13	60.0
14	66.0
15	62.0

To initialize the exponential smoothing process, the initial forecast is required. The first smoothed forecast to be used can be

1. First actual observations
2. An average of the actual data for a few periods

The manager decides to use a six-period average as the initial forecast Y'_7, with a smoothing constant of =0.40. Then

$$Y'_7 = (Y_1 + Y_2 + Y_3 + Y_4 + Y_5 + Y_6)/6$$
$$= (60 + 64 + 58 + 66 + 70 + 60)/6 = 63$$

Note that $Y_7 = 70$. Then Y'_8 is computed as follows:

$$Y'_8 = \alpha Y_7 + (1 - \alpha)Y'_7$$
$$= (0.40)(70) + (0.60)(63)$$
$$= 28.0 + 37.80 = 65.80$$

Similarly,

$$Y'_9 = \alpha Y_8 + (1 - \alpha)Y'_8$$
$$= (0.40)(74) + (0.60)(65.80)$$
$$= 29.60 + 39.48 = 69.08$$

and

$$Y'_{10} = \alpha Y_9 + (1 - \alpha)Y'_9$$
$$= (0.40)(62) + (0.60)(69.08)$$
$$= 24.80 + 41.45 = 66.25$$

By using the same procedure, the values of Y'_{11}, Y'_{12}, Y'_{13}, Y'_{14}, and Y'_{15} can be calculated. The following shows a comparison between the actual sales and predicted sales by the exponential smoothing method.

Comparison of Actual Sales and Predicted Sales

Time Period (t)	Actual Sales (Y_t)	Predicted Sales (Y'_t)	Difference $(Y_t - Y'_t)$	Difference^2 $(Yt - Y'_t)^2$
1	$60.0			
2	64.0			
3	58.0			
4	66.0			
5	70.0			
6	60.0			
7	70.0	63.00	7.00	49.00
8	74.0	65.80	8.20	67.24
9	62.0	69.08	−7.08	50.13
10	74.0	66.25	7.75	60.06
11	68.0	69.35	−1.35	1.82
12	66.0	68.81	−2.81	7.90
13	60.0	67.69	−7.69	59.14
14	66.0	64.61	1.39	1.93
15	62.0	65.17	−3.17	10.05
				307.27

How do I determine the best smoothing constant?

A higher or lower smoothing constant (α) can be used in order to adjust the prediction to large fluctuations in the data series. For example, if the forecast is slow in reacting to increased sales (if the difference is negative), a higher value might be called for. For practical purposes, the optimal α may be picked by minimizing what is known as the mean squared error (MSE), which is the average sum of the variations between the historical data and forecast values for the corresponding periods. MSE is computed as follows:

$$\text{MSE} = \sum (Y_t - Y'_t)^2/(n - i)$$

where i = the number of observations used to determine the initial forecast (in our example, i = 6).

In the previous example, i = 6 and

$$\text{MSE} = 307.27/(15 - 6) = 307.27/9 = 34.14$$

What to do: Try to select the α that minimizes MSE.

Can a computer help?

Managers will be confronted with complex problems requiring large sample data. Try different values of α for exponential smoothing. A computer can be of assistance here. Virtually all forecasting software has an exponential smoothing routine. To demonstrate, consider the following data:

Time Period	Actual Sales (in Thousands of Dollars)
1	117
2	120
3	132
4	141
5	140
6	156
7	169
8	171
9	174
10	182

Figure 11.1 is a printout of an exponential smoothing program. The best α for this particular example is 0.9, as it gives the least MSE.

Figure 11.1 Exponential Smoothing Program

Please enter the number of observations.
?10
Enter your data now.
The data should be separated by commas.
?117, 120, 132, 141, 140, 156, 169, 171, 174, 182
Enter the number of periods over which you compute the average to be used as the first forecast value.
?1

**********Exponential smoothing Program-single smoothing**********

Jae K. Shim

Period	Actual Value	Estimated Value	Error
1	117.00	.00	
2	120.00	117.00	

The value of the exponential smoother is .1

3	132.00	117.30	14.70
4	141.00	118.77	22.23
5	140.00	120.99	19.01
6	156.00	122.89	33.11
7	169.00	126.20	42.80
8	171.00	130.48	40.52
9	174.00	134.54	30.46
10	182.00	138.48	43.52

The total absolute error in estimate is 255.34
The mean squared error is 1136.48

The value of the exponential smoother is .2

3	132.00	117.60	14.40
4	141.00	120.48	20.52
5	140.00	124.58	15.42
6	156.00	127.67	28.33
7	169.00	133.33	35.67
8	171.00	140.47	30.53
9	174.00	146.57	27.43
10	182.00	152.06	29.94

The total absolute error in estimate is 202.24
The mean squared error is 690.23

Figure 11.1 (cont.)

The value of the exponential smoother is .3

3	132.00	117.90	14.10
4	141.00	122.13	18.87
5	140.00	127.79	12.21
6	156.00	131.45	24.55
7	169.00	138.82	30.18
8	171.00	147.87	23.13
9	174.00	154.81	19.19
10	182.00	160.57	21.43

The total absolute error in estimate is 163.66
The mean squared error is 447.49

The value of the exponential smoother is .4

3	132.00	118.20	13.80
4	141.00	123.72	17.28
5	140.00	130.63	9.37
6	156.00	134.38	21.62
7	169.00	143.03	25.97
8	171.00	153.42	17.58
9	174.00	160.45	13.55
10	182.00	165.87	16.13

The total absolute error in estimate is 114.16
The mean squared error is 308.97

The value of the exponential smoother is .5

3	132.00	118.50	13.50
4	141.00	125.25	15.75
5	140.00	133.12	6.88
6	156.00	136.56	19.44
7	169.00	146.28	22.72
8	171.00	157.64	13.36
9	174.00	164.32	9.68
10	182.00	169.16	12.84

The total absolute error in estimate is 114.16
The mean squared error is 226.07

The value of the exponential smoother is .6

3	132.00	118.80	13.20
4	141.00	126.72	14.28
5	140.00	135.29	4.71
6	156.00	138.12	17.88

Figure 11.1 (*cont.*)

7	169.00	148.85	20.15
8	171.00	160.94	10.06
9	174.00	166.98	7.02
10	182.00	171.19	10.81

The total absolute error in estimate is 98.13
The mean squared error is 174.23

The value of the exponential smoother is .7

3	132.00	119.10	12.90
4	141.00	128.13	12.87
5	140.00	137.14	2.86
6	156.00	139.14	16.86
7	169.00	150.94	18.06
8	171.00	163.58	7.42
9	174.00	168.77	5.23
10	182.00	172.43	9.57

The total absolute error in estimate is 85.76
The mean squared error is 140.55

The value of the exponential smoother is .8

3	132.00	119.40	12.60
4	141.00	129.48	11.52
5	140.00	138.70	1.30
6	156.00	139.74	16.26
7	169.00	152.75	16.25
8	171.00	165.75	5.25
9	174.00	169.95	4.05
10	182.00	173.19	8.81

The total absolute error in estimate is 76.05
The mean squared error is 117.91

The value of the exponential smoother is .9

3	132.00	119.70	12.30
4	141.00	130.77	10.23
5	140.00	139.98	.02
6	156.00	142.25	3.75
7	169.00	154.40	14.60
8	171.00	167.54	3.46
9	174.00	170.65	3.35
10	182.00	173.67	8.33

The total absolute error in estimate is 68.30
The mean squared error is 102.23

Figure 11.1 (cont.)
Summary Results

The exponential smoother	.1	with a mean squared error of 1136.48
The exponential smoother	.2	with a mean squared error of 690.23
The exponential smoother	.3	with a mean squared error of 447.49
The exponential smoother	.4	with a mean squared error of 308.97
The exponential smoother	.5	with a mean squared error of 226.07
The exponential smoother	.6	with a mean squared error of 174.23
The exponential smoother	.7	with a mean squared error of 140.55
The exponential smoother	.8	with a mean squared error of 117.91
The exponential smoother	.9	with a mean squared error of 102.23

11.3 REGRESSION ANALYSIS FOR SALES AND EARNINGS PROJECTIONS

What is regression analysis?

Regression analysis is a statistical procedure for mathematically estimating the average relationship between the dependent variable and the independent variable(s). Simple regression involves one independent variable—price or advertising—in a demand function, whereas multiple regression involves two or more variables—that is, price and advertising together.

Following is a discussion of simple (linear) regression, defined by the following equation:

$$Y = a + bX$$

Where

Y = dependent variable

X = independent (explanatory) variable

a = a constant or Y intercept of regression line

b = the slope of the regression line

How do I use the method of least squares?

The method of least squares attempts to find a line of best fit for the graph of a regression equation. To better explain this, let us define error, or u, as the difference between the observed and estimated values of sales or earnings. Symbolically,

$$u = Y - Y'$$

where

Y = observed value of the dependent variable

Y' = estimated value based on $Y' = a + bX$

The least-squares criterion requires that the line of best fit be such that the sum of the squares of the errors (or, in Figure 11.2, the vertical distance) from the observed data points to the line) is a minimum, that is,

$$\text{Minimum: } \sum u^2 = \sum (Y - a - bX)^2$$

Using differential calculus, the following equations, called normal equations, are obtained:

$$\sum Y = na + b\sum X$$
$$\sum XY = a\sum X + b\sum X^2$$

Figure 11.2 Actual (Y) versus estimated (Y')

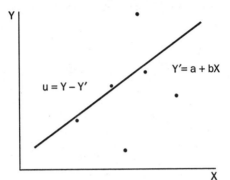

Solving the equations for b and a yields

$$b = \frac{n\sum XY - (\sum X)(\sum Y)}{n\sum X^2 - (\sum X)^2}$$

$$a = \overline{Y} - b\overline{X}$$

where

$$\overline{Y} = \frac{\sum Y}{n} \text{ and } \overline{X} = \frac{\sum X}{n}$$

Example 11.7

To illustrate the computations of b and a, we will refer to the data in Table 11.1. All the sums required are computed and shown below.

Table 11.1 Original Data and Computed Sums

Advertising X (000)	Sales Y (000)	XY	X²	Y²
$9	15	135	81	225
19	20	380	361	400
11	14	154	121	196
14	16	224	196	256
23	25	575	529	625
12	20	240	144	400
12	20	240	144	400
22	23	506	484	529
7	14	98	49	196
13	22	286	169	484
15	18	270	225	324
17	18	306	289	324
$174	$225	3,414	2,792	4,359

From Table 11.1:

$$\sum X = 174; \sum Y = 225; \sum XY = 3{,}414; \sum X^2 = 2{,}792.$$
$$\overline{X} = \sum X/n = 174/12 = 14.5;$$
$$\overline{Y} = \sum Y/n = 225/12 = 18.75.$$

Substituting these values into the formula for b first,

$$b = \frac{n\sum XY - (\sum X)(\sum Y)}{n\sum X^2 - (\sum X)^2}$$

$$= \frac{(12)(3{,}414) - (174)(225)}{(12)(2{,}792) - (174)^2} = \frac{1{,}818}{3{,}228} = 0.5632$$

$$a = \overline{Y} - b\overline{X} = 18.75 - (0.5632)(14.5)$$
$$= 18.75 - 8.1664 = 10.5836$$

Thus,

$$Y' = 10.5836 + 0.5632\, X$$

Assume that the advertising of $10 is to be expended for next year; the projected sales for the next year would be computed as follows:

$$Y' = 10.5836 + 0.5632\, X$$
$$= 10.5836 + 0.5632\,(10)$$
$$= \$16.2156$$

Note: $\sum Y^2$ is not used here, but rather is computed for r-squared (R^2).

How can I use trend analysis?

Trends are the general upward or downward movements of the average over time. These movements may require many years of data to determine or describe them. They can be described by a straight line or by a curve. The basic forces underlying the trend include technological advances, productivity changes, inflation, and population change. Trend analysis is a special type of simple regression. *Note:* This method involves a regression whereby a trend line is fitted to a time series of data.

The linear trend line equation can be shown as

$$Y = a + bt$$

where $t = $ time.

The formula for the coefficients a and b are essentially the same as the cases for simple regression. However, for regression purposes, a time period can be given a number so that $\sum t = 0$. When there is an odd number of periods, the period in the middle is assigned a zero value. If there is an even number, -1 and $+1$ are assigned the two periods in the middle, so that again $\sum t = 0$.

With $\Sigma t = 0$, the formula for b and a reduces to the following:

$$b = \frac{n\Sigma tY}{n\Sigma t^2}$$

$$a = \frac{\Sigma Y}{n}$$

Example 11.8

Case 1 (odd number)

	20X1	20X2	20X3	20X4	20X5
t =	−2	−1	0	+1	+2

Case 2 (even number)

	20X1	20X2	20X3	20X4	20X5	20X6
t =	−3	−2	−1	+1	+2	+3

In each case, $\Sigma t = 0$.

Example 11.9

Consider ABC Company, whose historical sales follow:

Year	Sales (in millions)
20X1	$10
20X2	12
20X3	13
20X4	16
20X5	17

Since the company has five years' worth of data, which is an odd number, the year in the middle is assigned a zero value.

Year	t	Sales (in millions) (Y)	tY	t^2	Y^2
20X1	−2	$10	−20	4	100
20X2	−1	12	−12	1	144
20X3	0	13	0	0	169
20X4	+1	16	16	1	256
20X5	+2	17	34	4	289
	0	68	18	10	958

$$b = \frac{(5)(18)}{5(10)} = 90/50 = 1.8$$

$$a = \frac{68}{5} = 13.6$$

Therefore, the estimated trend equation is

$$Y' = \$13.6 + \$1.8\,t$$

To project 20X6 sales, we assign +3 to the t value for the year 20X6.

$$Y' = \$13.6 + \$1.8(3)$$
$$= \$19$$

A summary of the five forecasting methods described in this chapter is provided in Figure 11.3. *Remember this:* Use the following table as a guide for determining which method is best for your specific circumstances.

11.4 STATISTICS TO LOOK FOR IN REGRESSION ANALYSIS

A variety of statistics can be used to illuminate the accuracy and reliability of the regression results. Three are described in this section:

1. Correlation coefficient (R) and coefficient of determination (R^2)

2. Standard error of the estimate (S_e) and prediction confidence interval

3. Standard error of the regression coefficient (S_b) and t-statistic

How can I measure the goodness of fit for the regression equation?

The correlation coefficient R measures the degree of correlation between Y and X. The range of values it takes on is between −1 and +1. More widely used, however, is the coefficient of determination, designated R^2 (read as r-squared). Simply put, R^2 indicates how good the estimated regression equation is. In other words, it is a measure of "goodness of fit" in the regression. *Rule of thumb:* The higher the R^2, the more confidence we have in our estimated equation.

The coefficient of determination represents the proportion of the total variation in Y that is explained by the regression equation. It has the range of values between 0 and 1.

Figure 11.3 Summary of More Commonly Used Forecasting Methods

Technique	Moving Average	Exponential Smoothing	Trend Analysis	Regression Analysis
Description	Each point of a moving average of a time series is the arithmetic or weighted average of a number of consecutive points of the series, where the number of data points is chosen so the effects of seasonals or irregularity or both are eliminated.	Similar to moving average, except that more recent data points are given more weight. Descriptively, the new forecast is equal to the old one plus some proportion of the past forecasting error. Effective when there are random demand and no seasonal fluctuations in the data series.	Fits a trend line to a mathematical equation and then projects it into the future by means of this equation. There are several variations: the slope-characteristic method, polynomials, logarithms, and so on.	Functionality relates sales to other economic, competitive, or internal variables and estimates an equation using the least-squares technique. Relationships are primarily analyzed statistically, although any relationship could be selected for testing on a rational ground.
Accuracy:				
Short-term (0–3 months)	Poor to good	Fair to very good	Very good	Good to very good
Medium-term (3 months–2 years)	Poor	Poor to good	Good	Good to very good
Long-term (2 years and over)	Very poor	Very poor	Good	Poor

Identification of turning point	Poor	Poor	Poor	Very good
Typical application	Inventory control for low-volume items	Production and inventory control, forecast of sales, and financial data.	New product forecasts (particularly intermediate and long-term).	Forecasts of sales by product classes, forecasts of income, and other financial data.
Data required	A minimum of two years of sales history if seasonals are present. Otherwise, fewer data. (Of course, the more history the better.) The moving average must be specified.	The same as for a moving average.	Varies with the technique used. However, a good rule of thumb is to use a minimum of five years' annual data to start. Thereafter, the complete history.	Several years' quarterly history to obtain good, meaningful relationships. Mathematically necessary to have two more observations than there are independent variables.
Cost of forecasting with a computer	Very minimal	Minimal	Varies with application	Varies with application
Is calculation possible without a computer?	Yes	Yes	Yes	Yes
Time required to develop an application and make forecasts	1 day–	1 day–	1 day–	Depends on ability to identify relationships

Example 11.10

The statement "Sales is a function of advertising expenditure with $R^2 = 70$ percent" can be interpreted as "70 percent of the total variation of sales is explained by the regression equation, or the change in advertising, and the remaining 30 percent is accounted for by something other than advertising, such as price and income."

The coefficient of determination is computed as

$$R^2 = 1 - \frac{\sum(Y - Y')^2}{\sum(Y - \overline{Y})^2}$$

In simple regression situation, this short-cut formula can be used:

$$R^2 = \frac{[n\sum XY - (\sum X)(\sum Y)]^2}{[n\sum X^2 - (\sum X)^2][n\sum Y^2 - (\sum Y)^2]}$$

Comparing this formula with the one for b, it is clear that the only additional information needed to compute R^2 is $\sum Y^2$.

Example 11.11

Refer to the table in Example 11.7. With Y^2, compute R^2 can be computed using the short-cut formula as follows:

$$R^2 = \frac{(1,818)^2}{[3,228][(12)(4,359) - (225)^2]}$$

$$= \frac{3,305,124}{[3,228][52,308 - 50,625]} = \frac{3,305,124}{(3,228)(1,683)}$$

$$= \frac{3,305,124}{5,423,724} = 0.6084 = 60.84\%$$

Interpretation: About 60.84 percent of the total variation in sales is explained by advertising, and the remaining 39.16 percent is still unexplained. A relatively low R^2 indicates that there is a lot of room for improvement in the estimated forecasting formula ($Y' = \$10.5836 + \$0.5632X$). Price or a combination of advertising and price might improve R^2.

Remember: A low R^2 is an indication that the model is inadequate for explaining the y variable.

The general causes for this problem are

1. Use of a wrong functional form

2. Poor choice of an X variable as the predictor

3. The omission of some important variable or variables from the model

How can I measure the accuracy of management predictions?

Use the standard error of the estimate, designated S_e, and defined as the standard deviation of the regression. It is computed as

$$S_e = \sqrt{\frac{\sum(Y - Y')^2}{n - 2}} = \sqrt{\frac{\sum Y^2 - a\sum Y - b\sum XY}{n - 2}}$$

This statistic can be used to gain some idea of the accuracy of our predictions.

Example 11.12

Going back to our example data, S_e is calculated as

$$S_e = \sqrt{\frac{\sum Y' - a\sum Y - b\sum XY}{n - 2}}$$

$$= \sqrt{\frac{4,359 - (10.5836)(225) - (0.5632)(3,414)}{12 - 2}}$$

$$= \sqrt{\frac{54,9252}{10}}$$

$$= 2.3436$$

Suppose management wants to make a prediction regarding an individual Y value—such as a prediction about the sales when an advertising expense = \$10. Usually, we would like to have some objective measure of the confidence we can place in our prediction, and one such measure is a confidence (or prediction) interval constructed for Y.

A confidence interval for a predicted Y, given a value for X, can be constructed in the following manner:

$$Y' \pm t\, S_e \sqrt{1 + \frac{1}{n} + \frac{(X_p - X)^2}{\sum X^2 - \frac{(\sum X)^2}{n}}}$$

where

Y' = the predicted value of Y given a value for X;

X_p = the value of independent variable used as the basis for prediction.

Note: t is the critical value for the level of significance employed. For example, for a significant level of 0.025 (which is equivalent to a 95 percent confidence level in a two-tailed test), the critical value of t for 10 degrees of freedom is 2.228 (see Table 11.3 at the end of this chapter). As can be seen, the confidence interval is the linear distance bounded by limits on either side of the prediction.

If a 95 percent confidence interval of the prediction is desired, the range for the prediction, given an advertising expense of $10, would be between $10,595.10 and $21,836.10, determined as follows (note that from Example 4.2, $R' = \$16.2156$). The confidence interval is therefore established as follows:

$$\$16.2156 \pm (2.228)(2.3436)\sqrt{1 + \frac{1}{12} + \frac{(10 - 14.5)^2}{2,792 - \frac{(174)^2}{12}}}$$

$$= \$16.2156 \pm (2.228)(2.3436)\,(1.0764)$$

$$= \$16.2156 \pm 5.6205$$

This means that the range for the prediction, given an advertising expense of $10, would be between $10.5951 and $21.8361. Note that $\$10.5951 = \$16.2156 - 5.6205$ and $\$21.8361 = \$16.2156 + 5.6205$.

How can I test the appropriateness of the regression coefficient?

The standard error of the regression coefficient, designated S_b, and the t-statistic are closely related. S_b is calculated as

$$S_b = \frac{S_e}{\sqrt{(X - \bar{X})^2}}$$

or, in short-cut form,

$$S_b = \frac{S_e}{\sqrt{X^2 - \bar{X}\sum X)}}$$

S_b gives an estimate of the range where the true coefficient will "actually" fall.

The t-statistic (or t-value) is a measure of the statistical significance of an independent variable X in explaining the dependent variable Y. This value is determined by dividing the estimated regression coefficient, b, by its standard error, Sb. It is then compared with the table t-value (see Table 11.3 at the end of this chapter). Thus, the t-statistic measures how many standard errors the coefficient is away from zero.

Rule of thumb: Any t-value greater than +2 or less than -2 is acceptable. The higher the t-value, the greater the confidence we have in the coefficient as a predictor. Low t-values are indications of low reliability of the predictive power of that coefficient.

Example 11.13

The S_b for this example is

$$S_b = \frac{S_e}{\sqrt{X^2 - (\bar{X}\sum X)}} = \frac{2.3436}{\sqrt{2,792 - (14.5)(174)}}$$

$$= \frac{2.3436}{\sqrt{2,792 - 2,523}} = 0.143$$

Thus,

$$\text{t-statistic} = \frac{b}{S_b} = \frac{0.5632}{0.143} = 3.94$$

Conclusion: Since t = 3.94 > 2, we conclude that the b coefficient is statistically significant. As was indicated previously, the table's critical value (cut-off value) for 10 degrees of freedom is 2.228 (from Table 11.3, at the end of this chapter).

To review,

1. The t-statistic is more relevant to multiple regressions that have more than one b.

2. R^2 tells how good the forest (overall fit) is, while t-statistic tells how good an individual tree (an independent variable) is.

In summary, the table t-value, based on a degree of freedom and a level of significance, is used

1. To set the prediction range—upper and lower limits—for the predicted value of the dependent variable.

2. To set the confidence range for regression coefficients.

3. As a cutoff value for the t-test.

Figure 11.4 shows an Excel regression output that contains the statistics discussed so far.

Figure 11.4 Excel Regression Output

SUMMARY OUTPUT

Regression Statistics	
Multiple R	0.77998
R Squared	0.60837 (R^2)
Adjusted R Squared	0.56921
Standard Error	2.34362 (S_e)
Observations	12

ANOVA

	df	SS	MS	Significance F
Regression	1	85.32434944	85.3243	0.002769
Residual	10	54.92565056	5.49257	
Total	11	140.25		

Figure 11.4 (cont.)

	Coefficients	Standard Error (S_b)	t Stat	Lower 95%	Upper 95%	Upper 95.0%
Intercept	10.5836	2.17960878	4.85575	5.727171	15.4401	15.4401
Advertising	0.5632	0.142893168	3.94139	0.244811	0.88158	0.88158

(1) R-squared (R^2) = .608373 = 60.84%

(2) Standard error of the estimate (S_e) = 2.343622

(3) Standard error of the coefficient (S_b) = 0.142893

(4) t-value = 3.94

All of the above values are the same as the ones manually obtained.

11.4.1 Statistics to Look for in Multiple Regressions

In multiple regressions that involve more than one independent (explanatory) variable, take note of the following statistics when doing multiple regression:

- t-statistics
- R-bar squared ($\overline{R}^2$) and F-statistic
- Multicollinearity
- Autocorrelation (or serial correlation)

What do the t-statistics show?

Even though the t-statistic was discussed in the previous section, it is taken up again here because it is more valid in multiple regression. The t-statistic shows the significance of each explanatory variable in predicting the dependent variable. In a multiple regression situation, the t-statistic is defined as

$$t\text{-statistic} = \frac{b_i}{S_{b_i}}$$

where $i = i_{th}$ independent variable. *Rule of thumb:* It is desirable to have as large (either positive or negative) a t-statistic as possible for each independent variable. Generally, a t-statistic greater than $+2.0$ or less than -2.0 is acceptable. Explanatory variables with low t-value can usually be eliminated from the regression without substantially decreasing R^2 or increasing the standard error of the regression. Table 11.2 (at the end of this chapter) provides t-value for a specified level of significance and degrees of freedom.

How do I measure goodness of fit?

For multiple regressions, goodness of fit is best represented by R-bar squared ($\overline{R}^2$):

$$\overline{R}^2 = 1 - (1 - R^2)\frac{n - 1}{n - k}$$

where

n = the number of observations

k = the number of coefficients to be estimated

An alternative test of the overall significance of a regression equation is the F-test.

The F-statistic is defined as

$$F = \frac{(Y' - \overline{Y}^2)/k}{(Y - Y')^2/(n - k - 1)}$$

$$= \frac{\text{Explained variation}/k}{\text{Unexplained variation}/(n - k - 1)}$$

If the F-statistic is greater than the table value, it is concluded that the regression equation is statistically significant in overall terms. *Note:* Virtually all computer programs for regression analysis show $\overline{R}^2$ and F-statistic.

How can I be sure the independent variables are unrelated?

When using more than one independent variable in a regression equation, there is sometimes a high correlation between the independent variables themselves. Multicollinearity occurs when these variables interfere with each other. This is a pitfall because the equations with multicollinearity may produce spurious forecasts.

Multicollinearity can be recognized when

- The t-statistics of two seemingly important independent variables are low.

- The estimated coefficients on explanatory variables have the opposite sign from that which would logically be expected.

There are two ways to get around the problem of multicollinearity:

- One of the highly correlated variables may be dropped from the regression.

- The structure of the equation may be changed using one of the following methods:

  - Divide both the left- and right-hand side variables by some series that will leave the basic economic logic but remove multicollinearity.

  - Estimate the equation on a first-difference basis.

  - Combine the collinear variables into a new variable, which is their weighted sum.

What is autocorrelation (serial correlation)?

Autocorrelation is another major pitfall often encountered in regression analysis. It occurs where there is a correlation between successive errors. The Durbin-Watson statistic provides the standard test for autocorrelation. Table 11.2, at the end of this chapter, provides the values of the Durbin-Watson statistic for specified sample sizes and explanatory variables. Table 11.2 gives the significance points for d_L and d_U for tests on the autocorrelation of residuals (when no explanatory variable is a lagged endogenous variable).

Generally speaking,

Durbin-Watson Statistic	*Autocorrelation*
Between 1.5 and 2.5	No autocorrelation
Below 1.5	Positive autocorrelation
Above 2.5	Negative autocorrelation

Autocorrelation usually indicates that an important part of the variation of the dependent variable has not been explained. *What to do:* The best solution to this problem is to search for other explanatory variables to include in the regression equation.

An example showing applications of all the tests discussed in this section can be found in Section 11.6.

11.5   MEASURING THE ACCURACY OF YOUR FORECASTS

The performance of a forecast should be checked against its own record, or against the performance of other forecasts. There are various statistical measures that can be used to measure performance of the model. Of course, the performance is measured in terms of forecasting error, where error is defined as the difference between a predicted value and the actual result:

$$\text{Error (e)} = \text{Actual (A)} - \text{Forecast (F)}$$

What measures are commonly used for summarizing errors?

Two measures are commonly used for summarizing historical errors: the mean absolute deviation (MAD) and the mean squared error (MSE). The formulas used to calculate MAD and MSE are

$$\text{MAD} = \sum |e|/n$$
$$\text{MSE} = \sum e^2/(n-1)$$

The following example illustrates the computation of MAD and MSE.

Example 11.14

Sales data of a microwave-oven manufacturer are as follows:

Period	Actual (A)	Forecast (F)	e(A − F)	|e|	e^2
1	217	215	2	2	4
2	213	216	−3	3	9
3	216	215	1	1	1
4	210	214	−4	4	16
5	213	211	2	2	4
6	219	214	5	5	25
7	216	217	−1	1	1
8	212	216	−4	4	16
			−2	22	76

Using the figures,

$$\text{MAD} = \sum |e|/n = 22/8 = 2.75$$
$$\text{MSE} = \sum e^2/(n-1) = 76/7 = 10.86$$

One way in which these measures are used is to evaluate forecasting ability of alternative forecasting methods. For example, using either MAD or MSE, a forecaster could compare the results of exponential smoothing with alphas and elect the one that performed best in terms of the lowest MAD or MSE for a given set of data. Also, MAD or MSE can help select the best initial forecast value for exponential smoothing.

How do I choose the best forecasting equation?

Choosing among alternative forecasting equations basically involves two steps. The first step is to eliminate the obvious losers; the second is to select the winner among the remaining contenders.

How to eliminate losers
1. Does the equation make sense? Equations that do not make sense intuitively or from a theoretical standpoint must be eliminated.
2. Does the equation have explanatory variables with low t-statistics? These equations should be reestimated or dropped in favor of equations in which all independent variables are significant. This test will eliminate equations in which multicollinearity is a problem.

3. How about a low $\overline{R}^2$? The $\overline{R}^2$ can be used to rank the remaining equations in order to select the best candidates. A low $\overline{R}^2$ could mean

   - A wrong functional was fitted.
   - An important explanatory variable is missing.
   - Other combinations of explanatory variables might be more desirable.

How to choose the best equation
1. *Best Durbin-Watson statistic.* Given equations that survive all previous tests, the equation with the Durbin-Watson statistic closest to 2.0 can be a basis for selection.

2. *Best forecasting accuracy.* Examining the forecasting performance of the equations is essential for selecting one equation from those that have not been eliminated. The equation with the best prediction accuracy in terms of measures of forecasting errors, such as MAD or MSE generally provides the best basis for forecasting.

It is important to note that neither Lotus 1-2-3 nor Quattro Pro calculates many statistics, such as R-bar squared ($\overline{R}^2$), F-statistic, and the Durbin-Watson statistic. For these calculations, go to regression packages such as Statistical Analysis System (SAS), MINITAB, and Statistical Packages for Social Scientists (SPSS), to name a few. These packages all come in PC versions.

11.6 HOW TO USE A COMPUTER STATISTICAL PACKAGE FOR MULTIPLE REGRESSIONS

Are computers helpful for regression analyses?

Software packages can greatly assist decision makers and forecasters with a variety of statistical analyses.

How does the computer handle multiple regression?

Following is an example of how a computer handles multiple regression. *Remember this:* Each software package is a little different. For this example, we use SPSS, one of the most popular programs. Figure 11.5 shows a computer listing containing the input data and output results using three independent variables. Illustrative comments have been added where applicable.

Example 11.15

Stanton Consumer Products Corporation wants to develop a forecasting model for its dryer sale by using multiple regression analysis. The marketing department has prepared sample data, which appear in the following table, using three independent variables: sales of washers, disposable income, and savings.

Month	Sales of Washers (X_1)	Disposable Income (X_2)	Savings (X_3)	Sales of Dryers (Y)
January	$45,000	$16,000	$71,000	$29,000
February	42,000	14,000	70,000	24,000
March	44,000	15,000	72,000	27,000
April	45,000	13,000	71,000	25,000
May	43,000	13,000	75,000	26,000
June	46,000	14,000	74,000	28,000
July	44,000	16,000	76,000	30,000
August	45,000	16,000	69,000	28,000
September	44,000	15,000	74,000	28,000
October	43,000	15,000	73,000	27,000

Figure 11.5 SPSS Regression Output

Variables Entered/Removed[b]

Model	Variables Entered	Variables Removed	Method
1	SAVINGS, sales, INCOME[a]	.	Enter

[a] All requested variables entered.
[b] Dependent Variable: SALESDRY

Model Summary[b]

Model	R	R Squared	Adjusted R Squared	Std. Error of the Estimate	Durbin-Watson
1	.992[a]	.983	.975	286.1281	2.094

[a] Predictors: (Constant), SAVINGS, sales, INCOME
[b] Dependent Variable: SALESDRY

Figure 11.5 *(cont.)*

<table>
<tr><th colspan="7" style="text-align:center">Coefficients[a]</th></tr>
<tr><th></th><th></th><th colspan="2" style="text-align:center">Unstandardized
Coefficients</th><th style="text-align:center">Stan-
dardized
Coeffi-
cients</th><th></th><th></th></tr>
<tr><th>Model</th><th></th><th>B</th><th>Std.
Error</th><th>Beta</th><th>t</th><th>Sig.</th></tr>
<tr><td>1</td><td>(Constant)</td><td>−45796.3</td><td>4877.651</td><td></td><td>−9.3989</td><td>.000</td></tr>
<tr><td></td><td>Sales</td><td>.597</td><td>.081</td><td>.394</td><td>7.359</td><td>.000</td></tr>
<tr><td></td><td>INCOME</td><td>1.177</td><td>.084</td><td>.752</td><td>13.998</td><td>.000</td></tr>
<tr><td></td><td>SAVINGS</td><td>.405</td><td>.042</td><td>.508</td><td>9.592</td><td>.000</td></tr>
</table>

[a] Dependent Variable: SALESDRY

The forecasting equation. From the SPSS output we see that

$$Y' = -45{,}796.35 + 0.597X_1 + 1.177X_2 + 0.405X_3$$

Suppose that in November the company expects

$$X_1 = \text{sales of washers} \quad = \$43{,}000$$
$$X_2 = \text{disposable income} = \$15{,}000$$
$$X_3 = \text{savings} \qquad\qquad = \$75{,}000$$

Then the forecast sales for the month of November would be

$$Y' = -45{,}796.35 + 0.597(43{,}000) + 1.177(15{,}000)$$
$$+ \, 0.405(75{,}000)$$
$$= -45{,}796 + 25{,}671 + 17{,}655 + 30{,}375$$
$$= \$27{,}905.35$$

The coefficient of determination. Note that the SPSS output gives the value of R, R^2, and R^2 adjusted. In our example,

$$R = 0.992 \text{ and } R^2 = 0.983$$

In the case of multiple regression, R^2 is more appropriate, as was discussed previously.

$$\overline{R}^2 = 1 - (1 - R^2)\frac{n-1}{n-k}$$

$$= 1 - (1 - 0.983)\frac{10-1}{10-3} = 1 - 0.017\,(9/7)$$

$$= 1 - 0.025 = 0.975$$

This tells us that 97.5 percent of total variation in sales of dryers is explained by the three explanatory variables. The remaining 2.2 percent was unexplained by the estimated equation.

Table 11.2 Values of the Durbin–Watson d for Specified Samples Sizes (T) and Explanatory Variables
Significance Level = 0.01

Number of Residuals	$K = 1$		$K = 2$		$K = 3$		$K = 4$		$K = 5$	
T	d_L	d_U	d_L	d_U	d_L	d_U	d_L	d_U	d_L	d_U
15	1.08	1.36	0.95	1.54	0.82	1.75	0.69	1.97	0.56	2.21
16	1.10	1.37	0.98	1.54	0.86	1.73	0.74	1.93	0.62	2.15
17	1.13	1.38	1.02	1.54	0.90	1.71	0.78	1.90	0.67	2.10
18	1.16	1.39	1.05	1.53	0.93	1.69	0.82	1.87	0.71	2.06
19	1.18	1.40	1.08	1.53	0.97	1.68	0.86	1.85	0.75	2.02
20	1.20	1.41	1.10	1.54	1.00	1.68	0.90	1.83	0.79	1.99
21	1.22	1.42	1.13	1.54	1.03	1.67	0.93	1.81	0.83	1.96
22	1.24	1.43	1.15	1.54	1.05	1.66	0.96	1.80	0.86	1.94
23	1.26	1.44	1.17	1.54	1.08	1.66	0.99	1.79	0.90	1.92
24	1.27	1.45	1.19	1.55	1.10	1.66	1.01	1.78	0.93	1.90
25	1.29	1.45	1.21	1.55	1.12	1.66	1.04	1.77	0.95	1.89
26	1.30	1.46	1.22	1.55	1.14	1.65	1.06	1.76	0.98	1.88
27	1.32	1.47	1.24	1.56	1.16	1.65	1.08	1.76	1.01	1.86
28	1.33	1.48	1.26	1.56	1.18	1.65	1.10	1.75	1.03	1.85
29	1.34	1.48	1.27	1.56	1.20	1.65	1.12	1.74	1.05	1.84
30	1.35	1.49	1.28	1.57	1.21	1.65	1.14	1.74	1.07	1.83

31	1.36	1.50	1.30	1.57	1.23	1.65	1.16	1.74	1.09	1.83
32	1.37	1.50	1.31	1.57	1.24	1.65	1.18	1.73	1.11	1.82
33	1.38	1.51	1.32	1.58	1.26	1.65	1.19	1.73	1.13	1.81
34	1.39	1.51	1.33	1.58	1.27	1.65	1.21	1.73	1.15	1.81
35	1.40	1.52	1.34	1.58	1.28	1.65	1.22	1.73	1.16	1.80
36	1.41	1.52	1.35	1.59	1.29	1.65	1.24	1.73	1.18	1.80
37	1.42	1.53	1.36	1.59	1.31	1.66	1.25	1.72	1.19	1.80
38	1.43	1.54	1.37	1.59	1.32	1.66	1.26	1.72	1.21	1.79
39	1.43	1.54	1.38	1.60	1.33	1.66	1.27	1.72	1.22	1.79
40	1.44	1.54	1.39	1.60	1.34	1.66	1.29	1.72	1.23	1.79
45	1.48	1.57	1.43	1.62	1.38	1.67	1.34	1.72	1.29	1.78
50	1.50	1.59	1.46	1.63	1.42	1.67	1.38	1.72	1.34	1.77
55	1.53	1.60	1.49	1.64	1.45	1.68	1.41	1.72	1/38	1.77
60	1.55	1.62	1.51	1.65	1.48	1.69	1.44	1.73	1.41	1.77
65	1.57	1.63	1.54	1.66	1.50	1.70	1.47	1.73	1.44	1.77
70	1.58	1.64	1.55	1.67	1.52	1.70	1.49	1.74	1.46	1.77
75	1.60	1.65	1.57	1.68	1.54	1.71	1.51	1.74	1.51	1.77
80	1.61	1.66	1.59	1.69	1.56	1.72	1.53	1.74	1.51	1.77
85	1.62	1.67	1.60	1.70	1.57	1.72	1.55	1.75	1.52	1.77
90	1.63	1.68	1.61	1.70	1.59	1.73	1.57	1.75	1.54	1.78
95	1.64	1.69	1.62	1.71	1.60	1.73	1.58	1.75	1.56	1.78
100	1.65	1.69	1.63	1.72	1.61	1.74	1.59	1.76	1.57	1.78

The standard error of the estimate (S_e). This is a measure of dispersion of actual sales around the estimated equation. The output shows

$$S_e = 286.1281.$$

Computed t. We read from the output

	t-Statistic
X_1	7.359
X_2	13.998
X_3	9.592

All t values are greater than a rule-of-thumb table t value of 2.0. (Strictly speaking, with $n - k - 1 = 10 - 3 - 1 = 6$ degrees of freedom and a level of significance of, say, 0.01, it can be seen from Table 11.3 that the table t-value is 3.707.) For a two-sided test, the level of significance to look up was .005. In any case, the conclusion is that all three explanatory variables selected were statistically significant.

F-test. From the output, it can be seen that

$$F = \frac{(Y' - \overline{Y})^2/k}{(Y - Y')^2/(n - k - 1)}$$

$$= \frac{\text{Explained variation}/k}{\text{Unexplained variation}/(n - k - 1)}$$

$$= \frac{29.109/3}{0.491/6} = 9.703/0.082$$

$$= 118.517 \text{ (which is given in the printout)}$$

At a significance level of 0.01, this F-value is far above the value of 9.78 (which is from Table 11.4), so it can be concluded that the regression as a whole is highly significant.

Conclusion. Based on statistical considerations, we see that

- The estimated equation had a good fit.
- All three variables are significant explanatory variables.
- The regression as a whole is highly significant.
- The model developed can be used as a forecasting equation with a great degree of confidence.

Table 11.3 Critical Values for the *t* Statistic

d.f.	$t_{0.100}$	$t_{0.050}$	$t_{0.025}$	$t_{0.010}$	$t_{0.005}$	d.f.
			Values of t			
1	3.078	6.314	12.706	31.821	63.657	1
2	1.886	2.920	4.303	6.965	9.925	2
3	1.638	2.353	3.182	4.541	5.841	3
4	1.533	2.132	2.776	3.747	4.604	4
5	1.476	2.015	2.571	3.365	4.032	5
6	1.440	1.943	2.447	3.143	3.707	6
7	1.415	1.895	2.365	2.998	3.499	7
8	1.397	1.860	2.306	2.896	3.355	8
9	1.383	1.833	2.262	2.821	3.250	9
10	1.372	1.812	2.228	2.764	3.169	10
11	1.363	1.796	2.201	2.718	3.106	11
12	1.356	1.782	2.179	2.681	3.055	12
13	1.350	1.771	2.160	2.650	3.012	13
14	1.345	1.761	2.145	2.624	2.977	14
15	1.341	1.753	2.131	2.602	2.947	15
16	1.337	1.746	2.120	2.583	2.921	16
17	1.333	1.740	2.110	2.567	1.898	17
18	1.330	1.734	2.101	2.552	2.878	18
19	1.328	1.729	2.093	2.539	2.861	19
20	1.325	1.725	2.086	2.528	2.845	20
21	1.323	1.721	2.080	2.518	2.831	21
22	1.321	1.717	2.074	2.508	2.819	22
23	1.319	1.714	2.069	2.500	2.807	23
24	1.318	1.711	2.064	2.492	2.797	24
25	1.316	1.708	2.060	2.485	2.787	25
26	1.315	1.706	2.056	2.479	2.779	26
27	1.314	1.703	2.052	2.473	2.771	27
28	1.313	1.701	2.048	2.467	2.763	28
29	1.311	1.699	2.045	2.462	2.756	29
Inf.	1.282	1.645	1.960	2.326	2.576	Inf.

Note: The *t* value describes the sampling distribution of a deviation from a population value divided by the standard error.

Degrees of freedom (*d.f.*) are in the first column. The probabilities indicated as subvalues of *t* in the heading refer to the sum of a one-tailed area under the curve that lies outside the point *t*. For example, in the distribution of the means of samples of size *n* = 10, *d.f.* = n − 2 = 8; then 0.0025 of the area under the curve falls in one tail outside the interval *t* ± 2.306.

Table 11.4

Values of F_P for specified probabilities P and degrees of freedom in the numerator n_1 and degrees of freedom in the denominator n_2

F_P is the value of the Snedecor F random variable such that the probability of obtaining a sample F value at least as large as F_P is P. In the first comprehensive table, the level of significance P is 0.05 *for all lightface entries* and 0.01 *for all boldface entries*. This table continues on three pages with the degrees of freedom in the numerator specified across the top and the degrees of freedom in the denominator specified along the side. The areas are shown in the illustration at the right. For example, given $n_1 = 4$ and $n_2 = 9$, the value of F is 3.63 when 5% of the total area is in the right tail of the distribution.

These Tables Show →

F Distribution

	n_1 = degrees of freedom for numerator = k								n_2 = degrees of freedom for denominator = $n - k - 1$			
	1	2	3	4	5	6	7	8	9	10	11	12
1	161	200	216	225	230	234	237	239	241	242	243	244
	4,052	**4,999**	**5,408**	**5,625**	**5,764**	**5,559**	**5,928**	**5,981**	**6,023**	**6,054**	**6,082**	**6,106**
2	18.51	19.00	19.16	19.25	19.30	19.33	19.36	19.37	19.38	19.39	19.40	19.41
	98.49	**99.01**	**99.17**	**99.25**	**99.30**	**99.33**	**99.34**	**99.36**	**99.38**	**99.40**	**99.41**	**99.42**
3	10.13	9.55	9.28	9.12	9.01	8.94	8.88	8.84	8.81	8.78	8.76	8.74
	34.12	**30.81**	**29.46**	**28.71**	**28.24**	**27.91**	**27.67**	**27.49**	**27.34**	**27.23**	**27.13**	**27.06**
4	7.71	6.94	6.59	6.39	6.26	6.16	6.09	6.04	6.00	5.96	5.93	5.91
	21.20	**18.00**	**16.69**	**15.98**	**15.52**	**15.21**	**14.98**	**14.80**	**14.66**	**14.54**	**14.45**	**14.37**

5	6.61	5.79	5.41	5.19	5.05	4.29	4.88	4.82	4.78	4.74	4.70	4.68
	16.26	**13.27**	**12.06**	**11.39**	**10.37**	**10.67**	**10.45**	**10.27**	**10.15**	**10.05**	**9.96**	**9.89**
6	5.99	5.14	4.76	4.53	4.39	4.28	4.21	4.15	4.10	4.06	4.03	4.00
	13.74	**10.92**	**(9.78)**	**9.15**	**8.76**	**8.47**	**8.26**	**8.10**	**7.98**	**7.87**	**7.79**	**7.72**
7	5.59	4.74	4.35	4.12	3.97	3.87	3.79	3.73	3.68	3.63	3.60	3.57
	12.25	**9.55**	**8.45**	**7.85**	**7.44**	**7.19**	**7.00**	**6.84**	**6.71**	**6.62**	**6.54**	**6.47**
8	5.32	4.48	4.07	3.84	3.69	3.58	3.50	3.44	3.39	3.34	3.31	3.28
	11.26	**8.64**	**7.69**	**7.01**	**6.63**	**6.37**	**6.19**	**6.03**	**5.91**	**5.82**	**5.74**	**5.67**
9	5.12	4.26	3.86	3.63	3.48	3.37	3.29	3.23	3.18	3.13	3.10	3.07
	10.66	**8.02**	**6.99**	**6.42**	**6.06**	**5.30**	**5.62**	**5.47**	**5.35**	**5.26**	**5.18**	**5.11**
10	4.96	4.10	3.71	3.48	3.33	3.22	3.14	3.07	3.02	2.97	2.94	2.91
	10.04	**7.54**	**6.55**	**5.99**	**5.64**	**5.39**	**5.21**	**5.06**	**4.95**	**4.85**	**4.78**	**4.71**
11	4.84	3.98	3.59	3.36	3.20	3.09	3.01	2.95	2.90	2.86	2.82	2.79
	9.65	**7.20**	**6.22**	**5.67**	**5.32**	**5.07**	**4.88**	**4.74**	**4.63**	**4.54**	**4.46**	**4.40**
12	4.75	3.88	3.49	3.26	3.11	3.00	2.92	2.85	2.80	2.76	2.72	2.69
	9.33	**6.93**	**5.95**	**5.41**	**5.04**	**4.82**	**4.65**	**4.50**	**4.39**	**4.30**	**4.22**	**4.16**
13	4.67	3.80	3.41	3.18	3.02	2.02	2.84	2.77	2.72	2.67	2.63	2.60
	9.07	**6.70**	**5.74**	**5.20**	**4.86**	**4.62**	**4.44**	**4.30**	**4.19**	**4.10**	**4.02**	**3.96**
14	4.60	3.74	3.34	3.11	2.96	2.85	2.77	2.70	2.65	2.60	2.56	2.53
	8.86	**6.51**	**5.56**	**5.03**	**4.69**	**4.46**	**4.28**	**4.14**	**4.03**	**3.94**	**3.86**	**3.80**
15	4.54	3.68	3.29	3.06	2.90	2.79	2.70	2.64	2.59	2.55	2.51	2.48
	8.62	**6.36**	**5.42**	**4.89**	**4.56**	**4.32**	**4.14**	**4.00**	**3.89**	**3.80**	**3.73**	**3.67**
16	4.49	3.63	3.24	3.01	2.85	2.74	2.66	2.59	2.54	2.49	2.45	2.42

Table 11.4 (cont.)

	8.53	**6.23**	**5.29**	**4.77**	**4.44**	**4.20**	**4.03**	**3.89**	**3.78**	**3.69**	**3.61**	**3.55**
17	4.45	3.59	3.20	2.96	2.81	2.70	2.62	2.55	2.50	2.45	2.41	2.38
	8.40	**6.11**	**5.18**	**4.67**	**4.34**	**4.10**	**3.93**	**3.79**	**3.68**	**3.59**	**3.52**	**3.45**
18	4.41	3.55	3.16	2.93	2.77	2.66	2.58	2.51	2.46	2.41	2.37	2.34
	8.26	**6.01**	**5.09**	**4.58**	**4.25**	**4.01**	**3.86**	**3.71**	**3.60**	**3.51**	**3.44**	**3.37**
19	4.38	3.52	3.13	2.90	2.74	2.63	2.55	2.48	2.43	2.38	2.34	2.31
	8.18	**5.98**	**5.01**	**4.50**	**4.17**	**3.94**	**3.77**	**3.63**	**3.52**	**3.43**	**3.36**	**3.30**
20	4.35	3.49	3.10	2.87	2.71	2.60	2.52	2.45	2.40	2.35	2.31	2.28
	8.10	**5.86**	**4.94**	**4.43**	**4.10**	**3.87**	**3.71**	**3.56**	**3.45**	**3.37**	**3.30**	**3.23**
21	4.32	3.47	3.07	2.84	2.68	2.57	2.49	2.42	2.37	2.32	2.28	2.25
	8.02	**5.78**	**4.87**	**4.37**	**4.04**	**3.81**	**3.65**	**3.51**	**3.40**	**3.31**	**3.24**	**3.17**
22	4.30	3.44	3.05	2.82	2.66	2.55	2.47	2.40	2.35	2.30	2.26	2.23
	7.94	**5.72**	**4.82**	**4.31**	**3.99**	**3.76**	**3.69**	**3.45**	**3.35**	**3.26**	**3.18**	**3.12**
23	4.28	3.42	3.03	2.80	2.64	2.53	2.45	2.38	2.32	2.28	2.24	2.20
	7.88	**5.64**	**4.76**	**4.28**	**3.94**	**3.71**	**3.54**	**3.41**	**3.30**	**3.21**	**3.14**	**3.07**
24	4.26	3.40	3.01	2.78	2.62	2.51	2.43	2.36	2.30	2.26	2.22	2.18
	7.82	**5.61**	**4.72**	**4.22**	**3.90**	**3.67**	**3.50**	**3.36**	**3.25**	**3.17**	**3.09**	**3.03**
25	4.24	3.38	2.99	2.76	2.60	2.49	2.41	2.34	2.28	2.24	2.20	2.16
	7.77	**5.57**	**4.68**	**4.13**	**3.86**	**3.63**	**3.46**	**3.32**	**3.21**	**3.13**	**3.05**	**2.99**
26	4.22	3.37	2.98	2.74	2.59	2.47	2.39	2.32	2.27	2.22	2.18	2.15
	7.72	**5.83**	**4.64**	**4.14**	**3.82**	**3.59**	**3.42**	**3.29**	**3.17**	**3.09**	**3.02**	**2.96**

CHAPTER 12

Making Use of Quantitative Decision Making

Quantitative methods (or models) are used in operations research or management science. They refer to sophisticated mathematical and statistical techniques for solving problems pertaining to managerial planning and decision making. Numerous such techniques are available, eight of which are discussed in this chapter. They are

- Decision making under certainty and conflict
- Decision making under uncertain conditions
- Decision theory
- Linear programming and shadow prices
- Learning curve
- Inventory planning and control
- Queuing models

12.1 DECISION MAKING UNDER CERTAINTY AND CONFLICT

Decision making involves managing three major elements:

- *Decision strategy*. A decision maker implements a decision strategy, which utilizes known existing organizational resources.
- *States of nature*. Elements of the environment over which the manager has little or no control. States of nature include the weather, political environment, economy, technological developments, and so on. They can dramatically affect the outcome of any decision strategy.

- *Outcome.* The result of the interaction of the implementation of a decision strategy with the states of nature. Because of the variable nature of the states of nature, outcomes can be extremely difficult to forecast. Thus, outcome of a decision strategy, O, the dependent variable, is a function of the interaction of the two independent variables: D, decision strategies; and S, the states of nature. Figure 12.1 shows a decision matrix. The rows are strategic choices a manager can make, while the columns represent decision outcomes. An outcome O_{ij} is a function of a decision strategy D_i and state of nature S_j.

Figure 12.1 Decision Matrix

	States of Nature					
Strategies	S_1	S_2	S_3	.	.	S_n
D_1	O_{11}	O_{12}	*	*	*	O_{1n}
D_2	O_{21}	O_{22}	*	*	*	O_{2n}
D_3	*	*				*
.	*	*				*
.						
.						
D_m	O_{i1}	O_{i2}	*	*	*	O_{mn}

Mathematically, this relationship can be expressed as

$$O_{ij} = f(D_i \, S_j)$$

What is decision making under certainty?

This is the simplest type of decision making because it has a known state of nature. Therefore, the outcomes are the direct result of the chosen decision strategy and can be predicted with certainty. In reality, this situation rarely occurs.

The manager simply evaluates all the available decision strategies and then chooses the one that best meets the outcome criteria. Various optimization techniques can be utilized to maximize a decision strategy.

Decision making under certainty occurs with problems that can be analyzed using basic inventory models, break-even analysis, linear programming, incremental analysis, and other methods where an outcome with one state of nature can be determined.

What is decision making under conflict?

In this situation, the decision maker is opposed by another party who is designing state-of-nature strategies to offset the decision maker's strategy to gain a competitive advantage. The decision maker must develop decision strategies to defeat an opponent's state-of-nature control strategy.

This is the ideal setting for developing game strategies. Games are dependent on rules governing a competitive situation where the number of players, strategies, states of nature between the players, and degree of conflict control the outcomes.

What are the types of games?

Games are classified according to the degree of conflict of interest between the opponents. A zero-sum game has a perfect inverse relationship between the gains and losses of the opponents. One opponent's gain is the other's loss. The total sum remains the same.

In nonzero-sum games, the gains of one participant do not necessarily represent a comparable loss for the other party of the game. In the business environment, most competitive situations are nonzero-sum games.

How does a zero-sum game work?

In a zero-sum game the gains and losses are always equal. No player can gain more than the other player loses. Therefore, the game is always in equilibrium.

The simplest type of zero-sum game is the two-person zero-sum game. Each player has a choice of game strategies. Because each player's gain will equal the other's loss, the outcome for each game strategy is known to each player.

In the two-person zero-sum game, the outcomes can be expressed numerically. A two-person zero-sum game outcome matrix is shown in Example 12.1. A positive number indicates a payoff to the player for row A, and a negative number indicates a payoff to the player for column B. In Example 12.1, the maximum any player can win or lose is 11.

Example 12.1

Two-player zero-sum game outcome matrix

| | **Player B** | |
	Strategy F r_1	Strategy H r_2
Player A		
Strategy D p_1	A wins 5	A wins 8
Strategy E p_2	A wins 6	B wins 2
		(or A loses 2)

What is a pure strategy?

A pure strategy exists when there is one strategy for player A and one for player B that will be played every time. An equilibrium point is reached when it is at an optimum point for each respective player. This is termed a saddle point. A saddle point occurs at both the smallest numerical value in its row and the largest numerical value in its column.

Example 12.2

Example 12.2 shows a sample saddle point in a two-person zero-sum game. Because 13 is the row minimum and the column maximum, it is the saddle-point strategy. The value of this game is 13. As the first choice, Player A gains 13 while Player B loses 13.

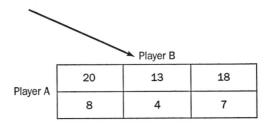

Player A	20	13	18
	8	4	7

What is a mixed strategy?

When no player has one strategy that will be used each time, there is no pure strategy used in the zero-sum game. When this happens, the optimum point—or saddle point—is found using a mixed strategy. In this case, each player's strategy is chosen using a random number process. Nonetheless, no player's gain is another player's loss.

Example 12.3

Using the two-player zero-sum game outcome matrix in Example 12.1, it is possible to establish a mixed strategy. Assuming p_1 and p_2 are the probabilities for A's strategies, and n_1 and n_2 are the probabilities for B's strategies, their values can be determined using the process discussed in Section 12.2.

12.2 DECISION MAKING UNDER UNCERTAIN CONDITIONS

Under what conditions are decisions made?

Decisions are made under certainty or under uncertainty (risk). Under certainty implies that there is only one event and therefore only one outcome for each action. Under uncertainty, which is more common realistically, several events are involved for each action, and with each comes a different probability of occurrence. *What to do:* Under uncertainty, it is often helpful to compute the following:

- Expected value
- Standard deviation
- Coefficient of variation

What does expected value tell me?

For decisions involving uncertainty, the concept of expected value ($\bar{r}$) provides a rational means for selecting the best course of action. Expected value is defined as a weighted average using the probabilities as weights. It is found by multiplying the probability of each outcome by its payoff:

$$\bar{r} = \sum r_i p_i$$

where r_i is the outcome for i_{th} possible event and p_i is the probability of occurrence of that outcome.

Note: A rational economic decision maker (one completely guided by objective criteria) will use expected monetary value to maximize gains under conditions of uncertainty because (s)he is risk-neutral. Expected value represents the long-term average payoff for repeated trials. The best choice is the one with the highest expected value (sum of the products of the possible outcomes and their respective probabilities).

What is the significance of the standard deviation?

Whenever we talk about the expected value, one statistic that is included is standard deviation. Standard deviation is a statistic that measures the tendency of data to be spread out. It is also a measure of the dispersion of a probability distribution. The smaller the deviation, the tighter the distribution, and the lower the riskiness of the project. The standard deviation is intuitively a margin of error associated with a given expected value. MBAs can make important inferences from past data using this measure. It is the square root of the mean of the squared deviations from the expected value ($\bar{r}$). The standard deviation, denoted with the Greek letter σ, read as *sigma*, is calculated as follows:

$$\sigma = \sqrt{(r_1 - \bar{r})^2 p_i}$$

To calculate σ, we proceed as follows:

Step 1. First compute the expected rate of return (r̄).

Step 2. Subtract each possible return from r̄ to obtain a set of deviations $(r_i - \bar{r})$.

Step 3. Square each deviation, multiply the squared deviation by the probability of occurrence for its respective return, and sum these products to obtain the variance (σ^2):

$$\sigma^2 = \sum(r_i - \bar{r})^2 p_i$$

Step 4. Finally, take the square root of the variance to obtain the standard deviation (σ).

The standard deviation can be used to measure the variation of such items as the expected profits, expected contribution margin, or expected cash flows. It can also be used to assess the absolute risk associated with investment projects. *Rule of thumb:* The higher the standard deviation, the higher the risk.

What does the coefficient of variation mean?

The coefficient of variation is a popular measure of relative dispersion, or relative risk. It represents the degree of risk per unit of return. It is computed by dividing the standard deviation by the expected value:

$$\sigma / \bar{r}$$

Example 12.4

Consider two investment proposals, A and B, with the following probability distribution of cash flows in each of the next three years:

	Cash Inflows		
Probability	(.2)	(.6)	(.2)
Project A	$200	300	400
Project B	$100	300	500

The expected value of the cash inflow is computed as follows.

Project A:

$200(.2) + 300(.6) + 400(.2) = $300

Project B:

$100(.2) + 300(.6) + 500(.2) = $300

The standard deviations are computed as follows.
  For A:

$$\sigma A = \sqrt{\begin{array}{l}(\$200 - 300)^2(.2) + (300 - 300)^2(.6) \\ + (400 - 300)^2(.2)\end{array}}$$

$$= \$63.25$$

  For B:

$$\sigma B = \sqrt{\begin{array}{l}(\$100 - 300)^2(.2) + (300 - 300)^2(.6) \\ + (500 - 300)^2(.2)\end{array}}$$

$$= \$126.49$$

The coefficients of variation are computed as follows.
  For A:

$$\$63.25/\$300 = .21$$

  For B:

$$\$126.49/\$300 = .42.$$

Conclusions: Proposal B is more risky than proposal A because its standard deviation is greater. And, because the coefficient is a relative measure of risk, the degree of risk is also greater for Project B.

12.3 DECISION THEORY

What is decision theory?

Decision theory refers to a systematic approach to making decisions, particularly under conditions of uncertainty. While statistics such as expected value and standard deviation are essential for making the best choice, the decision problem can best be approached using decision theory. Decision theory utilizes an organized approach such as a decision matrix (or payoff table). It is characterized by

- *The row.* Each row represents a set of available alternative courses of action.

- *The column.* Each column represents the "state of nature," or conditions that are likely to occur and over which one has no control.

- *The entries.* These appear in the body of the table and represent the outcome of the decision, known as payoffs. These may be in the form of costs, revenues, profits, contribution margins, or cash flows.

By computing expected value of each action, we will be able to pick the best one.

Example 12.5

Assume the following probability distribution of daily demand for strawberries:

Daily Demand	0	1	2	3
Probability	.2	.3	.3	.2

Also assume that unit cost = $3, selling price = $5 (that is, profit on sold unit = $2), and salvage value on unsold units = $2 (that is, loss on unsold unit = $1). The company can stock zero, one, two, or three units. The problem is this: How many units should be stocked each day? Assume that units from one day cannot be sold the next day. The payoff table can be constructed as follows:

	State of Nature				
Demand	0	1	2	3	Expected Value
Stock (probability)	(.2)	(.3)	(.3)	(.2)	
0	$0	0	0	0	$0
Actions 1	−1	2	2	2	1.40
2	−2	1*	4	4	$1.90**
3	−3	0	3	6	1.50

*Profit for (stock 2, demand 1) equals (no. of units sold)(profit per unit) − (no. of units unsold)(loss per unit) = (1)($5 − 3) − (1)($3 − 2) = $2 − $1 = $1
**Expected value for (stock 2) is: −2(.2) + 1(.3) + 4(.3) + 4(.2) = $1.90

The optimal stock action is the one with the highest expected monetary value—that is, stock two units.

What is the role of perfect information in decision theory?

Suppose it is possible to obtain a perfect prediction of which event (state of nature) will occur. The expected value with perfect information would be the total expected value of actions selected on the assumption of a perfect forecast. The expected value of perfect information (EVPI) can then be computed as

EVPI = Expected value with perfect information minus the expected value with existing information.

Example 12.6

From the payoff table in Example 12.5, with perfect information, the following analysis can be made:

	State of Nature				
Demand	0	1	2	3	Expected Value
Stock	(.2)	(.3)	(.3)	(.2)	
0	$0				$0
Actions 1		2			0.6
2			4		1.2
3				6	1.2
					$3.00

Alternatively,

$$\$0(.2) + 2(.3) + 4(.3) + 6(.2) = \$3.00$$

Conclusions: The optimal stock action is stock two, with the highest expected value of $1.90. Thus, with existing information, the best that can be done is to select stock two units to obtain $1.90. With perfect information (forecast), one could make as much as $3. Therefore, the expected value of perfect information (EVPI) = $3.00 − $1.90, or $1.10. This is the maximum price that should be paid for additional information.

Can you use a decision tree?

A decision tree is another approach used in discussions of decision making under uncertainty. A decision tree is a pictorial representation of a decision situation. As in the case of the decision matrix approach discussed earlier, a decision tree shows decision alternatives, states of nature, probabilities attached to the state of nature, and conditional benefits and losses. The decision-tree approach is most useful in a sequential decision situation.

Example 12.7

XYZ Corporation wants to introduce one of two products to the market this year. The probabilities and present values (PV) of projected cash inflows are given below:

Product	Initial Investment	PV of Cash Inflows	Probabilities
A	$225,000		1.00
		$450,000	0.40
		200,000	0.50
		−100,000	0.10
B	80,000		1.00
		320,000	0.20
		100,000	0.60
		−150,000	0.20

A decision tree analyzing the two products is given in Figure 12.2.

Figure 12.2 Decision Tree

	Initial Investment (1)	Probability (2)	PV of Cash Inflows (3)	PV of Cash Inflows (2) X (3) = (4)
Product A	$225,000	0.40	$450,000	$180,000
		0.50	$200,000	100,000
		0.10	−$100,000	−10,000
			Expected PV of Cash Inflows	$270,000
Product B	$80,000	0.20	$320,000	$64,000
		0.60	$100,000	60,000
		0.20	−$150,000	−30,000
			Expected PV of Cash Inflows	$94,000

Choice A or B

Based on the expected NPV, product A should be chosen over product B. *Note:* This analysis fails to recognize the risk factor in project analysis.

12.4 LINEAR PROGRAMMING AND SHADOW PRICES

12.4.1 Linear Programming

What is linear programming?

Linear programming (LP) is a mathematical technique designed to determine an optimal decision (or an optimal plan) chosen from a large number of possible decisions. The optimal decision is the one that meets the specified objective of the company, subject to various restrictions or constraints. LP concerns itself with the problem of allocating scarce resources among competing activities in an optimal manner. The optimal decision yields the highest profit, contribution margin (CM), or revenue, or the lowest cost.

What does linear programming consist of?

A linear-programming model consists of two important ingredients:

1. *Objective function.* The company must define the specific objective to be achieved.

2. *Constraints.* Constraints are in the form of restrictions on availability of resources or meeting minimum requirements. As the name linear programming indicates, both the objective function and constraints must be in *linear* form.

Example 12.8

A firm wants to find an optimal product mix. The optimal mix would be the one that maximizes the firm's total profit or contribution margin (CM) within the allowed budget and production capacity. Or, the firm may want to determine a least-cost combination of input materials while meeting production requirements, employing production capacities, and using available employees.

What are applications of linear programming?

Applications of LP are numerous. They include

1. Selecting least-cost mix of ingredients for manufactured products

2. Developing an optimal budget

3. Determining an optimal investment portfolio (or asset allocation)

4. Allocating an advertising budget to a variety of media

5. Scheduling jobs to machines

6. Determining a least-cost shipping pattern

7. Scheduling flights

8. Blending gasoline

9. Optimal manpower allocation

10. Selecting the best warehouse location to minimize shipping costs.

What is involved in the formulation of LP?

To formulate an LP problem, certain steps are followed. They are

1. Define the decision variables you are trying to solve for.

2. Express the objective function and constraints in terms of these decision variables.

Note: All the expressions must be in *linear* form.

In the following example, we will use this technique to find the optimal product mix.

Example 12.9

The Omni Furniture Manufacturing Company produces two products: desks and tables. Both products require time in two processing departments—the Assembly Department and the Finishing Department. Data on the two products follows:

| | Products | | Available |
Processing	*Desk*	*Table*	*Hours*
Assembly	2	4	100 hours
Finishing	3	2	90
Contribution margin per unit	$25	$40	

The company wants to find the most profitable mix of these two products.

Step 1
Define the decision variables as follows:

A = Number of units of desks to be produced

B = Number of units of tables to be produced

Step 2
The objective function to maximize total contribution margin (CM) is expressed as

$$\text{Total CM} = 25A + 40B$$

Step 3
Then, formulate the constraints as inequalities:

$$2A + 4B \leq 100 \text{ (Assembly constraint)}$$
$$3A + 2B \leq 90 \text{ (Finishing constraint)}$$

In addition, implicit in any LP formulation are the constraints that restrict A and B to be nonnegative, that is,

$$A, B \geq 0$$

Our LP model is

Maximize: Total CM = 25A + 40B
Subject to: 2A + 4B ≤ 100
3A + 2B ≤ 90
A, B ≥ 0

How do I solve LP problems?

There are several methods available to solve LP problems. Following are two common methods:

- *The simplex method.* This is the most commonly used method of solving LP problems. It uses an algorithm, which is an iteration method of computation, to move from one solution to another until it reaches the best one.

- *The graphical method.* This solution is easier to use but limited to the LP problems involving two (or at most three) decision variables.

To use the graphical method, follow these five steps:

1. Change inequalities to equalities.
2. Graph the equalities. To graph the equality, (1) set one variable equal to zero and find the value of the other, and then connect those two points on the graph; and (2) mark these intersections on the axes and connect them with a straight line.
3. Identify the correct side for the original inequalities by shading. Repeat Steps 1–3 for each constraint.
4. Identify the feasible region, or the area of feasible solutions.
5. Solve the constraints (expressed as equalities) simultaneously for the various corner points of the feasible region. Determine the profit or contribution margin at all corners in the region.

Example 12.10

Using the data and the LP model from Example 12.9, obtain the feasible region (shaded area) by going through Steps 1–4. Then evaluate all the corner points as follows:

	Corner Points		Contribution Margin
	A	*B*	*$25A + $40B*
(a)	30	0	$25(30) + $40(0) = $750
(b)	20	15	25(20) + 40(15) = 1,100
(c)	0	25	25(0) + 40(25) = 1,000
(d)	0	0	25(0) + 40(0) = 0

Conclusion: The corner 20A, 15B produces the most profitable solution (see Figure 12.3).

Figure 12.3 The Feasible Region and Corner Points

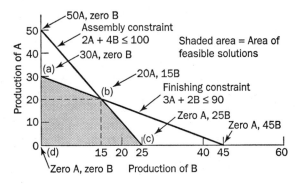

12.4.2 Shadow Prices (Opportunity Costs)

What are shadow prices (opportunity costs)?

After solving an LP problem, management might still want to know whether it pays to add capacity in hours in a particular department. For example, there may be an interest in the monetary value to the company of adding, say, an hour per week of assembly time. This monetary value is usually the additional contribution that could be earned—the shadow price of a given resource. Shadow prices constitute a form of opportunity cost when thought of as the contribution margin that would be lost by not adding capacity.

To justify a decision in favor of a short-term capacity decision, management must be certain that the shadow price exceeds the actual price of that expansion. For example, suppose the shadow price of an hour of assembly capacity is $6.50, while the actual market price is $8.00. That means it does not pay to obtain an additional hour of the assembly capacity.

Here is how to compute shadow prices (or opportunity cost):

1. Add one hour (or, preferably, more than one hour to make it easier to show graphically) to the constraint of a given LP problem under consideration.

2. Resolve the problem and find the maximum CM.

3. Compute the difference between the CM of the original LP problem and the CM determined in Step 2, which is the shadow price.

Example 12.11

Using the data in Example 12.10, compute the shadow price of the assembly capacity. To make this easier to show graphically, add eight hours of capacity to the assembly department rather than one hour. The new assembly constraint and the resulting feasible region are shown in Figure 12.4.

Then evaluate all the corner points in the *new* feasible region in terms of their CM, as follows:

	Corner Points		**Contribution Margin**
	A	B	$25A + $40B
(a)	30	0	$25(30) + $40(0) = $750
(b)	18	18	25(18) + 40(18) = 1,170
(c)	0	27	25(0) + 40(227) = 1,080
(d)	0	0	25(0) + 40(0) = 0

The new optimal solution, Corner b (18A, 18B) has total CM of $1,170 per week. The shadow price of the assembly capacity is $70 ($1,170 − $1,100 = $70), or $8.75 per hour ($70/8 hours = $8.75). *Conclusion:* The company would be willing to pay up to $70 to obtain an additional eight hours of the assembly capacity per week, or $8.75 per hour per week. In other words, the company's opportunity cost of not adding an additional hour is $8.75.

Figure 12.4 The Feasible Region and Corner Points

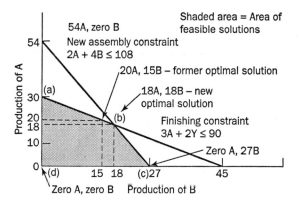

12.4.3   How to Use the Computer for Linear Programming

A computer LP software package, such as LINDO (Linear Interactive and Discrete Optimization) (www.lindo.com), What's Best! (www.AnalyCorp.com), or Microsoft Excel can be used to quickly solve an LP problem.

Figure 12.5 shows a computer output by an LP software program for out LP model. Figure 12.6 presents the Excel LP solution.

Note: The printout shows the following optimal solution:

$$A = 20 \text{ units}$$
$$B = 15 \text{ units}$$
$$CM = \$1,100$$

Figure 12.5 The LP Computer Output

INFORMATION ENTERED

NUMBER OF CONSTRAINTS	2	*Note:*
NUMBER OF VARIABLES	2	$X_1 = A$
NUMBER OF ≤ CONSTRAINTS	2	$X_2 = B$
NUMBER OF = CONSTRAINTS	0	
NUMBER OF ≥ CONSTRAINTS	0	

MAXIMIZATION PROBLEM
$$25 \times 1 \qquad +40 \times 2$$

SUBJECT TO
$$2 \times 1 \qquad + 4 \times 2 \qquad \leq 100$$
$$3 \times 1 \qquad + 2 \times 2 \qquad \leq 90$$

RESULTS

VARIABLE	VARIABLE VALUE	ORIGINAL COEFF.	COEFF. SENS.	Solution:
X1	20	25	0	$X_1 = A = 20$
X2	15	40	0	$X_2 = B = 15$

CONSTRAINT NUMBER	ORIGINAL RHS	SLACK OR SURPLUS	SHADOW PRICE
1	100	0	8.75
2	90	0	2.5

Shadow price of the assembly capacity

OBJECTIVE FUNCTION VALUE: 1100 = CM
SENSITIVITY ANALYSIS
OBJECTIVE FUNCTION COEFFICIENTS

VARIABLE	LOWER LIMIT	ORIGINAL COEFFICIENT	UPPER LIMIT
X1	20	25	60
X2	16.67	40	50

RIGHT-HAND SIDE

CONSTRAINT NUMBER	LOWER LIMIT	ORIGINAL VALUE	UPPER LIMIT
1	60	100	180
2	50	90	150

Shadow prices are

Assembly capacity = $8.75

Finishing capacity = $2.50

12.5 LEARNING CURVE

How does the learning curve work to estimate labor hours?

In manufacturing, labor hours are often observed to decrease in a definite pattern as labor operations are repeated. More specifically, as the cumulative production doubles, the cumulative average time required per unit will be reduced by some constant percentage, ranging typically from 10 percent to 20 percent. This reduction and its related costs are referred to as the learning-curve effect.

How do I properly express the learning-curve relationship?

By convention, learning curves are referred to in terms of the complements of their improvement rates. For example, an 80 percent learning curve denotes a 20 percent decrease in unit time with each doubling of repetitions.

Example 12.12

Suppose a project is known to have an 80 percent learning curve. It has just taken a laborer ten hours to produce the first unit. Then, each time the cumulative output doubles, the time per unit for that amount should be equal to the previous time, multiplied by the learning percentage. An 80 percent learning curve is shown in Figure 12.7.

Unit	Unit time (hours)
1	10
2	0.8(10) = 8
4	0.8(8) = 6.4
8	0.8(6.4) = 5.12
16	0.8(5.12) = 4.096

Take note: As production quantities double, the average time needed per unit reduces 20 percent from its immediately previous time.

Figure 12.6 The Excel LP Input and Output

Target Cell (Max)

Cell	Name	Original Value	Final Value
E5	Unit Contribution Margin:TotalCM:	$0	$1,100

Adjustable Cells

Cell	Name	Original Value	Final Value
B4	Number to make: Desk	0	20
C4	Number to make:Table	0	15

Constraints

Cell	Name	Cell Value	Formula	Status	Slack
D8	Assembly Used	100	D8< = E8	Binding	0
D9	Finishing Used	90	D9< = E9	Binding	0
B4	Number to make: Desk	20	B4> = 0	Not Binding	20
C4	Number to make:Table	15	C4> = 0	Not Binding	15

Adjustable Cells

Cell	Name	Final Value	Reduced Gradient
E4	Number to make: Desk	20	0
C4	Number to make: Table	15	0

Constraints

Cell	Name	Final Value	Lagrange Multiplier
D8	Assembly Used	100	8.75
D9	Finishing Used	90	2.5

Cell	Target Name	Value
E5	Unit Contribution Margin:TotalCM:	$1,100

Cell	Adjustable Name	Value	Lower Limit	Target Result	Upper Limit	Target Result
$3$4	Number to make: Desk	20	0	600	20	1100
C4	Number to make: Table	15	0	500	15	1100

Figure 12.7 An 80% Learning Curve

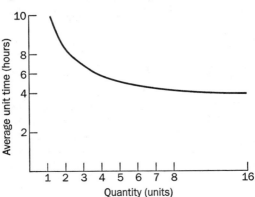

Example 12.13

Big Mac Electronics Products, Inc., finds that new product production is affected by an 80 percent learning effect. The company has just produced fifty units of output at one hundred hours per unit. Costs break down as follows:

Materials—50 units @ $20	$1,000
Labor and labor-related costs:	
Direct labor—100 hours @ $8	800
Variable overhead—100 hours @ $2	200
	$2,000

The company has just received a contract calling for another fifty units of production. It wants to add a 50 percent markup to the cost of materials, labor, and labor-related costs. To determine the price for this job, the first step is to build up the learning curve table.

Quantity	Total Time (hours)	Average Time (per unit)
50	100	2 hours
100	160	1.6 (.8 × 2 hours)

Thus, the new fifty-unit job takes sixty hours in total. The contract price is

Materials—50 units @$20	$1,000
Labor and labor-related costs:	
Direct labor—60 hours @$8	480
Variable overhead—60 hours @$2	120
	$1,600
50 percent markup	800
Contract price	$2,400

In what other ways can I use the learning curve?

CHECKLIST OF APPLICATIONS
FOR THE LEARNING CURVE

The learning curve theory has found useful applications in many areas, including

1. Budgeting, purchasing, and inventory planning
2. Scheduling labor requirements
3. Setting incentive wage rates
4. Pricing new products
5. Negotiated purchasing
6. Evaluating suppliers' price quotations

12.6 INVENTORY PLANNING AND CONTROL

Why are inventory planning and control important?

One of the most common problems facing operations managers is inventory planning. This is understandable; inventory usually represents a sizable portion of a firm's total assets and, more specifically, on the average, more than 30 percent of total current assets in U.S. industry. Excessive money tied up in inventory is a drag on profitability. The purpose of inventory planning is to develop policies that will achieve an optimal investment in inventory. You can do this by determining the optimal level of inventory necessary to minimize inventory-related costs.

What kinds of costs are associated with inventory?

Inventory costs fall into three categories. They are

- *Ordering costs*. These include all costs associated with preparing a purchase order.
- *Carrying (holding) costs*. These include storage costs for inventory items, plus the cost of money tied up in inventory.
- *Shortage (stockout) costs*. These are costs incurred when an item is out of stock. These include the lost contribution margin on sales, plus lost customer goodwill.

When and how much should I order?

Several inventory planning models are available to answer these questions. Three such models are

- Economic order quantity (EOQ)
- Reorder point (ROP)
- Determination of safety stock.

How does the economic order quantity (EOQ) model work?

The economic order quantity (EOQ) determines the order size that minimizes the sum of carrying and ordering costs.

Assumptions: Demand is assumed to be known with certainty, and to remain constant throughout the year. Order cost is also known to be fixed. Also, unit carrying costs are assumed be constant. Because demand and lead time (time interval between placing an order and receiving delivery) are assumed to be determinable, no shortage costs exist. No quantity discounts are allowed.

The EOQ is computed as

$$EOQ = \sqrt{\frac{2\,DO}{C}}$$

where C = carrying cost per unit, O = ordering cost per order, and D = annual demand (requirements) in units.

If the carrying cost is expressed as a percentage of average inventory value (say, 12 percent per year to hold inventory), the denominator value in the EOQ formula would be 12 percent times the price of an item. *Note:* When an item is made instead of purchased, the EOQ model is used to determine the economic production run size where O = cost per setup.

Example 12.14

Assume the Los Alamitos Store buys sets of steel at $40 per set from an outside vendor. It will sell 6,400 sets evenly throughout the year. The store's carrying cost is $8 per unit per year. The ordering cost is $100 per order. Therefore,

$$EOQ = \sqrt{\frac{2(6,400)(\$100)}{\$8.00}} = \sqrt{160,000} = 400 \text{ sets}$$

$$
\begin{aligned}
\text{Total number of orders per year} &= D/EOQ \\
&= 6,400/400 \\
&= 16 \text{ orders}
\end{aligned}
$$

$$
\begin{aligned}
\text{Total inventory costs} &= \text{Carrying cost} \\
&\quad + \text{Ordering cost}
\end{aligned}
$$

$$
\begin{aligned}
&= C \times (EOQ/2) + O\,(D/EOQ) \\
&= (\$8.00)(400/2) + (\$100)(6,400/400) \\
&= \$1,600 + \$1,600 = \$3,200
\end{aligned}
$$

Based on these calculations, the Los Alamitos Store's inventory policy should be the following:

1. The store should order 400 sets of steel each time it places an order, and order sixteen times during a year.

2. This policy will be most economical and cost the store $3,200 per year.

How do I determine the reorder point?

The reorder point (ROP) determines when a new order should be placed. However, this requires knowing the lead time from placing to receiving an order. Reorder point (ROP) is calculated as follows:

Reorder point = (average demand per unit of lead time × lead time) + safety stock

This indicates the level of inventory at which a new order should be placed. First, multiply average daily (or weekly) demand by the lead-time in days (or weeks) yielding the lead time demand. Then, add safety stock to this to provide for the variation in lead-time demand to determine the reorder point. *Note:* If average demand and lead time are both certain, no safety stock is necessary and should be dropped from the formula.

Example 12.15

Using the preceding example, assume lead time is constant at one week. There are fifty working weeks in the year.

The reorder point is

128 sets = (6,400 sets/50 weeks) × 1 week

Conclusion: When the inventory level drops to 128 sets, a new order should be placed. Suppose, however, that the store is faced with variable demand for its steel and requires a safety stock of 150 additional sets to carry. Then the reorder point will be 128 sets plus 150 sets, or 278 sets.

Figure 12.8 shows this inventory system when the order quantity is 400 sets and the reorder point is 128 sets.

Figure 12.8 Basic Inventory System with EOQ and Reorder Point

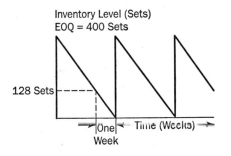

When are these models realistic to use?

The EOQ model described here is appropriate for a pure inventory system—that is, for single-item, single-stage inventory decisions for which joint costs and constraints can be ignored. EOQ and ROP assume that lead time and demand rates are constant and known with certainty. *Caution:* This may be unrealistic. Still, these models have been proven useful in inventory planning for many companies. There are, for instance, many businesses for which these assumptions hold to some extent. They include

- Subcontractors who must supply parts on a regular basis to a primary contractor
- Automobile dealerships, in which demand varies from week to week, but tends to even out over a season

Caveat: When demand is not known precisely or other complications arise, do not use these models. Instead, refer to probabilistic models.

What about quantity discounts?

EOQ does not take quantity discounts into account, which is often unrealistic in actual practice. Usually, the more that is ordered, the lower the unit price paid. A typical price discount schedule follows:

Order Quantity (Q)	Unit Price (P)
1 to 499	$40.00
500 to 999	39.90
1,000 or more	39.80

What to do: If quantity discounts are offered, weigh the potential benefits of reduced purchase price and fewer orders that will result from buying in large quantities against the increase in carrying costs caused by higher average inventories. Hence, the buyer's goal in this case is to select the order quantity which will minimize total costs, where total cost is the sum of carrying cost, ordering cost, and product cost:

$$\text{Total cost} = \text{Carrying cost} + \text{Ordering cost} + \text{Product cost}$$

$$= C \times (Q/2) + O \times (D/Q) + PD$$

where P = unit price, and Q = order quantity.

Use the following steps to find economic order size with price discounts:

- Compute the common EOQ, when price discounts are ignored, and the corresponding costs using the new cost after discount.
- Compute the costs for those quantities greater than EOQ at which price reductions occur.
- Select the value of Q that will result in the lowest total cost.

Example 12.16

Using the information from the preceding examples and the discount schedule shown previously, try to determine the EOQ. Recall that EOQ = 400 sets without discount. The total cost for this is

Total cost = $8.00(400/2) + $100(6,400/400)

$$+ \$40.00(6,400)$$

$$= \$1,600 + 1,600 + 256,000 = \$259,200$$

The further we move from the point 400, the greater will be the sum of the carrying and ordering costs. Thus, 400 is obviously the only candidate for the minimum total cost value within the first price range. Q = 500 is the only candidate within the $39.90 price range, and Q = 1,000 is the only candidate within the $39.80 price bracket. These three quantities are evaluated below, and pictured in Figure 12.9.

Annual Costs with Varying Order Quantities

Order Quantity (Q)	400	500	1,000
Purchase price (P)	$40	$39.90	$39.80
Carrying cost (C × Q/2) $8 × (order quantity/2)	$1,600	$2,000	$4,000
Ordering cost (O × D/Q) $100 × (6,400/order quantity)	1,600	1,280	640
Product cost (PD) Unit price × 6,400	256,000	255,360	254,720
Total cost	$259,200	$258,640	$259,360

Note that C = $8.00, O = $100, and D = 6,400 for all possible orders.

Figure 12.9 Costs with Quantity Discount Problem

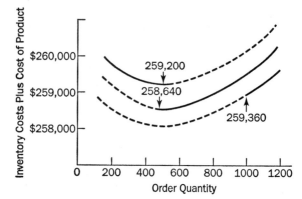

Conclusion: The EOQ with price discounts is 500 sets. The manufacturer is justified in going to the first price break, but the extra carrying cost of going to the second price break more than outweighs the savings in ordering and in the cost of the product itself.

What can I do when lead time and demand are uncertain?

When lead time and demand are not certain, carry extra units of inventory, called safety stock, as protection against possible stockouts. To determine the appropriate level of safety stock size, consider the service level or stockout costs.

Service level can be defined as the probability that demand will not exceed supply during the lead time. Thus, a service level of 90 percent implies a probability of 90 percent that demand will not exceed supply during lead time. Figure 12.10 shows a service level of 90 percent.

Following are three cases for computing the safety stock. The first two do not recognize stockout costs; the third does.

Case 1: Variable demand rate, constant lead time

$$\text{ROP} = \text{Expected demand during lead time} + \text{safety stock}$$
$$= \overline{u} \, LT + z \, \sqrt{LT \, (\sigma_u)}$$

where

$\overline{u}$ = average demand

LT = lead time

σ_u = standard deviation of demand rate

z = standard normal variate as defined in Table 12.1 (later in this chapter)

For a normal distribution, a given service level amounts to the shaded area under the curve to the left of ROP in Figure 12.10.

Figure 12.10 Service Level of 90 Percent

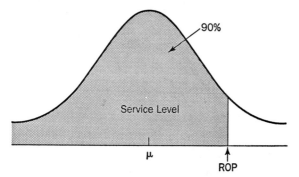

Table 12.1 Values of Z_p for Specified Probabilities P

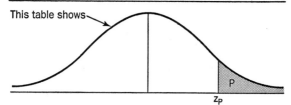

P	z_P	P	z_P	P	z_P
0.0005	3.29053	0.005	2.57583	0.11	1.22653
0.0010	3.09023	0.010	2.32635	0.12	1.17499
0.0015	2.96774	0.015	2.17009	0.13	1.12639
0.0020	2.87816	0.020	2.05375	0.14	1.08032
0.0025	2.80703	0.025	1.95996	0.15	1.03643
0.0030	2.74778	0.030	1.88079	0.16	0.99446
0.0035	2.69684	0.035	1.81191	0.17	0.95417
0.0040	2.65207	0.040	1.75069	0.18	0.91537
0.0045	2.61205	0.045	1.69540	0.19	0.87790
0.0050	2.57583	0.050	1.64485	0.20	0.84162
0.006	2.51214	0.06	1.55477	0.25	0.67449
0.007	2.45726	0.07	1.47579	0.30	0.52440
0.008	2.40892	0.08	1.40507	0.35	0.38532
0.009	2.36562	0.09	1.34076	0.40	0.25335
0.010	2.32635	0.10	1.28255	0.45	0.12566

Example 12.17

Norman's Pizza uses large cases of tomatoes at an average rate of fifty cans per day. The demand can be approximated by a normal distribution with a standard deviation of five cans per day. Lead time is four days. Thus,

$$\bar{u} = 50 \text{ cans per day.}$$
$$LT = 4 \text{ days}$$
$$\sigma_u = 5 \text{ cans}$$

How much safety stock is necessary for a service level of 99 percent? And what is the ROP? For a service level of 99 percent, z = 2.33 (from Table 12.1). Thus,

$$\text{Safety stock} = 2.33 \sqrt{4 \, (5)} = 23.3 \text{ cans}$$
$$\text{ROP} = 50(4) + 23.3 = 223.3 \text{ cans}$$

Figure 12.11 Service Level of 99 Percent

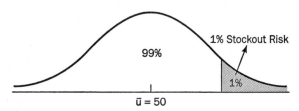

99%

1% Stockout Risk

1%

$\bar{u} = 50$

Case 2: Constant demand, variable lead time

$$\text{ROP} = \text{Expected demand during lead time} + \text{safety stock}$$
$$= u \, \overline{LT} + z \, u \, (\sigma_{LT})$$

where

$$u = \text{constant demand}$$
$$\overline{LT} = \text{average lead time}$$
$$\sigma_{LT} = \text{standard deviation of lead time}$$

Example 12.18

SVL's Hamburger Shop uses ten gallons of cola per day. The lead time is normally distributed with a mean of six days and a standard deviation of two days. Thus,

$$u = 10 \text{ gallons per day.}$$
$$\overline{LT} = 6 \text{ days}$$
$$\sigma_{LT} = 2 \text{ days}$$

How much safety stock is necessary for a service level of 99 percent? And what is the ROP?

For a service level of 99 percent, z = 2.33. Thus,

$$\text{Safety stock} = 2.33\,(10)(2)$$
$$= 46.6 \text{ gallons}$$
$$\text{ROP} = 10(6) + 46.6$$
$$= 106.6 \text{ gallons}$$

(Note: z = 2.33 at 99 percent service level.)

Case 3: Incorporation of stockout costs

This case specifically recognizes the cost of stockouts or shortages, which can be quite expensive. Lost sales and disgruntled customers are examples of external costs. Idle machine and disrupted production scheduling are examples of internal costs. *What to do:* The probability approach can be used to determine the optimal safety stock size in the presence of stockout costs. Here is an example.

Example 12.19

Refer to Example 12.15. The total demand over a one-week period is estimated as follows:

Total Demand	Probability
78	0.2
128	0.4
178	0.2
228	0.1
278	0.1
	1.00

A stockout cost is estimated at $12 per set. Recall that the carrying cost is $8 per set.

Figure 12.12 shows the computation of safety stock. *Conclusion:* The computation shows that the total costs are minimized at $1,200, when a safety stock of 150 sets is maintained. Thus, the reorder point is

$$128 \text{ sets} + 150 \text{ sets} = 278 \text{ sets}$$

Figure 12.12 Computation of Safety Stock

Safety Stock Levels in Units	Stockout and Probability	Average Stockout in Units	Average Stockout Costs	No. of Orders	Total Annual Stockout Costs	Carrying Costs	Total
0	50 with .2 / 100 with .1 / 150 with .1	35*	$420**	16	$6,720***	0	$7,140
50	50 with .1 / 100 with .1	15	180	16	2,880	400****	3,280
100	50 with .1	5	60	16	960	800	1,760
150	0	0	0	16	0	1,200	1,200

*50(.2) + 100(.1) + 150(.1) = 10 + 10 + 15 = 35 units.

**35 units × $12.00 = $420.

***$420 × 16 times = $6,720.

****50 units × $8.00 = $400.

442

12.7 QUEUING (WAITING LINE) MODELS

What is the purpose of queuing theory?

Queuing, or waiting-line, theory investigates the everyday hassle of waiting in line. Operating, marketing, or production managers can apply this tool should waiting time involve them.

Like EOQ, queuing theory involves minimization of overall costs; that is, the sum of waiting costs borne by customers or businesses, and the cost of providing extra service facilities and/or attendants.

What are the applications of queuing theory?

The applications of queuing theory are numerous. For example, it can be used to determine the number of doctors who should be on call at a clinic.

What are some queuing models?

Before investigating queuing models, know three things. They are

- The company's experience with the daily ebb and flow of customers
- The probability assumptions as the nature of this process unfolds; for example, what the chances are of experiencing an unusually large bunching of arrivals
- Determination of costs associated with waiting and improving the rate of service

There are many queuing models from which to choose. One, called the single-channel exponential service time model, assumes a Poisson arrival rate and infinite source. For this model, use the following symbols:

$$A = \text{mean arrival rate}$$
$$S = \text{mean service rate}$$

Queuing experts have developed the following equations for this single-channel model:

- System utilitization = probability that the servers are busy = $\dfrac{A}{S}$
- Average number in the system = number of units in the queue plus number being served = $\dfrac{A}{(S - A)}$

- Average number waiting for service to begin = number of units in the queue = $\dfrac{A^2}{S(S-A)}$

- Average time spent waiting in the system = queue time plus service time = $\dfrac{1}{S-A}$

- Average time spent waiting before service begins = time in queue = $\dfrac{A}{S(S-A)}$

- Percent of idle time = $1 - \dfrac{A}{S}$

Example 12.20

Los Alamitos Car Wash is an automatic operation with a single bay. On a typical Saturday morning, cars arrive at a mean rate of nine per hour, with arrivals tending to follow a Poisson distribution. Service time, including manual drying time, is assumed to be exponentially distributed. Past experience suggests that the mean service time should average five minutes. Thus,

$$A = 9 \text{ cars per hour}$$
$$S = 1 \text{ per 5 minutes or 12 per hour}$$

The following can be determined:

- System utilization = $\dfrac{9}{12}$ = 75%. This means the system is busy 75 percent of the time.

- Average number of cars in line and service = $\dfrac{9}{12-9}$ = 3 cars

- Average number of cars in line = $\dfrac{9^2}{12(12-9)} = \dfrac{81}{36}$ = 2.25 cars

- Average time cars spend waiting in line and for service = $\dfrac{1}{121-9}$ = 1/3 hour, or 20 minutes

- Average time cars spend waiting for service = $\dfrac{9}{12(12-9)}$ = 9/36 = 1/4 or 15 minutes

- Percent of idle time = $1 - 0.75 = 0.25$ or 25%

The following is Microsoft Excel's queuing output for this example.

M/M/s queuing computations

Arrival rate	9
Service rate	12
Number of servers	1 (max of 40)

Assumes Poisson process for arrivals and services

Utilization	75.000%	System utilization
P (0), probability that the system is empty	0.2500	Percent of idle time
Lq, expected queue length	2.2500	Average no. of cars in line
L, expected number in system	3.0000	Average no. of cars in line and service
Wq, expected time in queue	0.2500	Average time cars spend waiting for service
W, expected total time in system	0.3333	Average time cars spend waiting in line and for service
Profitability that a customer waits	0.7500	

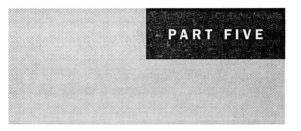

PART FIVE

Economics and Multinational Issues

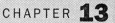

CHAPTER 13

Economics

13.1 MAJOR ECONOMIC AREAS: MICROECONOMICS AND MACROECONOMICS

What is microeconomics?

Microeconomics is the study of the individual units of the economy—individuals, households, companies, and industries. Microeconomics focuses on economic variables such as the prices and outputs of specific firms and industries, the expenditures of consumers or households, wage rates, competition, and markets. Questions that arise in the study of microeconomics include the following: What determines the price and output of individual goods and services? What factors determine supply and demand of a product? How do government policies such as price controls, subsidies, and excise taxes impact the price and output levels of individual markets?

What is macroeconomics?

Macroeconomics is the study of the whole national economy, or of its major sectors. Macroeconomics takes into account such areas as output, employment, national price, inflation, and exports. It looks at the forest instead of the trees. Questions to consider in macroeconomics include the following: What may be done to combat recession? What may be done to minimize inflationary effects? Why is the inflation rate so high? What are the important variables to national income and employment?

13.1.1 Importance of Business Economics

MBAs must stay abreast of economic trends and directions and attempt to see how these affect their businesses. Unfortunately, there are too many economic indicators and variables to be analyzed. Each has its own significance; in many cases, these variables could give mixed signals about the future of the economy. Various government agencies and private firms tabulate the appropriate economic data and calculate various indices. Sources for these indicators are easily subscribed at an affordable price or can be found in local public and college libraries. They include daily local newspapers and national newspapers such as *USA Today, The Wall Street Journal, Investor's Business Daily, Los Angeles Times,* and *The New York Times,* and periodicals such as *Business Week, Forbes, Fortune, Money, Worth, Barron's, Smart Money, Nation's Business,* and *U.S. News and World Report.* Internet users can look at the White House Web site's Economic Statistics Briefing Room, which provides easy access to current federal economic indicators. The Briefing Room is at www.whitehouse.gov/fsbr/esbr.html.

> *How can I keep track of the economy with economic and monetary indicators?*

To sort out the confusing mix of statistics that flow almost daily from the government, and to help keep track of what is going on in the economy, we examine various economic and monetary indicators.

Economic and monetary indicators reflect where the economy has been, and where it seems to be headed. Each month government agencies, including the Federal Reserve Board, and several economic institutions publish various indicators. These may be broken down into six broad categories, detailed in the following sections.

13.2 MEASURES OF OVERALL ECONOMIC PERFORMANCE

Measures of overall economic performance include gross domestic product (GDP), industrial production, personal income, housing starts, unemployment rate, and retail sales.

Gross Domestic Product
Gross Domestic Product (GDP) measures the value of all goods and services produced by the economy within its boundaries. This is the nation's broadest gauge of economic health. GDP is normally stated in annual

terms, though data are compiled and released quarterly. The Department of Commerce compiles GDP. It is reported as a "real" figure—that is, economic growth minus the impact of inflation. The figure is tabulated on a quarterly basis, coming out in the month after a quarter has ended. It is then revised at least twice, with those revisions being reported once in each of the months following the original release.

GDP reports appear in most daily newspapers and online at services such as America Online. Also visit the Federal Government Statistics Web site on the Internet at http://www.fedstats.gov/. GDP is often a measure of the state of the economy. For example, many economists speak of recession when there has been a decline in GDP for two consecutive quarters. The GDP in dollar and real terms is a useful economic indicator. An expected growth rate of 3 percent in real terms would be very attractive for long-term investment, and would affect the stock market positively. Because inflation and price increases are detrimental to equity prices, a real growth of GDP without inflation is favorable and desirable.

The following diagram charts a series of events leading from a rising GDP to higher security prices.

GDP up → Corporate profits up →
Dividends up → Security prices up.

A word of caution: GDP fails the timely release criterion for useful economic indicators. Unfortunately, there is no way of measuring whether we are currently in a recession or prosperity, based on the GDP measure. Only after the quarter is over can it be determined if there was growth or decline. Experts look upon other measures, such as unemployment rate, industrial production, durable orders, corporate profits, retail sales, and housing activity to look for a sign of recession.

Industrial Production
This index shows changes in the output of U.S. plants, mines, and utilities. Detailed breakdowns of the index provide a reading on how individual industries are faring. The index is issued monthly by the Federal Reserve Board.

Personal Income
This shows the before-tax income—such as wages and salaries, rents, and interest and dividends, and other payments such as unemployment and Social Security—received by individuals and unincorporated businesses. Personal income represents consumers' spending power. When personal income rises, consumers will usually increase their purchases, which will in turn favorably affect the economic climate. *Note:* Consumer spending makes a

major contribution (67 percent) to the nation's GNP. Personal-income data are released monthly by the Commerce Department.

Housing Starts

Housing starts is an important economic indicator that offers an estimate of the number of dwelling units on which construction has begun. The figures are issued monthly by the Bureau of Census. When an economy is about to take a downturn, the housing sector (and companies within it) is the first to decline. Housing starts data indicate the future strength of the housing sector of the economy. At the same time, the indicator is closely related to interest rates and other basic economic factors.

Unemployment Rate, Initial Jobless Claims, and Help-Wanted Index

Unemployment is the nonavailability of jobs for people able and willing to work at the prevailing wage rate. This is an important measure of economic health, because full employment is generally considered a desired goal. When the various economic indicators are mixed, many analysts look to the unemployment rate as being the most important. Weekly initial claims for unemployment benefits are another closely watched indicator, along with the unemployment rate, to judge the jobless situation in the economy. The help-wanted advertising index tracks employers' advertisements for job openings in the classified sections of newspapers in fifty or so labor-market areas. The index represents job vacancies resulting from turnover in existing positions, such as workers changing jobs or retiring, and from the creation of new jobs. The help-wanted figures are seasonally adjusted.

The unemployment rate is the number of unemployed workers divided by total employed and unemployed who constitute the labor force. Both statistics are released by the Department of Labor. The help-wanted advertising figures are obtained from classified advertisements in newspapers in major labor markets.

These figures are frequently reported in daily newspapers, in business dailies, on business television shows, and through online services. Labor Department releases can also be found at www.stats.bls.gov.

The effects of unemployment on the economy are summarized below.

UNEMPLOYMENT EFFECTS

1. *Less Tax Revenue:* Fewer jobs means less income tax to the state and nation, which means a bigger U.S government deficit. This forces states to make cuts in programs to balance their budgets.

2. *Higher Government Costs.* When people lose jobs, they often must turn to the government for benefits.

3. *Less Consumer Spending.* Without jobs, individuals can't afford to buy cars, computers, or houses, or to take vacations.

4. *Empty Stores.* Retailers and homebuilders can't absorb lower sales for long. Soon they have to lay off workers and, in more serious shortfalls, file for bankruptcy.

5. *Manufacturing Cuts.* The companies that make consumer products or housing materials are forced to cut jobs, too, as sales of their goods fall.

6. *Real Estate Pain.* As companies fail and as individuals struggle, mortgages and other bank loans go unpaid. That causes real estate values to go down and pummels lenders.

A word of caution: No one economic indicator is able to point to the direction in which an economy is heading. It is common that many indicators give mixed signals regarding, for example, the possibility of a recession.

But perhaps the best example of economic theory being turned on its head is the low unemployment figures in 1998 not creating inflationary pressures. Investors, and shoppers, can thank increased productivity and cheap foreign goods for that change.

Retail Sales
Retail sales is the estimate of total sales at the retail level. This estimate includes everything from groceries to durable goods, and is used as a measure of future economic conditions: a long slowdown in sales could spell cuts in production. Retail sales are a major concern because they represent about half of overall consumer spending. *Note:* Consumer spending accounts for about two-thirds of the nation's GNP. The amount of retail sales depends heavily on consumer confidence. The data are issued monthly by the Commerce Department.

13.3 PRICE INDICES

Price indices are designed to measure the rate of inflation. Various price indices are used to measure living costs, price level changes, and inflation. They are described as follows.

Consumer price index. The Consumer Price Index (CPI), the most well-known inflation gauge, is used as the cost-of-living index, which labor contracts and Social Security are tied to. The CPI measures the cost of buying a fixed bundle of goods (some four hundred consumer goods and services), representative of the purchase of the typical working-class urban family. The fixed basket is divided into the following categories: food and beverages, housing, apparel, transportation, medical care, entertainment, and other. Generally referred to as a "cost-of-living index," the CPI is published by the Bureau of Labor Statistics of the U.S. Department of Labor. The CPI is widely used for escalation clauses. The base year for the CPI index was 1982–84, at which time it was assigned 100.

Producer price index. Like the CPI, the PPI is a measure of the cost of a given basket of goods priced in wholesale markets, including raw materials, semifinished goods, and finished goods at the early stage of the distribution system. The PPI is published monthly by the Bureau of Labor Statistics of the Department of Commerce. The PPI signals changes in the general price levels, or the CPI, some time before they actually materialize. (Because the PPI does not include services, caution should be exercised when the principal cause of inflation is service prices.) For this reason, the PPI—and especially some of its subindexes, such as the index of sensitive materials—serves as one of the leading indicators that are closely watched by policy makers.

GDP deflator. This is the index of inflation used to separate price changes in GDP calculations from real changes in economic activity. The deflator is a weighted average of the price indexes used to deflate GDP so true economic growth can be separated from inflationary growth. Thus, it reflects price changes for goods and services bought by consumers, businesses, and governments. Because it covers a broader group of goods and services than do the CPI and PPI, the GDP deflator is a very widely used price index that is frequently used to measure inflation. The GDP deflator, unlike the CPI and PPI, is available only quarterly—not monthly. It is published by the U.S. Department of Commerce.

Employment cost index. This is the most comprehensive and refined measure of underlying trends in employee compensation as a cost of production. The ECI measures the cost of labor, and includes changes in wages and salaries and employer costs for employee benefits. ECI tracks wages and bonuses; sick and vacation pay, plus benefits such as insurance, pension, and Social Security; and unemployment taxes from a survey of 18,300 occupations at 4,500 sample establishments in private industry, and 4,200 occupations within about 800 state and local governments.

Price indices get major coverage in daily newspapers and business dailies, on business television programs such as *CNNfn* and *CNBC,* and on Internet financial news services. Government Internet Web sites www.stats.bls.gov and www.census.gov/econ/www/ also provide this data.

Check to see whether the inflation rate has been rising—a negative, or bearish, sign for stock and bond investors—or falling, which is bullish.

Rising prices are public enemy number one for stocks and bonds. Inflation usually hurts stock prices because higher consumer prices lessen the value of future corporate earnings, which makes shares of those companies less appealing to investors. By contrast, when prices rocket ahead, investors often flock to long-term inflation hedges such as real estate.

See how a chain of events leading from lower rates of inflation to increased consumer spending and, possibly, an up stock market:

Inflation is down, *so* real personal income is up, *so* consumer confidence jumps, *so* consumer spending goes up, *so* retail sales surge, *as* housing starts rise, *as* auto sales jump, *so* the stock market goes up.

Note: Federal Reserve Chairman Alan Greenspan is a big fan of the ECI as a good measure to see if wage pressures are sparking inflation.

A word of caution: Of course, if inflation disappears, that's no good in the long run, either. Deflation—that is, sharp falling prices—is a disastrous event. Think of Texas real estate in the 1980s, or California's property woes of the early 1990s. A broader example is the Great Depression of the 1930s. When demand for goods is so weak that merchants have to brutally slash prices just to stay in business, that's deflation. Deflation leads to layoffs and recession. That's bad for stock investors as profits shrink, but it is good for bond holders—as long as they own a bond backed by an issuer who can pay it back.

13.4 OTHER IMPORTANT ECONOMIC INDICATORS

13.4.1 Indices of Labor Market Conditions

Indicators covering labor market conditions are unemployment rate, average work week of production workers, applications for unemployment compensation, and hourly wage rates.

13.4.2 Money and Credit Market Indicators

The money and credit market indicators most widely reported in the media are money supply, consumer credit, the Dow Jones Industrial Average (DJIA), and the Treasury bill rate.

13.4.3 Index of Leading Indicators

This most widely publicized signal caller is made up of eleven data series. They are money supply, stock prices, vendor performance, average work week, new orders, contracts, building permits, inventory change, consumer confidence, change in sensitive prices, and change in total liquid assets. The index monitors certain business activities that can signal a change in the economy. A more detailed discussion will follow shortly.

13.4.4 Measures for Major Product Markets

These measures are designed to be indicators for segments of the economy such as housing, retail sales, steel, and automobile. Examples are ten-day auto sales, advance retail sales, housing starts, and construction permits.

Note: Indicators are only signals, telling the CEO something about the economic conditions in the country, a particular area, an industry and, over time, the trends that seem to be shaping up.

13.5 INDICES OF LEADING, COINCIDENT, AND LAGGING ECONOMIC INDICATORS

The Index of Leading Economic Indicators is the economic series of indicators that tend to predict future changes in economic activity; this is officially called the *Composite Index of 11 Leading Indicators*. This index reveals the direction of the economy in the next six to nine months. *Note:* If the index is rising, even only slightly, the economy is chugging along and a setback is unlikely. If the indicator drops for three or more consecutive months, look for an economic slowdown, and possibly a recession in the next year or so.

This series is the government's main barometer for forecasting business trends. Each of the series has shown a tendency to change before the economy makes a major turn—hence, the term "leading indicators." The index is designed to forecast economic activity six to nine months ahead (1982 = 100). The series is published monthly by the U.S. Department of Commerce, and consists of the following indicators:

1. *Average work week of production workers in manufacturing.* Employers find it a lot easier to increase the number of hours worked in a week than to hire more employees.

2. *Initial claims for unemployment insurance.* The number of people who sign up for unemployment benefits signals changes in present and future economic activity.

3. *Change in consumer confidence.* This measure is based on the University of Michigan's survey of consumer expectations. The index measures consumers' optimism regarding the present and future state of the economy, and is based on an index of 100 in 1966. *Note:* Consumer spending buys two-thirds of GDP (all goods and services produced in the economy), so any sharp change could be an important factor in an overall turnaround.

4. *Percent change in prices of sensitive crude materials.* Rises in prices of such critical materials as steel usually mean factory demands are going up, which means factories plan to step up production.

5. *Contracts and orders for plant and equipment.* Heavier contracting and ordering usually lead economic upswings.

6. *Vendor performance.* Vendor performance represents the percentage of companies reporting slower deliveries. As the economy grows, firms have more trouble filling orders.

7. *Stock prices.* A rise in the common stock index indicates expected profits and lower interest rates. Stock market advances usually precede business upturns by three to eight months.

8. *Money supply.* A rising money supply means easy money that sparks brisk economic activity. This usually leads recoveries by as much as fourteen months.

9. *New orders for manufacturers of consumer goods and materials.* New orders mean more workers hired, more materials and supplies purchased, and increased output. Gains in this series usually lead recoveries by as much as four months.

10. *Residential building permits for private housing.* Gains in building permits signal business upturns.

11. *Factory backlogs of unfilled durable goods orders.* Backlogs signify business upswings.

Note: These eleven components of the index are adjusted for inflation. Rarely do these components of the index all go in the same direction at once. Each factor is weighted. The composite figure is designed to tell only in which direction business will go. It is not intended to forecast the magnitude of future ups and downs.

What are coincident indicators?

Coincident indicators are the types of economic indicator series that tend to move up and down in line with the aggregate economy, and therefore are measures of current economic activity. They are intended to gauge current economic conditions. Examples are Gross Domestic Product (GDP), employment, retail sales, and industrial production.

What are lagging indicators?

Lagging indicators are those that follow or trail behind aggregate economic activity. There are currently six lagging indicators published by the government: unemployment rate, labor cost per unit, loans outstanding, average prime rate charged by banks, ratio of consumer installment credit outstanding to personal income, and ratio of manufacturing and trade inventories to sales.

13.6 OTHER IMPORTANT ECONOMIC INDICES

There are other important indices with which the CFO should be familiar. Some widely watched indices are given below.

What is the Dodge Index?

The Dodge Index (www.mag.fwdodge.com/graph.htm), prepared by the F. W. Dodge Division of McGraw-Hill, is a monthly market index (1996 = 100) that assesses the building industry in terms of the value of new construction projects.

What is the Forbes Index?

Forbes publishes the Forbes Index. This index (1976 = 100) is a measure of U.S. economic activity, composed of eight equally weighted elements: total industrial production, new claims for unemployment, cost of services relative to all consumer prices, housing starts, retail sales, the level of new orders for durable goods compared with manufactures' inventories, personal income, and total consumer installment credit.

What is the Institute for Supply Management's Index?

This index, based on a survey of 375 companies in 17 industries, measures new orders, inventories, exports, and employment in the service sector. Services account for five-sixths of the $10 trillion U.S. economy and include industries such as entertainment, utilities, health care, farming, insurance, retail, restaurants, and zoos.

What is the Purchasing Index?

The National Association of Purchasing Management releases its monthly Purchasing Index, which tells about buying intentions of corporate purchasing agents.

What is the Help-Wanted Index?

The Conference Board of New York, an industry-sponsored, nonprofit economic research institute, publishes two indices: The *Help-Wanted Advertising Index* and *Consumer Confidence Index.* The *Help-Wanted Index* measures the amount of help-wanted advertising in fifty-one newspapers and tells about changes in labor-market conditions.

What are two major consumer confidence indices?

The *Consumer Confidence Index* measures consumer optimism and pessimism about general business conditions, jobs, and total family income.

The University of Michigan Survey Research Center is another research organization that compiles its own index, called the *Index of Consumer Sentiment.* This measures consumers' personal financial circumstances and their outlook for the future. The survey is compiled through a telephone survey of five hundred households. The index is used by the Commerce Department in its monthly *Index of Leading Economic Indicators,* and is regularly charted in the department's *Business Conditions Digest.*

What is the Optimism Index?

The National Federation of Independent Business, a Washington-based advocacy group, publishes the Optimism Index, which is based on small-business owners' expectations for the economy. The benchmark year is 1978.

13.7 MONETARY INDICATORS AND HOW THEY IMPACT THE ECONOMY

What are monetary indicators?

Monetary indicators apply to Federal Reserve actions and the demand for credit. These are of particular importance to financial officers because they greatly impact firms in terms of the costs of debt and equity financing and security prices. These indicators involve consideration of long-term interest rates, which are important because bond yields compete with stock yields. Monetary and credit indicators are often the first signs of market direction. If monetary indicators move favorably, this is an indication that a decline in stock prices may be over. A stock market top may be ready for a contraction if the Federal Reserve tightens credit, making consumer buying and corporate expansion more costly and difficult.

Monetary indicators that are regularly watched are

- Dow Jones twenty-bond index
- Dow Jones utility average
- NYSE utility average
- T-bill yield

Bonds and utilities are yield instruments, and therefore are money-sensitive. They are impacted by changing interest rates. If the above-mentioned monetary indicators are active and pointing higher, it a sign the stock market will start to take off. In other words, an upward movement in these indicators takes place in advance of a stock market increase.

Following is a brief description of monetary and economic variables that should be carefully watched by MBAs.

What is the money supply?

The money supply is the level of funds available at a given time for conducting transactions in an economy, as reported by the Federal Reserve Board. The Federal Reserve System can influence money supply through its monetary policy measures. There are several definitions of the money supply: M1, which is currency in circulation, demand deposits, traveler's checks, and those in interest-bearing NOW accounts; M2, the most widely followed measure, which equals M1 plus savings deposits, money market deposit accounts, and money market funds; and M3, which is M2 plus large CDs. Moderate growth is thought to have a positive impact on the economy. Rapid growth is viewed as inflationary; in contrast, a sharp drop in the money supply is considered recessionary.

What are interest rates?

Interest rates represent the costs to borrow money. Interest rates come in many forms. There are long-term and short-term interest rates, depending on the length of the loan; there are interest rates on super-safe securities (such as U.S. T-bills), and there are interest rates on "junk bonds" of financially troubled companies; there are nominal (coupon) interest rates, real (inflation-adjusted) or risk-adjusted interest rates, and effective interest rates (or yields). Interest rates depend upon the maturity of the security. The longer the period, the higher the interest rate because of the greater uncertainty.

Some of the more important interest rates are briefly explained below.

- *Prime rate.* This is the rate banks charge their best customers for short-term loans. This is a bell-wether rate in that it is construed as a sign of rising or falling loan demand and economic activity. When the prime rate is climbing, it means companies are borrowing heavily and the economy is still on an upward swing.

- *Federal funds rate.* This is the rate on short-term loans among commercial banks for overnight use. The Fed influences this rate by open-market operations, and by changing the bank's required reserve.

- *Discount rate.* This is the charge on loans to depository institutions by the Federal Reserve Board. A change in the discount rate is considered a major economic event and is expected to have an impact on security prices, especially bonds. A change in the prime rate usually follows the change in the discount rate.

- *90-day Treasury bills.* This yield represents the direction of short-term rates, a closely watched indicator. When yields on ninety-day bills rise sharply, this may signal a resurgence of inflation. Subsequently, the economy could slow down.

- *10-year Treasury bonds.* The most widely watched interest rate in the world, the security known as the "T-bond" is seen as the daily barometer of how the bond market is performing. The ten-year Treasury bond is a fixed-rate direct obligation of the U.S. government. There are no call provisions on Treasury bonds. Traders watch the price of the U.S. Treasury's most recently issued ten-year bond, often called the "bellwether." The price is decided by a series of dealers who own the exclusive right to make markets in the bonds in U.S. markets. (The bond trades around the clock in foreign markets.) Bond yields are derived from the current trading price and its fixed coupon rate. Because of its long-term nature, the T-bond is extra sensitive to inflation, which could ravage the buying power of its fixed-rate payouts. Thus, the T-bond market also is watched as an indicator of where inflation may be headed. Also, T-bond rates impact fixed-rate mortgages somewhat. Still, the T-bond yield is also seen as a barometer for the housing industry, a key leading indicator for the economy.

Interest rates are controlled by the Fed's monetary policy. The Fed's monetary policy tools involve: (1) changes in the required reserve ratio; (2) changes in the discount rate; and (3) open market operations— that is, purchase and sale of government securities. Cuts in the discount rate are aimed at stimulating the economy—a positive development for stocks. The effect of cutting the discount rate on the economy is presented next.

13.8 EFFECTS OF LOWERING THE DISCOUNT RATE

- *The players:* The Federal Reserve is the nation's central bank. It regulates the flow of money through the economy.
- *The action:* The discount rate is what the Federal Reserve charges on short-term loans to member banks. When the Fed cuts the discount rate, it means banks can get cash cheaper, and thus charge less on loans.
- *The first effect:* Within a few days, banks are likely to start passing on the discounts by cutting their prime rate, which is what banks charge on loans to their best corporate customers.

- *Impact:* Businesses are more likely to borrow. Second, adjustable consumer loans are tied to the prime, such as credit-card rates. These become cheaper, stimulating spending.

- *The second effect:* Within a few weeks, rates on mortgage, auto, and construction loans drop.

- *The third effect:* The lower rates go, the more investors move their cash to stocks, creating new wealth.

- *The goal:* To kick-start the economy. If lower interest rates cause businesses to start growing again, laid-off workers get jobs, retailers start selling, and the economy starts to roll again.

The following diagram summarizes the impact of open market operations on the money supply, level of interest rates, and loan demand.

Easy Money Policy

Fed buys securities → Bank reserve up →
Bank lending up → Money supply up →
Interest rates down → Loan demand up

Tight Money Policy

Fed sells securities → Bank reserve down →
Bank lending down → Money supply down →
Interest rates up → Loan demand down

13.8.1 Inflation

What is inflation?

Inflation is the general rise in prices of consumer goods and services. The federal government measures inflation by comparing prices today—measured in terms of the CPI, PPI, and/or GNP deflator—to a two-year period, 1982–84. As prices increase, lenders and investors will demand greater returns to compensate for the decline in purchasing power. Companies may reduce borrowing because of higher interest rates. This leads to fewer capital expenditures for property, plant, and equipment. As a result, output may decrease, resulting in employee layoffs. During inflation, selling prices may increase to keep pace with rising price levels, but the company's sales in real dollars remain the same. Management will still lose out, since the company's tax liability will increase.

Most likely, the Federal Reserve will tighten the money supply and raise interest rates (such as discount rate or federal-fund rate). It would be too expensive to borrow money. Therefore, there is less demand for products, which in turn pushes prices down. The following diagram shows how inflation affects the prices of products:

Inflation → Fed raises discount rate →
Interest rates up → Demand for money down →
Demand for products down → Prices down

Interest rates are no more than a reflection of what expectations are for inflation. Inflation, therefore, means higher interest rates, and thus higher borrowing cost to the company.

13.8.2 Productivity and Unit Labor Costs

The data on productivity and unit labor costs is released by the Labor Department. Increased productivity, or getting more worker output per hour on the job, is considered vital to increasing the nation's standard of living without inflation. Meanwhile, unit labor cost is a key gauge of future price inflation, along with the CPI, PPI, and GNP deflator.

13.8.3 Recession

What is recession?

Recession means a sinking economy. Unfortunately, there is no consensus definition and measure of recession. Three or more straight monthly drops of the Index of Leading Economic Indicators are generally considered a sign of recession. Or, two consecutive quarterly drops of GNP signals recession. Or, consecutive monthly drops of durable goods orders, which most likely results in less production and increasing layoffs in the factory sector, can signal recession. Recession tends to dampen the spirits of consumers, and thus depress prices of products and services.

To kick-start the economy, the Fed will loosen the money supply and lower interest rates, (such as the discount rate). When the Fed cuts the discount rate, it means banks can get cash cheaper, and thus charge less on loans.

Note: The size of the cut is a critical consideration. For example, a half-point discount rate cut itself is not strong enough to get the economy moving fast. External political conditions (such as the crisis in the Middle East), the federal deficit, and problems in the banking and savings and loan industries can make companies hesitant to start expanding again, and can also make consumers nervous for a longer time that the Fed might anticipate.

13.8.4 Federal Deficit

What is the federal deficit?

The national debt is the sum of all the money the government has borrowed to finance budget deficits. The only way for a government to reduce its debt is to run a budget surplus—to obtain more money than it spends. The surplus must then be used to pay off maturing debt (bonds, notes, and so on) rather than replacing them (rolling them over) with more debt. This federal deficit affects the economy as a whole.

Economists generally believe that larger federal deficits result in higher interest rates for two reasons. First, increased budget deficits raise the demand for the loanable funds, resulting in higher interest rates. Second, larger deficits are apt to lead to higher inflation. This may be true either because the sources of the increased deficits—larger government spending and/or lower taxes—result in greater pressure for loan demand, and therefore inflation, or because the deficit will induce the Fed to expand the money supply to help finance the deficit, thus causing inflation. In any case, if the increased deficit elevates the public's expectation of inflation, it will tend to raise the level of interest rates. Furthermore, the financing of the deficit by issuance of government debt securities will compete for funds to be raised by companies and will deter economic expansion. It also forces companies to borrow at higher interest rates. This is called the "crowding-out effect."

13.8.5 The U.S. Balance of Payments

What is the balance of payments?

A balance of payments is a systematic record of a country's receipts from, or payments to, other countries. The "balance of trade" usually refers to goods within the goods and services category. It also known as merchandise, or "visible," trade because it consists of tangibles such as foodstuffs, manufactured goods, and raw materials. The "services" part of the category is known as "invisible" trade, and consists of intangibles such as interest or dividends, technology transfers, services (such as insurance, transportation, financial), and so forth.

When the net result of both the current account and the capital account yields more credits than debits, the country is said to have a surplus in its balance of payments. When there are more debits than credits, the country has a deficit in the balance of payments. *Note:* When deficits persist, this generally depresses the value of the dollar, and can boost inflation. The reason for this is that a weak dollar makes foreign goods relatively expensive, often allowing U.S. makers of similar products to raise prices as well. It is necessary for a CFO to know the condition of a country's balance of payments because the resulting inflation and the value of the dollar will affect the company's product demand.

13.8.6 The Value of the Dollar

What is better, a strong dollar (appreciation in foreign exchange rate) or a weak dollar (depreciation in foreign exchange rate)?

The answer is, unfortunately, that it depends. This is a matter of concern, particularly to the CEOs and CFOs of multinational corporations. A strong dollar makes Americans' cash go further overseas and reduces import prices, which is generally good for U.S. consumers and for foreign manufacturers. If the dollar is overvalued, U.S. products are harder to sell abroad and at home, where they compete with low-cost imports.

A weak dollar can restore competitiveness to American products by making foreign goods comparatively more expensive. But too weak a dollar can spawn inflation, first through higher import prices and then through spiraling prices for all goods. Even worse, a falling dollar can drive foreign investors away from U.S. securities, which lose value along with the dollar. A strong dollar can be induced by interest rates. Relatively higher domestic interest rates than those abroad will attract dollar-denominated investments, which will raise the value of the dollar. Figure 13.1 summarizes the impacts of changes in foreign exchange rates on the company's products and services and portfolio investments.

Figure 13.1 The Impact of Changes in Foreign Exchange Rates

	Weak Currency (Depreciation/ Devaluation)	*Strong Currency (Appreciation/ Revaluation)*
Imports	More expensive	Cheaper
Exports	Cheaper	More expensive
Payables	More expensive	Cheaper
Receivables	Cheaper	More expensive
Inflation	Fuel inflation by making imports more costly	Low inflation
Foreign investment	Discourage foreign investment. Lower return on investments by international investors.	High interest rates could attract foreign investors.
The effect	Raising interest rates could slow down the economy.	Reduced exports could trigger a trade deficit.

CHAPTER 14

International Business and Finance

Many companies are multinational corporations (MNCs) that have significant foreign operations, thus deriving a high percentage of their sales overseas. The managers of MNCs must have an understanding of the complexities of international finance to make sound financial and investment decisions. International business and finance involve consideration of managing working capital, financing the business, control of foreign exchange and political risks, and foreign direct investments. Most importantly, the financial manager must consider the value of the U.S. dollar relative to the value of the currency of the foreign country in which business activities are being conducted. Currency exchange rates may materially affect receivables and payables, and imports and exports of the U.S. company in its multinational operations. The effect is more pronounced with increasing activities abroad.

14.1 FOREIGN OPERATIONS

What is unique about the financial management of a multinational corporation (MNC)?

- *Multiple-currency problem.* Sales revenues may be collected in one currency, assets denominated in another, and profits measured in a third.

- *Various legal, institutional, and economic constraints.* There are variations in such things as tax laws, labor practices, balance of payment policies, and government controls with respect to the types and sizes of investments, types and amount of capital raised, and repatriation of profits.

- *Internal control problem.* When the parent office of a MNC and its affiliates are widely located, internal organizational difficulties arise.

What are popular financial goals of MNCs?

The financial goals of MNCs are identified in the following order of importance:

1. Maximize growth in corporate earnings, whether total earnings, earnings before interest and taxes (EBIT), or earnings per share (EPS).
2. Maximize return on equity.
3. Guarantee that funds are always available when needed.

What types of foreign operations are right for me?

When strong competition exists in the U.S., a company may look to enter or expand its foreign base. However, if a company is unsuccessful in the domestic market, it is likely to have problems overseas as well. Further, the manager must be aware of local customs and risks in the international markets.

A large, well-established company with much international experience may eventually have wholly-owned subsidiaries. However, a small company with limited foreign experience operating in "risky areas" may be restricted to export and import activity.

If the company's sales force has minimal experience in export sales, it is advisable to use foreign brokers when specialized knowledge of foreign markets is needed. When sufficient volume exists, the company may establish a foreign branch sales office, including sales people and technical service staff. As the operation matures, production facilities may be located in the foreign market. However, some foreign countries require licensing before foreign sales and production can take place. In this case, a foreign licensee sells and produces the product. A problem with this arrangement is that confidential information and knowledge are passed on to the licensee, who can then become a competitor at the expiration of the agreement.

A joint venture with a foreign company is another way to proceed internationally and share the risk. Some foreign governments require that this path be followed to operate in their countries. The foreign company may have local goodwill to assure success. Drawbacks of this setup are less control over activities and a conflict of interest.

In evaluating the impact that foreign operations have on the entity's financial health, the controller should consider the extent of intercountry transactions, foreign restrictions and laws, tax structure of the foreign country, and the economic and political stability of the country. If a subsidiary is operating in a high-tax country with a double-tax agreement, dividend payments are not subject to further U.S. taxes. One way to transfer income from high-tax areas to low-tax areas is to levy royalties or management fees on the subsidiaries.

14.2 THE FOREIGN EXCHANGE MARKET

What is the foreign exchange market?

Except in a few European centers, there is no central marketplace for the foreign exchange market. Rather, business is carried out over telephone or telex. The major dealers are large banks. A company that wants to buy or sell currency typically uses a commercial bank. International transactions and investments involve more than one currency. Due to the foreign exchange market, the buyer may pay in one currency, while the seller can receive payment in another currency. For example, when a U.S. company sells merchandise to a Japanese firm, the U.S. company wants to be paid in dollars, but the Japanese company typically expects to receive yen.

What are spot and forward foreign exchange rates?

An exchange rate is the ratio of one unit of currency to another. An exchange rate is established between the different currencies. The conversion rate between currencies depends on the supply-and-demand relationship. Because of the change in exchange rates, companies are susceptible to exchange-rate fluctuation risks because of a net asset or net liability position in a foreign currency.

Exchange rates may be expressed in terms of dollars per foreign currency unit (called a direct quote), or in units of foreign currency per dollar (called an indirect quote). Therefore, an indirect quote, is the reciprocal of a direct quote, and vice versa.

$$\text{An indirect quote} = 1/\text{direct quote}$$
$$\text{Pound}/\$ = 1/(\$/\text{pound})$$

Example 14.1

Figure 14.1 presents a sample of indirect and direct quotes for selected currencies. A rate of 1.617/British pound means each pound costs the U.S. company $1.617. In other words, the U.S. company gets 1/1.617 = .6184 pounds for each dollar.

The spot rate is the exchange rate for immediate delivery of currencies exchanged, while the forward rate is the exchange rate for later delivery of currencies exchanged. For example, there may be a ninety-day exchange rate. The forward exchange rate of a currency will be slightly different from the spot rate at the current date because of future expectations and uncertainties.

Figure 14.1 Foreign-Exchange Rates (A Sample)—August 5, 20X3

Country	Contract	U.S. Dollar Equivalent	Currency per U.S. $
Britain	Spot	1.6124	.6202
(Pound)	30-day future	1.6091	.6215
	90-day future	1.6030	.6238
	180-day future	1.5934	.6276
Japan	Spot	.008341	119.89
(Yen)	30-day future	.008349	119.77
	90-day future	.008366	119.53
	180-day future	.008394	119.13

Forward rates may be greater than the current spot rate (premium), or less than the current spot rate (discount).

What are cross rates?

A cross rate is the indirect calculation of the exchange rate of one currency from the exchange rates of two other currencies. In other words, it is the exchange rate between two currencies derived by dividing each currency's exchange rate by a third currency.

Example 14.2

Hypothetical dollar-per-pound and yen-per-dollar rates are given in Figure 14.2. For example, if dollars per pound is $1.6124/£ and yens per dollar is ¥119.89/$, the cross rate between Japanese yen and British pounds is

$$\text{Cross rate between yen and pound} = \frac{\text{Dollars}}{\text{Pound}} \times \frac{\text{Yen}}{\text{Dollar}} = \frac{\text{Yen}}{\text{Pound}}$$

$$= \$/£ \times ¥/\$ = ¥/£$$

$$= 1.6124 \text{ dollars per pound}$$
$$\times 119.89 \text{ yen per dollar}$$
$$= 193.31 \text{ yen per pound}$$

Because most currencies are quoted against the dollar, it may be necessary to work out the cross rates for currencies other than the dollar. The cross rate is needed to consummate financial transactions between two countries.

Figure 14.2 Example of Key Currency Cross Rates

	British	Euro	Japan	U.S.
British	—	.7054	.05770	.62020
Euro	1.4176	—	.00733	.87920
Japan	193.31	136.36	—	119.89
U.S.	1.6124	1.1374	.00834	—

Note: The Wall Street Journal routinely publishes key currency cross rates, as shown in the hypothetical rates. These are also available on www.bloomberg.com. The cross-currency table calculator can be accessed at www.xe.net/currency/table.htm.

Example 14.3

On August 5, 20X3, forward rates on the British pound were at a discount in relation to the spot rate, while the forward rates for the Japanese yen were at a premium from the spot rate. This means that participants in the foreign exchange market anticipated that the British pound would depreciate relative to the U.S. dollar in the future, but the Japanese yen would appreciate against the dollar.

The percentage premium (P) or discount (D) is computed as follows.

$$P \text{ (or D)} = \frac{F - S}{S} \times \frac{12 \text{ months}}{n} \times 100$$

where F, S = the forward and spot rates and n = length of the forward contract in months.

If F > S, the result is the annualized premium in percent; otherwise, it is the annualized discount in percent.

Example 14.4

On August 5, 20X3, a thirty-day forward contract in Japanese yens (see Figure 14.1) was selling at a 1.15 percent premium:

$$\frac{.008349 - .008341}{.008341} \times \frac{12 \text{ months}}{1 \text{ month}} \times 100 = 1.15\%$$

How do you control foreign-exchange risk?

Foreign-exchange rate risk exists when a contract is written in terms of the foreign currency or denominated in foreign currency. The exchange-rate fluctuations increase the riskiness of the investment and incur cash losses. The controllers must not only seek the highest return on temporary investments, but must also be concerned about changing values of the currencies invested. Managers do not necessarily eliminate foreign exchange risk; they may only try to contain it.

14.3 FINANCIAL STRATEGIES

In countries in which currency values are likely to drop, controllers of the subsidiaries should

- Avoid paying advances on purchase orders unless the seller pays interest on the advances sufficient to cover the loss of purchasing power.

- Not have excess idle cash—excess cash can be used to buy inventory or other real assets.

- Buy materials and supplies on credit in the country in which the foreign subsidiary is operating, extending the final payment date as long as possible.

- Avoid giving excessive trade credit. If accounts receivable balances are outstanding for an extended time period, interest should be charged to absorb the loss in purchasing power.

- Borrow local currency funds when the interest rate charged does not exceed U.S. rates, after taking into account expected devaluation in the foreign country.

What are three different types of foreign-exchange exposure?

MNCs' controllers are faced with the dilemma of three different types of foreign exchange risk.
They are

- *Translation exposure.* Often called accounting exposure, this measures the impact of an exchange-rate change on the firm's financial statements. An example would be the impact of a British pound devaluation on a U.S. firm's reported income statement and balance sheet.

- *Transaction exposure.* This measures potential gains or losses on the future settlement of outstanding obligations that are denominated in a foreign currency. An example would be a U.S. dollar loss after the Euro devalues, on payment received for an export invoiced in Euros before that devaluation.

- *Operating exposure.* Often called economic exposure, this is the potential for change in the present value of future cash flows due to an unexpected change in the exchange rate.

14.4 TRANSLATION EXPOSURE

A major purpose of translation is to provide data regarding expected impacts of rate changes on cash flow and equity. In the translation of the foreign subsidiaries' financial statements into the U.S. parent's financial statements, the following steps are involved:

1. The foreign financial statements are put into U.S. generally accepted accounting principles.
2. The foreign currency is translated into U.S. dollars.

Current FASB rules require translation by the current rate method. Under the current rate method

- All balance-sheet assets and liabilities are translated at the current rate of exchange in effect on the balance-sheet date. If a current exchange rate is not available at the balance-sheet date, use the first exchange rate available after that date.

- Income statement items are usually translated at an average exchange rate for the reporting period.

- All equity accounts are translated at the historical exchange rates that were in effect at the time the accounts first entered the balance sheet.

- Foreign currency translation gains or losses are presented under "other comprehensive income.

14.5 TRANSACTION EXPOSURE

Foreign-currency transactions may result in receivables or payables fixed in terms of the amount of foreign currency to be received or paid. Transaction gains and losses are reported in the income statement.

Foreign-currency transactions are those transactions whose terms are denominated in a currency other than the entity's functional currency. Foreign-currency transactions take place when a business

- Buys or sells on credit goods or services, the prices of which are denominated in foreign currencies.
- Borrows or lends funds, and the amounts payable or receivable are denominated in a foreign currency.
- Is a party to an unperformed forward-exchange contract.
- Acquires or disposes of assets, or incurs or settles liabilities denominated in foreign currencies.

Note: Transaction losses differ from translation losses, which do not influence taxable income.

What is long versus short position?

When there is a devaluation of the dollar, foreign assets and income in strong currency countries are worth more dollars, as long as foreign liabilities do not offset this beneficial effect.

Foreign-exchange risk may be analyzed by examining expected receipts or obligations in foreign-currency units. A company expecting receipts in foreign-currency units ("long" position in the foreign-currency units) has the risk that the value of the foreign-currency units will drop. This results in devaluing the foreign currency relative to the dollar. If a company is expecting to have obligations in foreign-currency units ("short" position in the foreign-currency units), there is a risk that the value of the foreign currency will rise, and the company will need to buy the currency at a higher price.

If net claims are greater than liabilities in a foreign currency, the company has a "long" position—it will benefit if the value of the foreign currency rises. If net liabilities exceed claims with respect to foreign currencies, the company is in a "short" position—it will gain if the foreign currency drops in value.

What is the monetary position?

Monetary balance is avoiding either a net-receivable or a net-payable position. Monetary assets and liabilities do not change in value with devaluation or revaluation in foreign currencies.

A company with a long position in a foreign currency will be receiving more funds in the foreign currency. It will have a net monetary asset position (monetary assets exceed monetary liabilities) in that currency.

A company with net receipts is a net monetary creditor. Its foreign-exchange-rate risk exposure has a net-receipts position in a foreign currency that is susceptible to a drop in value.

A company with a future net obligation in foreign currency has a net monetary debtor position. It faces a foreign-exchange risk of the possibility of an increase in the value of the foreign currency.

What are some ways to neutralize foreign-exchange risk?

Foreign-exchange risk can be neutralized or hedged by a change in the asset and liability position in the foreign currency. Following are some ways to control exchange risk.

Entering a money-market hedge. The exposed position in a foreign currency is offset by borrowing or lending in the money market.

Example 14.5

XYZ, an American importer, enters into a contract with a British supplier to buy merchandise worth £4,000. The amount is payable on the delivery of the goods, thirty days from today. The company knows the exact amount of its pound liability in thirty days. However, it does not know the amount payable in dollars. Assume that the thirty-day money-market rates for both lending and borrowing in the U.S. and the U.K. are .5 percent and 1 percent, respectively. Assume further that today's foreign-exchange rate is $1.7350 per pound.

In a money-market hedge, XYZ can take the following steps:

1. Buy a one-month U.K. money-market security, worth of 4,000/(1 + .005) = £3,980. This investment will compound to exactly £4,000 in one month.

2. Exchange dollars on today's spot (cash) market to obtain the £3,980. The dollar amount needed today is £3,980 × $1.7350 per pound = $6,905.30.

3. If XYZ does not have this amount, it can borrow it from the U.S. money market at the going rate of 1 percent. In thirty days XYZ will need to repay $6,905.30 \times (1 + .1) = \$7,595.83$.

Note: XYZ need not wait for the future exchange rate to be available. On today's date, the future dollar amount of the contract is known with certainty. The British supplier will receive £4,000, and the cost of XYZ to make the payment is $7,595.83.

Hedging by purchasing forward- (or futures) exchange contracts. A forward-exchange contract is a commitment to buy or sell, at a specified future date, one currency for a specified amount of another currency (at a specified exchange rate). This can be a hedge against changes in exchange rates during a period of contract, or against exposure to risk from such changes. More specifically, this allows a company to do the following: (1) Buy foreign-exchange forward contracts to cover payables denominated in a foreign currency, and (2) sell foreign-exchange forward contracts to cover receivables denominated in a foreign currency. This way, any gain or loss on the foreign receivables or payables due to changes in exchange rates is offset by the gain or loss on the forward-exchange contract.

Example 14.6

In the previous example, assume that the thirty-day forward exchange rate is $1.7272. XYZ may take the following steps to cover its payable.

1. Buy a forward contract today to purchase £4,000 in thirty days.
2. On the thirtieth day, pay the foreign-exchange dealer £4,000 $\times$ $1.7272 per pound = $6,908.80 and collect £4,000. Pay this amount to the British supplier.

Note: Using the forward contract, XYZ knows the exact worth of the future payment in dollars ($6,908.80).

Note: The basic difference between futures contracts and forward contracts is that futures contracts are for specified amounts and maturities, whereas forward contracts are for any size and maturity desired.

Hedging by foreign-currency options. Foreign-currency options can be purchased or sold in three different types of markets: (a) options on the physical currency, purchased on the over-the-counter (interbank) market; (b) options on the physical currency, on organized exchanges such as the Philadelphia Stock Exchange and the Chicago Mercantile Exchange; and (c) options on futures contracts, purchased on the International Monetary Market (IMM) of the Chicago Mercantile Exchange. *Note:* The difference between using a futures contract and using an option on a futures contract is that with a futures contract, the company must deliver one currency against another, or reverse the contract on the exchange, while with an option the company may abandon the option and use the spot (cash) market if that is more advantageous.

Repositioning cash by leading and lagging the time at which an MNC makes operational or financial payments. Often, money- and forward-market hedges are not available to eliminate exchange risk. Under such circumstances, leading (accelerating) and lagging (decelerating) may be used to *reduce* risk. *Note:* A net asset position (that is, assets minus liabilities) is not desirable in a weak or potentially depreciating currency. In this case, expedite the disposal of the asset. By the same token, lag or delay the collection against a net asset position in a strong currency.

Maintaining balance between receivables and payables denominated in a foreign currency. MNCs typically set up "multilateral netting centers" as a special department to settle the outstanding balances of affiliates of an MNC with each other on a net basis. This is the development of a "clearing house" for payments by the firm's affiliates. If there are amounts due among affiliates, they are offset insofar as possible. The net amount would be paid in the currency of the transaction. The total amounts owed need not be paid in the currency of the transaction; thus, a much lower quantity of the currency must be acquired. *Note:* The major advantage of this system is a reduction of the costs associated with a large number of separate foreign-exchange transactions.

Positioning of funds through transfer pricing. A transfer price is the price at which an MNC sells goods and services to its foreign affiliates or, alternatively, the price at which an affiliate sells to the parent. For example, a parent that wishes to transfer funds from an affiliate in a depreciating-currency country may charge a higher price on the goods and services sold to this affiliate by the parent or by affiliates from strong-currency countries. Transfer pricing affects not only transfer of funds from one entity to another, but also the income taxes paid by both entities.

14.6 OPERATING EXPOSURE

Operating (economic) exposure is the possibility that an unexpected change in exchange rates will cause a change in the future cash flows of a firm and its market value. Operating exposure differs from translation and transaction exposures in that it is subjective and thus not easily quantified. *Note:* The best strategy to control operation exposure is to diversify operations and financing internationally.

What are some key questions to ask that help to identify foreign-exchange risk?

A systematic approach to identifying an MNC's exposure to foreign-exchange risk is to ask a series of questions regarding the net effects on profits of changes in foreign-currency revenues and costs.

The questions are

- Where is the MNC selling? (Domestic vs. foreign sales share)
- Who are the firm's major competitors? (Domestic vs. foreign)
- Where is the firm producing? (Domestic vs. foreign)
- Where are the firm's inputs coming from? (Domestic vs. foreign)
- How sensitive is quantity demanded to price? (Elastic vs. inelastic)
- How are the firm's inputs or outputs priced? (Priced in a domestic market or a global market; the currency of denomination)

14.7 IMPACTS OF CHANGES IN FOREIGN-EXCHANGE RATES

Figure 14.3 summarizes the impacts of changes in foreign-exchange rates on the company's products and financial transactions.

Figure 14.3 The Impacts of Changes in Foreign-Exchange Rates

	Weak Currency (Depreciation)	*Strong Currency (Appreciation)*
Imports	More expensive	Cheaper
Exports	Cheaper	More expensive
Payables	More expensive	Cheaper
Receivables	Cheaper	More expensive

Can foreign-exchange rates be forecast?

The forecasting of foreign-exchange rates is a formidable task. Most MNCs rely primarily on bank services for assistance and information in preparing exchange-rate projections. The following economic indicators are considered to be the most important for the forecasting process:

- Recent rate movements
- Relative inflation rates
- Balance of payments and trade
- Money supply growth
- Interest-rate differentials

14.8 INTEREST RATES

Interest rates have an important influence on exchange rates. In fact, there is an important economic relationship between any two nations' spot rates, forward rates, and interest rates. This relationship is called the interest rate parity theorem (IRPT). The IRPT states that the ratio of the forward and spot rates is directly related to the two interest rates.

Specifically, the premium or discount should be

$$P \text{ (or D)} = -\frac{r_f - r_d}{1 + r_f}$$

where r_f and r_d = foreign and domestic interest rates. (When interest rates are relatively low, this equation can be approximated by: $P \text{ (or D)} = -(r_f - r_d)$).

The IRPT implies that the P (or D) calculated by the equation should be the same as the P (or D) calculated by

$$P \text{ (or D)} = \frac{F - S}{S} \times \frac{12 \text{ months}}{n} \times 100$$

Example 14.7

On August 5, 20X3, a thirty-day forward contract in Japanese yen (see Figure 14.1) was selling at a 1.15 percent premium:

$$\frac{.008349 - .008341}{.008341} \times \frac{12 \text{ months}}{1 \text{ month}} \times 100 = 1.15\%$$

The thirty-day U.S. T-bill rate is 8 percent annualized. What is the thirty-day Japanese rate?

Using the equation

$$P \text{ (or D)} = -\frac{r_f - r_d}{1 + r_f}$$

$$.0115 = \frac{.08 - r_f}{1 + r_f}$$

$$.0115 \,(1 + r_f) = .08 - r_f$$

$$.0115 + .0115 \, r_f = .08 - r_f$$

$$-.0685 = -.9885 r_f$$

$$r_f = .0693$$

The thirty-day Japanese rate should be 6.93 percent.

14.9 INFLATION

Inflation, which is a change in price levels, also affects future exchange rates. The mathematical relationship that links changes in exchange rates and changes in price level is called the purchasing power parity theorem (PPPT). The PPPT states that the ratio of the forward and spot rates is directly related to the two inflation rates:

$$\frac{F}{S} = \frac{1 + P_d}{1 + P_f}$$

where

F = forward exchange rate (e.g., $/foreign currency)

S = spot exchange rate (e.g., $/foreign currency

P_d = domestic inflation rate

P_f = foreign inflation rate

Example 14.8

Assume the following data for the U.S. and the U.K.:

Expected U.S. inflation rate = 5%

Expected U.K. = 10%

S = $1.6124/U.K.

Then,

$$\frac{F}{1.6124} = \frac{1.05}{1.10}$$

So

$$F = \$1.5391/U.K.$$

Note: If the U.K. has the higher inflation rate, the purchasing power of the pound is declining faster than that of the dollar. This will lead to a forward discount on the pound relative to the dollar.

How are foreign investments analyzed?

Foreign investment decisions are basically capital budgeting decisions at the international level. The decision requires two major components:

- *The estimation of the relevant future cash flows.* Cash flows are the dividends and possible future sales price of the investment. The estimation depends on the sales forecast, the effects on exchange-rate changes, the risk in cash flows, and the actions of foreign governments.
- *The choice of the proper discount rate (cost of capital).* The cost of capital in foreign investment projects is higher due to the increased risks of
  - Currency risk (or foreign-exchange risk)—Changes in exchange rates. This risk may adversely affect sales by making competing imported goods cheaper.
  - Political risk (or sovereignty risk)—Possibility of nationalization or other restrictions with net losses to the parent company.

14.10 EXAMPLES OF POLITICAL RISKS

Following are some examples associated with political risks.

- Expropriation of plants and equipment without compensation or with minimal compensation that is below actual market value
- Nonconvertibility of the affiliate's foreign earnings into the parent's currency—the problem of "blocked funds"
- Substantial changes in the laws governing taxation
- Government controls in the host country regarding wages, compensation to personnel, hiring of personnel, the sales price of the product, making of transfer payments to the parent, and local borrowing

How is political risk measured?

Many MNCs and banks have attempted to measure political risks in their businesses. Some even hire or maintain a group of political-risk analysts. Several independent services provide political-risk and country-risk ratings:

- *Euromoney* magazine's annual *Country Risk Rating* is based on a measure of different countries' access to international credit, trade finance, political risk, and a country's payment record. The rankings are generally confirmed by political-risk insurers and top syndicate managers in the Euromarkets.

- Rating by *Economist Intelligence Unit,* a New York–based subsidiary of the *Economist Group,* London, is based on such factors as external debt and trends in the current account, the consistency of the government policy, foreign-exchange reserves, and the quality of economic management.

- *International Country Risk Guide,* published by the PRS Group (www.prsgroup.com/icrg/icrg.html), offers a composite risk rating as well as individual ratings for political, financial, and economic risk for 140 countries. The political variable—which makes up half of the composite index—includes factors such as government corruption and how economic expectations diverge from reality. The financial rating looks at such things as the likelihood of losses from exchange controls and loan defaults. Finally, economic ratings consider such factors as inflation and debt-service costs.

What are the methods for dealing with political risk?

To the extent that forecasting political risks is a formidable task, what can an MNC do to cope with them? There are several methods:

- *Avoidance.* Try to avoid political risk by minimizing activities in or with countries that are considered to be of high risk. Use higher discount rates for projects in riskier countries.

- *Adaptation.* Try to reduce risk by adapting the activities (for example, by using hedging techniques discussed previously).

- *Diversification.* Diversify across national borders, so that problems in one country do not severely damage the company.

- *Risk transfer.* Buy insurance policies for political risks.

Example 14.9

Most developed nations offer insurance for political risk to their exporters. Following are some examples:

- In the U.S., the Exurban offers policies to exporters that cover such political risks as war, currency inconvertibility, and civil unrest. Furthermore, the Overseas Private Investment Corporation (OPIC) offers policies to U.S. foreign investors to cover such risks as currency inconvertibility, civil or foreign war damages, or expropriation.

- In the U.K., similar policies are offered by the Export Credit Guarantee Department (ECGD); in Canada, by the Export Development Council (EDC); and in Germany, by an agency called Hermes.

14.11 INTERNATIONAL FINANCING

What are international sources of financing?

A company can finance its activities abroad, especially in countries in which it is operating. A successful company in domestic markets is more likely to be able to attract financing for international expansion.

The most important international sources of funds are the Eurocurrency market and the Eurobond market. Also, MNCs have access to national capital markets in which their subsidiaries are located. Figure 14.4 presents an overview of international financial markets.

The Eurocurrency market is a largely short-term (usually less than one year of maturity) market for bank deposits and loans denominated in any currency except the currency of the country in which the market is located. For example, in London, the Eurocurrency market is a market for bank deposits and loans denominated in dollars, yen, francs, Marks, and any other currency except British pounds. The main instruments used in this market are CDs, time deposits, and bank loans. *Note:* The term "market" in this context is not a physical marketplace, but a set of bank deposits and loans.

The Eurobond market is a long-term market for bonds denominated in any currency except the currency of the country in which the market is located. Eurobonds may be of different types, such as straight, convertible, and with warrants. While most Eurobonds are fixed-rate, variable-rate bonds also exist. Maturities vary, but ten to twelve years is typical.

Although Eurobonds are issued in many currencies, try to select a stable, fully convertible, and actively traded currency. In some cases, if a Eurobond is denominated in a weak currency, the holder has the option of requesting payment in another currency.

Sometimes large MNCs establish wholly owned offshore finance subsidiaries. These subsidiaries issue Eurobond debt, and the proceeds are given to the parent or to overseas operating subsidiaries. Debt service goes back to bondholders through the finance subsidiaries.

If the Eurobond is issued by the parent directly, the U.S. requires a withholding tax on interest. There may also be an estate tax when the bondholder dies. These tax problems do not arise when a bond is issued by a finance subsidiary incorporated in a tax haven. Hence, the subsidiary may borrow at less cost than the parent.

In summary, the Euromarkets offer borrowers and investors in one country the opportunity to deal with borrowers and investors from many other countries, buying and selling bank deposits, bonds, and loans denominated in many currencies.

Figure 14.5 provides a list of funding sources available to a foreign affiliate of an MNC (debt and equity).

Figure 14.4 International Financial Markets

Market	Instruments	Participants	Regulator
International monetary system	Special drawing rights; gold; foreign exchange	Central banks; International Monetary Fund	International Monetary Fund
Foreign-exchange markets	Bank deposits; currency; futures and forward contracts	Commercial and central banks; firms; individuals	Central banks in each country
National money markets (short-term)	Bank deposits and loans; short-term government securities; commercial paper	Banks; firms; individuals; government agencies	Central bank; other government agencies
National capital markets	Bonds; long-term bank deposits and loans; stocks; long-term government securities	Banks; firms; individuals; government agencies	Central bank; other government agencies

Eurocurrency markets (short-term)	Bank deposits; bank loans; short-term and rolled-over credit lines; revolving commitment	Commercial banks; firms; government agencies	Substantially unregulated
Euro-commercial paper markets (short-term)	Commercial paper issues and programs; note-issuing facility; revolving underwritten facilities	Commercial banks; firms; government agencies	Substantially unregulated
Eurobond market (medium and long-term)	Fixed coupon bonds; floating-rate notes; higher-bound bonds; lower-bound bonds	Banks; firms; individuals; government agencies	Substantially unregulated
Euroloan market (medium and long-term)	Fixed-rate loans; revolving loans; revolving loans with cap; revolving loans with floor	Banks; firms; individuals; government agencies	Substantially unregulated

Figure 14.5 International Sources of Credit

Borrowing	Domestic Inside the Firm	Domestic Market	Foreign Inside the Firm	Foreign Market	Euromarket
Direct, short-term	Intrafirm loans, transfer pricing, royalties, fees, service charges	Commercial paper	International intrafirm loans, international transfer pricing, dividends, royalties, fees	Euro-commercial paper
Intermediated short-term		Short-term bank loans, discounted receivables	Internal back-to-back loans	Short-term bank loans, discounted receivables	Euro short-term loans
Direct, long-term	Intrafirm loans, invested in affiliates	Stock issue Bond issue	International intrafirm long-term loans, foreign direct investment	Stock issue Bond issue	Eurobonds
Intermediated long-term		Long-term bank loans	Internal back-to-back loans	Long-term bank loans	Euro long-term loans